RR

A Guide to the Socialist Economies

A Guide to the Socialist Economies

Ian Jeffries

Routledge
London and New York

First published 1990
by Routledge
11 New Fetter Lane, London EC4P 4EE

Simultaneously published in the USA and Canada
by Routledge
a division of Routledge, Chapman and Hall, Inc.
29 West 35th Street, New York, NY 10001

© 1990 Ian Jeffries

Page-set and laser printed directly from the publisher's w-p disks by
NWL Editorial Services, Langport, Somerset, England

Printed in Great Britain by
Richard Clay Ltd, Bungay, Suffolk

British Library Cataloguing in Publication Data
Jeffries, Ian
A guide to the socialist economies.
1. Communist countries. Economic policies
I. Title
330.9171'7

ISBN 0-415-00746-1

Library of Congress Cataloging in Publication Data

Jeffries, I.
A guide to the socialist economies / Ian Jeffries
    p.   cm.
Bibliography: p.
Includes index.
ISBN 0-415-00746-1
1. Communist countries—Economic policy.   2. Soviet
Union—Economic policy—1917–   3. Central planning—Communist
countries.   4. Central planning—Soviet Union.   I. Title
HC704.J34   1989   89–1037
338.9'009171'7—dc19   CIP

Contents

12 The People's Republic of China   203

13 Cuba   245

14 Democratic People's Republic of Korea   261

15 The Mongolian People's Republic   271

16 Socialist Republic of Vietnam   279

Part IV: Conclusion

17 Summing up   299

    Bibliography   303

    Index   317

Figures

Tables

Preface

Any person analysing fourteen countries deserves, I believe, a little credit for even making the attempt and for exposing himself to attack from specialists in the various fields. Nevertheless, the author, fully aware of the pitfalls, extends a positive welcome to any constructive comments.

I am indebted to my friend and colleague Dr Manfred Melzer, who vetted the chapter on the GDR, Alan Jarvis, the Editor, who made many invaluable suggestions, and a particularly thorough anonymous referee appointed by the publishers. My colleague Professor Russell Evans was extremely kind to transfer the text from one set of disks to another.

The amount of reading material used has been phenomenal and one essential for this type of book is rapid and reliable access to the various sources. The library staff at the University College of Swansea have gone well beyond the call of duty in this regard; I do not think it an exaggeration to say that they helped make this venture possible. The following deserve particular praise (in alphabetical order): Gwenda Bailey, Elaine Brown, Merlyn Brown, Rosalyn Condon, Fred Cowley, Margaret Gillett, Beryl Jones, David Painting, Hazel Pember, Ann Preece, Linda Pritchard, Jane Richards and Carole Williams.

Other typically unsung heroes are the porters ('the boys') in the Abbey and in Fulton House who went out of their way to ensure early morning availability of the quality newspapers. The porters in the library, too, were always ready to oblige with things like packaging.

My friends and colleagues in the Department and Centre gave constant encouragement. Mary Griffiths and Siân Davies did the typing in the early stages.

Introduction

The justification for writing a general textbook on the socialist[1] economies is not very difficult to find. Of the five billion plus world population, China alone accounts for some 1.1 billion, while the Soviet Union is the third largest country in this regard (286.7 million) and first with respect to land area, covering a sixth of the world's land surface excluding Antarctica. The Soviet Union is now, of course, one of the two 'superpowers', its General Secretary is a household name, and *glasnost'* is a word that has been adopted by many other languages.

There is general awareness that major events by any standard are taking place in the society and economy of the Soviet Union and China and that the post-war era has been shaped by the clash between 'capitalism' and 'socialism'. The 'Iron Curtain' fenced off Eastern Europe and led to events such as the 1948–49 Berlin blockade and airlift, the Korean War of 1950–53, the 1956 Hungarian Revolution, the 1968 Warsaw Pact invasion of Czechoslovakia and the brief initial rise of Solidarity in Poland in the early 1980s. Today there is a vague general awareness that Yugoslavia seems to be in a mess politically and economically and that Romania seems to be a harsh place to live in. Albania and Mongolia are among the least known of the socialist countries and arouse some interest for that reason.

The basic aim of this book is to give the reader some idea of the rich variety of economic systems to be found among socialist countries today and to highlight and explain some of the major problems facing them. On the eve of their socialist development, these countries, with the exception of the German Democratic Republic and Czechoslovakia, were basically agrarian in nature. Since all the socialist countries, to varying degrees, either adopted or had imposed upon them a traditional Soviet-type system, it seems sensible to start by outlining that system and the problems it engendered. This, together with an analysis of reforms in the Soviet Union itself, provides a valuable reference point for understanding the reasons for and nature of the reforms undertaken or proposed in all the other countries.

There are three main sections. Part I deals with the traditional Soviet system, its reform in the Soviet Union itself and an analysis of foreign trade. Chapter 1 attempts to explain the essence of a command economy, where decision-making with respect to resource allocation is highly centralized, money plays an essentially passive role, and the main function of the production unit (the enterprise) is to fulfil the state plan. While such a system enabled the Soviet Union rapidly to attain superpower status, such severe problems arose that reforms became necessary. These problems have, to varying degrees, affected all the socialist economies. Chapter 2 traces the reform process in the Soviet Union up to the present and discusses Gorbachev's remedies. The 1990s will show a marked departure from the traditional model if the reforms are actually implemented. Chapter 3 is devoted to foreign trade. In the traditional system trade is a state monopoly and this leads to the phenomenon of 'goods inconvertibility' (on top of currency inconvertibility), which, in turn, helps explain the prevalence of bilateralism. Comecon members are forced to base their foreign trade prices on world levels. Consideration is given to current preoccupations and solutions proposed at recent Comecon meetings. There are such extreme difficulties in foreign trade decision-making that it could be argued that only a radical move towards market methods would overcome them.

Part II looks in turn at each of the other countries of Eastern Europe (Albania, Bulgaria, Czechoslovakia, the GDR, Hungary, Poland, Romania, and Yugoslavia). Part III examines four countries in Asia (China, North Korea, Mongolia, and Vietnam) and one in the Caribbean (Cuba). It would be misleading to rank the countries on some percentage reform scale, but it was clear that in the late 1980s Yugoslavia, Hungary, and China led the field in this regard, while Albania and North Korea are at the other extreme. The Soviet Union, Poland, and Vietnam seemed far more anxious to do something about this than the GDR, Romania, and Cuba, while Bulgaria and Czechoslovakia were dragging their feet. Mongolia will no doubt follow the Soviet lead eventually.

It is useful to look for two broad themes, namely departures from the traditional system and the nature and origins of current problems. Most of the chapters that follow are arranged thus:

1. Political and economic background.
2. Departures from the traditional system, subdivided into two sections
   i. Reform of the planning mechanism: industrial reform; the allocation of manpower; the financial system, with analysis of prices, banking, monetary and fiscal policy, and inflation; agriculture; foreign trade, with analysis of planning, joint equity ventures and foreign debt.
   ii. Changes in ownership: the private, non-agricultural sector.

This enables the reader interested in, say, agricultural policy with regard to private plots, to know broadly where to look. Where useful, statistical survey tables can be found before the notes at the end of chapters.

Notes

1. 'Socialist' as opposed to 'communist', since the latter refers to the final Marxian stage of human development, a utopia on earth not yet attained.

Glossary

agrarno-promishlen komplex (APK)   Agro-industrial complex in Bulgaria. Normally a horizontal integration of cooperative farms, state farms and their servicing centres.

Basic Organization of Associated Labour (BOAL)   The basic legal and economic unit in Yugoslavia. The smallest unit producing a marketed or marketable product.

bilateral trade   The balancing of trade between two countries over a period of time: characterizes trade between command economies.

centrala   'Central' in Romania, usually the result of a country-wide, horizontal integration of one large enterprise with smaller ones.

chuch'e   The North Korean policy of 'self-reliance'.

Comecon (CMEA)   Council of Mutual Economic Assistance. Set up in 1949, there are ten full members: the Soviet Union, Bulgaria, Czechoslovakia, Hungary, Poland, Romania, the GDR, Mongolia, Cuba and Vietnam.

Commune ('people's commune')   Key institution during the Chinese Great Leap Forward.

'Comprehensive' (Complex) Programme   A 1971 Comecon programme for the further extension and improvement of co-operation and development of socialist integration to the year 2000.

control figures   Initial, tentative output targets passed down by the State Planning Commission.

Cultural Revolution   Officially covered the period 1966–76 in China, but the more extreme elements were ended by 1969.

currency inconvertibility   The currencies of command economies are not convertible into each other, into gold or into Western currencies; that is they are not freely bought and sold in foreign exchange markets.

danwei   The workplace in China, not only a production unit, but historically represents an important provider of housing and the chief provider of welfare services.

doi moi   'Renovation' (Vietnam).

Durzhavenski Stopanski Obedineniya   State Economic Organization. The basic production unit in Bulgaria, comprising horizontally integrated enterprises.

economic levers   Prices, taxes, interest rates and so on, used to steer the economy indirectly.

edinonachalie   The principle of one-man responsibility and control, applying to the management of the Soviet enterprise by the director.

extensive growth   Growth of the economy achieved mainly through increasing inputs.

GATT   General Agreement on Tariffs and Trade.

glasnost'   Openness.

glavki   Chief administrations – bodies linking ministries and enterprises in the traditional Soviet economic system.

GLF   Great Leap Forward in China 1958–60.

'goods inconvertibility'   If one command economy has a trade surplus with another, this cannot be automatically converted into a claim on particular goods in the latter country, because of the lack of direct and free exchange between ultimate purchaser and supplier. This claim can only be met by negotiations and provisions in central plans.

Gosbank   The Soviet State Bank.

Gosplan   The Soviet State Planning Commission.

Gospriomka   The Soviet State Quality Commission.

Gossnab   The Soviet State Committee for Material-Technical Supply. Re-established in 1965; a similar organization had existed 1947–53.

goszakazy   State orders in the Soviet Union.

hard commodities   Those commodities particularly sought after within Comecon, because the internal price system undervalues them and they can be sold and purchased on the world market for hard (convertible) currencies (e.g. foodstuffs, fuels, raw materials).

higher-level co-operative   In Vietnamese agriculture this differs from the 'lower-level co-operative' in that labour is the sole source of remuneration.

higher-type agricultural co-operative   A transitional institution in Albania towards a full state farm, differing from the traditional co-operative in ways such as the fact that it receives state budgetary grants instead of repayable long term loans.

HRS   Household responsibility system. The household is now the basic production unit in Chinese agriculture. After meeting state sales quotas, tax obligations and payments for collective services, the household is able to make its own output and input decisions.

IMF   International Monetary Fund.

initial (primary) stage of socialism   The stage in China that started in the 1950s and which could last beyond the mid twenty-first century: a process of gradually moving towards a modern industrial economy.

intensive growth   Output increases largely accounted for by increases in the efficiency of input use, especially by means of an improvement in the application of modern science and technology.

Intensivierung   Intensification. In the GDR approximately equivalent to 'intensive growth'.

Junta Central de Planification (Juceplan)   Cuban Central Planning Board.

khozraschyot   Economic accounting. On this basis the Soviet industrial enterprise is a financially separate and accountable unit for the purpose of efficiently implementing the tekhpromfinplan.

kolkhoz   The Soviet collective farm.

kombinat   The GDR combine. A horizontal and vertical amalgamation of enterprises under the unified control of a director general.

lower-level co-operative (production collective)   A farm in Vietnam where individual income depends on both labour and contributed land and means of production.

material balances   The basic planning technique used in command economies, involving the drawing up of the major sources of supply and demand for a particular commodity with the aim of attaining a rough balance.

materials allocation   The administrative distribution of raw materials, intermediate goods, and capital goods.

MOFERT   The Chinese Ministry of Foreign Economic Relations and Trade.

'moral economy' stage   During the Cuban development of 1966–70, emphasis was placed on moral incentives and collective interests rather than individual material incentives.

naryad   Soviet allocation certificate for non-labour inputs.

NEP   The New Economic Policy period in the Soviet Union (1921–28) characterized by considerable concessions to private enterprise and the restoration in large part of the market mechanism.

Net material product   The Soviet 'material product system' differs from the 'system of national accounts' recommended by the United Nations and used in the West in that it excludes so-called non-productive services. These include (with some variation) defence, general administration, education, finance and credit, and transport and communications serving households. 'NMP produced' minus exports plus imports, measured in domestic prices, and minus losses due to abandoned construction and accidental damage, gives 'NMP utilized'. As a very rough approximation, the Soviet definition gives a figure about 20 per cent less than its Western counterpart.

Neues Ökonomisches System The GDR's NES 1963–70, a period that saw the greatest use to date of indirect steering of the economy by means of mainly monetary instruments.

New Economic Mechanism Introduced in Hungary on 1 January 1968. The term was also used in Bulgaria throughout the 1970s, but resemblance to the Hungarian system is in name only.

new economic zones Resettlement plan in Vietnam to move mainly northern people to zones in central and south Vietnam.

nomenklatura A system whereby the communist party makes all important appointments, including those in the economy.

normative net output Required as opposed to actual wage costs, social insurance, and profit. A sort of 'shadow price' that can be used to determine the entire NNO for the enterprise by multiplying it by actual output.

Noul Mecanism Economico-Financiar The Romanian New Economic and Financial Mechanism, introduced at the start of 1979.

Nov Sistem na Rukovodstvo The Bulgarian New System of Management.

NPK The Bulgarian 'scientific-productive complex', incorporating scientific institutes.

obedineniye The Soviet association, a mainly horizontal amalgamation of enterprises.

'open door' policy Introduced in China in 1978 to open the economy to foreign trade, capital, technology, and know-how.

Pak The Bulgarian 'industro-agrarian complex', a vertical merger of farms with industrial enterprises processing and selling agricultural products.

perestroika The Soviet term for the restructuring of the whole of economic and social life. All-around economic and social reforms.

Plan tekniko-industrial financiar The Albanian industrial enterprise's technical-industrial-financial plan.

Planungsordnung The GDR's Order of Planning.

polny khozraschyot 'Full economic accounting'. All expenditures incurred by the Soviet enterprise, including investment, have to be covered from revenue earned or credits borrowed.

predpriyatiye The Soviet enterprise.

Preisausgleich 'Price equalization'. The mechanism by which exports and imports are involved in a sort of price equalization with world and domestic prices respectively.

prestavba The Czech term for *perestroika*.

Prinzip der Einzelleitung   Principle of individual management. The GDR
        equivalent of *edinonachalie*.

prodrazvyorstka   Compulsory requisitioning of agricultural products used
        during the Soviet War Communism period, 1918–21.

raspilenie sredstv   'Scattering' (excessive spread) of investment resources.
        Construction projects whose completion times are excessive
        relative both to plan and to those taken in the West.

ratchet effect ('base-year approach'; 'planning from the achieved level')   This
        period's achievement by the enterprise is the starting point for
        next period's plan.

samofinansirovanie   Soviet 'self-financing'. Both operating costs and
        capital expenditures have to be covered out of revenue earned by
        the enterprise; investment is normally to be financed out of
        retained profit or from credits that have to be repaid.

samookupaemost   This concept entails at least a minimum rate of return on
        Soviet investment, whatever the source of finance.

samoupravleniye   Soviet 'self-management'. The workforce takes a more
        active part in enterprise plan formulation and in the election of
        management.

second economy   The non-regulated sector, including both legal and illegal
        activity.

self-management   Self-management of the 'socially owned' Yugoslav
        industrial enterprise by the workers via an elected workers'
        council.

SEZs   Special Economic Zones in China. An important feature of China's
        'open door' policy.

shturmovshchina   The Soviet term for 'storming': a mad rush by enterprises
        to fulfil the plan towards the end of the planning period.

Sistema de Dirección de la Economia   The Cuban System of Economic
        Management and Planning.

soft budget constraint   State financial support in the form of subsidies, price
        increases or tax reductions is forthcoming to cover any losses
        made by enterprises.

soft commodities   The reverse of hard commodities (see above). Includes
        examples such as low quality, obsolete machinery and equipment.

sovkhoz   The Soviet state farm. Literally, 'Soviet economic unit'.

stavka   Basic wage rate set for a particular branch of Soviet industry.

structural (commodity) bilateralism   The balancing of trade in 'hard' and
        'soft' goods separately.

taut planning   Implies pressure to maximum output from given resources.

tekhpromfinplan   The technical-industrial-financial plan to be fulfilled by
        the enterprise in the traditional Soviet economic system.

togrog   The Mongolian currency unit. Equals 100 mongo.

tolkachi   Soviet 'pushers': unofficial supply agents.

transferable rouble   A unit of account used in transacting intra-Comecon trade.

trudoden   The Soviet agricultural 'work day'. Not literally a calendar day, but each particular piece of work is valued at so many 'work days'.

turnover tax   Essentially the difference between the wholesale and retail price. Typically the tax is price-determined, that is a residual resulting from attempts to equate supply and demand.

valovaya produktsiya   The Soviet term for gross output. Measures the value of finished output plus net change in the value of goods in the process of production.

valuta   Foreign currency.

Vervollkommnung   'Perfecting' of planning, management and economic accounting in the GDR.

vstrechnye plany   'Counter plans'. Designed as an inducement to enterprise managers to adopt more demanding targets than those set out in the five-year plan.

Vyrobni hospodarska jednotka (VHJ)   The Czechoslovak industrial association.

war communism   The period 1918–21 in the Soviet union, characterized by extreme nationalization and an attempt at a form of moneyless administration.

wielkie organizacje gospodarcze   Polish 'large economic organizations'.

zayavka   The Soviet indent (request) for non-labour inputs.

zjednoczenie   Polish 'association' of enterprises.

zrzeszenie   Polish 'amalgamation' of enterprises.

zveno   The Soviet 'link': a small agricultural group that is given responsibility for a piece of land or livestock unit, allocated inputs and set broad output targets. The group is paid for results, but is not set work assignments.

Part one

The Soviet Union

Chapter one

The traditional Soviet economic system

Background

On the eve of the First World War Russia was still a relatively backward, agrarian country. This was despite considerable industrial growth over the previous thirty years, the rate of which had doubled during the 1890s. Today the Soviet Union is one of the world's two 'superpowers'.

Various indicators may be used to assess the level of development of Russia in 1913. Per capita income was less than 40 per cent of France's, about 33 per cent of Germany's, 20 per cent of Britain's and 10 per cent US per capita income (Gregory and Stuart, 2nd edn, 1981: 25). In 1913 Russia accounted for only just over 4 per cent of world industrial output, compared to 10 per cent in 1941 and about 20 per cent today. In 1917 Russia ranked as the fifth industrial power in the world and the fourth in Europe (Aganbegyan 1988a: 45–47). Today the Soviet Union's national income is around 66 per cent of that of the United States; Western estimates are lower, in the range of 50–55 per cent (Aganbegyan 1988a: 224). More recent official Soviet figures show a decline in the ratio of Soviet to US net material product (NMP) from 66 per cent in 1986 to 64 per cent in 1987 (Treml 1988: 80). A high birth rate of around 44 per thousand in 1913 was coupled with a relatively high death rate of around 27 per thousand, the infant mortality rate being about 237 per thousand. Sixty per cent of the population over the age of 10 was illiterate (Gregory and Stuart 1986: 41–42). The commodity structure of foreign trade was typical of a poor country, with exports of primary commodities, especially grain, paying for imports of manufactures, especially capital goods. Agriculture employed 72 per cent of the workforce (82 per cent of the population was rural) and contributed over 50 per cent of national product (Gregory and Stuart 1986: 41); in 1928 agriculture contributed 60 per cent of national income (Aganbegyan 1988a: 21). Serfdom had been abolished only in 1861, and the attempted switch to capitalist agriculture after 1906 came too late.

This vast country, however, had enormous economic potential in the shape of a rich and varied natural resource endowment, despite climatic, transport and soil difficulties.[1]

3

The Bolsheviks, under Lenin, came to power in October 1917 with no detailed economic blueprint from the works of Marx and Engels.[2] Marx saw society inevitably progressing through various stages of development, namely primitive society, slavery, feudalism, capitalism, socialism and communism. Marx essentially provided a critique of capitalism, but socialism was only vaguely defined. There was to be the 'conscious social regulation of production' (as opposed to the 'anarchy' of the market), the 'common' ownership of the means of production, and distribution according to work (as opposed to need under communism).

The early years after the revolution saw state takeovers (without compensation) in banking, foreign trade and key industries like iron and steel. All land was nationalized, and the national debt, equivalent to 120 per cent of national income in 1917, was repudiated. The period of 'war communism' lasted from 1918 to 1921. The overriding aim was to win the civil war against the Whites who were aided by capitalist intervention (e.g. Germany occupying the Ukraine). Nationalization was taken to extremes, with enterprises employing only one person in some cases. The market was replaced by a form of moneyless administration, local authorities mainly, with the central state practising campaign methods. Labour was directed and increasingly paid in kind, while agricultural products were compulsorily requisitioned (the *prodrazvyorstka*). Although allowing resources to be concentrated at the front, war communism was not sustainable as a peacetime mechanism, and gave way to the New Economic Policy (NEP; 1921–28), the study of which is topical today because of Gorbachev's interest in the period. Concessions were made to private enterprise, especially in retail trade, although the state still retained control of the commanding heights like metallurgy, armaments, fuels, and banking. The market mechanism was restored to a large extent. There were even (not very successful) attempts to attract foreign capital and enterprise. One of the world's classic hyperinflations was checked by output increases, an end to exclusive reliance on the printing press, and confidence inspired by a new currency. The pre-First World War output levels were broadly regained towards the end of the NEP period, planning institutions such as Gosplan were established, planning techniques were developed and the future was explored in the rigorous 'industrialization debate'.

The traditional Soviet economic system

It is useful to examine the traditional economic system in terms of goals, strategy, and institutional framework.

Goals

Being the only socialist country in what was perceived to be a hostile capitalist environment and thus in danger of an all-out invasion, the basic aim was to catch up with and surpass the leading capitalist countries, especially in terms of heavy industrial capacity and military power. This was encapsulated in a famous 1931 speech by Stalin: 'We are fifty or a hundred years behind the advanced countries. We must make good this distance in ten years. Either we do it, or we shall go under' (quoted in Ellman 1989: 13). This goal was to be achieved by means of the chosen strategy and institutional framework. Stalin maintained that it was possible to build 'socialism in one country', socialism being, as shown above, the penultimate stage on the path to communism where there is distribution according to need and no class conflict. There were other goals, of course, such as full employment and the absence of the extremes of income and wealth associated with capitalism. As is shown below, however, significant wage differentials are an important aspect of labour policy in the traditional system.

Strategy

During the 1930s the state used its allocative powers to devote the historically high figure of around a quarter of national output to investment (Bergson 1961: 237). Consumption was held down to a level judged adequate to maintain political stability and work incentives. Sectoral priority was awarded to industry, specifically about 40 per cent of total investment (Kaplan 1953: 52). The share in total industrial production of producer goods rose from 39.5 per cent in 1928 to 61.2 per cent in 1940 (Ellman 1989: 139). The 'leading links' were iron and steel, heavy engineering, mining, electric power generation, and armaments. In a quantitative sense, foreign trade did not play a large strategic role; exports reached their lowest share in national income of only 0.5 per cent in 1937. Nevertheless, the Soviet Union was able to import vital capital goods embodying the latest technology.

The institutional framework

Command planning

The economic problem, as conventionally defined – namely that of choosing which of an essentially infinite number of needs are to be met with the limited (scarce) resources available – is one that faces all societies. In a system of command planning the basic allocative decisions about what to produce and in what quantities are taken by the state, but in reality the whole economic hierarchy has to be involved in decision-making.[3] In highly simplified form the pyramid has the State Planning Commission (Gosplan) at its apex, ministries ('commissariats' before 1946) at the intermediate level and enterprises (production units) at its base (see Figure 1.1). Before embarking on this analysis it is important to understand the crucial role of the Communist Party in formu-

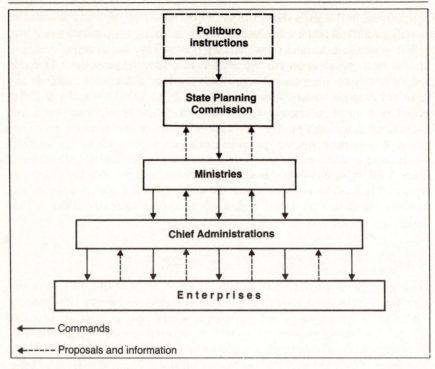

Figure 1.1 The economic hierarchy

lating and implementing policies, dominating economic, political, and social life in a one-party state.

The State Planning Commission (SPC)

The SPC receives instructions about basic economic magnitudes from the party, especially the Politburo, relating to growth rates of national income and of its sub-categories of consumption, investment, and defence, and to vitally important goods. These instructions are relayed via the state apparatus, especially the Council of Ministers, and Gosplan combines these with the data/requests/proposals flowing upwards from the hierarchy to draw up plans of varying duration by means of 'material balances'. The annual, quarterly and monthly plans are operational; medium (five-year) plans and perspective plans of at least 15 years' duration are much more highly aggregated and are only operational in relation to the investment plan, since many projects cover a number of years. More recently annual plans are meant to be drawn up within the context of the allegedly more important five-year plan, but in reality changing targets and environmental and economic conditions ensure that the annual plan is still the operational one. The basic aim is to draw up a balanced plan that fulfils the goals set by the Politburo.

Table 1.1 illustrates a material balance in simplified form. The major sources of supply and demand for a particular commodity are drawn up with the aim of attaining a rough balance. Production is typically by far the major source of supply, since 'taut' planning is exercised and imports are only important for certain commodities, such as capital goods during the 1930s. It is useful to distinguish between intermediate and final demand at this stage, since later on we shall be studying input-output analysis. Intermediate inputs are used up in the course of producing other goods.

Table 1.1 The Soviet Union: a material balance

	Supply		Demand
1.	Production	1.	Intermediate use
2.	Stocks at the beginning of the plan period	2.	Final demand use
			a. Consumption
			b. Fixed investment
3.	Imports		c. Stocks at the end of the plan period
			d. Exports

The Soviet economy suffers endemic supply problems (see pp. 14 for the effects) and one reason is the crudity of the material balance technique. Balances are heavily aggregated, the number of balances being far fewer than the number of 'commodities'. Even by 1981 the annual plan involved Gosplan drawing up material balances for only 2,044 products, Gossnab 7,500, and ministries 25,000 (Schroeder 1982: 75). Then there is the 'iterative' problem. If, for example, the output of a particular good was increased, in the early years of planning usually only the first-order iteration (repetition) was carried out (i.e. estimates made of the effects on direct inputs). Further iterations (effects on the inputs needed to produce the increased inputs and so on) were ignored. For this reason excess demand was tackled as much as possible by, for example, reducing both the use of inputs per unit of output ('tightening of norms') and the consumption element of final demand, as opposed to changing supply (i.e. increasing output).

The allocation of most non-labour inputs is handled by the 'materials allocation' system – the administrative distribution of raw materials, intermediate goods and capital goods. The supplying and using enterprises are matched centrally, and the all-important document is the *naryad* (allocation certificate), which specifies the quantity of the product and the supplying organization.

Command planning is well named in the sense that the enterprise eventually receives plan targets in the shape of a technical-industrial-financial plan (*tekhpromfinplan*). But since it is impossible for central planners to produce detailed, concrete plans in the abstract, the economic hierarchy has to be involved, with the emphasis in the traditional system on vertical as opposed to horizontal (i.e. enterprise to enterprise) linkage. More specifically tentative output targets ('control figures') are passed down the planning pyramid to be increasingly disaggregated (made more detailed) by ministries and enterprises. Suggestions/requests (the *zayavka* is an input indent, for example) are made at each echelon and passed back up the hierarchy. While the centre's major allocative decisions are preserved, this process can be influential, as in suggested input substitution to meet a given output target. Annual plans are often late and are frequently changed; failure to fulfil by one enterprise has repercussions on others. It is worth noting at this point the importance of informal linkages that oil the wheels of the economic mechanism in reality. Examples include, as is to be seen below, shady deals and downright illegal relationships between enterprises.

Before exploring the role of the enterprise, it is interesting to note that two areas of the economy have been left, in more normal times, largely to the market mechanism, namely the distribution of consumer goods and the allocation of manpower. These are interrelated in both a micro- and macro-economic sense. Wages and salaries paid out in the production sector constitute the main means of payment for the consumer goods and services made available in the plan (which, in turn, provide the main incentive to work), while avoidance of inflation means matching the cash (rouble notes and coins) injected into the economy with the aggregate supply of consumer goods and services at established prices.

Distribution of consumer goods

There is essentially consumer choice (as opposed to sovereignty) in the command economy. This means that consumers can choose among the consumer goods and services made available in the plan, rather than being able to determine the allocation of resources, as in a competitive market economy.

Figure 1.2 shows how the distribution of a particular good may be handled. The supply curve is drawn parallel to the vertical axis, that is perfectly inelastic with respect to price, to represent planned supply. A shift to the right of the schedule would indicate a decision to increase planned supply. The demand curve is estimated, and the market would be cleared at the equilibrium price of P_1.

Although planners often attempt to set price at the market clearing level, this is typically not achieved, either because the demand curve is wrongly estimated in the first place or it may have shifted over time; prices are often set for extended periods of time (see p. 18).[4] If the price is too low (P_2), then excess demand AB results and other forms of market clearing, such as queues, have to be employed. If the price is set too high (P_3), then excess supply CD causes stockpiles of commodities. The poor quality of many Soviet consumer goods,

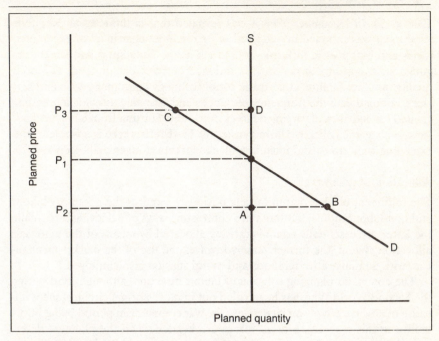

Figure 1.2 The distribution of a particular good

the reason for which will be analysed later, may be seen to be reflected in this context as a demand curve well to the left of that estimated by planners (this latter estimated curve would go through point D), producing the above result. Note that in this case the turnover tax becomes a 'tax by difference', the difference between the wholesale and retail price less trade margins. In some cases, however, it is more like an excise tax.

It is important to note that the state deliberately underprices some commodities and these are distributed either through queues, literally or in the form of long waiting lists, or formally rationed. Foodstuffs (such as bread, dairy products, and meat), transport fares, and housing rents are typically heavily subsidized in socialist economies and remain constant for decades for political and income distribution reasons. For example, Soviet consumers receive state subsidies amounting to over 50 billion roubles annually for basic foodstuffs and services (Nikolai Shmelev, *Novy Mir*, no. 6, June 1987: 152), while in 1985 rents for state housing, fixed in 1928, took up only 3 per cent of an average family budget (Trehub 1987: 29). Queues are usually allowed to form for foodstuffs. There have been periods when rationing has been general, such as in the Soviet Union in the first half of the 1930s. Even today, however, a coupon system for the sale of products such as meat, sugar, and butter exists in eight of the fifteen republics of the Soviet Union (*Pravda*, 1 September

1988, p. 3). In December 1988 it was revealed that in the Russian Republic itself meat was rationed in one third of its regions, sugar in 67 of its 86 territories and butter even in fertile areas such as the Volgograd and Rostov regions. State housing, in contrast, is rationed on the basis of need. The poor quality, non-availability, and erratic supply of many consumer goods and services, coupled with the frequency of queues and rationing, provide a breeding ground for activities of varying degrees of legality. Starting from legal mechanisms, such as the collective farm market for foodstuffs, there is a whole gamut extending right up to and including black markets (Katsenelinboigen 1977).

Allocation of manpower

The fulfilment of plan output targets obviously requires the necessary labour and non-labour inputs, but there are contrasting ways of achieving this. While the latter are essentially administratively allocated by means of the materials allocation system, the former mainly involves the use of the market mechanism, with administrative methods and moral suasion also employed.[5]

The command planning solution of labour direction, although used during the Second World War, has been ruled out in more normal circumstances because of adverse effects on incentives (the war communism period being informative in this respect). Market forces are heeded when the planners determine basic wage differentials, while the state controls the education system, including the number of places available for particular courses of study. The state is able to use this combination, for example, to induce the increased supply of labour of the required skill needed to meet an altered production plan.

Figure 1.3 shows the demand and supply schedules for a particular type of skilled worker. The demand curve is shown as perfectly inelastic on the grounds that, with existing technology, the number of workers required is given by the planned level of output. Assume initially that supply equals demand, but that the new plan calls for increased output which, with labour a derived demand, leads to a shift to the right of the demand curve to D_2. If the total supply of skilled labour were not increased, the wage rate would have to rise to W_2 to regain equilibrium, by attracting workers with the required skill from other sectors. But if the supply curve could be shifted to the right, by a combination of increasing the number of training places available and party propaganda for example, as well as the inducement of higher wages to learn a new skill, the equilibrium wage rate becomes W_3 and the increased supply N_1N_2 is the result of two sources, N_1N_3 from other sectors and N_3N_2 from the newly skilled.

The industrial worker's pay crudely consists of two parts: (1) a state-guaranteed basic wage, which varies according to industrial branch, skill and region; and (2) the residual. This is affected by bonuses, related to such factors as plan fulfilment and the nature of the job (dangerous working conditions, for example). A basic rate (*stavka*) is set for a particular branch of industry,

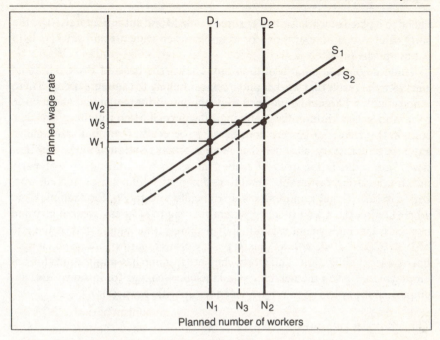

Figure 1.3 Demand and supply schedules for a particular type of skilled worker

Source: Adaptation of the model used by McConnell, R. and Brue, S. (1986) *Contemporary Labour Economics*, New York: McGraw-Hill, pp. 557–8.

which determines the wage of the least skilled and therefore lowest paid worker. A tariff (scale) then establishes higher skill rates as a percentage of the basic rate, and there is also a set of regional coefficients with which to multiply the standard rate by. This formal system enables the state to encourage labour to move to desired industries and regions and to adopt the desired skills. In addition, there is *de facto* room to manoeuvre by the enterprise manager, even within the constraints of an enforced wage fund, by manipulating norms and skill designations for example. In the early period piece rates, as opposed to time rates, were dominant; a 100 per cent fulfilment of the norm, or output quota, would earn the *stavka* (Filtzer 1989: 90).

The non-market elements in manpower allocation have varied enormously over time. Forced labour camps were full as a result of the collectivization of agriculture and Stalin's purges. Although used for activities such as mining in inhospitable places, the camps served a mainly political function. High labour turnover during the 1930s, seen as a threat to plan fulfilment, was combated by means such as the 'work book'. This was introduced in 1938 and held by the enterprise manager; without it a worker could not, in principle, find another job. Increasingly harsh legislation eventually made even absenteeism and lateness criminal offences. Graduates of universities and technical schools are as-

11

signed to a place of work for two or three years. Moral suasion exercised by the party can be seen in operation, for example, when students and workers help out at harvest time.

Trade unions are an arm of the state. They are organized along industrial lines with the result that worker and manager belong to the same union. There is no collective bargaining between trade unions and management about basic wage and salary differentials, although the former exercise some marginal consultative roles. Strikes are considered to be counter-revolutionary and in any case unnecessary, although they are not actually outlawed in the constitution. This reduces the role of trade unions to the transmission of party policies, ensuring favourable conditions for plan fulfilment, protecting workers' interests (legal requirements as to health and safety, for example) and administering the social security system relating to sickness, work injury and pensions. Unemployment was officially declared to be eliminated by the end of 1930 (*CDSP*, 1988, vol. XL, no. 4, p. 4); work is regarded not only as a right but as a legal obligation. The Gorbachev programme has implications for unemployment,[6] given the need for rapid technical change for instance, and unemployment pay has been reintroduced for specific purposes.[7]

The industrial enterprise

Private enterprise was severely limited as regards:

1. Area: Handicrafts, agriculture and certain consumer services were acceptable, but selling goods made by other people was not allowed.
2. Employment: The employment of another person outside the immediate family in the production of goods for sale was illegal.
3. Income: Direct taxes were heavier than normal.

Thus the industrial enterpise was a state-owned plant, operating on the principle of one-man responsibility and control (*edinonachalie*) by a director appointed by the state or more strictly the party: positions of any importance were to be found on its *nomenklatura* or list. Lower levels of management included the deputy director and chief engineer, complemented by the party cell and the trade union branch.

The basic function of the industrial enterprise was to fulfil its 'technical, industrial and financial plan' (*tekhpromfinplan*). The operational plans (annual, quarterly and monthly) were expressed in terms of plan targets (success indicators), varying over time in terms of number and priority as particular problems arose. Output targets, however, were paramount. This is explicable in terms of the goals discussed earlier: the fact that a high proportion of production is used as inputs by other enterprises, the need to equate supply and demand via the use of material balances, and the difficulty of measuring quality. Gross output (*valovaya produktsiya*) measured the value of finished output plus net change in the value of goods in the process of production;

output in physical terms involved units of measurement such as weight, numbers and length; and targets for more heterogeneous output were broken down into main assortment indicators. On the input side there was a plan for material-technical supply and for labour utilization indicators, namely the wage fund (the total amount to be paid out in the plan period), productivity, average wage and number of workers by skill brackets. There were usually many other indicators, such as cost reduction, profit (as a percentage of cost rather than capital), investment, innovation, delivery schedules, and equipment utilization.

The industrial enterprise was a financially separate and accountable unit operating on a *khozraschyot* (economic accounting) basis, for the purpose of efficiently implementing the plan. Prices were fixed by the state and the enterprise account had to be kept in the local branch of the State Bank (Gosbank). The purpose of the latter was to help ensure plan compliance, the idea being that only payments in conformity with the plan should be permitted. Budgetary grants covered fixed capital needs and Gosbank had a monopoly over the granting of short-term credit, available at a nominal rate of interest which was fixed only to cover administrative costs. Management motivation involved negative consequences for non-fulfilment of plan, such as loss of bonuses, expulsion from the party and its associated privileges, and possible imprisonment or even capital punishment for 'economic sabotage' during the darkest periods. Positive incentives were associated with fulfilment and overfulfilment. Bonus, socio-cultural and investment funds were linked to success indicators, especially output.

Enterprises producing goods for export or using imported commodities were shielded from the world market by the state monopoly of foreign trade and payments. The industrial enterprise was assigned to a foreign trade corporation. The FTC, in turn, was subject to the authority of the Ministry of Foreign Trade and the ministry to the State Planning Commission. The price paid to the enterprise producing the good for export was the domestic and not the world price; imports were paid for at the prices of comparable domestic commodities. This divorce of domestic and world market prices, coupled with arbitrarily determined exchange rates,[8] led to accounting 'profits' and 'losses' being made by the FTCs. Due to a penchant for overvaluation of the rouble these were typically losses on exports and profits on imports. This is the mechanism by means of which exports and imports are involved in a sort of price equalization (*Preisausgleich*) with world and domestic prices, respectively. This separation of Soviet and foreign industrial firms greatly aggravated the problems already experienced with product quality. Although the traditional system played a crucial role in carrying out Stalin's goals, micro-economic problems of a severe kind arose.

Neglect of user need. Output only had to be produced and not sold in the traditional Soviet economic system, while emphasis on one indicator led to neglect of others. The result was that quantity was stressed at the expense of quality. For example, physical indicators such as weight, number, or length resulted in too large, small, or narrow objects respectively being produced, relative to user need. Gross output provides an incentive to use expensive inputs if these are reflected in product price and to orientate product assortment towards those goods incorporating large amounts of these inputs. This neglect of the qualitative aspects of production was especially acute in low-priority sectors involved in heterogeneous output, such as textiles, and helps explain the seemingly paradoxical phenomenon of stockpiles of unsaleable products in a situation of general consumer goods scarcity. Even today there is a problem – only between 7.0 and 18 per cent of Soviet manufacturing output meets world standards (Nikolai Shmelev, *Novy Mir*, no. 6, June 1987, p. 148).

A tendency to understate productive capacity. The director has an incentive to provide such false information in the hope of achieving a 'slack' plan, one that calls for less than feasible output,[9] since no bonuses were paid for anything less than 100 per cent fulfilment. Although extra bonuses were available for overfulfilment, the director was careful not to overfulfil by too much since this would endanger fulfilment of subsequent plans. The 'ratchet effect', known in Eastern Europe as the 'base-year approach', means that this period's achievement is the starting point for next period's plan – 'planning from the achieved level', as it is also called (Birman 1978). The ratchet effect has been a persistent problem because of its simplicity of use by data-deficient planners.

A tendency to overindent for non-labour inputs and to hoard these as well as labour. Manpower was hoarded to meet unforeseen needs or the frequent changes in plans. Non-labour inputs too were hoarded, due, for example, to the horrendous supply problems associated with the materials allocation system and the fact that capital was a free factor to the enterprise. This led to such phenomena as *tolkachi* (expediters, unofficial supply agents, who barter with each other among other things) and a powerful inducement to self-sufficiency in the supply of inputs; parts of Soviet industry are notoriously non specialized.

Storming (shturmovshchina). This is the mad rush to fulfil plans at the end of the planning period (such as the month), explained by such factors as the bonus system, delays in receiving inputs from other enterprises and the unwillingness of enterprises to show early eagerness in an environment where plans typically arrive late and are frequently changed (Bleaney 1988: 63).

Anti-innovation bias at the micro level. Innovation is the application of new ideas about products and techniques to the production process. While new priority large-scale technologies (in armaments, for example) are readily dealt with by command economies, vital, spontaneous, micro level innovation is hindered by the traditional Soviet economic system:

1. There is no competitive pressure to stay in business as in market economies.
2. The incentive system means jeopardizing short-term plan fulfilment and the prospect of 'ratchet effects'.
3. State-determined prices may mean adverse effects on value indicators.
4. There were the aforementioned problems of input supply.
5. R&D, traditionally taking place in specialized organizations within ministries, was separated from production (Berliner 1976).

Thus it seems that the interests of enterprise, user and state often conflict in the command economy, but it is important to note (Nove 1986) the impossibility of central planners generally knowing what is needed in precise, disaggregated detail. The price system (see p. 18) is denied this informational role and this is at the root of the reform problem. According to Shmelev (*Novy Mir*, no. 6, June 1987, p. 136), there are currently around 24 million items in Soviet industrial production.

The financial system

Any economy that wishes to reap the benefits of extensive specialization and exchange needs money to function as a medium of exchange, unit of account, store of value and standard for deferred payments. The command economy uses money (the experience of war communism was influential here), but, given that resources are largely centrally allocated, it plays an essentially passive role. This is best illustrated by repeating the point that an enterprise's non-labour inputs are distributed administratively; it is the *naryad* that is the vital piece of paper, money being automatically forthcoming. Price tags are attached to items of expenditure and revenue in order to be able to draw up the account necessary for purposes of evaluation and control. Note, however, that since market elements are important in these areas, differential wage rates actively influence manpower allocation, and consumers often exercise choice over the goods and services made available in the plan. Money is needed because it is impossible to plan physically the output of every single good and in order to monitor performance.

The concept of the total money supply in the Soviet economy is not very meaningful because there are two payments circuits, 'household cash' and 'deposit transfer'. The latter circuit comprises the bookkeeping changes that cover practically all inter-enterprise transactions, while the former has implications for macro financial equilibrium. The state is concerned to keep a bal-

15

ance between the cash injected into the economy, largely via the paying out of wages and salaries, and the supply of consumer goods and services made available in the plan at established prices, in order to avoid inflationary pressures. This can be expressed with the aid of an equation: $PQ = Y + TP - S - T$, where P is the general retail price level (i.e. average retail price); Q is the quantity of consumer goods and services; Y is household income in the form of wages and salaries earned in the production of all goods and services; TP is transfer payments, such as pensions, paid out to households; S is household savings; and T is direct taxes levied on households.

In principle the Soviet Union is thus able to prevent open and repressed inflation. It is interesting and instructive, therefore, to examine why significant open inflation was a feature of the 1930s. While plans for the production of consumer goods were generally underfulfilled, there was a large leakage of cash into the system through the overdrawing of wage funds. This originated in (1) the high level of labour turnover, which itself was the result of a predominantly undisciplined labour force, recently arrived from the countryside, in search of higher earnings; and (2) the plight of enterprise directors desperate for labour to fulfil the all-important output targets. Managers indulged in all sorts of activities, such as artificial upgrading, to get around state determined wage rates. The State Bank allowed wage fund transgressions for fear of jeopardizing output plans.[10]

There were attempts to correct the financial imbalance by encouraging household savings (S), including what were in effect forced bond sales, but the massive increases in direct taxes that would have been needed were ruled out by the necessity to preserve work incentives. What was left was P – retail prices were increased to move nearer to market clearing levels (thus causing turnover taxes, which were usually price determined, to increase) and to soak up some of the excess purchasing power. It is worth noting that in the 1930s the Soviet Union experienced full employment and open inflation, while the reverse situation existed in the capitalist West.

Y is worth exploring a little further because wages and salaries are paid out not only to people working in sectors producing consumer goods and services, but also to those not, namely in investment, social consumption and defence. These have to be absorbed by indirect taxes, direct taxes, or savings (Ellman 1989: 233). If the latter two are ruled out, then indirect taxation must involve an average markup (m) over the costs of production of consumer goods and services given by the following equation:

$$m = \frac{Wsc + Wi + Wd}{Whc}$$

where W represents wages and salaries paid out in social consumption (sc), investment (i), defence (d) and household consumption (hc). The introduction of direct taxes and savings means that a lower markup would be needed.

Note that the actual markup involves mainly the turnover tax and profit.

If retail prices are not raised sufficiently to achieve financial equilibrium, the result is repressed inflation, which takes the form of queues, rationing and blocked purchasing power (i.e. forced savings). The extent to which repressed inflation has existed in the Soviet Union in recent decades, however, is a very controversial point. The sceptics point to the coexistence of stockpiles and queues, and consider rapidly rising savings accounts as normal consumer behaviour.

The budget

Real resource flows are determined in the plan, but are also reflected in the consolidated budget at all levels of government. The major elements of expenditure are for the 'national economy', especially capital grants and subsidies, and for socio-cultural purposes, such as health and education. The budgetary category of defence significantly underestimates the real total, with elements such as weapons research tucked away under other headings. On the revenue side, the outstanding point to note is the overwhelming reliance on indirect rather than direct taxes. One important reason for this was to preserve the wage differentials needed for incentives in a market environment. The turnover tax was more important than profit payments in the early years. Since resource allocation is determined in the plan, the budget plays a role in the quest for financial equilibrium.

The banking system

Banking is a state monopoly. The State Bank (Gosbank) is a *monobank*, that is there is not the separation between the central bank and private commercial banks to be found in the West. Gosbank fulfils the following functions in that it:

1. issues cash;
2. has a monopoly of gold and foreign exchange reserves (command economies typically have a specialized Foreign Trade Bank to deal with international payments);
3. acts as the fiscal agent of government, collecting budgetary revenue and disbursing current expenditures (a separate Construction Bank handles the doling out of investment grants);
4. has a monopoly on short-term credits for working capital purposes in line with the state plan; and
5. monitors plan fulfilment by enterprises by means of the obligatory account.

The Savings Bank services the needs of individuals. The overriding task then, reflecting the essentially passive role of money, is to aid plan fulfilment. Contrast this with the active exercise of monetary (and fiscal) policy in market economies.

Price determination

In the traditional system industrial prices are formally fixed by the state on the basis of planned branch *average* cost of production and a small profit markup on costs. Average cost is used in order to ensure overall branch profitability, while providing an incentive to lower costs. Costs include labour, raw materials, intermediate inputs, interest on short term credits, and depreciation (though not allowing for technical obsolescence), but exclude a capital charge and a rental charge reflecting favourable location or plant modernity.[11] For consumer goods the difference between the wholesale price, including the markup of the wholesale organization where appropriate, and the retail price, less the retail markup, is the 'turnover tax'. Since the general rule is to try to set the retail price at market clearing levels, the turnover tax is generally price-determined (i.e. a residual). The tax is only price determining when it is in effect an excise tax of a given amount. Retail prices reflect demand to varying extents, but wholesale prices ignore demand because of persistent shortages. The latter are based on average rather than marginal cost (though not based on all costs), and are fixed for long periods of time, partly for administrative reasons and partly to be better able to assess enterprise performance over time. Wholesale prices are, therefore, not efficiency prices,[12] but they are not, of course, meant to play an important allocative role, factor substitution being one area where they are active. Instead, in line with the essential passivity of money, they serve as a means of control and evaluation (*khozraschyot* and value indicators, for example). As already noted, domestic prices are separated from world prices by the state foreign trade monopoly. Radical price reform only becomes essential when a significant decentralization of decision-making is considered.

Agriculture

All land in the Soviet Union belongs to the state, although other bodies are allowed use of it. The main production unit in the early system was not the state farm (*sovkhoz*), but the collective farm (*kolkhoz*). Collectivization during the 1930s was forced, bloody and brutal. Only a nominally independent co-operative, the *kolkhoz* was subject to state plans and delivery quotas (the latter being concentrated upon after the mid-1950s) at state-determined prices which sometimes bordered on the confiscatory. In 1936 the compulsory procurement price for wheat, plus handling costs, was 15 roubles a tonne; this wheat was sold to state milling enterprises at 107 roubles per tonne, the turnover tax thus amounting to 92 roubles (Nove 1961: 99). During the 1930s the compulsory procurement price for potatoes of 3.6 roubles a tonne contrasted with free market prices varying between 37 and 200 roubles a tonne.

Peasant income for work on the collective farm was residual in nature, constituting that remaining from gross revenue after deduction of all other costs, including social security and equipment. The workday (*trudoden*) was not literally a calendar day, but each particular piece of work was valued at so many workdays. Its value was not known until the end of the year, the residual being divided by the total number of workdays earned. This uncertainty, the infrequency and low levels of remuneration (in kind as well as money), the negligible impact of individual effort on total farm income, and the fact that the burden of a poor harvest was placed on the shoulders of the peasants (there was even a man-made famine in areas such as the Ukraine) had a disastrous effect on incentives. Collective farm peasants did not receive state pensions until 1964. Peasants devoted so much time to their private plots that a minimum number of days of collective work had to be introduced. Although severely restricted in terms of size and livestock holdings, these plots were a vital source of peasant cash income and of supply of such products as fruit and vegetables, dairy products and meat, which were either consumed in the household or sold on the free market.

There is still controversy about the role of agriculture as a source of forced savings, but collectivization provided food for the rapidly growing urban labour force, raw materials (like cotton) for industry and agricultural products for export (generally at relatively low cost to the state), and encouraged the movement of labour necessary for rapid industrialization. It was also hoped that collectivization would reap the benefits of industrial mechanization applied to large scale farming units and secure party control in the countryside.

The cost of collectivization, however, was great. In the short term there was a reduction in agricultural output of around a fifth during 1928–32 and a massive slaughter of livestock by unwilling peasants. The long run health of the sector also suffered, agriculture often being described as the Achilles' heel of the economy. Apart from the income distribution system, the central planning of agriculture faces special problems, including the variety of constantly changing local conditions and difficulties of supervision, the vital importance of a timely supply of inputs in a sector dominated by seasonal factors (such as spare parts for repair and maintenance), and the fact that land and produce may be put to better use, as far as farmers are concerned.

Conclusion

Despite an industrial spurt in the late Tsarist era, the economy in 1917 and in 1928, after a recuperative period, was still basically agrarian. The traditional Soviet economic system adopted by Stalin after 1928 sought to achieve the main goal of rapidly matching the capitalist powers in terms of heavy industrial capacity and military strength. Implementation involved a strategy of investing a historically high proportion of national output and giving sectoral priority to heavy industry, coupled with a limited role assigned to foreign trade. The institutional framework was that of a command economy, in which decision-making with respect to resource allocation was highly centralized. The distribution of consumer goods and the allocation of manpower, however, involved substantially market methods in more normal times. The prime function of the state industrial enterprise was to fulfil state plan targets, while the private sector was severely curtailed. Money plays an essentially passive role in a command economy, but the possibility of inflation is raised.

The traditional economic system enabled the Soviet Union rapidly to attain superpower status, albeit at the expense of serious economic problems. Chapter 1 has discussed the neglect of user need, understatement of productive capacity, hoarding of inputs, 'storming' and anti-innovation bias. The beginning of Chapter 2 follows this up with other problems such as the scattering of investment resources and declining growth rates.

Notes

1. The Soviet Union occupies a sixth of the earth's land surface, excluding Antarctica. In 1917 the population was 143 million (with a different land area), compared with the 286.7 million on 12 January 1989.
2. According to the Julian calendar, which was used until February 1918, the start of the Bolshevik Revolution was 25 October 1917, but thereafter was celebrated on 7 November. The so-called 'bourgeois revolution' of February 1917 actually overthrew Tsarism. The Treaty of Brest-Litovsk was signed on 3 March 1918 with Germany, Austria-Hungary, Turkey and Bulgaria, but was annulled 13 November 1918.
3. The enterprise manager, for example, has some decision-making autonomy with regard to input substitution and production choice within the aggregate plan target. Contracts drawn up between enterprises include things like delivery times and the detailed product mix. Kroll (1988: 360) views the main functions of contracts as to economize on information costs and to strengthen the customer's position, although a sellers' market and the paramount importance of the production plan marginalizes the role of contracts in the command economy.
4. Queues can also be due to other factors, such as a restricted number of poorly organized distribution outlets. Velikanova (*Literaturnaya Gazeta*, no. 16, 20 April 1988, p. 14) gives a figure of 65 billion man-hours a year spent shopping in the Soviet Union today.
5. The *nomenklatura* system, whereby the party makes all important appointments, including those in the economy, was described as having 'outlived its usefulness' at the Nineteenth Party Conference in 1988.
6. In 1987 a million people in Uzbekistan and a quarter of a million in Azerbaijan, for example, and an overall unemployment rate of 3 per cent according to Nikolai Shmelev (*Novy Mir*, no. 6, June 1987, p. 148). Western estimates are to be found in Gregory, P. and Collier, I. (1988) 'Unemployment in the Soviet Union: evidence from the Soviet interview project', *American Economic Review* (September). Gregory and Collier calculate the one-month-or-more unemployment rate for 1974–79 from a survey of 2,793 Soviet emigres to the United States to be 1.2 to 1.3 per cent; this compares with Wiles' estimate for 1962–63 of 1.1 to 1.8 per cent and Granick's for the late 1970s of 1.5 to 3.0 per cent (p. 625).
7. The first case involved those losing their jobs as a result of ministerial reorganization in 1985, being eligible for full pay for three months without affecting pension and

other social security rights (normally pension rights are adversely affected if unemployment lasts more than a month).

8. The rouble is an inconvertible currency and is not, therefore, subject to supply and demand forces in world foreign exchange markets (see chapter three).

9. 'Taut' planning prevails in general, with pressure to maximize output from given resources.

10. The leak associated with Y was later plugged by tighter regulations, which specified, for example, that overspending had to be made good within a matter of months.

11. In reality it is possibly the case that most prices of manufactured goods reflect individual enterprises' costs of production, due to deals between the enterprise and the centre (Hewett 1988: 195–96); again, the reality is that the centre actually only sets the prices of a few major products, such as raw materials, fuels, food, oil and grain. Most prices are actually set by ministries and enterprises on the basis of centrally given rules, only a few price proposals are seriously analysed by the overburdened centre (Hewett 1988: 192).

12. In market economies prices are determined by supply and demand, thus reflecting both costs and utility. Prices play crucial informational, incentive and allocative functions. changing supply and demand conditions, have an incentive to respond in an efficient manner and are able to reallocate scarce resources.

References

Some general references on the first three chapters include:

Aganbegyan, A. (1988) *The Challenge: Economics of Perestroika*, London: Hutchinson.

Bleaney, M. (1988) *Do Socialist Economies Work? The Soviet and East European Experience*, Oxford: Basil Blackwell.

Dyker, D. (1985) *The Future of the Soviet Planning System*, London: Croom Helm.
—— (ed) (1987) *The Soviet Union under Gorbachev: Prospects for Reform,* London: Croom Helm.

Gregory, P. , and Stuart, R. (1986) *Soviet Economic Structure and Performance*, 3rd edn, New York: Harper & Row (2nd edn 1981).

Hare, P. (1987) 'Resource allocation without prices: the Soviet economy', *Economic Review*, 5, no. 2.

Hewett, E. (1988) *Reforming the Soviet Economy: Equality versus Efficiency*, Washington, D.C.: Brookings Institution.

Nove, A. (1986) *The Soviet Economic System*, 3rd edn, London: Allen & Unwin.

Ofer, G. (1987) 'Soviet economic growth: 1928–85', *Journal of Economic Literature*, XXV (December).

Schroeder, G (1986) *The System versus Progress*: Soviet Economic Problems, London: Centre for Research into Communist Economies.

Smith, A. (1983) *The Planned Economies of Eastern Europe*, London: Croom Helm.

Zimbalist, A., Sherman, H., and Brown, S. (1989) *Comparing Economic Systems: A Political-Economic Approach*, 2nd edn, New York: Harcourt Brace Jovanovich. Part Three (pp. 93– 316).

Chapter two

Reform of the traditional economic system

Reasons for reform

The serious micro-economic problems associated with the neglect of user need, understatement of productive capacity, hoarding of inputs, storming, and an anti-innovation bias, have already been discussed at length.[1] As Gorbachev puts it: 'The gross output drive, particularly in heavy industry, turned out to be ... just an end in itself ... the consumer found himself totally at the mercy of the producer and had to make do with what the latter chose to give him' (1987: 19). 'Our rockets can find Halley's comet and fly to Venus with amazing accuracy, but ... many Soviet household appliances are of poor quality' (1987: 21). He also continually attacks bureaucracy, including 'over-management' (there was one manager for every six workers in 1987), and the irrationality of prices – this induces such phenomena as loaves of bread being used as footballs. Slyunkov (*CDSP*, 1987, vol. XXXIX, no. 24, p. 2) notes that fuel and raw materials prices are between one-third and two-thirds of the world level, while on average foodstuff prices only cover a half of production costs. Mention should also be made of the 'scattering' (excessive spread) of resources (*raspilenie sredstv*), construction projects whose completion times are excessive relative both to plan norms and to those taken in the West. Various factors are responsible for this:

1. The greater ease involved in obtaining resources to complete projects (whose prospective benefits are typically exaggerated and whose initial cost estimates are understated), as opposed to starting them, encourages overbidding; supply difficulties make it necessary to keep options open.
2. The absence of a capital charge before the mid-1960s.
3. The tendency of output-orientated indicators to reward starting more than finishing.
4. The ambitions of self-interested departments.
5. The absence of the threat of bankruptcy in the event of investment failure.
6. New plants do not jeopardize short-term plan fulfilment, as does innovation (Winiecki 1988: 18).

22

At the macro-economic level, the Soviet economy has become more complex and has experienced declining rates of growth of net material product (NMP),[2] as can be seen in Table 2.1. Official figures for the annual average rate of growth of 'NMP utilized'[3] show a falling trend. Aganbegyan (1988: 177) considers that, after taking account of factors such as hidden price increases, economic development came to a standstill at a point between the 1970s and 1980s. Western calculations, though lower and differing among themselves, also show this downward trend.

Table 2.1 The Soviet Union: average annual rate of growth of NMP (utilized) and GNP

Source	1951–5	1955–58	1958–61	1961–5	1966–70	1971–5	1976–80	1981–5	1986	1987*	1988
Official Soviet figures	11.0	10.2	7.3	6.0	7.1	5.1	3.9	3.2	4.1	2.3	4.4
Joint Economic Committee of US Congress	5.5	—	—	5.1	5.2	3.8	2.7	2.4	3.9	0.5	1.5
Ofer		1950–60 5.7		1960–70 5.2		1970–5 3.7		1975–80 2.6		1980–5 2.0	

Sources: Schroeder (1986: 20); Ofer (1987: 1778); Dyker, *The Soviet Economy* (1976), London: Crosby, Lockwood, Staples, p. 18.
*See note 4 at end of chapter.

Soviet growth has been of an 'extensive' type (largely due to increases in inputs, rather than to greater efficiency in the use of inputs, i.e. increasing factor productivity). Gregory and Stuart (1986: 423) estimate that only one-third of growth is accounted for by a rise in efficiency, compared with around two-thirds in the West. Ofer concludes that during the period 1928–85 the growth of factor productivity accounted for only 24 per cent of total GNP growth, falling to 20 per cent in the post-war period and to zero from 1970 on when productivity growth stagnated or even became negative. Aganbegyan (1988) gives the following figures for the proportion of economic development arising from the growth of resources: 1971–85, two-thirds (thus only a third occurred because of an increase in efficiency); 1971–5, three-quarters; 1976–80, two-thirds; 1981–5, three-fifths (1988a: 10–11, 73). The drying up of the traditional sources of inputs[5] has put massive pressure on the Soviet Union to adopt a more 'intensive' pattern of growth. The fall in the world price of oil since the end of 1985 has reduced badly needed hard currency earnings (oil alone accounts for over 60 per cent of the total) and adds to the pressure for reform.

Industrial reform

It is easy to be overwhelmed by the vast number of amendments, but the Soviet economy in 1987 was still, in essence, a command economy. Stalin's death in 1953 and Khrushchev's denunciation of the cult of personality at the famous Twentieth Party Congress in 1956 were landmark events, but debate about economic reform surged after the publication of Liberman's article in *Pravda* (9 September 1962). Liberman wanted to ensure that the interests of society and of the enterprise coincided. His proposals were often vague, but involved ending 'petty tutelage' over enterprises by allowing management greater decision-making powers over details (deliveries, main assortment and profit would remain as plan indicators), while profitability, subject to fulfilling the other indicators, was to determine the amount of retained profit feeding the incentive funds. Reform experiments started in 1964 with the Bolshevichka and Mayak clothing plants, for which sales (the result of directly negotiated contracts with retail outlets) and profitability were the main targets and which were allowed greater contact with customers and some limited scope for price alteration. The experiments were expanded in 1965. These preceded the 1965 Kosygin (then prime minister) reforms, which were to be applied to all enterprises by 1970.

Essential features of this reform included a restoration of Gosplan's powers; ministries and *glavki* beginning to operate on a *khozraschyot* basis; a reduction in the traditionally large number of success indicators to only eight, with the aim of decentralizing decision-making to a limited extent (for example, over assortment details); talk, hopelessly optimistic in light of the retention of materials allocation more or less intact, of letting decentralized investment eventually amount to 20 per cent of the total; moving, without a timetable, towards wholesale trade. The indicators were value of sales (as opposed to gross output); profit (usually profitability, but sometimes profit increases); main assortment; wage fund; contributions to and receipts from the state budget; centralized investment and the introduction of new productive capacity; basic tasks for the introduction of new techniques; and material supply obligations. Profitability and the percentage increase in either sales or profits were to determine retained profits, although subject to fulfilment of the other indicators (note that profit was seen as a measure of the efficiency with which the other indicators were achieved). Three incentive funds were fed, namely the material incentive, socio-cultural and housing, and production development. Even these mild reform measures (a glance at the indicators show how all important areas of decision-making were still centrally controlled) were whittled away by the end of the decade. Only the Ministry of Instrument-making, Automation Equipment and Control Systems and several *glavki* were on *khozraschyot* by 1970. Materials supply remained and 'sales' was not a significant improvement in conditions of acute supply scarcity. There was no radical price reform.

The old familiar problems remained unsolved, including plan changes and ratchet effects. The latter was supposed to be overcome by the use of more stable and uniform norms associated with the enhanced role of the five year plan: in reality norms came to be reassessed on an annual basis and were differentiated for each enterprise (Aganbegyan 1988: 59). Ministries continued to meddle. Hewett makes the important point that this is inevitable as long as ministries are held responsible for the performance of their enterprises (1988: 97); ministries still had to meet gross output targets, for instance (1988: 240). Aganbegyan points out that reform was only partially applied – for example, the attempt to transfer the new system to construction was not successful (1988: 62). The reforms envisaged a movement towards long-term credits and away from capital grants. By 1974, however, bank credit accounted for less than 8.0 per cent of total industrial centralized investment finance (Dyker 1988: 92). Labour was still hoarded, although mention should be made of the 1967 *Shchekino* (chemical complex) experiment to help combat this problem. Here manpower reduction was reflected in increased bonus payments to the remaining workforce based on a given percentage of the wages saved (for a more detailed analysis see Arnot 1988). A more recent variation involves the railway system, beginning with the one in Belorussia. Here the benefit accrues in the form of an increase in the tariff element of wage, supposedly less subject to ministerial interference (Trehub 1987: 10).

During the 1970s emphasis was given to improving management and planning by means of a movement towards an integrated, computerized information and control system. Extra success indicators were imposed on enterprises (such as labour productivity in 1973) due to wage increases considerably exceeding productivity increases, and in 1971–72, the low percentage of output meeting world quality standards. Indicators such as main products in physical terms remained important. Decentralized investment was actually abandoned in 1976 because of supply problems. After the mid-1970s the material incentive fund was linked to contract fulfilment (still relatively ineffective in a sellers' market it should be noted), with sales revenue reduced in the event of contract violations; the payment of managerial bonuses linked to other plan targets was also made conditional on contract fulfilment (Kroll 1988: 359).

The 1973 decree designated the *production association* (*proizvodstvennoe obedineniye*) as the main production unit. These are mainly horizontal amalgamations of enterprises and are of three types, all on a *khozraschyot* basis: (1) production associations, currently comprising about four enterprises on average; (2) science-production associations, with integrated R&D institutes; and (3) industrial (administrative) associations, financed by profit deductions from enterprises and a replacement for the glavki (although the aim was for a more homogeneous enterprise membership). In 1984 the first two accounted for about half of both industrial output and employment (Nove 1986: 72); the remainder were taken care of by independent enterprises, mostly coming under industrial associations. The chief benefits are seen as the streamlining of the planning system by a reduction in the number of units to be centrally controlled, economies of scale, and encouragement given to technical progress. The average size of associations or enterprises is relatively large, at more than 800 workers (Aganbegyan 1988: 168).

Counter-plans (vstrechnye plany), introduced in 1971, are a device to overcome managerial preference for 'slack plans', to induce enterprises to adopt more demanding targets than those set out in their five year plan. Under this plan bonuses for fulfilment are higher than for overfulfilment of original targets. The problem was that managers now had a greater incentive to bargain for even lower initial targets, and ministries continued to alter plans in reality. In 1978 enterprises had to submit counter-plans when the regular plans were formulated in order to overcome supply problems; by 1981 only 7 per cent of industrial enterprises were offering counter-plans (Bleaney 1988: 60, quoting Bornstein).

There was a resurgence of interest in net output to combat the excessive use of components and materials. Experiments involving *normative net output* (NNO) can be traced back to the 1960s. This is the sum of *required* (specified in centrally determined norms, as opposed to actual) wage costs, social insurance, and profit. The idea is that a reduction in non-labour inputs and less than norm expenditure on wages will increase profit and, therefore, incentive funds. Normative net output is a sort of 'shadow' price that can be used to determine the entire NNO for the enterprise by multiplying it by actual output. The 1979 decree used this concept both as a indicator and as a unit of measurement (for labour productivity and quality mix, for example). Three main indicators determined bonuses: labour productivity, quality mix, and fulfilment of delivery plans in volume terms of the most important products according to supply contracts. Other indicators, however, included volume of output in physical terms of the most important products, sales, profit, cost reduction, investment and introduction of new techniques. Norms, used to identify inefficiencies, were tightened and greatly expanded in number to encourage greater efficiency in the use of inputs. Renewed emphasis was given to five year plans. The idea here is that annual plans should be firmly based on the five-year plan. More stable norms should be fixed, for example for payments out of profit to the state budget, in order to overcome the 'free remainder' problem. This remains after the capital charge, rental charge, and incentive fund retentions have been deducted from gross profit and renders fines for contract violation, for example, meaningless, since the sum would have gone to the state anyway. The decree saw the ultimate transfer to 'full' *khozraschyot*, covering investment as well as current expenditures and state obligations from own revenue.

There was an upgrading in the role of both counter-plans and of 'comprehensive' or 'programme goal' approaches to planning and management.

These would deal with problems such as those relating to technological innovation and/or to the regions, and cross-sectoral boundaries. On 26 August 1987 a programme was announced for the development of the area from Lake Baikal to the Pacific Ocean up to the end of the century (served by the Baikal-Amur railway). Another so-called 'territorial production complex' is based on the West Siberian oil and gas fields. Thirty per cent of the 232 billion rouble investment would be devoted to infrastructure projects such as housing, schools and cultural facilities to reduce the high level of labour turnover. The aim is to make the area largely self-sufficient in terms of energy and important agricultural commodities such as meat, dairy products and vegetables. Industrialization is to revolve around the processing of minerals, agricultural products and fish: the fishing industry is to be concentrated on the Pacific coast. In 1984 there were seven territorial production complexes, including west Siberia. A major problem is the lack of authority of the co-ordinating agencies, since production units are still subject to ministerial control (Nove 1986: 68).

There was increasing stress on worker brigades in enterprises after 1979, with the proportion of the industrial work-force affected increasing from 34 per cent to 71.7 per cent in 1984 (Slider 1987: 394–5). In 1987 80 per cent of the workforce in industry and construction was affected, although the economic accountability form covered only a third of brigades in industry and around a half in construction (*CDSP*, vol. XL, no. 10, 1988, p. 21). These groups of about 20 workers typically set their own work schedules according to assigned tasks and with supplied inputs. The aim is to increase incentives and discipline because of payments by result (such as completed houses) and powers to distribute collective bonuses among themselves, with workers disciplining themselves in effect through peer pressure. The experiment started in 1970 in the construction industry, where brigades benefited from a share in any savings achieved, but also bore any losses (Arnot 1988: 203).

The Andropov era

Andropov (November 1982–February 1984) succeeded Brezhnev (who, in turn, succeeded Khrushchev in October 1964) as General Secretary of the CPSU. His short period of office, during which he was ill, was mainly significant for the impact he made on his protégé, Gorbachev. Andropov stressed order and discipline, running campaigns against absenteeism from work (even involving a six-week police drive), drunkenness and corruption. He also emphasized the need for a strong link between remuneration and both effort and skills. In the July 1983 decree, which began to be implemented on 1 January 1984 in two all-union and three republican ministries, the main enterprise success indicators were contractual deliveries (in the sense that only sales that satisfied contracts were valid), labour productivity, cost reduction, the introduction of science and technology and quality mix (bonuses were to be reduced if the last two were not met). The Socio-cultural Fund was linked to the growth of labour productivity (measured by NNO). Stable norms were to be fixed for a five-year period, such as those relating the wage fund to the growth of NNO (thus linking pay and performance). Decentralized investment was reinstated and financed out of the development fund, depreciation reserves and credits, while preferential input supply was to be guaranteed. Wage fund economies accruing through job rationalization schemes were to be used to reward suitably skilled and productive workers. Efficient enterprises were not to be penalized as a means of supporting weaker brethren.

The Chernenko era

Chernenko (General Secretary February 1984 – March 1985) cautiously echoed Andropov's call for greater efficiency, effort, organization, order and discipline. The Andropov reform was extended in 1985, with 12 per cent of industrial output affected by the start of the year. It was applied to all industry in January 1987.

Dyker summarizes the Gorbachev July 1985 follow-on measures: the payment of managerial bonuses for other reasons should not be dependent on the fulfilment of contractual deliveries, as under the Andropov scheme; a system of price surcharges and discounts related to quality of products (including exportables); fines for or the costs of correcting defective products to affect the bonus fund adversely (1987: 69–70). In June 1986 new measures were adopted in order to strengthen contract fulfilment. For example, if suppliers refused to sign contracts relating to the delivery of goods specified in planning orders, such goods would count as unfulfilled delivery obligations; and delivery obligations had to be totally met before any bonus was paid to managers who had fulfilled the total sales plan (Kroll 1988: 360).

The Gorbachev era

Since he was appointed General Secretary on 11 March 1985 (also becoming Chairman of the Presidium of the Supreme Soviet or President on 2 October 1988), Mikhail Gorbachev has profoundly altered the atmosphere and rhetoric in the Soviet Union. Nevertheless, in 1988 a command economy essentially remained. Terms familiar even to Western ears are: 1. *perestroika* or 'restructuring' of the whole of economic and social life, that is all-around economic and social reforms, or as Gorbachev (1987) defines the term, ' ... a policy of accelerating [*uskorenie* is the Russian for 'acceleration'] the country's social and economic progress and renewing all spheres of economic life'; 2. *glasnost'* ('having a voice', openness); and 3. 'democratization'. Gorbachev describes democracy as legality, the strict observance of the law, but it includes in general increased discipline and mass participation in decision-making, and specific aspects such as multiple candidates, an enhanced role for soviets (people's councils), experiments with elected management, greater involvement of enterprises and their work-forces in the planning process and secret ballots. The connection is that there has to be open admittance of problems before reforms can be introduced to overcome them, with *glasnost'* and democratization seen as the prerequisites for successful restructuring. The willingness to be more frank about problems was dramatically illustrated during the Twenty-seventh Congress of the CPSU (25 February – 6 March 1986).

Gorbachev has highlighted the relative stagnation of the Brezhnev period (note, not that of Andropov). The era is now formally known as the 'period of stagnation'. Gorbachev (1987: 18–19) claims a loss of momentum, especially in the latter half of the 1970s, and a fall in growth rates to a level close to economic stagnation by the start of the 1980s. He has continually attacked and dismissed many of those who oppose his ideas, those in ministries in particular. In a speech to the Komsomol (youth wing of the party) Congress in April 1987, Gorbachev, although denying political opposition as such, pinpointed nests of those who are slow to adapt and who delay reconstruction as being in the Central Committee, government, ministries, republics, provinces, work collectives and in the Komsomol itself. A constant theme that runs through his speeches is the need to remove those who do not intend to adjust and who are, therefore, an obstacle to change.

Gorbachev's remedies

The 1985 Party Programme (outline of party policy to the year 2000) contrasts strikingly with Khrushchev's utopian 1961 version: 'a communist society will, in the main, be built by 1980'. More realistic, though still ambitious targets were set. For instance, aggregate output is to double by the year 2000 (achieved mainly by means of 'intensification') and individual housing is to be available for practically every family. Many of the proposals below were outlined in the programme and have subsequently been extended and elaborated upon:

The need to create a new 'psychology of economic activity'

Gorbachev has attacked what he calls the peculiar psychology of the Brezhnev period ('how to improve things without changing anything') and the prevalence of inertia, bureaucracy, irresponsibility, bribery, theft and parasitism. What is needed is increased discipline, effort, responsibility and accountability. Practical steps taken include the anti-alcoholism campaign, which involves restrictions on hours and number of sales outlets and rising prices, although the policy was subsequently eased as a result of problems such as illegal distilling and consequent sugar shortages. Enhanced importance was also given to cost accounting. In March 1987 the Leningrad Building Association actually closed one of its enterprises for failing to meet its targets for costs, completion times and quality, and transferred its 2,000 workers to other jobs. In May a Moscow research centre specializing on the construction industry was also closed down. In January 1988 a cigarette factory was closed (Bill Keller, *IHT*, 22 September 1988, p. 13). Official estimates put the number of 'superfluous' personnel to be released from goods production at 16 million by the year 2000 (taken up by the expansion of services) and three million during the current five-year plan (see, for example, Kostakov, 1988). A 50 per cent staff cut in republican ministries and departments is foreseen, along with a 30 to 35 per cent cut at the provincial level.

Under the terms of the January 1988 decree, enterprises are obliged to give at least two months' notice of redundancy and to try to place the affected person in other work in the same enterprise. If this is not possible or the employee refuses the offer, the employee may go to a job placement agency (the enterprise providing all relevant information) or find work for him- or herself. Severance pay amounts to one month's average earnings; average wages will be paid during the job placement period, but no longer than two months from the day of dismissal. A third month is possible by decision of the placement agency, provided the employee applied within two weeks of dismissal and the agency is not able to find a job. If enterprises are liquidated, average wages can be paid for up to three months, counting the one month's severance pay. A nationwide system of job placement, retraining, and vocational guidance was to be introduced in 1988. The centres and bureaus will be on a *khozraschyot* basis, financed by payments from enterprises.[6]

Economic management

It is worth mentioning at the outset Gorbachev's reminder at the 1986 Congress that there should be 'no retreat from the principles of planned guidance, but only a change in its methods'. Nevertheless, the broad themes in his reform strategy were discernible:

(a) An increase in the decision-making powers exercised by the centre and by the production units at the expense of the obstructive ministries. This 'two-link' management system or 'double-thrust strategy' involves a concentration of and hence improved control over strategic decisions at the centre and delegation of operational matters to production units. The latter should face fewer obligatory targets and have the ability to sell above-plan output to other enterprises or to the public. There should be greater financial accountability and a greater use of economic levers for indirect steering, inducing economic agents to perform in desired ways. In current Soviet phraseology, the essence of *perestroika* lies in the transition from administrative to economic methods of management, with a greatly enhanced role for prices, finance, credit and work incentives (Aganbegyan 1988: 23). At the Nineteenth Party Conference in 1988, Gorbachev stressed the need for the party to refrain from interference in the day-to-day management of the economy, for the party to be freed from 'economic-administrative' functions and to shift to 'political methods of leadership' (*CDSP*, 1988, vol. XL, no. 30, p. 4). This is to be ensured by the abolition of the present division of the party apparatus by spheres of management (i.e. departments that issue instructions to enterprises and farms). An important theme at the conference was that political reform was a prerequisite for successful economic reform. At a special plenum of the Central Committee held on 30 September 1988 six new 'commissions' were set up, for socio-economic, agricultural, personnel, ideology, foreign policy and legal affairs. These replaced or subsumed the 22 departments that supervised and tended to duplicate ministries. The commissions are headed by Central Committee Secretaries who are also Politburo members. They are involved in decision-making and reform implementation, but are, supposedly, to avoid the day-to-day interference associated with the departments.

(b) Greater decision-making autonomy is to be allowed to production units involved in light industry, services and retail trade (fewer plan targets, greater ability to react to changes in demand) than to those in the heavy and defence industries.

(c) There will be greater regional decision-making autonomy, especially in the production of consumer goods, since local planning authorities are in a much better position to know local circumstances and needs, and in the provision of improved infrastructure to attract a larger and more stable labour force (to Siberia for instance). In 1988, for example, the Estonian Republic was granted greater autonomy in a number of branches of industry (only 10 per cent of industry was then locally controlled) and in fuel and energy, transport, public services, education, culture, forestry, and the environment. Local authorities are to be allowed to receive a portion of the profits of enterprises within their areas plus a part of the turnover tax revenue derived from the sale of local goods, excluding wine, spirits and tobacco (Aganbegyan 1988a: 121). The three Baltic Republics of Estonia, Latvia, and Lithuania, Belorussia, the city of Moscow, Sverdlovsk province and the Tatar Autonomous Republic are to be the subject of experiments involving 'territorial self-financing'. Revenue sources will be formed on the basis of long term normatives, including receipts from all enterprises located in these areas (Gostev, *CDSP*, 1988, vol. XL, no. 45, p. 11). At the Nineteenth Party Conference it was decided that republics generally should be on a *khozraschyot* basis, which will enable them to determine net contributions to or receipts from the central budget. In his Krasnoyarsk speech of 16 September 1988,

Gorbachev outlined the idea of possible 'joint enterprise zones ' for the Soviet Far East, where joint equity ventures would enjoy special privileges, such as direct links with foreign partners, tax concessions and more relaxed controls on hard currency transactions and customs regulations (Quentin Peel, *FT*, 26 July 1988, p. 4; 17 September 1988, p. 1; and 28 September 1988, p. 2). It is even possible that 100 per cent foreign ownership will be permitted. The first special economic zone is planned to be set up in the Saimaa Canal area (currently leased to Finland), free of both customs duties and the need for commuting workers to have visas. (Olli Virtanen, *FT*, 29 November 1988, p. 11)

A stronger link between the performance of production units and workers and their remuneration

Gorbachev has criticized the practice of wage and salary levels being maintained even when unsaleable goods are produced, the payment of automatic bonuses and equal pay for the conscientious and the negligent/incompetent, and the existence of inadequate differentials between skilled and unskilled. 'It is hardly a secret to anyone that many people even now receive wages for just showing up at work and hold their posts without having their actual labour contribution taken into account' (18 February 1988 speech, *CDSP*, 1988, vol. XL, no. 7, p. 7). At present graduate engineers and technicians in construction receive slightly lower pay than manual workers, while in industry the pay of engineers and technicians is only 10 to 15 per cent higher than that of a labourer (Aganbegyan 1988: 167). Thirty years ago scientists were the highest paid members of the work force; they are now relegated to the fourth rank behind workers in transport, construction and industry (Kostakov 1988: 96). Shcherbakov describes how bonuses have been primarily linked to work norms rather than enterprise plans. Since work norms have been infrequently revised, they have been increasingly easy to overfulfil, despite problems with plan fulfilment (Shcherbakov 1987: 76). At present the incentive fund, on average, makes up only a twelfth of the wage fund (in the best enterprises, such as Sumy, the fund reaching 15 per cent: Aganbegyan 1988a: 162).

Practical steps taken include basing the remuneration of scientists, technicians and industrial designers more (up to 50 per cent of pay) on their contribution to research and its application to industry, rather than academic degree and length of service. Over the period 1986–90 pay scales for engineers, technicians, and white-collar workers are to be increased by 30 to 35 per cent, while those of manual workers are to rise by only 20 to 25 per cent (Aganbegyan 1988a: 167). Teachers' salaries are being raised by 30 per cent and those of doctors and medical workers by 40 per cent (Aganbegyan 1988a: 18–19). The October 1986 wage decree increased the proportion of total income accounted for by basic wage rates and widened these rates to take account of skills. The targets for consumer goods and services set for the 1986–90 five-year plan were revised upwards in August 1988 for the sake of material incentives. In 1989 a progressive tax is likely to be introduced on enterprises' wage increases in excess of productivity increases, due to concern about the inflationary consequences of the former exceeding the latter.

A need to increase the quality of production

The continuing concern with quality has led to the establishment of the State Quality Commission (Gospriomka), subordinate to the State Committee for Standards and operative since 1 January 1987. Initially applied to 1,500 enterprises covering 20 per cent of industrial production, the commission's scope has since been extended. This method of tackling the problem was adapted from the defence sector, and is admittedly still bureaucratic and able to refer only to existing designs, however obsolete. Nevertheless, many enterprises subjected to its scrutiny have failed to meet production targets and workers have lost bonuses. This has led to strikes. Those in October 1987 at a bus assembly plant in Likino and at the Chekhov bus station illustrate the problems of apportioning blame – workers cite faulty equipment and lack of spares.

The need for intensive growth

Intensive growth involves output increases due largely to greater efficiency of input use, especially by means of the application of modern science and technology. An improvement in quality is another aspect. A practical result of this policy is that increasing emphasis is placed on modernizing the existing capital stock rather than enlarging it. Specifically, the plan is to raise the proportion of capital investment devoted to technical reconstruction from a little more than a third to more than a half over the period 1986–90 (Aganbegyan 1988a: 14). This means increased priority for sectors such as machine tools, instrument making, electronics and electrical engineering, while intensification is also to be achieved by making better use of resources in general, by tightening norms, increasing emphasis on net output, and so on. The volume of capital investment in machine building increased by 24 per cent during 1981–85 and the aim is 80 per cent during 1986–90 (Aganbegyan 1988a: 14). Only 5 per cent of all capital investment went into machine building during 1981–85 (Aganbegyan 1988a: 104); output of the sector is to treble during 1986–2000 (Aganbegyan 1988a: 220). Depreciation rates are to be stepped up in order to further technical progress. In 1985 71 per cent of the stock of machinery and equipment in civil mechanical engineering was obsolete, but only 3.1 per cent of production ceased and was replaced by new models – this renewal rate is to be raised to 13 per cent by 1990 (Aganbegyan 1988: 183). In other words, in 1985 only 29 per cent of machine building production was up to the best international standards, while the aim is 80 to 90 per cent by 1990. Over the period 1981–85 only 9 per cent of all equipment was renewed; this figure is to rise to 40 per cent over 1986–90 (Aganbegyan 1988a: 14). In the whole of industry in

1985 only 1.3 per cent of the capital stock was written off/replaced (Aganbegyan 1988a: 100).

Industrial reform

In order to streamline planning and management (reduction of overlapping, duplication, and narrow departmental interests), to further scientific and technical progress, to raise quality, to encourage specialization and to improve materials supply, Co-ordinating Bureaus have been set up. These bureaus, which have been influenced by organizations in the defence sector, are the following: Gosagroprom, the State Agro-industrial Committee, formed out of the merger of four ministries and a committee in November 1985; the Bureau for Machine Building (October 1985); the Bureau for the Fuel and Energy Complex (March 1986); and the USSR State Committee for Construction (September 1986). The latter three were formed in order to co-ordinate the activities of the various ministries involved.

Experiments at the VAZ (Volga car plant) at Togliatti and the Frunze machine tool enterprise at Sumy were extended to another 200 enterprises at the beginning of 1987. The VAZ plant, for example, has now been included in the foreign trade decentralization reforms, but even before this 40 per cent of hard currency earnings were allowed to be retained for imports (currently 70 per cent; Aganbegyan 1988a: 151). Delivery, productivity and quality indicators are important, and the bonuses dependent on them are paid out to work brigades for distribution to individuals.[7] Norms are stable, such as those relating to the distribution of net profit between the state budget, the ministry and the enterprise (47.5, 5.0 and 47.5 per cent, respectively, in the case of the Frunze association). Major problems include the lack of control over prices and supply difficulties. At the Sumy plant the incentive fund accounts for a third of total labour remuneration (double the average), while the development fund amounts to 5 per cent of the value of the capital stock (Aganbegyan 1988a: 164). Under the Vaz/Sumy system the enterprise or association is responsible for nearly all investment, except for entirely new plants (Dyker 1988: 101). Ministries are not allowed to redistribute funds between enterprises (Dyker 1987: 75).

From 1 January 1987 five industrial ministries and more than thirty individual and amalgamated enterprises were placed on 'full economic accounting' (*polny khozraschyot*). All expenditures (including investment) have to be covered from revenue earned (or credits borrowed) and ministries are not allowed to transfer profits from profitable to loss-making enterprises. Stable norms dictate the share of profits going to the state budget and that retained by the enterprise. On 1 January 1988 the Lvov Conveyor Combine in the Ukraine became the first enterprise to grant its workers a share (3 per cent) of monthly profit unrelated to the fulfilment of plan targets. This overcomes the problem that non-fulfilment of targets may be due to external problems such as non-delivery of inputs (*FT*, 11 December 1987, p. 3).

In June 1987 a new *'Law on Enterprises'* was adopted.[8] There was to be a transitional period during 1988–90, and 1991–5 was to be the first full five-year plan period when the entire system was operational. Gosplan is to become the nation's 'economic headquarters', focusing on strategic matters, the main national economic proportions, inter-sectoral co-operation, long-term science and technology programmes, structural investment policy, and balance in the national economy. These ideas are to be embodied in perspective plans of fifteen years' duration and five-year plans that are also to take into account the needs of enterprises as expressed via ministries and republics. Increasing use is to be made of economic levers to steer the economy indirectly, including competitive state contracts, prices (new wholesale prices to be introduced on 1 January 1990 and new retail prices on 1 January 1991) and monetary policy.

Monetary policy is to be carried out in the context of the 1988 reorganization of the banking system. Gosbank is to assume a role more akin to a Western central bank, with more independent banks comprising the Industry and Construction Bank (Promstroibank), the Agro-Industrial Bank (Agroprombank), the Bank for Housing and Municipal Services and Social Development (Zhilsotsbank), and the Bank of Labour Savings and Credit Services to the Population (Sberbank). The Bank for Foreign Economic Activity (Vneshekonombank) replaced the Foreign Trade Bank. Interest rates are to be raised and a stricter control is to be exercised over the repayment of credits, with most capital expenditures eventually being financed out of enterprise revenues or bank credit. All banks are expected to be run profitably and credit allocation is to be influenced by the expected profitability of projects (Panova 1988). Co-operative banks, with a minority share held by a state bank, are being set up to encourage innovation.

Gorbachev (1987: 33) defines the restructuring of economic management as a shift in emphasis from primarily administrative to primarily economic management methods at every level. Ministries are not to interfere in the day-to-day operation of the enterprises or to redistribute profits from efficient to less efficient enterprises. They are to move to a full *khozraschyot* basis and deal with aspects such as raising technical levels, increasing exports, improving quality, and labour retraining. The administrative associations and *glavki* are destined to be replaced by 'state production enterprises', which operate on a *khozraschyot* basis and supervise a number of large enterprises and production associations involved in R&D, production, transportation, and marketing of related products; the related firms may be in the same area (Schroeder 1988a: 185). To be more precise, the June 1987 decree saw a future in which the industrial structure would be characterized by a few hundred giant, vertically integrated enterprises operating in national-level markets, and thousands of republican and local enterprises handling regional and local markets and some of the needs of the national enterprises (Hewett 1988: 331, 352). The first interbranch state associations have been created: *Energomash* (Power Machinery) and *Tekhnokhim* (Chemical Equipment) are based in Leningrad, and *Kvantemp* (Quantum Electromechanical Production) is based in Moscow (*CDSP*, 1989, vol. XLI, no. 5, p. 13). *Kvantemp*, for example, involves 24 widely-spread enterprises from 3 ministries, and employs 50,000 (*CDSP*, 1989, vol. XLI, no. 6, p. 25).

The association is the basic production unit, operating on the following principles:

1. 'Self-management' (*samoupravlenie*). The idea is that work-forces will take a more active part in enterprise plan formulation and in the election of management.
2. 'Full economic accountability' and 'self-financing' (*samofinansirovanie*). Both operating costs and capital expenditures are to be covered out of revenue earned. Investment is normally to be financed out of retained profit or from credits that have to be repaid out of earned revenue. Centralized investment is to be restricted to things like the creation of new branches of production, major projects, transport infrastructure and urban reconstruction (Aganbegyan 1988a: 120).
3. *Samookupaemost*. This entails at least a minimum rate of return on investment financed from whatever source (Hewett 1988: 326).

Enterprises are able to choose between two basic models of wage determination. 1. The wage fund is directly related to normative net output and the residual is left for (priority) taxes and interest payments and, after that, for the enterprise funds. 2. Wage payments are the final residual after payments for taxes, interest and the enterprise funds according to norms (Hewett 1988: 331). Because of the extra risk involved, only 172 of the average 50,000 enterprises in each of the 30 or so branches of industry have opted for the latter (reported by John Lloyd in *FT*, 16 August 1988. p. 2).

By 1990 managerial personnel are to be elected by the whole membership of the enterprise labour collective, including the director, although the elected director must be confirmed by the 'superior organ' (nominations seem to be controlled by the regional party organization) and the heads of enterprise subdivisions such as foremen and brigade leaders must be approved by the enterprise director (Bova 1987: 82). Bova also notes the 1983 'law on labour collectives', which made compulsory biannual general meetings of the labour collective, and created the legal requirement for the election of 'production conferences' (to discuss and evaluate enterprise operations in an advisory capacity) in all economic institutions of more than 300 employees (1987: 78). A new, elected body called the 'labour collective council', open to all members of the collective, operates between general meetings, dealing with such matters as improving labour discipline and increasing productivity (Bova 1987: 82).

The enterprise is to draw up its own annual and five-year plans and to conclude contracts, based on:

1. Control figures. These are broad, non-mandatory targets, such as output, profits and scientific and technological progress, emanating from the central five-year plan.
2. State orders (*goszakazy*). In Makorov's opinion, the state order is intended to be 'a contractual agreement between Gosplan, the ministries or the republican authorities on the one hand, and the enterprise on the other, with mutual obligations – in other words an economic contract, freely entered into by both sides ... the intention is that state orders will not encompass anywhere near all of national output; rather they will be limited to ensuring supplies for the most important projects in the social sphere, state investment projects, and defence' (1988: 458). Thus, as far as obligations are concerned, the state body ensures input supply, foreign currency allocations, capital investments, and profitable sales (Aganbegyan 1988a: 113). The idea is that contracts should be competed for when the new system is well established (Aganbegyan 1988a: 113). Abalkin, too, stresses that state orders should be limited to satisfying high priority strategic and social needs, should be the most profitable orders to the enterprise, and should be awarded, as a rule, on a competitive basis (*CDSP*, vol. XL, no. 8, pp. 16–17).
3. Direct orders from customers, which will become increasingly important.
4. Stable, long-term normatives (*normativy*) are to be fixed for at least a five-year period after 1991 and are to be uniform over entire branches and sectors, rather than being applicable to individual enterprises, as is the case during the transitional period. These relate to the size of the wage fund, which is linked to enterprise performance, budgetary payments, charges for working capital, the use of natural resources and so on, and to profit flows to the state and ministries and into the enterprise bonus, socio-cultural and investment funds. In general normatives for the formation of economic incentive funds are tied to profits and gross income.[9] The ultimate aim is to replace normatives relating to the formation of the wage fund and the distribution of profits with taxes and state benefits (Gorbachev's speech of 29 July 1988; *CDSP*, 1988, vol. XL, no. 30, p. 8).

Wholesale trade (i.e. a market in non-labour inputs, in which purchases are made from Gossnab wholesale stores) is gradually to become, within five to six years, the basic form of material-technical supply (in 1988 wholesale trade accounted for 15 per cent of the total volume of sales of 'production-and-technical output': *CDSP*, 1989, vol. XLI, no. 5, p. 13). It is to account for around two-thirds of the volume of resources sold through the supply system by 1992 (*CDSP*, 1988, vol. XXXIX, no. 52, p. 6). Note, however, that the sectors accounting for about a quarter of the economy (defence, energy and communications etc.), would still be subject to direct state contracts. Aganbegyan (1988a: 137–8) puts the timetable for wholesale trade at 60 per cent of all production by 1990 and 80 to 90 per cent by 1992. This would need to be gradually phased in because of the current excess money holdings of enterprises and the lack of price reform. State orders will gradually decline in importance in favour of direct ties between producer and consumer.

Enterprises accounting for around 60 per cent of Soviet industrial output were operating under the new system of self-financing as of 1 January 1988. The others were to have been included by the start of the next five-year plan, but this was brought forward to the start of 1989 as a result of the Nineteenth Party Conference. Major problems include the temptation to use control figures as compulsory targets and the reality that state orders may mean that little is different from the old system of plan target fulfilment. Furthermore, there have been numerous complaints about the proportion of an enterprise's capacity taken up by state orders. Gorbachev is aware of the problem:

> Officials at the centre are still clinging tenaciously to gross output indices, are manifesting administrative fiat through state orders, and are making attempts to turn economic methods of management into veiled forms of command. There are instances in which assignments are issued in violation of the Law on State Enterprises.
>
> (18 February 1988 speech, *CDSP*, vol. XL, no. 7, p. 6)

At the All-Union Party Conference (28 June–1 July 1988), the first since 1941, Gorbachev claimed that enterprises were being compelled by means of state orders to manufacture goods that were not in demand because they wanted to attain gross output targets. He promised that strict controls would be placed on ministries' ability to issue state orders and that wholesale trade in energy and raw materials would be introduced before 1990. Makarov recognizes that the use of state orders during the transitional period as a vehicle for conveying five-year plan targets 'departs from the principles of the reform, continuing the old system of plan commands to enterprises' (1988: 458). During a December 1987 discussion involving directors of the Moscow enterprises which were part of the early experiment, it emerged that state orders in some cases exceeded 100 per cent of productive capacity. Directors accepted such high orders because they represented the only way of ensuring inputs. Abalkin is also aware of the attempts to use state orders as output assignments and control figures as mandatory goals. One of the causes of this is the fact that ministries are still held responsible for providing the goods specified in their product lists (*CDSP*, 1988, vol. XL, no. 8, pp. 15–19).[10] There have been reports of enterprises refusing to accept state orders (see *The Economist*, 24–30 September 1988, p. 66; *FT*, 20 September 1988, p. 1; *FT*, 16 January 1989, p. 12).

The July 1988 decree limited the percentage of an enterprise's output that could be taken up by state orders to 67 per cent and restricted the ordering to Gosplan alone. Vid (Deputy Chairman of Gosplan) envisages a declining share between 1988 and 1989 for the following sectors: engineering (86 to 25 per cent); fuel and power (95 to 59.4 per cent); metallurgy (86 to 42 per cent); chemical and timber (87 to 34 per cent); light industry (96 to 34 per cent); and building materials (66 to 51 per cent) (1988: 14).

Foreign trade reform

Aganbegyan (1988a: 141–42) gives some interesting general figures relating to Soviet foreign trade. In 1986 exports accounted for 12 per cent of national income. Exports consisted of fuels, mainly oil and gas, and electricity (53 per cent); other raw materials such as ores and timber (9 per cent); and machines, equipment, and vehicles (14 per cent). Imports comprised foodstuffs and raw materials (over 20 per cent), metals and manufactures (over 8 per cent), industrial goods for mass consumption (around 12 per cent) and machines, equipment and vehicles (a little more than a third). While the Soviet Union's share of world industrial output is about 20 per cent, its share of world trade is only 5 per cent (Aganbegyan 1988a: 148); the socialist countries accounted for 67 per cent of the Soviet Union's foreign trade in 1986, the CMEA 60 per cent (Aganbegyan 1988a: 153).

Under a decree published on 23 September 1986, the Council of Minister's State Foreign Economic Commission (SFEC) was set up to co-ordinate the activities of all organizations having economic, financial, cultural, scientific and technical relations with foreign countries, the aim being to streamline and improve management. In January 1988 the Ministry of Foreign Economic Relations was formed out of the Ministry of Foreign Trade (which had previously lost a number of foreign trade enterprises) and the State Committee on Foreign Economic Relations; it has 25 FTCs instead of the previous 45.

The first day of January 1987 saw the start of an experiment to foster direct links between Soviet and foreign organizations. Twenty ministries and departments (such as Gosagroprom, the Ministry of the Chemical Industry, and Gossnab and 76 major individual enterprises (such as the VAZ plant and Uralmash, a heavy engineering plant in Sverdlovsk) and amalgamated enterprises were granted the right of direct participation in export-import transactions in the world market and to retain a portion of foreign exchange earnings. More recent figures are 65 and 105 respectively (Yuri Pekshev, deputy chairman of the SFEC of the Council of Ministers, 1988: 13). A major extension of the scheme was announced in December 1988: as of 1 April 1989 any state or co-operative enterprise whose output is competitive on the foreign market will be able to trade independently, while Vneshekonombank will be able to lend up to 5 million roubles in foreign exchange in order to encourage exports (the bank is also to be allowed to conduct foreign exchange auctions). (Aganbegyan states that in the socialist world market every business can export independently; 1988: 184.) They have their own foreign trade enterprises operating on an economic accounting basis and are self-supporting with regard to hard currency dealings. Credits from the Bank for Foreign Economic Activity have to be repaid and responsibility has to be taken for any losses incurred. Imports of capital goods to modernize plants are encouraged, although as of 1989 10 per cent of enterprise hard currency earnings may be allowed to be used for imported consumer goods. It is still not clear, however, where final authorization over the use of hard currency actually lies, since the Bank for Foreign Economic Activity handles the accounts. Foreign trade agencies are now being set up in the fifteen Soviet republics, oriented towards the export of local products (Oleg Milyukov, *Guardian Survey*, 24 June 1988, p. 16). Sovintrade was set up in October 1988, a body jointly owned (by the six state banks, the Ministry of Finance, foreign trade associations, and enterprises that are permitted to export directly) and not subject to the state plan. Its functions include the provision of financial assistance, the identification of potential markets and acting as a clearing house for countertrade (Quentin Peel, *FT*, 12 October 1988, p. 7).

It is worth noting that on 5 January 1988 the Soviet Union, via the Bank, entered the international bond market for the first time since 1917, a 100 million Swiss franc bond to purchase Swiss machine tools. This excludes the London based Moscow Narodny Bank, however, which, for technical reasons, is classified as a British bank. The aim, declared in January 1988, is to meet around 2 per cent of investment needs from hard currency sources in general.

The background to these changes is the dependence of the Soviet Union on primary commodities, especially oil, sold for US dollars when exported to the West. The hope is to improve the quality and saleability of its manufactures in order to widen its sources (and types) of convertible currencies. The Soviet Union's net hard currency debt was $21.2 billion at the end of 1986 (*EIU Country Profile*, 1987–88, p. 36), compared with $0.6 billion in 1971 (Holzman 1987: 5). Clyde Farnsworth (*IHT*, 4 December 1987, p. 2), quoting a US Congress report, gives a figure of $23.2 billion, ignoring the $25 billion owed by less developed countries. The UN Economic Commission for Europe reports a rise from $23 billion to $25 billion in 1987 (*IHT*, 24 March 1988, p. 1). The *IHT* of 4 March 1988 (p. 17) gives a 1987 total net debt of $38 billion, with a debt-service ratio of 23 per cent. *The Economist* estimates gold reserves at $30 billion (7 January 1989, p. 82).

These initial experiments covered only about 6 per cent of hard currency trade (i.e. products such as basic raw materials and foodstuffs were excluded) and all the organizations are still subject to the ultimate authority of the new Committee. Petrov (*Guardian Survey*, 6 November 1987, p. 18) estimates that the 22 ministries and 77 of what he called 'enterprises and organizations' accounted for about 20 per cent of total Soviet foreign trade in 1987. Over 65 per cent of machinery and equipment exports were already directly supplied by their manufacturers rather than through the Ministry of Foreign Trade. According to Gostev, most ministries and departments, all union republics and more than 100 associations, enterprises, and organizations have received the right of direct access to the foreign market (*CDSP*, 1988, vol. XL, no. 45, p. 13).

Similar considerations explain the (unsuccessful) mid-1986 application of the Soviet Union to seek observer status at the current Uruguay round of GATT negotiations. In mid-1988 the Soviet Union's plans seemed to involve a trade and co-operation accord with the European Community in the near future, an application to join GATT within two years and the achievement of rouble convertibility by the year 2000. There was also some interest expressed in future membership of the IMF, the World Bank, and the Multi-fibre Agreement as well. Official US policy, as expressed in the January 1988 *Annual Report on National Security*, is that until the Soviet Union translates talk of economic reform into positive action, the Soviet system remains fundamentally incompatible with membership of these organizations (it should be added that there was also no explicit link made between trade and human rights). At the Nineteenth Party Conference in 1988 Gorbachev called for rouble convertibility in the long term and for increasing trade with capitalist, developing, and (as the immediate priority) socialist countries. In December it was announced that there was to be a future devaluation of the rouble for certain international trade transactions: a uniform exchange rate should replace the thousands of 'coefficients' (effectively exchange rates) by 1991.

Even more striking is the ability to set up joint equity ventures with Western companies, first permitted as of 1 January 1987 (*CDSP*, vol. XXXIX, no. 6, pp. 15–16, 23).[11] The exact initial terms varied from deal to deal, but joint ventures were free to determine their own output and input plans. Western ownership was restricted to a maximum of 49 per cent and the managing director had to be a Soviet citizen. The first two years were tax free (amended in September 1987 to two years after a profit is first made), as is profit placed in reserve and in funds for R&D and technology, but there is a 30 per cent tax on the remainder of profit. Repatriated profit is normally liable to an additional 20 per cent tax.

Problems include the differing interests of the partners. The Soviet Union is mainly interested in improving the quality and exportability of manufactured goods (by means of Western capital, technology and management techniques), in order to increase via exports its hard currency earnings and to save on them via import substitution, since there is pressure to use domestic components. (Note also the advantage of avoiding the debt repayments associated with foreign borrowing.) Originally all foreign exchange outlays, including repatriated profits, had to stem from export revenue; hard currency loans also have to be repaid out of export earnings. It is now possible, however, for export earnings to be more indirect, as in the case of the enterprise set up by the

US company Honeywell and the Soviet Ministry of Mineral Fertilisers. The venture provides process control systems for fertilizer plants to help export their products. Subsequent amendments have enabled the remittance of profits to be in hard currency or in kind. In mid-1988 agreement was reached to allow the foreign exchange earned by one venture to be transferred to another producing for the domestic market. For example, in the American Trade Consortium the Chevron Oil Company's exports supply hard currency to its fellow members, that is only the group as a whole needs to be self-financing in convertible currency earnings. In December a scheme was announced for four-monthly hard currency auctions to be organized by Vneshekonombank; all enterprises with surpluses are eligible sellers.

Western companies, on the other hand, are primarily interested in breaking into the domestic Soviet market, arguing that import substitution saves on convertible currency. According to Valery Prokopov, a new law allows joint ventures that sell import-replacing products solely on the domestic market to repatriate profits in the form of currency or goods (*Guardian Survey*, 13 December 1988, p. 20). Supplies of raw materials were originally secured through the competent foreign trade organization at state-determined prices, although this took account of world prices. Capital goods are not guaranteed in the state plan and, therefore, have to be imported from the Western country concerned (unlike the situation for socialist joint enterprises). It is now possible for joint ventures to undertake their own domestic buying and selling with a mutually agreed currency (Prokorov, *Guardian Survey*, 13 December 1988, p. 20).

The first agreement to be signed was between Intourist (the Soviet travel agency) and Finnair to refurbish the Hotel Berlin in Moscow (a hard currency earner), but others concluded include chemicals and petro-chemicals (development of oil and gas wealth is a priority), publishing, engineering, banking, sawmills, clothing, footwear, fruit juice, refrigeration equipment, retail trade and restaurants. Negotiations going on include Volkswagen car engines, for example. According to Ivan Ivanov, Vice-chairman of the State Committee on External Economic Relations, the Soviet Union has registered 70 joint ventures; six of these are actually operating (*Kommunist*, August 1988, no. 12, p. 38); eleven socialist countries are involved, including Hungary and Yugoslavia (p. 45). By 15 February 1989 the number of registered joint ventures had risen to 248 (*PlanEcon Report*, 24 March 1989, vol.V, nos 10–11–12, p. 1). According to Hanson (1989: 10), these have to date brought in less than one tenth of one per cent of the annual flow of investment.

Likely changes in 1989 include up to 80 per cent foreign ownership, possibly 100 per cent at some time in the future in the 'special economic zones'. The formal end of the 49 per cent ceiling and of the requirement that a Soviet citizen be chairman or managing director was announced in December 1988; there were also tariff concessions, an extension of the tax exemption to three years after a profit is made, special tax provisions for the Soviet Far East, and a relaxation of labour regulations, while permission was given to pay foreign workers' accommodation in roubles.

Non-state activity

Although 1986 saw a crackdown on illegally earned income (checks on large items of expenditure, increased fines), the following year saw a considerable relaxation in the laws governing private and (independent and voluntary) co-operative activity.[12] The aim was to improve rapidly the supply of scarce consumer goods and services (and thus provide an incentive to work hard) and to provide the state with tax and licence revenue from previously black market sources.[13]

Originally co-operatives involved the following types of people: housewives, students over 16 years of age, pensioners, and, to a limited extent, state employees on a part-time basis. The last were eligible in order to protect the labour-short state sector. Food can be purchased by co-operative restaurants from state and collective farms, state retail outlets, or the free market. The 1 July 1988 decree on co-operatives relaxed state regulations by allowing broader rights in price formation, although centralized prices were to remain for state orders and products made with state allocated inputs; the expansion of activities to include homes, roads and cultural clubs; the issuing of shares to both members and contracted employees; involvement in foreign trade, although formal permission was then still required; lawsuits; joint ventures with state enterprises and foreign companies; and the hiring of full-time workers laid off by state enterprises. On the other hand, a progressive income tax was promised – at present there is a flat rate income tax of 3 per cent on individuals, while the high marginal rates on co-operatives of up to 90 per cent proposed in April 1988 are not to be accepted. Also promised was a local flat rate tax in order to reduce resistance by local authorities, while in the same month licence fees were made to vary with the level of profit. A figure of 14,000 co-operatives employing 150,000 people was given by Gorbachev in his 23 March 1988 speech (*CDSP*, 1988, vol. XL, no. 12), while Premier Ryzhkov reported that in 1987 they accounted for 0.3 per cent of consumer goods production, 0.3 per cent of public catering and 0.6 per cent of the volume of consumer services sold (*CDSP*, 1988, vol. XL, no. 22, p. 13). Between 1 July 1987 and 1 July 1988 the number of co-operatives increased from 3, 709 to 32,561 (Kunelsky, *Ekonomicheskaya Gazeta*, no. 34, August 1988, p. 12). By the end of 1988 almost 2 million were employed in 'cooperatives and independent enterprise', compared with 117.5 million workers and office employees, and 12.2 million collective farmers (*CDSP*, 1989, vol. XLI, no. 4, p. 12).

'Individual labour activity' (the law on which came into effect 1 May 1987) is now permitted in certain defined fields (the local authorities decide precisely which may be allowed through the issue of licences). These include house, car and appliance repairs; public catering; tailoring; furniture making; private cars used as taxis; dressmaking; shoes; private tuition in subjects on official curricula; restaurants; pottery and ceramics; medical consultancy; nursing; and translation and secretarial work. Activities still banned include trade in goods produced by others, copying of video tapes, gambling, weapons repair, and discotheque management. The October 1987 regulations specifically banned publishing and printing co-operatives.[14] A 30 December 1988 decree on co-operatives also listed the following banned areas: the making and selling of firearms, explosives, alcohol, religious artefacts, and most jewellery; the production of films and videos, the sale of which is authorized only under contract with a state enterprise; schools; and medical diagnostic work, obstetrics and the treatment of cancer and venereal disease. Shortly afterwards it was announced that co-operatives fulfilling state orders and those charging prices no higher than those of the state would be given preference in terms of bank credit, input supply, and tax rates.

Individual labour activity is generally confined to 'jointly residing family members' over the age of 16, housewives, students, pensioners, the disabled and all citizens over the age of 18 who have a state job (i.e. part-timers). Thus, there are restrictions in the shape of a general ban on the employment of non-family workers[15] and on the use of sophisticated automated equipment. There is a system of progressive taxation: zero tax on income of less than 70 roubles a month; and 13 per cent, the highest marginal rate on state sector wages and salaries, on income between 70 and 250 roubles a month, rising to 65 per cent over 500 roubles a month. Note that a high licence fee may be substituted where income is difficult to check, such as in the case of taxi services. Resentment is caused by the high prices inevitably associated with deficient supply in the short run, while there is a problem with supplies, state enterprises being encouraged to provide recycled and waste materials. Since September 1987 private individuals have been able to rent shops and kiosks and space in some state stores.

Prices

The infrequent wholesale price changes usually involve increases in order to reflect rising costs and to reduce subsidies, the aim being to allow most enterprises to operate profitably. Prices, however, are still generally fixed on a cost-plus basis, although the profit markup is now on capital and is high enough to allow for the payment of a capital charge. This was introduced in 1965 and is normally 6 per cent of the undepreciated value of an enterprise's fixed and working capital. The charge is not formally counted as a cost, but is reflected in price indirectly through the higher markup. Rental charges are also now paid by those industrial enterprises particularly favourably situated and/or endowed with modern machinery.

Deviations from standard practice include a move towards marginal cost pricing in extractive industries (oil, natural gas and iron ore). Since 1967, for example, oil prices have been based on the costs of average-sized enterprises working under worse-than-average conditions, with the more favourably situated fields making rental payments to the state.

In 1964 'analogue' pricing was introduced generally for new and improved products. This involves pricing in relation to improvements, in the form of higher quality, lower costs and so on, compared with the most analogous product. A lower limit (roughly the old cost plus basis) and an upper limit (based on the improvements in use value) are fixed with prices set nearer the upper limit the greater the shortage of the products, thus taking some account of demand.

At the 1986 Congress Gorbachev suggested that prices should not only reflect outlays, but also the consumer properties of goods, the degree to which they meet the needs of society and consumer demand. Consideration should be given to the high level of subsidies for housing and foodstuffs and there should be greater use of ceiling and contract prices. Actual price developments include a system of producer price surcharges for above standard quality and price reductions for below standard goods.

In the 1987 proposals on wholesale prices it was envisaged that goods such as fuels, energy, and basic raw materials would still be state determined and raised substantially, relating them to world levels in order to encourage a more efficient use. There would be scope, however, for prices between purchaser and supplier to be above the norm when quality is higher or innovation is involved. Thus a three-tier system of prices is in prospect: fixed (for basic goods), maximum (or range), and free (for luxury goods).

Gorbachev has personally attacked the receipt of the same price for goods of very different quality. He has also criticized:

1. The high subsidies on basic foodstuffs at the retail level. In 1989 total food subsidies are likely to amount to 88 billion roubles or 17.8 per cent of total planned budgetary expenditure. These benefit higher-income families disproportionately because of their higher spending on these items and exacerbate shortages by diverting household expenditure.
2. The case of a pair of ladies' boots costing 120 to 130 roubles, or the same as the annual average consumption (62 kg) of meat;
3. Bread for being so cheap that children use loaves as footballs, a variation on the illegal feeding of bread instead of fodder to livestock because the former is cheaper than the latter (see report of the Murmansk speech in *CDSP*, 1987, vol. XXXIX, no. 40, p. 5).

At the Nineteenth Party Conference in 1988, Gorbachev stressed the need for price reform in order to assess the costs and results of production, to stimulate technical progress, to encourage savings of resources and to reduce subsidies (the retail prices of many food products, notably of meat and milk, were lower than production costs and procurement prices). Housing rents were fixed in 1928, bread, sugar and eggs in 1954 and meat in 1962. The 5 kopek Moscow underground fare was fixed in 1935. Valentin Pavlov (Chairman of the State Committee for Prices) revealed that subsidies were first introduced for food in 1965 (*FT*, 26 November 1987, p. 3). The average price of a kilo of meat in a state shop is 1.80 roubles, which represents a subsidy of 3 roubles, the same applying to dairy products and bread. In 1986 subsidies for food products came to 57 billion roubles, out of a total state budget of 430 billion roubles (Aganbegyan 1988: 181).

New industrial wholesale prices were to be introduced on 1 January 1990 and new retail prices and agricultural procurement prices on 1 January 1991. It is stressed that retail price rises will be compensated by increases in money incomes. Aganbegyan states that there are 24 million types of goods and services and that the prices of around 500,000 of them are set by the central government alone (1988a: 134). The aim is to confine centrally set prices to the most essential products, such as fuels, electricity, vital raw materials and some consumer goods (1988a: 119). Prices are to be reviewed at least every five years, or earlier if conditions alter sharply (1988a: 135).

Agriculture

There is a dramatic difference between the agriculture of the Stalinist era and that of today.[16] Although still a problem sector, it is now highly subsidized. Investment is heavy, although often inefficiently used. The state farm has steadily increased in importance, although the differences between it and the collective farm have lessened. Since 1966, for instance, collective farmers have been given monthly payments for work done based on state farm rates of pay. A noteworthy event is the growing importance of the *'autonomous (or normless) link'* (*beznaryadnoye zveno*), in the sense of working without daily assignments. There are group variations in name or substance known as the contract brigade, team, small (typically around six) work group, group contract, collective contract, and even family contract. This growth is at the expense of the 100-plus-strong brigades, where there is only a tenuous relationship between individual effort and reward.

Links vary, but can involve, for example, a small group of people, self-selected or even family members (there is also a tendency for these activities to overlap with work on the private plot), who are given responsibility for a piece of land or livestock unit, supposedly allocated inputs, supposedly set broad output targets for five years and paid by results (Gagnon 1987). Work assignments are not set, however. Production in excess of target may be sold to the farm at a higher price or sold on the free market. Links have a history that can be traced back to the 1930s, but these fell into total disfavour by 1950. A revival began in the form of experiments in the late 1950s. Opposition then set in, a further revival took place in the late 1970s and Gorbachev, as the Party Secretary in charge of agriculture, gave his endorsement in March 1983 (Nove 1987: 21). Problems include input supply and a diminution in the authority of farm chairmen, whose responsibilities and remuneration remain unaffected (Johnson 1988a: 208). As a whole they accounted for about a half of the agricultural work-force in 1985 and 76 per cent by the end of 1987 (Charles Hodgson, *FT*, 26 January 1988, p. 28). Wädekin provides the following information on 'normless links' and 'contract brigades': by 1984 19 per cent of the agricultural work-force was involved, with six and twenty four members respectively on average (1988: 208).

In his 23 March 1988 speech Gorbachev highlighted the 'family contract' and the 'rental or lease contract' (where both land and the means of production are leased; *CDSP*, 1988, vol. XL, no. 41, p. 4). He outlined farm policy as follows:

1. the lifting of restrictions on auxiliary activities such as processing, services and consumer goods;
2. the ability of collective farms to lease, both to other enterprises and to private citizens, part of the land assigned to them and also some of their fixed assets;
3. the ability to engage in foreign economic operations;
4. the possibility of revoking a co-operative's right to use land and even to liquidate the inefficient; and
5. further encouragement given to the private plot.

Gorbachev spoke favourably of experiments where a multi-layer structure is being set up. Small groups are at the bottom ('primary co-operatives') and are on an economic accounting basis (including a separate bank account). Agro-industrial, inter-unit associations organized on a horizontal and vertical basis are in the middle and there is a similar organization at the provincial level. Note, however, there will still be state guidance in forms such as tax and credit policy, state contracts and state orders (*CDSP*, 1988, vol. XL, no. 12, pp. 4–7).

The administrative mechanism of the *agro-industrial complex*, experiments dating from 1974, was basically established by 1982. This was part of the May Food Programme of that year. This involved a drive to increase food production and thus reduce food and foodstuffs imports, stemming in part from the US grain embargo of January 1980 to April 1981.[17] The aim of the complex was to co-ordinate farm production, input supply and other services, procurement, rural construction, transport, storage, food processing and sales. There is a vertical hierarchy at the federal, republican, provincial and district level (Rapo). The hoped-for benefits include increased output and an amelioration of the problems of input supply and lack of farm specialization. In his 29 July 1988 speech Gorbachev, in fact, criticized the agro-industrial complex and recommended a changeover to the voluntary creation of joint management agencies by collective and state farms and to co-operative forms of service provision (*CDSP*, 1988, vol. XL, no. 30, p. 7). In November 1985 the State Agro-Industrial Committee (Gosagroprom) was established, enveloping the previously separate bodies such as ministries (though a number of ministries survived as separate units) and service organizations, with the aim, among other things, of improving the co-ordination of input supplies. These bodies in fact survived, albeit under new names (Nove 1987: 22). *Gosagropromy* were also to be created at the republican and provincial levels, dovetailing with the existing Rapos at district level (Dyker 1987: 106).

The *private plot* accounts for about a quarter of total agricultural output[18] and only 3 per cent of sown area. Note there are urban as well as rural plots. In 1984 they accounted for 58 per cent of potatoes, 30 per cent of vegetables, meat, eggs, and milk, and 24 per cent of wool (*EEN*, 1988, vol. 2, no. 1, p. 2). Their fortunes have fluctuated considerably over time, depending on factors such as the political climate and the performance of the socialized sector, but present policy is one of encouragement through means such as increased credits and a wider use of lease contracts by collective and state farms that provide additional plots of land on a long-term basis to sell produce under contract to farms and consumer co-operatives (*CDSP*, 1987, vol. XXXIX, no. 40, p. 16). Since 1981 private individuals have been able to obtain young animals and complementary inputs from farms under contracts that specify expected return sales of final products and at particular prices (Roucek 1988: 54). *The Economist* reports that there is now no limit on the number of animals that can be kept on each plot (*Survey* 1988: 54).

At the Nineteenth Party Conference in 1988 Gorbachev stressed the need to promote *leasing arrangements* (*CDSP*, 1988, vol. XL, no. 26, p. 8) and elaborated upon this at the follow-up Central Committee Plenum held on 29 July. The experiments country-wide involved around a fifth of the 50,000 or so state and collective farms, typically with land leasing of around five years and inputs purchased from and sales made to the farm. Rentals were used extensively until their abolition in the mid-1930s. These experiments had proven successful because leasing overcame the feeling that the means of production belonged to no one and forged a link between remuneration and performance, while socialism was preserved because state ownership remained: 'a person becomes the true master of the land and has a stake in seeing to it that the land and other means of production he rents are used with the maximum effectiveness and produces the highest returns' (Gorbachev, *CDSP*, 1988, vol. XL, no. 30, p. 6). He contrasts this with the situation where the average annual gross output of agriculture for 1986–87 grew by only 41 per cent over the average annual level for 1966–70, while over the same period capital investment increased by 140 per cent (*CDSP*, 1988, vol. XL, no. 41, p. 2). The period of the land lease should be up to 50 years. The leasing applies to small groups or families (leases can be passed on to children), while Gorbachev also recommended an extension of the system of leasing of shops and plants in industry (*CDSP*, 1988, vol. XL, no. 30, p. 6).[19] The subsequent decree also approved the purchasing of machinery and the hiring of seasonal labour. 'Collective farms and state farms must be integrated with the individual sector through contracts' (Gorbachev, *CDSP*, 1988, vol. XL, no. 41, p. 8).

The Gorbachev era has seen farmers being paid a price bonus for major products (50 per cent for meat and milk for example and 100 per cent for grain) on sales above the average level actually achieved in the period 1981–85, rather than income being tied to the fulfilment and over fulfilment of delivery plans. Provincial authorities now have the power to set the prices of fruit and vegetables in their state outlets, while farms are now able to sell up to 30 per cent of their delivery quotas of fruit and vegetables (instead of just above-plan deliveries) on the free market or via co-operatives. Farm managers are now able to earn bonuses of up to 25 per cent of normal pay. Designers of machinery applied by farms are now able to share up to half of the extra profits forthcoming (*FT*, 14 August 1987, p. 20). In 1988 agricultural science and research and design centres began to move to a self-financing basis. Since July 1987 urbanites have been able to rent empty village houses and their adjacent plots, although an agreed quota of produce must be delivered to the *kolkhoz*, which is also to be allowed to rent or sell equipment and buildings to individual members and to develop direct trading links with agricultural co-operatives overseas (Hodgson, *FT*, 26 January 1988, p. 28). There have been experiments with wholesale trade in the means of production, such as in Lithuania, while *The Economist* survey (1988: 10) discusses the Estonian experiment. Here the state supports agriculture by means of higher product prices instead of input subsidies in order to favour those who produce more rather than those who make larger losses. Estonia is also the first republic to introduce land rent that varies with land quality.

There have been experiments in both state and collective farms involving 'shareholders' associations', whereby part of the work-force contributes funds and, in return, receives dividends (dependent on profits) and regular reports from the director; the association board determines the use of funds (*CDSP*, 1988, vol. XL, no. 22, p. 22).

The Central Committee meeting on 15–16 March 1989 resolved to:

1. Abolish Gosagroprom on the grounds of bureaucracy and overcentralization, replacing it with a commission of the Council of Ministers.
2. Encourage leasing in the general context of diversified forms of organization.
3. Raise procurement prices from January 1990, while holding state retail prices of basic foodstuffs steady for two to three years.
4. Introduce 'more flexible prices' for seasonal products (e.g. fruit and

vegetable prices to be set contractually between local authorities and farms).

The period 1988–89 will see the changeover of all collective and state farms to full economic accountability and self-financing (*CDSP*, 1987, vol. XXXIX, no. 40, p. 16). As of 1988 more than 60 per cent of all farms had switched over to the new management methods (*CDSP*, 1988, vol. Xl, no. 12, p. 5).

Conclusion

The traditional Soviet economic system encountered severe economic problems, not only those outlined in Chapter 1, but also others such as the 'scattering' of investment resources and declining rates of growth of national income. There is increasing need for a more intensive pattern of growth.

There have been a bewildering number of reforms, but the Soviet economy in 1988 essentially still operated on the command principle. The June 1987 legislation promises a significant departure from the traditional system, but it is important to be aware of the fact that much of it still remains on paper and that a complete transition to the new system is by no means a foregone conclusion. Nevertheless, some changes already introduced are remarkable in their historical context, particularly the permitting of joint equity ventures with Western companies, the erosion of the state monopoly of foreign trade and the expansion of the private and independent co-operative sectors. The proposal to introduce leasing on a grand scale in agriculture, if carried out, would mean a fundamental departure from the traditional structure.

Gorbachev faces tremendous resistance to his reforms, not in the sense of organized political opposition, but rather from a general lethargy and lack of individual initiative plus a more positive aversion to reform in the middle and lower ranks of the bureaucracy anxious to preserve their privileged positions. Many managers and workers too are not keen to expose themselves to increased uncertainty, responsibility and inequalities, especially given the lack of adequate material incentives due to continuing shortages in the supply of consumer goods and services. With the gradualist approach to reform the transitional stage is awkward in that new elements may disturb the operation of the old system. Many of the more cautious individuals at the top have been dismissed or demoted, perhaps the best recent example of the latter being the case of Yegor Ligachev. Formerly regarded as 'Number Two' with his control over ideology and personnel, Ligachev was instead put in charge of agriculture at the emergency plenum of the Central Committee held on 30 September 1988.

On the domestic political scene Gorbachev places great hope in the new Congress of People's Deputies (2,250 members) and its standing Supreme Soviet (542 members) with executive Chairman (President). The soviets (councils) are to be endowed with substantially enhanced decision-making powers.

The general aim is to separate party and state, in order to prevent the former from interfering in day-to-day affairs. Gorbachev has had to deal with events such as the April 1986 Chernobyl accident, but he seems to have the knack of turning them to his advantage, as can also be illustrated by the Mathias Rust affair of May 1987. Here the military was taken to task for its inability to prevent the landing of a German light aircraft in Red Square. Perhaps the Armenian earthquake of December 1988 may also prove to be an example given the criticisms levelled at the Soviet relief effort and the high profile of foreign aid. Unrest in some of the republics (especially demands for greater autonomy in the Baltic Republics of Estonia, Latvia, and Lithuania, but also demonstrations in Georgia, and the strife between Armenia and Azerbaijan over the latter's autonomous province of Nagorno Karabhak), however, is possibly the greatest threat to Gorbachev's position.

Table 2.2 The Soviet Union: statistical survey

(Annual average rate of growth NMP (utilized) (%)								
1951–55	1961–65	1966–70	1971–75	1976–80	1981–85	1986	1987	1988
11.0	6.0	7.1	5.1	3.9	3.2	4.1	2.3	4.4

	1971	1987
Net hard currency debt	$0.6 billion	$25 billion
Share of world trade (1986, %)	5.0	

Joint equity ventures (end of November 1988)	139 registered, about 12 operating

Independent co-operatives (1987)	0.3% of consumer goods production, 0.37 % of public catering and 0.67% of the volume of consumer services sold.

Agricultural output (1985, %)	Collective farms	State farms	Private plots
	35	40	25

Population (12 January 1989)	286.7 million

Sources: See Table 2.1; Aganbegyan (1988a: 148); IHT, 4 March 1988, p. 17; CDSP, 1988, vol. XL, no. 22, p. 13; Schroeder (1988a: 180).

On the international level Gorbachev has become a household name. The urgent need to devote as much time and energy as possible to the enormous problems facing the Soviet Union at home is an important factor in explaining Gorbachev's quest for improved international relations. The December 1987 INF Treaty involved the scrapping of land-based, intermediate nuclear missiles. Soviet troops were withdrawn from Afghanistan by 15 February 1989 as promised, while pressure seems to have been used to encourage the withdrawal of Cuban troops from Angola and Vietnamese from Kampuchea. Gorbachev and Deng Xiaoping agreed to meet on 15–18 May 1989, 30 years after Khrushchev and Mao Zedong met in Beijing. A prime aim is to switch resources from the military to the civilian sector of the economy. The dramatic announcement in his speech to the United Nations on 7 December 1988 of a unilateral reduction in troops and weapons was supplemented by a proposal to experiment with the conversion of several armaments plants to civilian production.

Postscript

For further information see pp. 72–3.

Notes

1. Linz uses interviews with Soviet emigrants to examine these factors in the two decades prior to Gorbachev. This method has obvious limitations, but she concludes that there had been a reduced scope for enterprise management autonomy, due to the enhanced technical expertise of ministerial personnel and the huge documentation required of enterprises during annual plan negotiations. As a result, enterprise management was unable, to any significant extent, to overindent for inputs, understate productive capacity, attain lower output targets or falsify data. During the 1970s light industry had to receive the trade organization's permission to change assortment plans, while the decade was characterized by government attempts to offset falling growth rates by increasing central controls rather than decentralizing decision-making (1988: 190–91). Linz has also published a complementary essay dealing with organizational change ('The impact of Soviet economic reform' in Linz and Moskoff 1988).
2. NMP differs from the United Nations 'system of national accounts', mainly because of the exclusion of so-called non-productive services, such as defence, general administration, education, finance and credit, and transport and communications serving households.
3. 'NMP produced' minus exports plus imports, measured in domestic prices, and minus losses due to abandoned construction and accidental damage, gives 'NMP utilized'.
4. In 1987 growth officially defined on a Western GNP basis for the first time was calculated to be 3.3 per cent (5 per cent in 1988). By contrast, the CIA and DIA report to the US Congress estimated Soviet GNP growth to be 3.9 per cent in 1986, 0.5 per cent in 1987, and 1.5 per cent in 1988. An explanation as to why growth estimates vary would involve factors such as data deficiencies, the lack of efficiency prices, which years' prices are used in time series, and the problem of new products. This is a complicated area and the interested reader is advised to consult the references cited.
5. Namely, influx of manpower from the countryside, increases in participation rates (especially among women) and increases in the proportion of national income devoted to investment. Aganbegyan places the decline in the potential of extensive growth via the growth of resources at the beginning of the 1970s (1988a: 23).
6. See *CDSP*, 1988, vol. XL, no. 4, pp. 1–7.
7. Brigades are becoming increasingly important in Soviet industry in general, offering advantages like group pressure on individuals not to let the colleagues down.
8. See *CDSP*, 1987, vol. XXXIX, nos 24, 27, 30; *EEN*, 1987, vol. 1, no. 2; Gorbachev 1987; Kaser 1987; Litvin 1987; Petrov in *The Guardian*, 6 November 1987, p. 18; Reut (Deputy Chairman of Gosplan) in *IHT*, 7–8 November 1987, p. 9; Tedstrom

1987; Aganbegyan 1988, 1988a; *CDSP*, 1988, vol. XXXIX, no. 52; Hewett 1988; Makorov 1988.

9. Note that all enterprises are expected to manufacture consumer goods.

10. Since the start of 1988 it has been possible for certain enterprises to issue non-equity shares to their own employees. The first was the Konveyer plant in Lvov; a variable dividend is payable and shares can be traded back to the plant bank at any time for their original value (David Remnick, *IHT*, 8 February 1989, p. 2; Quentin Peel, *FT*, 5 May 1989, p. 21 and 41). In his budget speech to the Supreme Soviet in October 1988 Finance Minister Boris Gostev outlined plans to extend share issues in order to mop up excess purchasing power, to improve attitudes towards state property and to provide alternative sources of enterprise finance. Shares would be differentiated according to an enterprise's own personnel and to other enterprises and organizations (*CDSP*, 1988, vol. XL, no. 45, p. 15). An individual worker's maximum would be 10,000 roubles' worth and shares would not involve any special voting rights. Shares in total could be up to 80 per cent of the value of an enterprise's fixed and working capital (a 30 per cent ceiling on own workers' shares and 50 per cent on other enterprises').

11. Comecon enterprises are also included, such as the first Polish-Soviet joint venture (manufacturing cosmetics in Poland), announced at the end of 1987. For a detailed analysis see UN Economic Commission for Europe (1988) *Economic, Business, Financial and Legal Aspects of East-West Joint Ventures*, Geneva.

12. See *CDSP*, 1986, vol. XXXVIII, no. 42 and 1987, vol. XXXIX, no. 18; Roucek, *Soviet Studies*, vol. XL, no. 1.

13. Tatyana Koryagina, head of the Social Research Department of Gosplan, values the black economy (excluding organized crime) at 90 billion roubles (see the report by Rupert Cornwell in *The Independent*, 13 August 1988, p. 7; this is equivalent to up to 15 per cent of produced national income). In services alone, the black economy provides 14 billion to 16 billion roubles compared with 45 billion in the official economy.

14. Note that it is still the case that income can only be paid out to members who actually work in the co-operative.

15. Artisans may still be fully self-employed, while citizens working on a self-employed basis may take on some categories of trainees (Aganbegyan, 1988a: 28). Local authorities are now able to grant permission for full-time self-employment, especially when scarce consumer goods are involved (p. 131).

16. Campaigns, like the Virgin Lands Campaign conceived by Khrushchev in 1954, tend to be overdone. The colossal scheme to divert water from north-flowing rivers to the Asiatic republics was scrapped in 1986.

17. The 1982 Food Programme up to 1990 mainly stressed the need to increase both infrastructural investment and farm prices (mushrooming subsidies cushioning retail prices), but also to decentralize decision-making to a greater extent to farms and within farms, and to encourage the private sector.

18. Collective farms account for around 35 per cent of total agricultural output (Schroeder 1988a: 180). In terms of marketed output the shares in 1985 were as follows: state farms 49 per cent; collective farms 41 per cent; and the private sector 10 per cent (p. 180).

19. Experiments with leasing have taken place in Estonia and in the Moscow area. The lease lasts for seven years on average and involves a group of workers or a whole plant making a fixed payment in exchange for the opportunity to use remaining profit at their own discretion (*The Economist*, 14 January 1988, p. 47).

Appendix

Planning techniques

Material balancing is still the core of command planning. Although this has been improved (by a greater number of iterations, for example), nevertheless, input-output analysis and linear programming also play a subsidiary role.

Input-output analysis

This technique is associated with Leontief, who took part in the early work on drawing up balances of inter-sectoral flows before leaving the Soviet Union in 1925. Due to Stalin's aversion to mathematical techniques, which he saw as a threat to political control, the first input-output table to be drawn up was for the year 1959.

An economy is characterized by inter-industry dependence. Thus coal is used as an input in other industries, while coal needs the output of other industries as inputs. Coal is also a final good, however, when used in the home for heating purposes, while primary inputs (e.g. labour) are also needed to produce coal. The question to be asked, then, is what the level of output of each industry should be in order to meet the total demand (intermediate and final) for that product.

Figure 2.1 shows a simplified input-output table for a closed economy (no foreign trade) with three sectors (industries). Reading across the rows we see how the gross output of each sector is used as an input in the three sectors (i.e. including itself) and for final demand purposes (consumption and investment). Reading down the columns, it can be seen that each sector uses intermediate inputs from the three sectors and primary inputs, namely labour, land and capital.

The heavily outlined section, designated as Quadrant I in tables, captures the inter-sectoral relationships. From the information contained in each cell, an input coefficient can be worked out specifying the amount of a particular input needed to produce a unit of output of a particular sector. Given targets for final demand, the process of matrix inversion enables mutually consistent gross output levels to be calculated, simultaneously meeting all the demands placed upon them. The effect of changes in final demand targets on the output levels of all sectors can be traced through.

When first worked on, greater hopes were held out for input-output analysis. Yet today it plays only a peripheral role in planning: (a) variant analysis (e.g. the effects of higher percentage shares of investment during a five year plan); and (b) in the final stages of planning for checking consistency. Its indirect effects on popularizing mathematical modelling and computer technology should not be forgotten, however. Major problems include:

1. The high degree of aggregation: the largest Soviet table so far is 600 x 600,

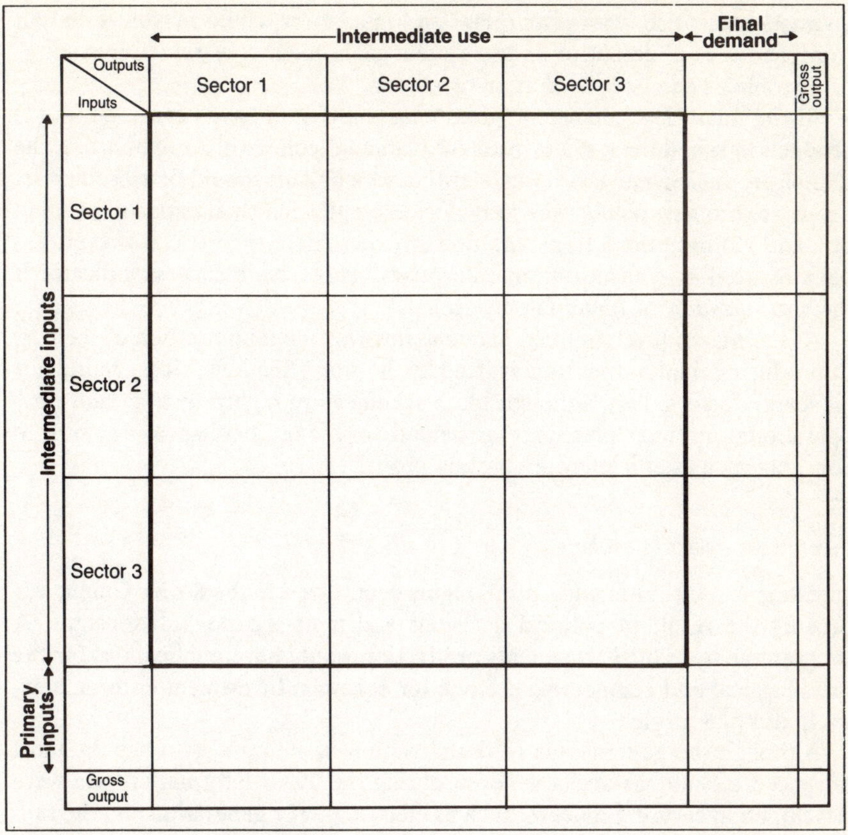

Outputs / Inputs	Intermediate use			Final demand	Gross output
	Sector 1	Sector 2	Sector 3		
Sector 1					
Sector 2					
Sector 3					
Gross output					

Figure 2.1 Input-output table

while over 20,000 material balances are drawn up centrally (Gosplan alone 2,000). The number of sectors is, of course, tiny compared to the vast number of commodities.

2. The assumption of constant input coefficients is unrealistic over longer periods of time since technology changes.
3. The fact that Soviet industry is highly non-specialized. Input-output is conceived in terms of 'pure' sectors, on a 'commodity by commodity' basis. To be of operational value, in the sense of providing plan targets for individual enterprises, account would have to be taken of enterprise-specific input-output coefficients and the timely inter-enterprise distribution of inputs.

Linear programming

This was invented by Kantorovich in 1939, the first example illustrating how a plywood enterprise, with given plant and machinery, could maximize output subject to the fulfilment of an assortment plan. Such constrained maximization problems can be looked at on two levels.

At the micro level, linear programming techniques have been used in: (1) production scheduling; (2) investment planning (this involves minimizing the cost of producing a given output, showing which plant should be closed or set up, where the new plants were to be located, and what their capacities should be); and (3) in optimal transportation schemes (here their use, however, has been resisted by transportation enterprises, whose main success indicator is the *maximization* of tonne-kilometres).

At the macro level, optimal planning involves the minimization of the cost of producing final output targets fixed by the state. Shadow prices emerge for all scarce factors, and, although these schemes are highly abstract and non-operational, optimal planning has helped overcome ideological aversion to concepts such as efficiency pricing and profit.

Investment decision-making

Investment decision-making is still highly centralized in the Soviet Union; it is broadly the result of political decisions and inter-sectoral relationships. A programme to reduce armaments production would have implications for the metallurgical and engineering sectors, for example. Investment criteria, however, also play a role.

Although the general rule of thumb within branches was to use the most advanced techniques available, even during the 1930s informal criteria were developed in certain branches, such as electric power generation and the railways, to help choose between different ways of achieving a given output target. Suppose the possible variants to be Project 1 (a hydro scheme) and Project 2 (coal-fired power stations), with the former involving a higher initial capital outlay (I_1), but a lower annual operating cost C_1 (including depreciation, but excluding a charge on capital) than the latter. The more capital intensive Project 1 will be chosen if the additional capital outlay can be recouped within a period of time equal to or smaller than the normative recoupment period fixed for that sector. More formally:

$$\frac{I_1 - I_2}{C_2 - C_1} = T \quad \text{(recoupment period: RP)}$$

If $T \leq T_n$ (normative recoupment period), then Project 1 is chosen; if $T > T_n$ then Project 2.

The reciprocal of T is called the 'coefficient of relative effectiveness' (CRE). Project 1 is selected if $\frac{1}{T} (= E) \geq \frac{1}{T_n} (= E_n)$, Project 2 if $E < E_n$. E represents the 'return' in the form of the savings on operating costs resulting from the additional capital outlay. For example, if $RP = 8$, then $E = 0.125$ ($\times 100 = 12.5$ per cent). If $RP_n = 10$, then $E_n = 0.1$ ($\times 100 = 10$ per cent), and Project 1 will be chosen.

Although a crude device (for example, there is no capital market in the Soviet Union, so the choice of E_n is arbitrary), the CRE at least recognizes that capital has an opportunity cost. It was formally accepted in the 1960 'Standard methodology for determining the economic effectiveness of capital investment and new technology', although other factors affect investment decisions, including political ones and physical indicators such as input utilization which may override CRE considerations. The 1969 amended version of the Standard Methodology also highlighted 'coefficients of absolute effectiveness', effectively incremental output-capital ratios $[\Delta Y/\Delta K]$ and profit-capital ratios $[\Delta \Pi/\Delta K]$, but these do not supersede conventional central allocative decisions and seem to be more a check on efficiency.

Chapter three

Foreign trade

In the traditional Soviet economic system the state has a monopoly on foreign trade and payments, the purpose being to help carry out party policy and shield the domestic from the international economy. With direct control exercised over exports and imports, tariffs lose their conventional significance as protectors of home industry and sources of budgetary revenue. Two-tariff schedules have been used by command economies, however, as bargaining levers with the West in the quest for 'most favoured nation treatment' (the lowest tariff applying to all). Czechoslovakia, Hungary, Poland and Romania belong to GATT and have agreed to increase imports so as to simulate the effects of tariff reductions.

The institutional hierarchy runs from the State Planning Commission to the Ministry of Foreign Trade and on to the foreign trade corporations (FTCs), which normally specialize in a particular product or group of products and which operate on a *khozraschyot* basis. The industrial enterprise that produces the good designated in its *tekhpromfinplan* as an export does not receive the world price, but the domestic wholesale price, with appropriate adjustments in case of factors such as quality differences. The ultimate user of an import is charged the price of its nearest domestic substitute. There is a multiple exchange rate system, with various rates for different products or groups of products. Exchange rates are arbitrarily determined, with a tendency towards overvaluation. In consequence, the higher level of domestic prices for tradeable goods than the world price level typically results in accounting 'profits' on imports and 'losses' on exports made by the FTCs.

The separation of original producer and ultimate purchaser, except for perhaps contact over minor details such as precise delivery times, severely aggravates the problem of quality in production and marketing. Industrial enterprises in command economies produce according to plan and are unaffected by either competition in or, in any automatic sense, the movement of prices on the world market.

Planning and foreign trade

In textbook market economies, international trade is based on specialization according to comparative advantage, with firms equally interested in exports or imports in the search for maximum profits. In the traditional Soviet system exports were viewed as a means of paying for the import of goods either totally unavailable or in short supply at home, goods deemed essential to fulfil national plans; exports are not seen, for example, as a means of achieving full employment. As Winiecki puts it, imports are largely determined by drawing up material balances that show the rough gaps between planned domestic demand and supply. These balances also show exportable surpluses; if it is not possible to reduce imports, it is the value of the imports needed to meet the planned growth rate that determines the value of exports (1988: 136). Inefficient domestic prices and arbitrarily determined exchange rates preclude a meaningful calculation of the gains from trade. The commodity structure of trade is determined by political factors (sales of armaments, for example), domestic resource endowment (the Soviet Union is the world's largest producer of oil) and the relative inefficiency of the economic system (command economies have difficulties selling manufactured goods in Western markets).

In 1937 Soviet exports reached an all-time low of 0.5 per cent of national product, although this was due to a combination of deliberate isolation ('socialism in one country'), Western embargoes and deteriorating commodity terms of trade (i.e. the prices of primary products falling relative to imported manufactures). The 'trade aversion' to which command economies are susceptible was especially evident in the early years. In contrast, Hungary today is heavily dependent on international trade.

Intra-Comecon prices

A fundamental feature is the use of some form of world prices, due to the lack of efficient domestic prices and meaningful exchange rates. The exact form has varied over time, although world prices are allegedly cleansed of so-called business cycle, and monopolistic and speculative influences, and adjustments are made to take account of such factors as differences in quality. The particular price formula is used to determine specific prices in the bilateral negotiations which also decide quantities. More specifically, current world market prices were used in 1949 and average prices of 1949–50 until 1956. Between 1958 and 1965 1957 prices were used, while average prices of 1960–64 were employed during the period 1966–70. Average 1965–69 prices were used over the period 1971–75, but 1975 saw a switch to a new system, namely an annually moving average of the previous five years (three in the case of some products). This system of price determination explains why the prices charged by the Soviet Union for oil deliveries to its Comecon partners lagged behind the upsurge in world prices after 1973–74 and 1979 and the decline after

November 1985.

Another feature of more recent pricing policies has been the policy of allowing, albeit still in a controlled fashion, domestic prices to reflect, to varying extents, changes in world prices. Within Comecon this has been taken to greatest lengths in Hungary.

Determination of exchange rates

In market economies operating on a floating exchange rate regime, the price of one national currency in terms of another is determined by supply and demand forces operating in foreign exchange markets. In the long run such exchange rates approximate 'purchasing power parity', units of the different national currencies buying roughly equal amounts of internationally traded goods and services (i.e. the prices of similar goods on the world and domestic markets being approximately the same at the prevailing exchange rates). In command economies national currencies are not convertible into each other, into gold or into Western currencies, so they are not bought and sold on world foreign exchange markets. The separation of domestic and world prices resulting from the state monopoly of foreign trade and payments thus ensures that exchange rates are arbitrarily determined. It should be noted, however, that tourist exchange rates differ from commercial ones in that the former have to take into account the effects of expenditure by tourists, who have the choice as to whether to buy the goods and services available. Nevertheless, the frequency of black markets indicates some overvaluation of the domestic currency even here. The commercial exchange rates are thus units of account that are needed to draw up a balance of payments, with export and import statistics valued in *valuta* (foreign currency) roubles or marks, say. The figures can be converted into domestic roubles or marks by means of state determined exchange rates.

Reforms in foreign trade decision-making

In command economies foreign trade decisions are still largely the result of material balance planning and trade agreements, but nowadays reforms have increased the degree of decentralized decision-making to trade and production enterprises, and planners use a number of foreign trade indices. These indices are fundamentally flawed in that they rely on inefficient domestic prices and the absence of market-determined exchange rates which approximate purchasing power parity: hence they have only a marginal effect on decision-making, helping to eliminate grossly unprofitable transactions by crudely estimating foreign exchange earnings per unit of domestic resource expenditure and savings in domestic resources per unit of foreign exchange expended.

In helping to decide whether it is profitable to import a commodity, the following simplified import efficiency index (M_e) can be used:

$$M_e = \frac{P_d \cdot E}{P_f}$$

The inherent defects in this index can be seen in the inefficient domestic price (P_d) and the lack of a meaningful exchange rate (E) with which to compare P_d and P_f (the foreign price expressed in terms of foreign currency). A crude ranking of imports can be derived by comparing $\frac{P_d}{P_f}$ for each commodity. The same sort of ranking procedure can be followed for exports, comparing foreign exchange earnings per unit of domestic resource expenditure. Winiecki makes the point that these indices may help avoid gross errors at the level of a narrow product group at best, since even serious price distortions are at least of a similar type (1988: 147).

Council of Mutual Economic Assistance

Comecon has ten full members: the Soviet Union, Bulgaria, Czechoslovakia, Hungary, Poland, Romania (who formed the original membership in January 1949), the GDR (joined 1950), Mongolia (1962), Cuba (1972) and Vietnam (1978). Albania joined in February 1949, but effectively ceased to be a member at the end of 1961 (membership has never formally been revoked). Yugoslavia is the only 'limited participant' – since 1964 it has had partial associate status, co-operating in most standing commissions, and is a member of other organs. The following have observer status: Afghanistan, Angola, China, Ethiopia, Laos, Mozambique (Mozambique has made a number of unsuccessful applications for membership, the first in 1981), Nicaragua, North Korea and South Yemen. Co-operation agreements have been signed with Finland, Iraq and Mexico.

Comecon was set up largely as a political response to the June 1947 Marshall Plan for the reconstruction of Europe and the 1948 split between the Soviet Union and Yugoslavia: Stalin feared possible imitators. Comecon was also the economic counterpart of the Organization for European Economic Co-operation (the OEEC subsequently became the OECD). Czechoslovakia, Hungary and Poland actually received invitations to participate, but Stalin blocked any positive response. Western boycotts after the 1948 Berlin blockade helped push the socialist countries together, and the official aim was 'to develop economic collaboration between the socialist countries and to co-ordinate their economic progress on the basis of equality of rights of all member states'.

Apart from occasional summits of leaders (General Secretaries), the main institutional bodies are as follows:

1. *The Council Session*. The chief body, although decisions are not binding; usually, since 1984, a biannual meeting of prime ministers.
2. *The Executive Committee*. Deputy prime ministers, meeting quarterly; the chief executive organ of the Council Session, representing it between Session meeting.
3. *Council Committees*. For planning, material-technical supply, scientific and technological co-operation, and machine-building).
4. *The Permanent Secretariat*. Headed by Vyacheslav Sychov. Comecon's only permanent body, acting as a sort of civil service.
5. *Standing Commissions*. For the chemicals industry, agriculture and construction, for example, dealing with detailed co-ordination in specific industries and areas. Increasing concern about damage to the environment caused by such factors as output indicators, heavy industry and nuclear accidents, led to the first meeting of the commission on environmental protection on 28–31 March 1988.

Countertrade

There is a wide variety of types of countertrade practised in the world at large (see *The Financial Times* surveys). The simplest is barter, a straight swap in kind of goods or services of equivalent value. Others include: 'counterpurchase', which requires a varying proportion of payment in kind, with cash dominant as a rule; 'buy-back', where deliveries of plant and equipment are wholly or partly repaid in the form of output forthcoming from the project; and 'switch' trading, where trade imbalances between two socialist countries, for example, are cleared by involving a Western country. Estimates of the present importance of countertrade in total world trade vary between 5 and 10 per cent. Major explanatory factors include: (1) the existence of command economies, with their currency and goods inconvertibility and difficulties experienced in exporting manufactures to the West; and (2) the debt crisis affecting many developing countries (as well as socialist countries) following the 1973–74 and 1979 oil price shocks. Rising interest rates on the massive credits granted by Western banks in their early recycling of OPEC trade surpluses, declining exports to Western countries in recession, and severe credit restrictions in the 1980s all contributed. Given the desperate shortage of hard currency earnings and reserves, countertrade helps maintain trade volume, even though this is relatively inefficient in comparison with multilateral trade under normal circumstances, where the full benefits of comparative advantage can be reaped. Even socialist countries themselves avoid countertrade with Western partners if they are able to sell their products in other markets for convertible currencies which can then be used to buy in the cheapest markets.

Bilateral trade

Bilateral trade still predominates in intra-Comecon trade. Here, trade is balanced between two countries over a period of time and is implemented via annual and longer-term, especially five-year, agreements. Multilateral trade, in contrast, involves surpluses and deficits with different partners which can be offset against one another through the use of convertible currencies. Bilateral trade still dominates despite its tendency to reduce the volume of trade (exchange limited to the country with the lesser export potential) and to force countries to accept goods of lesser value than could be otherwise obtained or bought at a lower price elsewhere. The situation within Comecon is complicated by the existence of so-called hard and soft commodities, stemming originally from the early stereotyped sectoral strategies of giving priorities to heavy industry. A radial pattern of trade developed, with the Soviet Union as the major supplier of fuels and raw materials. 'Hard' goods are those particularly sought after within Comecon, because the internal price system undervalues them and they can be sold on and purchased from the world market for convertible (hard) currencies; examples include foodstuffs, fuels and raw materials. 'Soft' goods, such as low-quality, obsolete machinery and equipment, are the reverse. 'Structural' or 'commodity' bilateralism exists because partners have an incentive to balance trade in each of the two types of commodity taken separately.[1] Holzman mentions the extreme case where a product, classified as soft, contains inputs from the West paid for in hard currency. Here the cost of these inputs has to be reimbursed in hard currency (1987: 100–101). Unplanned surpluses or deficits can be worked off by flows in subsequent periods, transfers of soft goods, or, more reluctantly on the deficit country's part, transfers of hard goods and payment in convertible currencies. The reluctance to use hard currencies is reflected in the very small percentage accounted for by multilateral trade.

The prevalence of bilateral trade can be explained by the following factors:

1. Such trade is administratively easier to handle by command economies. Five year and annual plans take account of the implications of trade agreements, although the frequency with which output plans are changed is reflected in the flexibility characteristic of annual trade agreements (themselves more specific than the five year trade protocols).
2. Minimization of the use of scarce hard currencies.
3. 'Currency inconvertibility'.
4. Currency inconvertibility is compounded by 'goods inconvertibility'. If one command economy has a trade surplus with another, this cannot be automatically converted into a claim on particular goods in the latter country (let alone in a Western country), because of the lack of direct and free exchange between ultimate purchaser and supplier. This claim can only be met by negotiations and provisions in central plans. Contrast this

with the US dollar, for illustrative purposes. Dollars can be freely converted into, say, French francs, which can be used by US buyers in free negotiations with French firms. Comecon countries, thus, have an incentive to avoid delivering hard goods to one another – these goods sold in the world market yield currencies that can be used to buy the best quality products at the lowest price. For multilateral trade to become the norm within the CMEA, this would require market-oriented economies using convertible currencies.[2]

The International Bank for Economic Co-operation (IBEC) was set up in 1964 to promote multilateral trade within the CMEA. The 'transferable rouble' was created as a unit of account to transact intra-Comecon trade, with the backing of the capital provided by members in the form of domestic currencies and gold. Annual bilateral negotiations should not attempt bilateral trade balances, but should be followed by a multilateral trade session to cancel out most surpluses and deficits. Remaining imbalances were to be removed by deficit exporting to surplus countries, the latter paying in accumulated transferable roubles (see especially Holzman 1987: 100). The failure of the IBEC to overcome bilateralism is due to the unchanging fundamentals of trading relationships. The transferable rouble is simply a unit of account for drawing up members' trade balances with each other. Trade imbalances have to be negotiated away as before – the transferable rouble is not convertible, goods inconvertibility remains, and all countries strive, therefore, to avoid building up a surplus. The International Investment Bank was established in 1971 in order to encourage co-operation in major investment projects. However, its credits, with the exception of hard currency loans of course, are mere reflections of negotiated transfers of capital goods, such as those used in Soviet energy projects.

Forms of Comecon co-operation

Stalin deliberately kept the Eastern European satellites separate. Thus until his death in 1953 Comecon played no effective role in co-ordinating trade, since it was restricted to such activities as registering bilateral agreements. Since the mid-1950s, however, the theme has been one of increasing plan co-ordination and economic integration, including investment, within Comecon. The problem is that the absence of markets has left administrative (plan) methods as the chief way to achieve these goals. This is complicated by the fact that Comecon is not a supranational planning agency. Khrushchev's 1962 suggestion to move towards such a system was thwarted by Romanian resistance especially. There is an 'interested party principle', which allows individual countries to opt out of any project. Individual countries still continue to draw up their own plans, although five year trade agreements and five year output plans coincide, and the former are reflected in the latter.[3] Nevertheless, the

Soviet economist Ruslan Grinsberg describes intra-Comecon trade as based on the 'left-over principle', where each country draws up its own five-year plan and then looks to partners for what it lacks (reported by Leslie Colitt in *FT*, 5 July 1988, p. 2). Holzman (1987: 21, 109) notes the antipathy to integration inherent in the command model, due to factors such as the unwillingness to close down large enterprises and whole industries and an aversion to migration and foreign ownership.

There are many cases and forms of co-operation, but they share the common feature of being essentially the result of bureaucratic negotiations. The Stalinist years saw the adoption of stereotyped sectoral investment strategies that favoured heavy industry and involved reliance on mainly Soviet fuels and raw materials. In joint stock (mixed) companies between the Soviet Union and the country possessing ex-German assets, the Soviet Union usually contributed these assets and its partner an equivalent amount. They were a resented but effective means of exercising Soviet control over key areas of the economy, such as Romanian oil. They began to be dismantled after 1953, and compensation payments were waived after 1956.

Attempts to overcome these parallel industrial structures have met with mixed results. In 1962 Romania flatly refused to specialize in primary products, for example, but there are many specialization agreements. These met with various degrees of success and focused mainly on finished goods, such as forklift trucks in Bulgaria, buses in Hungary and trams in Czechoslovakia. Administrative negotiations are performed by the standing commissions.

A common form of co-operation involves payment for plant and equipment, know-how and labour supplied by partner countries in the form of the output of the project. Thus the Soviet Union encourages such activity in the construction of oil and gas pipelines and the mining of raw materials. The Druzhba (friendship) oil pipeline connects the Soviet Union with Poland, Czechoslovakia, Hungary and the GDR. The Soyuz (Union) gas pipeline, completed in 1978, runs from Orenburg in the Soviet Union to the Czech border, while the Yamburg pipeline from Western Siberia to the Soviet Union's western border is the latest gas project. The Mir (Peace) is the united power grid. Many cases of joint R&D and standardization (including armaments) can be found. Comecon organizations such as Interchim indulge in the joint planning of particular sectors. Joint equity ventures go back as far as 1959, when the Haldex company was formed by Poland and Hungary to extract coal and building materials from Polish slag heaps. It is interesting to note that all the Eastern European Comecon countries, except the GDR, now permit joint equity ventures with Western countries: Romania was the first in 1971 and the Soviet Union is the most recent, on 1 January 1987.

The 1975 Agreed Plan for Multilateral Integration Measures, to apply to the 1976–80 plan era, related to ten major investment projects. These were to be integrated into the national plans of those countries involved in the form of 'special sections'. Eight were in the Soviet Union and mostly already begun, while most were related to Soviet energy, raw materials, and transport (Wallace and Clarke 1986: 105). The second plan, adopted in 1981 for the period 1981–85, concerned the implementation of previously established target programmes in energy and raw materials, engineering, food supply, industrial consumer goods, and the Comecon transport network (Wallace and Clarke 1986: 105).

Comecon preoccupations and solutions

The 1971 'Comprehensive (Complex) programme for further extension and improvement of co-operation and development of socialist integration by CMEA member countries' to the year 1990 emphasized integration – increasing the division of labour, reducing differentials in development levels and widening markets – as opposed to trade co-ordination. Other aims included encouraging multilateral trade by increasing the use of hard currencies in settling trade imbalances. This blueprint for long-term co-operation covered a wide range of activities, including joint investment projects and the joint planning of individual branches of the economy by 'interested' members. Harmonization of individual economic plans was to be enhanced by the submission of draft medium- and long-term plans to other members and to Comecon bodies for discussion. In 1976 the stress was on sectoral integration, with joint planning for integration restricted to particular sectors. Administrative negotiation has continued to be the mechanism for integration, however, and individual planning has remained dominant.

Eastern Europe generally followed a strategy of import-led (debt-led) growth during the 1970s, to stem the fall in growth rates experienced towards the end of the 1960s. Both investment and consumption growth targets were raised, the latter for incentives. Western credits were freely offered by banks, which were confident of Soviet backing and anxious to recycle OPEC surpluses, after the 1973–74 quadrupling of oil prices, to hitherto good repayers. These credits were sought in the hope of using imported capital goods, embodying the latest technology, to stimulate the hard currency exports needed to repay debt. Foreign technology was generally seen as a substitute for radical economic reform rather than the latter being a necessary accompaniment both for successful utilization and ongoing domestic innovation. Floating interest rates were the norm and they rose considerably during the second half of the 1970s. This factor, plus recession in the West, which restricted its importing and investment potential (the latter freeing OPEC funds), and unwarranted optimism about the prospects for exporting manufactured goods of sufficient quality to the West led to enormous repayment difficulties. The success in debt reduction in most countries in the early 1980s was due mainly to a contraction in imports. The Polish and Romanian debt rescheduling problems spilled over into the credit restrictions imposed on their CMEA partners. The Soviet Union was fortunate in having substantial gold reserves and hard currency earnings from oil and gas.

Comecon preoccupations have been reflected in recent meetings, such as the 12–14 June 1984 summit of party leaders, the first time they had met since April 1969 on Comecon business. The Soviet grievance at being the major supplier of 'hard' goods lay behind the agreement that contained supplies of Soviet raw materials and energy at a given level (note that Soviet oil deliveries were reduced by about 10 per cent in 1982) were to be dependent on comparable products from its Eastern European partners. 'Comparable' means world-quality machinery and equipment and industrial consumer goods, as well as food products and construction materials. The annual meeting of prime ministers in Havana on 29–31 October 1984 reiterated this agreement and witnessed a renewed Soviet call for East European investment in Soviet raw materials and fuels extraction, with the usual payment in output. Future developments should concentrate on co-ordination in electronics, automation, nuclear energy, raw materials and biotechnology. These choices reflected concern over a general technological lag behind the West and a general desire to encourage 'intensification', including the raising of labour productivity and the lowering of unit energy consumption.

The Warsaw meeting on 25–28 June 1985 to coincide with the start of the new five year plans took an even longer general view up to the year 2000. Themes included increased integration, reduction in energy and raw materials use, and the need to increase intra-Comecon innovation. The forty-first (special) session of the Comecon Council in Moscow on 17–18 December 1985 produced a 'comprehensive programme for scientific and technical progress', outlining a co-operative programme of co-ordinated R&D up to the year 2000. The chosen means included more co-ordinated investment plans and more joint ventures.

The emphasis on intensive growth is reflected in the goal of doubling labour productivity by means of a marked reduction in the input of energy and raw materials per unit of output and technological progress based largely on intra-Comecon efforts. Gorbachev stressed the need for 'technical independence from and invulnerability to pressure and blackmail by imperialism'. Soviet concern was enhanced by falling world oil prices after November 1985.

Five main areas were singled out for special attention: electronics, including the manufacture of super and personal computers and the use of optical fibres in communications systems; automation, including robots; nuclear energy, to reduce dependence on Soviet oil and gas; raw materials and components; and biotechnology. Three multilateral co-operation agreements were signed, namely computer-assisted production systems, optical fibre transmission systems and robot technology. The Complex Programme also stressed the need to develop 'direct links' between enterprises within Comecon.

The meeting of prime ministers on 3–4 November 1986 in Bucharest saw a repetition of the call for better quality products to be supplied to the Soviet Union, increased direct links and closer co-operation in production and science and technology. The nuclear energy programme was to go ahead despite Chernobyl. Ryzhkov, the Soviet premier, complained that several members were still trying to deliver substandard commodities to the Soviet Union, called for increased direct links and joint enterprises, and criticized Comecon for being incapable in its present form of the effective co-ordination and integration needed to achieve intensification.[4]

This Comecon meeting was, without precedent, quickly followed by one involving the party leaders, the first since June 1984. A very secret affair, it ended with only a brief pledge to increase living standards through more intensive economic, scientific, and technological co-operation. This was just one indication of the very real and continuing disagreements within the organization, not only Soviet complaints about quality, but other long-standing issues. These include the GDR's reluctance to integrate too closely with its less developed neighbours at the expense of its links with Western countries, especially the Federal Republic of Germany, and the pleas for preferential treatment and increased aid from Cuba, Vietnam and Mongolia.

The forty-third session of Comecon took place in Moscow on 13–14 October 1987. Particular attention was paid to the need to move in the direction of currency convertibility, itself seen as a way towards greater integration. While it was recognized that the transferable rouble was still to be used in most transactions in the foreseeable future, the plan was to try to make Comecon national currencies mutually convertible especially through the medium of joint ventures. In the future a common monetary unit may emerge that would be convertible into Western currencies.

At the meeting of prime ministers in Prague on 5–7 July 1988, the differing attitudes towards reform became very apparent, with Romania and the GDR taking a conservative position. The GDR stressed the need to co-ordinate five-year plans, while Romania actually failed to sign the final communique, which spoke of an 'understanding on gradually creating conditions for a mutual free movement of goods, services and other production factors, to create an integrated market'. The hope was for a gradual move towards a convertible rouble. Co-operation was to increase between the Soviet Union, Hungary, Poland and Czechoslovakia with Comecon reform in mind, while Cuba, Mongolia and Vietnam were promised increased technical assistance and credits. Nikolai Ryzhkov, the Soviet Prime Minister, informed the meeting that intra-Comecon trade had grown by only four per cent since 1985 and by 1.5 per cent in 1987.

The 'in' thing at the moment, stressed by Gorbachev himself, is the greater development of direct links between industrial enterprises, trading companies or research organizations in different Comecon countries for trade, joint production, component specialization or research and development. Experiments started in the early 1980s. This is seen as a move away from administrative methods of integration (more market orientated co-operation, for instance, may help overcome the poor specialization in component supply, unreliable supply from abroad encouraging countries to be as self-sufficient as possible); a means of helping to avoid a repetition of the acute debt crisis of the early 1980s, by improving the supply of 'hard' goods; and a way of swapping surplus-deficit inputs. The problem with direct linkage is providing enterprises with sufficient independence in decision-making to make such co-operation meaningful. Ministries, in reality, often have a considerable influence in establishing links. The exchange of know-how seems to to be the dominant form of collaboration (Pekshev 1988: 17). In March 1988, in a move towards overall convertibility, it was agreed that Czech and Soviet enterprises involved in such direct linkage (and joint ventures) could transact business in either the Soviet rouble or the Czech koruna (as opposed to the transferable rouble) at an exchange rate of 10.4 koruny to one rouble; particularly suitable transactions include one-off deliveries at agreed prices (Vetrovsky and Hrinda 1988: 13–14). Bulgarian and Soviet enterprises are also involved in a similar scheme. Joint equity ventures between socialist countries have a long history, but since 1 January 1987 these can be established on Soviet soil.

It is worth noting at this point that Czechoslovakia, the GDR, Poland, and the Soviet Union have recently imposed severe restrictions on the amount and types of consumer goods that are allowed to be taken out by visitors from socialist countries. This is due to domestic shortages as well as price distortions, and the lack of meaningful inconvertible currency exchange rates which lead to the opportunity of resale profits for the individuals concerned, Polish citizens being particularly suspect.

Comecon and the West

Comecon and the European Community

East-West trade accounts for just 4 per cent of world trade (*FT*, 22 June 1988, p. 2). Comecon accounts for only about 7 per cent of the EC's foreign trade, while the reverse trade figure is at least a third (*The Economist*, 18–24 June 1988, p. 56). In 1987 trade between the EC and Comecon amounted to $52 billion (*FT*, 20 December 1988, p. 3). Over 60 per cent of the CMEA's exports to the EC are fuels and raw materials (including raw materials used in the production of foodstuffs and condiments), and only about 7 per cent constitute machinery and equipment. In contrast, machinery accounts for more than 35 per cent of imports from the EC (Sychov, *CDSP*, 1988, vol. XL, no. 25, p. 21). Between 1957 (Treaty of Rome) and 1975, the EC was dismissed as the economic wing of NATO and a tool of Western imperialism and multinational corporations. While 1975 did not signify recognition, the signing of the Helsinki Accords saw Soviet and EC officials beginning to deal with particular problems, such as allegations of dumping. CMEA-EC talks began in 1977, but were broken off in 1981. The causes included the cooling post-Afghanistan atmosphere, conflicting interests – the Soviet Union wanted Comecon-EC trade negotiations, while the EC insisted on negotiations with individual Comecon countries, with organization-to-organization talks confined to marginal issues like environmental protection (including nuclear safety), information exchange and industrial standards. Comecon is not a supranational body and, unlike the EC, ironically, has no common commercial policy that it can enforce.

On 14 June 1985 a letter was sent by Vyacheslav Sychov (Secretary General of Comecon) to Jacques Delors (President of the European Commission) calling for a recommencement of talks. Agreement was reached in September 1985 and talks resumed a year later. The 24 November 1986 letter received by Willy de Clercq (the EC Commissioner for External Relations) signified a major breakthrough in that Comecon conceded the EC argument that mutual diplomatic recognition be coupled with EC negotiations with individual countries. Subsequent talks, starting in March 1987, however, ran into difficulties over the question of West Berlin. The Treaty of Rome explicitly included West Berlin as part of the EC, while the Soviet Union argued that the 1971 Quadripartite Agreement on Berlin precludes this. A joint declaration was eventually signed on 25 June 1988, the problem being solved by agreement to consider European Community territory as that defined by the Treaty of Rome and to state that the 1971 Agreement is unaffected. In October Comecon listed eight main areas for negotiation, namely technical standards, environmental protection, transport, science and technology, energy, nuclear power, statistics, and economic forecasting.

The European Community signed a trade pact with Romania in 1980.[5] In April 1989, however, the EC formally suspended talks on a full trade and economic agreement because of Romania's poor human rights record. In contrast, favourable treatment was promised countries like Poland (in light of the Roundtable Agreement). A ten-year trade (including agricultural products) and co-operation accord (including science but excluding technology) between Hungary and the EC was signed on 26 September 1988, with quotas on Hungarian imports into the EC being removed in three stages over the period up to the end of 1995. Dumping regulations still apply, however, while Hungary agreed to improve access to EC products and reduce the use of barter. On 19 December a four-year agreement on a number of industrial goods was signed by Czechoslovakia and the EC, involving increased imports and the supply of improved information by the former and quota concessions by the latter. Diplomatic recognition has now been extended by all the individual European Comecon members except Romania. The GDR has also requested negotiations about a general trade pact, with the aim of reducing its dependence on the FRG, while the Soviet Union, Poland and Bulgaria are interested in broader agreements.[6] Cuba established diplomatic relations on 29 September, although a trade accord has not been requested since the standard trade concessions for developing countries are already received. Note also that Soviet oil and gas, for example, are not subject to EC restrictions anyway.

In January 1988 the European Institute of the Soviet Academy of Sciences was established, another symptom of the now more positive attitude taken towards Western Europe in light of fears aroused by the prospective single EC market by 1992.

Dumping

In trade between market economies, 'dumping' usually refers to a situation where a country exports a product at a price below its home price, or below its cost of production when there are no domestic sales, and undercuts a similar good produced in the importing country. The difficulties in proving allegations are normally great, but pale in comparison with cases involving market and command economies, given the way in which prices and exchange rates are determined in the latter. Western countries have used a number of additional criteria in their trading relations with command economies, including the prices of similar products in 'comparable' countries, estimated costs of production, and the trade weighted average prices of a number of exporting countries. Holzman (1976; 1987: Chapter 4; Chapter 6) suggests that since foreign trade corporations in socialist economies are not interested in market disruption for its own sake and are simply forced to sell for what the Western market will bear, it is important to distinguish between short-run, crisis sales, justifying countervailing measures, and long-run supply at relatively low prices.

Coordinating Committee on Multilateral Export Controls

COCOM, a Paris-based organization was set up in 1950 and includes all the NATO countries (except Iceland) plus Japan. The aim is to prevent the export of goods and know-how (computers and computer software, for instance), that could be used for military purposes. Exemption sales need unanimous approval. Until November 1985 listed items were updated every three years, but since then there has been a continuous review. This reflects the rapidity of technological change and the increasing overlap in the civilian and military use of technologies in fields such as telecommunications and computers. In October 1985 an advisory body called STEM (Security and Technology Experts' Meetings) was established, reflecting this increasing complexity. There have been changes in targets over time, in terms of products and countries. The rules governing the export of non-sophisticated personal computers (e.g.

for educational use), have been relaxed, while separate, less strict lists are now drawn up for China.

In June 1988 agreement was reached on the sale of three A–310 jets by Airbus Industrie to Interflug (the East German airline), subject to strict conditions protecting technology: anything other than day-to-day maintenance is carried out by Lufthansa, the West German airline. This was followed in August by a leasing arrangement between Hungary and the Irish-based GPA group for three Boeing 737/200s and at the beginning of the new year by a Western bank loan that enabled Lot (the Polish airline) to purchase three Boeing 767s. Three of the latter aircraft were also involved in a purchase agreement in principle signed by Romania and Boeing in February 1989, while in the previous December Czechoslovakia began discussions about purchasing A–310 jets.

Conclusion

The main aim in devoting a separate chapter to foreign trade is to avoid tedious repetition of the severe endemic difficulties experienced by command economies in conducting international trade between themselves and with the West. The traditional system is a state monopoly of foreign trade and payments, the purpose being to help carry out party policy and to shield the domestic from the world economy, thus isolating the domestic production unit. Inefficient domestic prices and arbitrarily determined exchange rates have forced the use of (modified) world market prices. Comecon is analysed in the following ways: the reasons for the predominance of bilateral trade, such as currency and commodity inconvertibility; the forms of co-operation and integration; and current preoccupations and solutions, such as Soviet complaints about the poor quality of partner manufactures in return for energy and raw materials, and the recent stress on direct links between producing units in different countries. The chapter ends with a brief look at Comecon's relations with the European Community.

The general conclusion is that there are such extreme difficulties in foreign trade decision-making that it could be argued that only a radical move towards market systems would eradicate them. More open economies would, of course, expose the socialist economies to other sorts of problems.

Postscript

A surprising number of independent and radical deputies were elected to the Congress of People's Deputies, the first round of voting taking place on 26 March 1989. Sessions of the Congress especially but also of the Supreme Soviet have been likewise surprisingly lively and open. Gorbachev was voted President (unopposed) on 25 May. He visited China that month and the

Federal Republic of Germany in June.

Gorbachev has been plagued by a series of unfortunate events, including ethnic clashes between Georgians and the Abkhazian minority and between Uzbeks and the Meskhetian minority, loss of life in the suppression of demonstrations in Georgia, rail disasters and gas pipeline explosions. In July 1989 there were widespread strikes by coal miners, whose 'strike committees', bypassing the official trade union structure, put forward a long list of demands. These included improved supplies of basic foodstuffs and consumer goods such as soap, higher pay for night work, free Sundays, increased local decision-making autonomy, more retained profits and hard currency earnings, and improved housing, safety regulations, environment and amenities. Concessions quickly followed and were supplemented by promises to raise the wholesale price of coal and to step up imports of consumer goods. A threatened rail strike was averted by concessions relating to wages and living and working conditions. Gorbachev used the crisis to dismiss reform-resistant party and state officials, and to allow individual republics discretion over the timing of local elections. On 9 October 1989, the Supreme Soviet passed a law relating to labour disputes. Strikes (excluding politically inspired ones) are permitted – if a majority of the workforce votes in favour and after a conciliation process has been undertaken – except in key sectors such as transport, communications, fuel, energy and defence.

At the end of July 1989 approval in principle was given for the Baltic republics to enjoy greater autonomy in economic decision-making from 1 January 1990. The following month an experiment was announced, covering the remainder of 1989 and the whole of 1990, to pay collective and state farms hard currency for wheat in excess of average annual production during the period 1981–5 and for oilseeds for 1986–8. The aim is to increase output and to reduce imports (thus being a self-financing scheme).

Changes and supplements to the 'Law on the State Enterprise (Association)' were published in *Pravda* (11 August 1989, pp. 1–2). These include the following:

1. Enterprises are independently able to form concerns, consortia, inter-branch state associations and other large-scale organizational structures, including the participation of co-operatives and joint ventures with foreign firms. Enterprises maintain their economic independence within the new structures.
2. Enterprises have the right to extricate themselves from the subordination of branch and territorial administrations.
3. State orders must not reach 100 per cent of productive capacity. Conflicts between enterprises and higher bodies over orders are subject to arbitration.
4. The use of enterprise net income for investment and remuneration purposes is regulated by the tax system.
5. Enterprises have the right, in the prescribed manner, independently to engage in foreign trade, including that with capitalist and developing

countries. Trade can be transacted on a commission basis or by means of a newly created foreign trade organization acting on a *khozraschyot* basis.

Notes

1. The Soviet Union is exceptional in that it has frequently run up long-term overall surpluses, while supplying hard goods in exchange for soft.
2. Western citizens, such as tourists, diplomats, exchange students and sales representatives, can either use their own currencies to buy scarce consumer goods in 'hard currency shops', or can exchange these for Comecon currencies to buy those goods and services available in ordinary sales outlets. This introduces an active element in the determination of tourist exchange rates, in contrast to commercial ones.
3. Annual trade plans are more detailed than the five year protocols and have to exhibit flexibility because of the frequency with which annual output plans are changed.
4. This echoed Gorbachev's criticism at the 1986 Congress of the CPSU that Comecon had too many 'committees and commissions' and neglected 'economic levers, initiatives, socialist entrepreneurship and workers' collectives'.
5. The normal sequence is a trade agreement as a possible prelude to a full co-operation accord, which can include joint investment projects and technology transfer.
6. The following are full members ('contracting parties') of GATT, with entry dates in brackets: Cuba (founding member in 1947); Czechoslovakia (founding member); Hungary (1973); Poland (1967); Romania (1971); Yugoslavia (1966). Bulgaria and China applied in 1986, while on 15 August of that year the Soviet Union formally requested (in vain) observer status (see van Brabant 1988). Although there are obvious problems with planned economies being members, the relatively small size of these countries makes compromise much easier than in the case of the Soviet Union and China. Concessions asked of planned economies include increases in imports.

References

Comisso, D. and Tyson, L. (eds) (1986) *International Organisation*, 40, no. 2, (Spring): 187–598, devoted to the response of the socialist economies to international disturbances.

The Economist Survey on Comecon, 20 April 1985.

Ellman, M. (1989) *Socialist Planning*, 2nd edn, London: Cambridge University Press, Chapter 9.

The Financial Times Survey on East-West Trade, 13 December 1988.

Holzman, F. (1987) *The Economics of Soviet Bloc Trade and Finance*, Boulder CO and London: Westview Press. See especially the Introduction (pp. 1–29) and Chapter 4 (pp. 91–112).

Smith, A. (1983) *The Planned Economies of Eastern Europe*, London: Croom Helm.

—— (1987) 'Gorbachev and the world – the economic side', in D. Dyker (ed) *The Soviet Union under Gorbachev: Prospects for Reform*, London: Croom Helm.

van Brabant, J. (1980) *Socialist Economic Integration*, London: Cambridge University Press.

—— (1988) 'Planned economies in the GATT framework: the Soviet case', in *Soviet Economy*, 4 (Jan-March).

Wallace, W. and Clarke, R. (1986) *Comecon, Trade and the West*, London: Francis Pinter.

Eastern Europe

Chapter four

The People's Republic of Albania

Political background

Foreign domination has had a profound impact on political developments in the 'Land of the Eagle'. Roman and Byzantine rule was followed by incorporation into the Ottoman Empire from 1467 to 1912. Pre-war economic dependence on Italy culminated in the invasion of April 1939, and the Nazi occupation lasted from 1943 to 1944. The country's independence was attained by November 1944, without the help of foreign forces, and the People's Republic was formally set up in 1946. Enver Hoxha founded the Albanian Labour Party in 1941 and became General Secretary two years later. Until his death in April 1985 he maintained a Stalin-like control of Albania. Stalinist orthodoxy led to the break with Yugoslavia in 1948. Yugoslav leaders were described as 'anticommunist renegades', as a result of Tito's quarrel with Stalin. Albania broke with the Soviet Union in 1961 after the Sino-Soviet split, Khrushchev's denouncement of the cult of personality, acceptance of peaceful coexistence with the 'imperialist' United States (the Soviet Union became a 'social imperialist' power), and moves of reconciliation towards Yugoslavia in the late 1950s. Albania resisted Comecon plans for agricultural specialization and after 1961 trade with the Soviet Union fell from over 50 per cent to zero. Finally came the break with China in 1978. China had allegedly adopted 'social revisionism' after 'taking the capitalist path' in economic policy and had become more friendly towards the United States after President Nixon's visit in 1972. In 1967 Albania banned all religious institutions and practices and became the first atheistic state in the world, an important reason being to stamp out any possible threat to national unity represented by the varying allegiances of Muslims and Christians.[1]

Since Ramiz Alia assumed power as First Secretary in April 1985, something of a foreign relations thaw has set in. For example, diplomatic relations were established with Spain in September 1986 and with Canada and West Germany in the same month of the following year.[2] The technical state of war with Greece, which had existed since the Italian invasion of Greece in 1940, was lifted in August 1987, and the following April the two countries signed an agreement to encourage border trade, having already agreed to set up a ferry link with Corfu. Two accords have been signed with Turkey, one on economic, scientific and technological co-operation and the other on road transport. Albania took part in the Balkan Conference of Foreign Ministers on 24–26 February 1988. Hosted by Yugoslavia and attended by Bulgaria, Romania, Greece and Turkey, it aimed at increasing regional stability and co-operation in the spheres of economic and cultural relations, tourism, the environment and transport and communications. Albania's representative, Foreign Minister Reis Malile, stressed the need to respect the independence, national sovereignty, and territorial integrity of neighbouring states. Policy on national minorities and their treatment is an internal question for each country, although other countries may have a legitimate interest and seek to transform the question into one that encourages stability and cohesion at home and good relations between states.[3] Malile said there was scope for improving economic (small-scale expansion of border trade, and removal of tariffs and licences for some goods, for example), transport, communications, and water management links.[4]

Economic background

Pre-war Albania was the most backward country in Europe. According to Schnytzer (1982: 1), in 1938 industry accounted for only 4.4 per cent of national income. Only 150 industrial enterprises existed, which were thinly scattered over the country and nearly 50 per cent of them employed less than ten workers (p. 65). In 1927 per capita income was only $40 and 90 per cent of national income was derived from agriculture; in 1928 livestock products accounted for 65 per cent of exports (p. 14). In 1938 85 per cent of the population was rural and average life expectancy was 38 years; it was 71 by 1985. Socialist Albania inherited an illiteracy rate of 85 per cent and no railway network.

On the other hand, Albania is relatively well endowed with natural resources. There are fertile soils – although 70 per cent of the country is classified as hilly or mountainous, there is extensive land reclamation and irrigation. Fifty five per cent of arable land is currently under irrigation (Prescott 1986: 11). Resources also include energy (especially hydroelectric, but also coal, oil and gas), chrome (third only to the Soviet Union and South Africa in 1985), nickel, copper, iron ore and manganese.

Development strategy involved rapid rates of growth, especially industrial. The share of agriculture in net material product fell from 76.3 per cent in 1950 to 37.9 per cent in 1978 (Kaser 1986: 19) and achievements include allegedly stable prices (some prices have actually fallen). Transport and communications links with other countries have improved in recent years. For example, a freight ferry link with Italy was established in 1983 and a rail link with Yugoslavia in 1986; previous to this Albania was the only country in continental

Europe inaccessible by train.

In 1986 the population of around 3 million was the fastest growing in Europe (2.1 per cent), but had the lowest per capita income ($850 according to UN figures). In a July 1987 speech to the Central Committee Alia declared that Albania's development and foreign policy could not be separated from events in the rest of the world. He criticized the performance of some sectors of the economy, saying that export earnings were insufficient to purchase the new technology needed to develop industry.

Central planning and the industrial enterprise

According to Schnytzer (1982: 18), the centralized economy was only introduced gradually, and the traditional plan indicators did not operate until 1959 because of a lack of qualified cadres.

In 1966 a decentralization of decision-making took place, but not so much to enterprises (the number of success indicators was decreased) as to ministries and district councils. The number of indicators approved by the Council of Ministers was reduced from 550 to 77 for industry, 320 to 42 for agriculture and 500 to 100 for investment and construction. Formerly all indicators for each enterprise were approved by the Council of Ministers, which approved plans quarterly (as opposed to only annually after 1966). Ministries were responsible for disaggregating the central plans, which were then passed to district councils (the latter became responsible for an increasing number of smaller enterprise from the mid-1960s onwards and especially after 1970), for coordination and for overseeing implementation (Schnytzer 1982: 33–34). Before 1966 the plan process was begun by passing down the draft annual plan from the centre for disaggregation; after that date the enterprise and district councils sent up plan drafts, based on the five year plan (Schnytzer 1982: 30). Ministries and district councils formally now controlled enterprise investment funds instead of the State Bank (p. 50).

The industrial enterprise now has eight indicators to fulfil in its technical-industrial-financial plan (*plan tekniko-industrial financiar*): production, productive capacity, employment and payroll, material-technical supply and distribution of output, technical progress and scientific research work, cost plan, investment and basic construction, and financial plan; it operates on the principle of 'single management' (Kaser 1986: 9). By 1977 district councils began to lose their control over industry. By 1983 more than 200 material balances were drawn up by the State Planning Commission and notified by the Council of Ministers. The centre also drew up an 'urgent list' of imports for the Ministry of Foreign Trade (Kaser 1986: 9). Since November 1986 there has been some recognition of the need for economic reform. For example, in his 3 November 1986 report to the Ninth Party Congress Ramiz Alia acknowledged that

The lack of experience needed to know foreign markets with the international complications increased the difficulties for the development of the economy...the targets of the plan were not fully accomplished in particular branches of the economy, such as the oil industry, in some agricultural and livestock products, in financial income and in exports. As a consequence, some imbalance was created in the economy. There were shortcomings, also, in supplying goods for the people as the plan envisaged.

(quoted in Costa 1988: 235)

Mild measures already taken include the introduction in the late 1970s of bonuses of 2 to 30 per cent of wages for increased production, but in December 1987 Ramiz Alia formally ruled out the introduction of Soviet-type reforms. Even at the Ninth Congress he said, 'The main way for the increase of productive capacities is that of reconstructions or expansions of the existing ones' (Costa 1988: 235). A leading article in *Zëri i Popullit* (The People's Voice) gives a flavour of Albanian attitudes towards *perestroika*:

It was Khrushchev who, at the 20th Congress of the CPSU, began the great counter-revolutionary transformation, that process of 'reforms' which destroyed socialism, paved the way for the restoration of capitalism... Perestroika is broader in extent than all the 'reforms' undertaken by Gorbachev's predecessors ... [and] aims to eliminate everything that hinders the complete transition to unfettered capitalism.

(*Albanian Life*, 43, no. 3 (1988): pp. 37–40)

Until the split in 1978 Albania tended to mimic Chinese policy to some extent; the introduction of a form of workers' control in 1966 was a pale imitation of the Cultural Revolution. In order to pressurize managers into disclosing hidden reserves and to appease workers disappointed with consumption growth, workers' control involved the ability to give advice to management in the drawing up of the enterprise plan (Schnytzer 1982: 27). In 1968, however, after considerable criticism, workers' committees could be elected only on an ad hoc basis as specific problems cropped up and membership was confined to production workers only (p. 42). In 1970 the role of the mass meeting in enterprise annual plan formulation was reduced to submission of a draft plan to the State Planning Commission via the ministry (for centrally controlled enterprises) or the district council (for locally controlled enterprises) (Kaser 1986: 9). Kaser (1986: 3, 9) describes the post-1966 measures as a reversion to the traditional Soviet system. Today the trade union branch is able to recommend the sacking of a manager.

Note that there is no legal *private sector* in industry.

At the Ninth Congress in November 1986 it was reported that over the period of the Seventh Five-year Plan (1980–85) national income had increased by 16 per cent, while 45 per cent of investment had been devoted to industry (especially heavy industry) and 30 per cent to agriculture. The aim of the Eighth Five Year Plan (1986–90) is to devote 83 per cent of investment to industry and agriculture, with the latter receiving 32 percentage points (*Albanian Life*, December 1986: 6–7). During the 1980s engineering, as an aspect of import substitution, and chemicals, as a support for agriculture, have been given increased priority.

Manpower

Until the mid-1960s the sort of wage and salary differentials associated with the traditional Soviet model were typical. In 1966, however, a policy of far greater egalitarianism was followed, with actual reductions of salaries in the higher ranges implemented in 1967 and 1976. In 1976 the maximum 'vertical' pay scale differential was fixed at 1:2.5, and the maximum 'horizontal' range for laborious work or special locations at 1:1.66 to 1.233 (Kaser 1986: 13). Greater stress was laid on moral incentives; managers, however, continued to receive certain perquisites, such as the use of a company car (no private cars are allowed) and party members have special access to scarce commodities. The benefits of productivity increases have been given in the form of periodic price reductions (in 1950–69 and 1982–83, for example) rather than higher nominal wages.

Negative effects on work incentives, however, have led to complaints of absenteeism and declining work discipline and labour productivity. In 1980, as a consequence, a stronger link was forged between pay and performance in both state enterprises and agricultural co-operatives via the payment of bonuses and other benefits such as holidays for plan fulfilment. The 1986–90 five year plan envisages the increased use of such bonus payments.

Since 1958 there have been attempts to involve administrative employees (including management after 1968) in production on a paid basis. This, together with the encouragement given to young people to offer their services voluntarily, has been inspired by a desire to reduce the gap between town and countryside and between mental and physical labour (Schnytzer 1982: 36). Beginning in the early 1970s there was a programme to reduce the number of administrative personnel in the productive enterprises, while many office workers 'volunteered' to work an assembly line (Bowers 1989: 452). By 1975 the party's rotation effort had been extended to include even former deputy ministers and enterprise directors (p. 453).

The financial system

As is typical in the socialist world, taxes on state enterprises and co-operatives provide the bulk of budgetary revenue, there being no income tax since 1967. In 1984 96 per cent of revenue came from turnover tax and profit deductions (Kaser 1986: 15). On average, about a fifth of national income was devoted to defence during 1981–84 (*EEN*, 1988, vol. 2, no. 12, p. 5). There is extensive rationing of highly subsidized basic commodities and state housing (private housing exists and is especially common in the countryside). 'Luxury' consumer goods bear a heavy tax; the *EEN* reports the appearance of 20 foodstuffs for 'special' occasions at very high prices (1988, vol. 2, no. 21, p. 8).

Agriculture

In pre-socialist Albania 85 per cent of the population lived in the countryside, where 3 per cent of the rural population owned 40 per cent of arable land and 14 per cent owned no land at all (Prescott 1986: 5). In 1944–45 land above what was considered to be a family's needs was confiscated and redistribution took place. Private peasants, however, were subjected to compulsory delivery quotas. Collectivization began in November 1946, was accelerated in the late 1950s, and was completed in 1966, by which time all land was either collectively or state owned.

Private plots (maximum 200 square metres) are allowed in co-operatives, although they have decreased in size over time and peasants are not legally allowed to sell their produce in free markets. Instead, private output must be sold to the co-operative farms at state-determined prices. Note that the state has a monopoly of all trade. Collective farm peasants, however, have benefited from state pensions, lower input prices and increases in procurement prices. In 1971 monthly advances for co-operative peasants were introduced, with an end-of-year residual paid according to plan fulfilment. The 1975 experiment of combining family-owned livestock into joint herds subsequently spread. In 1986 pressure to transfer livestock to the co-operatives led to slaughtering and meat shortages. The following year saw encouragement given to the private plots. A 1986 concession involved acreage being turned over to collective farms for private tillage, provided that the crop was shared among brigade members. The *EEN* predicts a possible attempt to encourage food production by allowing co-operatives in general to sell more of their output themselves (and hence on more favourable terms) and those in remote areas farming poor land to charge higher prices (1988, vol. 2, no. 24, p. 6). Nine districts and two agricultural enterprises have been granted greater autonomy on an experimental basis. It is not clear exactly what the reforms involve in these districts, but they probably relate to enhanced local decision-making in crop production, work-force productivity deals, and modest price differentials depending on local conditions and availability of a particular crop (*EEN*, 1989, vol. 3, no. 1, p. 6). The ultimate aim is to eliminate private farming by means of the gradual transformation of co-operatives, whose members are permitted a plot, into state farms, where all property is state owned and where the loss of plots is allegedly compensated by wage security.

Although about 20 co-operatives a year are being converted, co-operative farms still dominate Albanian agriculture. In the mid-1980s state farms only accounted for some 25 per cent of agricultural output. In 1971 'higher-type agricultural co-operatives' were introduced, as transitional institutions towards full state farms. These 'higher types' differ from traditional co-operatives in a number of ways, in that they: (1) receive state budgetary grants instead of repayable long-term bank credits; (2) have exclusive use of a single Machine Tractor Station instead of having to share (the MTS is used to ensure state rather than co-operative ownership of large machinery and as a means of party propaganda); and (3) pay guaranteed piece-rate wages every fortnight amounting to 90 per cent of the planned payroll, the remaining 10 per cent being paid after the end-of-year accounting on successful fulfilment of plan targets. A number of co-operatives have now been transformed into full state farms, which own their own machinery and equipment and act as stock breeding and seed distribution centres.

Although uniform retail prices prevail, procurement prices are lower for co-operative farms operating in more favourable circumstances (Prescott 1986: 9). Thus a form of rent extraction is in operation. The present overall strategy for agriculture revolves around 'intensification', especially through the greater use of pesticides and fertilizers.

Albania claims to be 95 per cent self-sufficient in food, with agriculture accounting for around a quarter of exports (*EIU*, 1987–8: 32).

Foreign trade

Soviet aid and trade were important until 1961. According to Kaser (1986: 3), Albania started to open up trade with the West in the early 1970s, but after the mid-1970s import substitution was followed to extreme lengths. The desire for self-reliance and self-sufficiency increased after the split with China in 1978. Chinese aid ended in July 1978, but the rift started with China's invitation to President Nixon in 1971. The 1976 constitution actually incorporates a ban on loans or direct investment from capitalist countries, although *EEN* reports the acceptance in October 1987 of a DM 6 million grant from the FRG for 'technical assistance' (1987, vol. 1, no. 15, p. 8). The present strategy stresses the need to reduce imports, but recognizes the need to increase exports of its foodstuffs, raw materials and energy (such as electricity) in order to finance absolutely vital imports of the capital goods required to update the outmoded capital stock. Otherwise, domestic production of equipment is stressed: this is a change from the 1962 role of domestic production of spare parts for imported machinery (Kaser 1986: 8). Trade links with China were formally restored in 1983, and Western companies are helping to develop chromite and ferro-nickel processing. This strategy is preferred to joint equity ventures and any radical reform of the economy. In 1988 the following were signed: an agreement on economic co-operation with the FRG (June); an agreement on

economic, scientific, and cultural co-operation with Algeria (June); a proto-
col on economic co-operation and an agreement on international road transport with Turkey (August) (*Albanian Life*, 43, no. 3, 1988: 45). In August a
ten-year barter deal with the Philips Company was signed, involving the exchange of Albanian cement and tobacco for electronic components, measuring equipment and, at a later stage, colour television assembly kits and television lighting and studio equipment (*FT*, 18 August 1988, p. 2).

Albanian exports comprise 'industrial' products (three-quarters), especially oil and minerals; the rest are largely agricultural products; imports are
chiefly capital goods, materials, and consumer goods (*EIU*, 1987–88: 37–38).

Conclusion

A history of foreign domination helps explain Albania's economic and political isolation, its quarrels in turn with its one-time major allies the Soviet
Union and China. Despite some relaxation since the death of Enver Hoxha in
1985, the economy remains relatively isolated (although trade links are expanding), and the poorest country in Europe is still tightly controlled in every
sense. The following points are worth highlighting: Albania banned all religious institutions and practices in 1967; there is no legal private sector in industry and there is a state monopoly of domestic as well as foreign trade; the
country is in the process of converting agricultural co-operatives into state
farms, where all property belongs to the state and where there are no private
plots; and the constitution allows no loans or direct investment from capitalist
countries. There seems to be no prospect of market-oriented reforms in the
foreseeable future.

Notes

1. The 70 per cent who were Muslims (making Albania the only 'Islamic' country in
   Europe) looked towards Turkey, while 20 per cent were Greek Orthodox. There
   were also Catholics.
2. The FRG's Foreign Minister Genscher visited Albania in October 1987, the first
   Western minister to do so.
3. Observers took this to be a positive reference to Yugoslavia's autonomous province
   of Kosovo. Serbian demonstrations against alleged persecution and discrimination,
   as well as attempts (successful by March 1989) to reduce the autonomy enjoyed by
   Kosovo, however, have led to official Albanian protests.
4. See Malile's speech reproduced in *Albanian Life* (1988, 41, no. 1).

Chapter five

Bulgaria

Background

In 1878, with the help of Tsar Alexander II, Bulgaria was liberated from 500 years of Ottoman rule and Russia continued to safeguard the country's interests against British and French efforts to bolster Turkey. Bulgaria sided with Germany in the First World War. There was a fascist military-royalist coup in 1923 against the elected Agrarian Party government and Bulgaria joined the Axis Pact in the Second World War. It did not declare war on Russia, however. In fact, Russia declared war against Bulgaria on 5 September 1944, although three days later the latter did the same against Germany (McIntyre 1988: Chapter 2). Todor Zhivkov, who became First Secretary in March 1954 and President in 1971, has always been a loyal supporter of the Soviet Union.

Bulgaria's 9 million inhabitants live in a country that is relatively well endowed with fertile soils, although the rainfall is not dependable, and is relatively poor in energy and minerals. Some low-grade coal and copper, bauxite, and lead are to be found. In pre-socialist Bulgaria 75 per cent of the population was classified as rural, and agriculture contributed 65 per cent of national output. McIntyre (1988: 69, 97) makes the interesting point that the transition to a Soviet-type system in the post-war period was aided by a number of factors, such as active state intervention in the inter-war economy, a relatively even distribution of land and general poverty in the countryside, and a co-operative tradition in agriculture. Table 5.1 shows the official figures for average annual rates of growth of NMP.

Table 5.1 Bulgaria: average annual rate of growth of NMP (%)

1949–52	1953–7	1958–60	1961–65	1966–70	1971–75	1976–80	1981–85	1986	1987
8.4	7.8	11.6	6.7	8.8	7.8	6.1	3.7	5.5	5.1

Sources: Lampe (1986: 144); McIntyre (1988: xvi); *Bulgaria* (1988: January-March, p. 8).

Industrial reform

Bulgaria has undertaken a continuous stream of reforms (Kaser 1981; Dellin 1970; Feiwell 1979; Lampe 1986; Jackson 1986a; McIntyre 1988). In May 1963 a decree authorized the establishment of a horizontally integrated DSO (Durzhavenski Stopanski Obedineniya: State Economic Organization), later to become the basic production unit. In July of that year some 2,000 industrial enterprises were merged into 120 DSOs. The *December 1965 'Theses'* provided a blueprint of the New System of Management (Nov Sistem na Rukovodstvo). Although the economy was to remain highly centralized, organization was to become more efficient by means of a reduction in the number of production units, which also allowed the centre to have firm control over strategic decision-making, and an increase in the amount of details decided below. The number of compulsory indicators for the five-year plan was reduced to four, though these were very broad and readily open to further subdivision: physical output, ceiling on investment, ceiling on inputs and foreign trade targets. There was talk (only) of a tiered system of prices, fixed (on the basis of average cost plus a 2 per cent markup), range and a very restricted 'free' category. Profitability was to become a more important determinant of incentive funds (up to 70 per cent of profits could be retained) and there was to be a move away from investments financed by budgetary grants towards retained profits and interest-bearing credits, although investment decisions remained tightly controlled from above. A capital charge averaging 6 per cent of the value of enterprise fixed and working capital was introduced. The wage fund indicator was abandoned and replaced by a progressive income tax.

Even though pre-1968 rhetoric outstripped practice (a not uncommon feature in Eastern Europe), that year still marked a clear change of course, due mainly to a fear of loss of party control were reforms remotely approaching those of pre-invasion Czechoslovakia to be introduced. A labour shortage also became apparent at the start of the 1970s. The number of plan indicators was increased to include, for instance, a wage fund limit and deliveries in volume terms. The idea of tiered prices was abandoned. Lampe (1986: 204) points out that it was the DSO and not the ministries that supervised the new system of supply contracts between enterprises, with prices determined by enterprise bargaining. In November 1970 the number of DSOs was reduced from 120 to 64 (35 in industry) and the following month enterprises were shorn of their legal autonomy; larger ones became 'subsidiaries' (still allowed to sign contracts and hold bank accounts) and smaller ones became 'subdivisions' which were fully absorbed. The DSO became the basic production unit, dominating its constitutent parts, distributing inputs, allocating plan tasks, determining investment, and relegating the subsidiary to the role of executing plan targets, especially for volume, assortment and quality of output, input utilization and technical levels. Counter-planning was introduced in 1972. Apart from the DSO, a number of co-ordinating agencies and alternative 'economic organizations' were set up after 1974, such as vertically integrated combines. The main aim was to streamline the command planning system.

The term 'New Economic Mechanism' was used throughout the 1970s and beyond, but resemblance to Hungary is in name only. Bulgaria continues to be a command economy, although *the 1979 proposals*, first applied to agriculture, are worth noting (see Kaser 1981 in particular). The main objective in these and the 1982–83 measures was to achieve financial accountability and self-financing (including investment financed internally or from credit, both needing servicing out of revenue earned, and payments to the budget). In these 1979 proposals the ministry may officially impose only five broad indicators on the DSO or equivalent economic organization (instead of the previous 25), namely (1) 'realized production' (production in saleable form disposed of to recipients) in physical terms, subdivided into exports, co-operative deliveries and spare parts and deliveries to the domestic market; (2) net output in value terms; (3) foreign exchange earnings on exports and/or maximum foreign exchange expenditure; (4) limits on supplies of raw materials, intermediate inputs, energy and 'certain deficitary materials and equipment'; and (5) payments to the state budget. In turn, the DSO or equivalent imposes four indicators on its 'subdivisions', namely (1) production in physical units by type and quality; (2) 'normed cost of production per unit of output'; (3) tasks for the application of new techniques; and (4) maximum number of personnel. There is to be full self-accounting for all enterprises, and the wage fund is linked to productivity and allowed a share in profit increases. Management will benefit from plan overfulfilment, but suffer salary reductions for failure to fulfil norms. The DSO or other economic organization is able to sell above-plan output once its planned production targets have been fulfilled. Above-plan output may be sold in own shops, abroad (on commission or through a foreign trade corporation) or to a local government authority. A number of wholesalers are permitted to establish production plants. Economic organizations can apply for long-term (up to ten years) credit, although investment remains highly centralized. Decentralized investment is steered by the availability and cost of credit, and successful enterprises pay less interest than unsuccessful ones. There are also interest rate rebates for overfulfilling export targets, especially in hard currency markets. According to M. Jackson (1986a: 49), branch ministries reverted to state budget financing after being placed on an economic accounting basis in 1976. Within the enterprise brigades became increasingly placed on an economic accounting basis (M. Jackson 1988: 50). Increasing emphasis is being placed on worker brigades (as is common in other socialist countries); these average around 16 per enterprise in Bulgaria. They are provided with output targets and inputs, arrange their own work schedules, and are paid by results. In December 1986 the first direct elections were held by workers of their factory managers. In March of the previous year workers at enterprises failing to fulfil output targets were required to increase their working week from five to six days until the deficit had been eliminated (Miskiewicz 1987: 80).

There have been some interesting changes since 1979 (Lampe 1986: 217–8; McIntyre 1988: 119–22, 1988a: 602–4):

1. The *'initiation of small enterprises'* programme began in 1980–81. These are state-owned, semi-autonomous, small and medium-sized units within DSOs, with some flexibility to respond to changing market needs.[1] The Bulgarian Industrial Association (BIA) was set up in 1982 as a 'voluntary membership organization', providing managerial and consultancy services and playing an entrepreneurial role in the setting up of new enterprises where there are gaps in the market, initially in areas like clothing, small appliances and speciality foodstuffs, but more recently also in research and technical applications and computer services.

2. There are strong links between the BIA and the Mineral Bank–Bank for Economic Initiatives (MB) set up in 1986 and jointly owned by the Bulgarian National Bank (a half) and about 200 large economic organizations (the other half). The MB provides credit for above-plan investments in large enterprises that help achieve the plan more effectively, and for the small enterprise programme, based on criteria such as the payback period, energy savings and potential for foreign exchange earnings.

3. Measures were taken during 1982–83, mainly concerning financial incentives and prices. 'Final economic performance' (net income) is the major plan indicator, but there are also targets for tax payments, limits on input use and minimum export levels. The minimum wage has been abolished. Experiments are testing managerial performance in relation to net income over a five year period with demotion possible, while ministers' salaries now depend to some extent on the performance of their organizations. The Bulgarian National Bank is allowed to hold regional competitions for investment credits.

The New Economic Mechanism has thus been gradually modified since 1979. The general aim is to increase the importance of indirect steering and to allow the centre to concentrate on strategic matters, with production units (able to sign legally binding contracts) having greater decision-making authority, free from the petty tutelage typically exercised by ministries. Ministries have been amalgamated into fewer bodies in order to streamline the planning process, and to prevent both empire building and meddling in day-to-day enterprise management. For example, the new Ministry of Trade and Material Resources fused the ministries of construction, foreign trade, internal trade and material resources.

The financial system

A basic idea of the New Economic Mechanism is that bank credits should be increasingly based on the criterion of economic effectiveness. Capital investment credits require at least a 35 per cent contribution by an investor from own resources (Jackson 1986a: 52). In June 1987 a Hungarian-type two-tier *banking system* was established, with the Bulgarian National Bank (as a central bank) supervising eight commercial banks, which are owned by the National Bank and economic organizations, which elect bank directors and take part in shareholders'meetings. They are sector-oriented (such as electronics and transport), compete for customers and face the threat of bankruptcy. The state will still have to finance desired projects that do not meet commercial criteria; the commercial banks do not have to make loans to unprofitable companies, which have to resort to state subsidies or price support (Lev Kokushin in *Bulgaria*, November-December 1987, p. 34).

There is a tiered system of prices (Jackson 1986a: 53; Lampe 1986: 219): fixed prices for basic consumer goods, communal services, fuels, energy and raw materials; ceiling; range; and contract prices. Foreign trade organizations are able to contract freely with enterprises for above-plan output, and wholesalers and retailers are able to negotiate over the prices of non-essential products. Increasing regard is taken of changes in world prices.

Later amendments

The Thirteenth Party Congress in April 1986 saw an attack on the defects of the current system: corruption, bureaucracy, incompetence, inertia, irresponsibility, inefficiency, alcoholism and absenteeism. Sweeping personnel changes have taken place (younger and more technocratic people have been installed) and order, discipline, and responsibility are stressed. Subsequent changes include the establishment of new state councils for agriculture and forestry, intellectual development, social affairs and economic affairs. McIntyre (1988: 115, 118) suggests, however, that the closure of six major industrial ministries may be more apparent than real, especially in light of the creation, in May 1986, of five 'voluntary associations' in construction, trade, light industry, electronics and food and tobacco; these may possibly be mere subsections of the councils. In August of the following year, however, it was announced that these were to be scrapped along with three ministries (finance, trade and education) and five committees (research and technology, state planning, labour and social affairs, prices, and science) and replaced by four new ministries: economics and planning; foreign economic relations; agriculture and forestry; and culture, science and education. Within the enterprise, brigades were emphasized.

The 1987 reform proposals

The June 1987 plenum of the Central Committee approved the introduction of the 'Principles of the Concept of the Further Construction of Socialism in Bulgaria', to be phased in after 1 January 1988 (see especially Hristov 1987: 10–18). The basic idea is to leave 'strategic' matters to the centre, with planning to remain the principal instrument through which the state manages the economy (e.g. via 'state orders'). Current and executive affairs (including joint ventures with foreign companies) are to be left to self-managing economic organizations, the aim being to keep each function to the lowest level where it is able to be independently performed. There is a three-tier system of enterprise, corporation, and association. The last is the coordinator of general policy (in electronics, for example), while leaving, on the whole, a substantial measure of autonomy to constituent organizations, although in sectors such as power generation there is a highly centralized structure. Managerial decision-making at the corporation level is undertaken by a collective body called the 'economic council' and comprising enterprise directors. The same applies to the association, although day-to-day affairs are left to a chairman and a deputy chairman, both elected by the board of directors, plus a limited number of executives. Note that enterprise directors have been elected since late 1986, although the list of candidates is drawn up by 'public organizations'.

The state will still control the prices of 120 basic commodities, subsidizing them if necessary, but, as a rule, domestic prices must match those that could be obtained for the commodities on the world market. This applies to users of raw materials, although those producers operating under very unfavourable natural conditions will be subsidized. Interest rates, allegedly, will also match world levels. Bankruptcy is a possibility. The reforms will allow a higher proportion of profits to be retained; at present up to 80 per cent is taxed away, excluding local rates and taxes. Pay is to be tied to performance, with only a minimum wage remaining. The salaries of the techno-scientific intelligentsia and university graduates are to be increased, those of managerial personnel linked to indices such as profit margins and profit size, while heads of R&D units will be paid in accordance with the increased profits made by production units using these ideas. These are meant to overcome problems associated with the relatively low pay of administrative-managerial personnel.

Grandiose schemes for top government include increasing the role of the state *vis-à-vis* the party, with the National Assembly (parliament) turned into a 'collective working body of self-management'. There is the vague idea of somehow making the enterprise collective the formal owner of property. Multi-candidate elections have taken place, such as the February 1988 local elections. The Council of Ministers and the State Council would be abolished and replaced by a 'new headquarters of state power'. The Council of Ministers would be substituted by a 'national co-ordinating body'. In January 1988 the proposal was accepted of limiting all top party officials to two five-year terms, while since the first of that month municipal authorities have been financed directly from the central government rather than indirectly through regional councils.

Agriculture

Land belongs to the state except that around detached homes and weekend houses (McIntyre 1988: xix).The *collectivization process* came to an end by 1958, when collective farms accounted for 92 per cent of total arable land. Until that year members were compensated for loss of their land through a rental payment. The next two years witnessed an amalgamation of collectives into 957 large farms with an average of 4,500 hectares (Lampe 1986: 148–9). A decade later another merger programme was undertaken. In 1967 co-operative farmers were formed into fixed brigades specializing in one task as near to their own village as possible, and they were the first in Eastern Europe to receive state pensions and health benefits (Lampe 1986: 203). Collectives were then transformed into state farms; the former were eliminated as autonomous units by 1977 (McIntyre 1988: 99).

During the 1970s a *'process of industrialization'* of agriculture took place (after experiments in 1968–69) based on the 'agro-industrial complex' (Agrarno-Promishlen Komplex: APK), normally a horizontal integration of cooperative farms, state farms and their servicing centres (some vertical integration took place, such as agriculture, fertilizer production and final sales); and the 'industro-agrarian complex' (PAK), which vertically merged (backwards) industrial enterprises processing and selling agricultural products with farms (e.g. the DSO Rodopa; see Kaser 1981 and Wiedemann 1980). In the period 1970–72 the existing 800 state and collective farms were grouped into 170 APKs, the former two eventually losing their juridical autonomy and becoming mere operating sections of the latter (McIntyre 1988: 100); the number fell to a low of 153 in 1974, but subsequently increased (p. 101). Although still subject to the central plan when executing the most important targets, there is still considerable scope for independent decision-making with regard to details. The 'scientific-productive complex' (NPK) is particularly important for the incorporation of scientific institutes. Capital-intensive modern industrial farming methods were designed to reap economies of scale, to save on scarce labour and to increase processed agricultural product exports (Lampe 1986: 207). In 1976 the National Agro-Industrial Union was formed, absorbing the Ministry of Agriculture and Food three years later, whose purpose was to control the entire food sector, from farm production, to processing, and right through to marketing (Cook 1986a: 61).

The APK is divided into brigades and each one is assigned a particular land area or production line and on an economic accounting basis, with a wage fund linked to net income (Cook 1986a: 65). Under the New Economic Mechanism, which was first applied to agriculture in 1979, the number of central plan targets has been reduced from twenty-four to four: delivery quotas; minimum hard currency earnings coupled with import ceilings; payments to the state budget; and ceilings on domestic input use (Cook 1986a: 64). By 1982 the average APK covered 16,000 hectares, while the PAK and NPK were roughly twice this size (Lampe 1986: 207).

According to the *EEN* (1988, vol. 2, no. 8, p. 6), a November 1987 resolution divided the agro-industrial complexes into some 2,500 self-managing work teams designed to function as financially independent economic enterprises, although implementation has been delayed due to administrative bottlenecks. Future developments seem to revolve around the implementation of Soviet-type leasing arrangements of between 5- and 50-year duration (Judy Dempsey, *FT*, 5 May 1989, p. 2).

Private plots

There are still a few individual farms in mountainous areas. Private plots were first allowed in 1957; plot sizes range from 0.2 to one hectare; a further 0.1 hectares was granted for each head of cattle raised (McIntyre 1988a: 611). Active encouragement was given during the 1970s, such as the removal of restrictions placed on the number of livestock allowed in 1971. As as result they accounted for 14 per cent of cultivated land by 1980 (Lampe 1986: 210). In 1985 the private sector accounted for 13 per cent of arable land and a quarter of gross farm output; it was especially important (figures for 1986) in meat (42 per cent of total output), fruit (42 per cent), vegetables (37 per cent) and eggs (50 per cent) (Cochrane 1988: 50). Products can be sold on the free market, to the state or to agro-industrial complexes, with which contracts can be signed, bringing benefits in the form of seed and fodder at favourable prices. As in Hungary, the state sector and private plots are mutually supportive (this has been the case especially since 1974); the former provides the latter with inputs and services in return for contractual sales of much of the output, which is then sold through the state distribution system (McIntyre 1988: 102, 1988a: 610). There are also auxiliary farms run by industrial and other non-agricultural enterprises, especially for works canteens but possibly also for sale of the produce to their workers (McIntyre 1988a, p. 610). Direct leasing of plots to urban residents began in 1977 (McIntyre 1988a: 103). In 1981 further encouragement came in the following forms: socialized bodies were permitted to include output purchased from the private sector in their obligatory sales to the state, while the income derived from sales by private producers was rendered tax free (Cochrane 1988: 49). The series of harsh winters and summer droughts in the mid-1980s resulted in further incentives being offered to private production and rises in the prices of many consumer goods. The hiring of labour outside the immediate family is not allowed.

Foreign trade and payments

Although actually starting the decade with a relatively high level of debt, Bulgaria was not tempted into borrowing Western credits during the 1970s on such a large scale as its allies, although engineering was expanded and modernized and by 1976 the hard currency debt-service ratio of 44 per cent was actually the highest in Eastern Europe. Both the ratio and the net debt itself (a $3.7 billion peak at the end of 1979) were reduced, by a programme that especially concentrated on reducing imports and re-exporting Soviet oil (since the late 1970s), to 20 per cent and $1.8 billion respectively by the end of 1982 and $0.9 billion by the end of 1984. Bulgaria resumed borrowing in 1985, after the December 1979 cessation, and net debt climbed to $3.4 billion by the end of 1986 (*EIU*, 1987–8: 22–3), $5.3 billion in 1987 (when the debt-service ratio was 30 per cent: *IHT*, 4 March 1988, p. 17) and $6.4 billion in 1988 (*FT*, 1 March 1989, p. 8).

Comecon has always dominated Bulgaria's foreign trade, but by 1986 its share had risen to 79.2 per cent, the Soviet share alone to 59.2 per cent. The composition of exports has changed substantially over time. There has been a decline in the importance of foodstuffs, from around 49 per cent in the mid-1960s to 22 per cent two decades later. On the other hand the importance of manufactured products has risen (machinery not far short of 50 per cent), reflecting the overall strategy of development; this involves, in particular, capital goods (including hi-tech items like robots and computers), and chemicals (including petrochemicals). Bulgaria is one of the most enthusiastic supporters of intra-Comecon trade and technology collaboration, and has benefited from specialization agreements, forklift trucks being the best known example. Imports are dominated by Soviet raw materials and oil (reduced by 10 per cent in early 1983, partly to encourage a more efficient use by Bulgaria, but still adequate to allow for exports of oil and petrochemicals). Machinery, however, accounts for around a third. Bulgaria has not escaped Soviet complaints about the quality of products exchanged for ensured supplies of Soviet energy and raw materials. McIntyre (1988a: 7) estimates that total trade turnover has reached 100 per cent of national income in recent years.

The organization of foreign trade has been modified. Some enterprises such as Balkancar have their own trading organizations, while Machinoexport, for example, represents 17 industrial companies. Since 1987 interest has been expressed in joining GATT.

Joint equity ventures

Access to Western hi-tech and know-how is gained mainly through industrial co-operation agreements, but since March 1980 joint ventures with Western companies with majority foreign ownership of equity have been allowed. There has not been too much success so far. This is because of the restrictions imposed: the chairman of the management board must be Bulgarian and all decisions must be unanimous; the foreign tax rises from 20 per cent for profits retained in Bulgaria to 30 per cent for repatriated profits. Machinery and equipment imported by the foreign partner are now free of tariffs. Fifteen joint ventures were in operation at the end of 1987 (*FT*, 14 April 1988, p. 3). Actual examples include industrial robots, machine parts, hotels, chemicals and biotechnology. Since January 1989 state approval may be sought for a foreign share exceeding 49 per cent (Robin Gedye, *The Daily Telegraph*, 12 January 1989, p. 11).

The private non-agricultural sector

This is not a flourishing sector of the economy. In the early 1980s private restaurants were allowed to operate for a short time only in Black Sea resorts, while there were some unpublicized experiments in Sofia, the capital, in 1985. Co-operatives have especially benefited. For example, co-operative taxis compete with state taxi services, but must charge the same price as the latter and can only operate up to four hours a day on a part-time basis. According to the June 1987 'private labour decree' individuals or groups are allowed to set up, on a part-time basis, small workshops within state enterprises, and also retail shops, bakeries, laundries, repair shops, tailoring, cafes and restaurants and transport and building services; tourists can now be accommodated by families. The ban on employing outside labour applied here too, but in January 1989 an employment ceiling of ten was established for private enterprises (Judy Dempsey, *FT*, 12 January 1989, p. 3).

Table 5.2 Bulgaria: statistical survey

Average annual rate of growth of NMP (%)									
1949–52	1953–57	1958–60	1961–65	1966–70	1971–75	1976–80	1981–85	1986	1987
8.4	7.8	11.6	6.7	8.8	7.8	6.1	3.7	5.5	5.1

Net hard currency debt	1979 (peak) $3.7 billion	1984 $0.9 billion	1987 (Debt-service ratio, 30%)	1988 $6.4 billion

Joint equity ventures with Western companies (end 1987)	15

Private agriculture (1985) (including some private farms) The private non-agricultural sector is relatively small	Arable land 13%	Agricultural output 25%

Population (1987)	9 million

Source: Lampe (1986: 144); McIntyre (1988: xvi); Cochrane (1988: 50); *FT*, 14 April 1988, p. 3; *FT*, 1 March 1989, p. 8.

Conclusion

A loyal ally of the Soviet Union (Tsar Alexander II helped to achieve liberation from Ottoman rule in 1878), Bulgaria has undertaken a continuous stream of reforms that have not, however, radically altered the nature of its command economy. Even the 'Principles of the Concept of the Further Construction of Socialism in Bulgaria', gradually phased in since 1 January 1988, are not as in Hungary; they promise only that 'strategic matters' will be left to the centre and detailed decision-making to the enterprises. Interesting aspects include pioneering work in agro-industrial organization, the Hungarian-style symbiosis between socialized and private agriculture, the small enterprise scheme, progress in high technology and an easily manageable foreign debt. Joint equity legislation has not proved to be highly successful in attracting foreign capital and the private, non-agricultural sector is not flourishing.

Postscript

The mass exodus of ethnic Turks since May 1989 has led to serious labour shortages. One result was the 4 July Decree, which proclaimed that women aged 17 to 55 and men aged 18 to 60 were subject to conscription into work batallions (Thomas Goltz, *IHT*, 13 July 1989, p. 8).

Notes

1. Winiecki is highly critical of the programme. The managers of these enterprises are former deputy ministers and heads of various bureaus etc., whose managerial qualities are at best suspect but who have the right connections to input supplies; they subcontract as much as possible and earn significantly more than previously. 'The only thing that has happened is that the shortages have been rearranged among enterprises and part of the ruling stratum gets more than before' (Winiecki 1988a: 33).

Chapter six

Czechoslovakia

Background

The First World War resulted in the disintegration of the Habsburg Empire and Czechoslovakia emerged in 1918 (28 October) as a separate state under President Tomas Garrigue Masaryk. The Communist Party assumed complete power in February 1948, having actually done quite well in the free elections to the Constitutional National Assembly of 26 May 1946, which left it the strongest party with 38 per cent of the vote. The Munich Agreement, signed by Britain, France, Italy, and Germany on 30 September 1938, did away with Czech independence and left Nazi Germany in increasing control. The country is a federated socialist republic comprising the Czech and Slovak Socialist Republics.

Czechoslovakia was already an advanced industrialized country, although not particularly well endowed with raw materials, with a democratic tradition, at the start of the socialist era. By 1930 nearly 35 per cent of the working population was employed in industry (36.3 per cent in 1950) and in 1938 it was the only surviving democracy in central and south-east Europe (Teichova 1988: 33, 80). Czechoslovakia ranked in the top ten industrial producers, in the top seven suppliers of arms and, among European countries, in the top echelons for export dependency (Teichova 1988: 20). Winiecki (1988: 207) considers that here, at the turn of the twentieth century, was to be found one of the world's top five centres of heavy industry.

The 'Prague Spring' was ended by the Warsaw Pact (excluding Romania) invasion of 1968.[1] Gustav Husak became First Secretary in April 1969 (replacing Alexander Dubcek) and President in 1975. Dubcek replaced Antonin Novotny on 5 January 1968 (the latter had become General Secretary in 1953 and President four years later). Dubcek was expelled from the party in June 1970. On 17 December 1987 Husak himself lost his General Secretaryship to Milos Jakes, although retaining the Presidency. The 15.6 million population has one of the highest standards of living in the socialist world, but it was only with the advent of Gorbachev that meaningful political and economic reform has become a possibility. The Seventeenth Party Congress in March 1986 saw an attack on problems such as corruption, inertia, inefficiency and bureaucracy, similar to that at the Soviet Congress. The country depends heavily on imports of fuel and energy, especially from the Soviet Union. The economy is endowed with only limited raw materials, for example low grade coal is the sole energy resource of note, providing around 55 per cent of total energy. Despite Chernobyl, a major nuclear programme is under way. Nuclear energy is planned to account for 25 per cent of electricity by 1990 and over half by the year 2000 (*EEN*, 1988, vol. 2, no. 10, p. 7), compared to 6 per cent in 1980. Currently, lignite accounts for 70 per cent and hydroelectricity 5.0 per cent (*Abecor Country Report*, June 1988, p. 2). Table 6.1 shows officially estimated rates of growth of national income.

Table 6.1 Czechoslovakia: average annual rate of growth of NMP (%)

1951–55	1956–60	1961–65	1966–70	1971–75	1976–80	1981–85	1986	1987	1988
8.2	6.9	2.0	6.9	5.7	3.6	1.8	3.2	2.4	3.0

Sources: Abecor Country Report, June 1988 and June 1989: 1; Economist Intelligence Unit, *Country Profile*, 1987-88: 12; *Smith* (1983: 40).

Industrial reform

The fact that Czechoslovakia was a relatively industrialized country before the Second World War accounts, in part, for an early attempt to modify command planning. In the late 1950s enterprises were amalgamated into associations, emphasis was placed on financial planning and some small measure of decentralization of decision-making was allowed. The deep-seated ills were not cured and a negative growth rate in 1962 added to the list; the five-year plan was abandoned in August of that year. Batt (1988: 171) states that the main reason for the introduction of economic reforms in the mid-1960s was the need to preserve political stability – poor economic performance was a threat to party legitimacy. The most radical reform measures outside Yugoslavia were taken in 1966–67 (Feiwell 1968; Holesovsky 1968, 1973; Kyn 1970; Staller 1968; Teichova, 1988).

The 1966–67 measures largely abandoned directive planning and generally allowed enterprises to determine their own output and input mix in light of maximizing net value added. The industrial associations (VHJs; created in 1958) were amalgamated into trusts (Teichova 1988: 152). Workers' councils began to be set up in 1968. These included representatives of workers, management, banks, and state bodies, and were to have determined the main enterprise decisions and to have appointed managers. Batt (1988: 224–25) makes the point, however, that although there was a certain element of spontaneity in the establishment of workers' councils, started by CKD Praha and Skoda Plzen, the process was rather slow and popular interest only became keen after the Warsaw Pact invasion, when councils took on a patriotic aspect. The state exercised indirect control via instruments such as credit policy, capital charges (6.0 per cent on 'basic means' and 2.0 per cent on 'assets'; Teichova 1988: 153), a tax on value added, payroll surcharges (30 per cent on wage growth), and varying taxes on other uses of retained profit. The state intended to retain control of the overall share of investment and consumption in national income, but decentralized investment was to constitute as much as 40 per cent of total investment. Banks took account of commercial criteria as well as state guidelines and foreign trade considerations in allocating investment credits. A tiered system of prices was introduced. The first stage (1 January 1967) saw the introduction of fixed prices (15 per cent of important producer goods, such as raw materials, fuels and energy, and more than 75 per cent of consumer goods, mainly basic foodstuffs), limit prices (80 per cent of producer goods), and free prices (5.0 per cent of producer goods and 20 per cent of consumer goods). The second stage, which began in the summer of the same year, increased the importance of the limit category, introduced a standard sales tax, and envisaged the prices of around 50 per cent of all products being freed by 1969. It was also planned to narrow the gap between domestic and world prices (Teichova 1988: 154–55). The relationship between enterprise and association gave rise to difficulties, such as association influence over investment and financial transfers between enterprises, but it was intended eventually to make membership voluntary. Enterprises and foreign trade corporations were to be allowed to trade directly with foreign partners.

The *August 1968 Warsaw Pact invasion* (Soviet troops had been withdrawn in November 1945) quickly halted the whole liberalization process and by mid-1970 most of the economic reform had been abandoned. Batt traces the events. In October 1968 the government forbade the further extension of the 'experiment' in enterprise councils, and in May of the following year the concept of self-managing councils was formally rejected. In June and July 1969 it became apparent that enterprise autonomy and non-command planning were not acceptable; industrial associations were required to deliver specified goods to the state, while the 1970 plan targets, published in July, were to be mandatory. Central wage controls were reintroduced in the latter half of 1969, while a price freeze introduced in 1970 lasted for virtually a decade. Brezhnev and rest of the Soviet leadership disliked the continuation of 'spontaneous' post-invasion developments, such as the voluntary establishment of new associations (which started in December 1968 in engineering) and the work of the Federal Planning Ministry on a new law of planning, which continued up to mid-1969 (Batt 1988: 226–27).

Some 1967 elements remained, such as the stress on credits as opposed to budgetary grants in the financing of state-determined investments, and some enterprises being allowed to continue trading directly with foreign partners. In 1977 prices were based on average cost plus markups on capital and wage

costs. Prices of raw materials, fuels and electricity were raised in order to economize on their use and investment goods' prices lowered to stimulate factor
substitution and thus savings on scarce labour. Rising world prices of raw materials and fuels led to the 1978 'complex experiment', which involved 12 associations, covering 150 industrial enterprises, nine foreign trade corporations
and 21 research institutes. This provided the basis for the gradual introduction of the March 1980 *Set of Measures to Improve the System of Planned Management of the National Economy after 1980*' (Rychetnik 1981).

The industrial association (VHJ) became the basic production unit. It
usually involves a horizontal integration of enterprises, either a *koncern* (a
large enterprise alone or one linked with smaller ones) or a trust (where enterprises of comparable size are merged), but there is also the vertically integrated *kombinat*. The economy remains tightly controlled, with familiar plan
indicators, such as production, sales, technical development, fixed investment,
material inputs, labour, wages and financial tasks, still to be found. There are,
however, several interesting features echoing those in other Comecon countries. Norms and plans are supposed to be fixed for a five year period and value
added is to play an important role in wage bill determination, although basic
wage rates are to remain centrally controlled. The 'wage bill limit' consists of
two parts: a 'basic wage bill limit' linked to value added and an 'incentive component' related to profitability. Material incentives are also affected by: (1) a
'rewards fund' (a share of profits is dependent on meeting targets for product
quality and technical level and on labour economies); and (2) the 'cultural and
social needs fund' (this is linked to the wage bill, profit, labour productivity,
product assortment, exports, product quality and fixed asset utilization). Exports are encouraged by an 'export stimulation fund'. Payments to the state,
such as payments out of profit, a capital charge and social security contribution, have priority over material incentive funds. Decentralized investment
was abandoned and budgetary grants, as opposed to retained profits and credits, are supposed to be the exception rather than the rule. There has been no
radical price reform, though there have been attempts to take greater account
of movements in world prices, raw material and fuel prices have been increased and quality surcharges (and discounts) introduced. Bank credit policy,
including hard currency, has been geared to import saving, export promotion,
and restructuring.

The 1980 set of measures was formally destined to be replaced by a programme for the *'comprehensive restructuring (prestavba) of the economic mechanism'* when 37 'principles for the restructuring of the economic mechanism'
were laid down in January 1987 and adopted at the Central Committee session
in December 1987.[2] The State Enterprise Act was passed on 14 June 1988.
The programme is not designed to come fully into effect until the start of the
1991–95 five-year plan. Experiments began in 1987 with twenty-two enterprises taking almost 8 per cent of the output of centrally controlled industry,

99

mostly in the export-oriented consumer goods branches; a further 38 enterprises accounting for over 19 per cent of industrial output were placed on the new system in January 1988 (Janeba 1988: 46–47).

The centre should concentrate on 'strategic' decisions, the planning of overall social and economic development. An intensive type of development is of paramount importance, making full use of scientific and technological progress and a deepening of the international division of labour. The old-style directive aspects of the state plan are to be significantly curtailed, with a transition to a new mechanism primarily oriented towards indirect steering of the economy via the use of economic levers ('economic methods'), such as deductions into the state budget, prices, credit, and wages. The currently prevailing stress on the annual plan is gradually to give way to the primary role of the five-year plan.

Broadly speaking, economic and technical questions should be decided at the particular management level having responsibility and access to the necessary information. Ministries are to be confined to such aspects as investment projects affecting the branch of industry as a whole and should refrain from behaviour like redistributing profits from successful to less successful enterprises. There have been some ministerial amalgamations, such as metallurgy, engineering and technology. The state plan (e.g. 'state orders') forms the basis of the enterprise plan, but the latter should also take account of the economic contracts concluded, thus expanding the role of horizontal relationships. Within its area of business and after fulfilling state tasks, the enterprise has greater room for independent decision-making. There are to be only a limited number of key indicators, especially net output and profit, while enterprises are able to determine the total number of workers, the qualifications structure, and payment over the wage tariffs laid down.

A significant part of pay is to be dependent on the final results of the enterprise – specifically, 'disposable profit'. By 1990 the incentive portion of wages paid from disposable profit will have increased from the present average of 3 per cent to between 7 and 10 per cent at minimum, this figure gradually increasing over the course of the next five-year plan; this proportion will vary between categories of workers in order to widen differentials (Resolution, *Czechoslovak Economic Digest*, 1988, no. 1, p. 25). Enterprises are to be placed on the basis of 'full cost accounting' and 'self-financing': 'An enterprise shall defray its needs and costs from takings obtained primarily from its entrepreurial activities as well as from other sources' ('Law on state enterprise' in *Czechoslovak Economic Digest*, 1988, no. 6, p. 11, henceforth 'Law'). This implies a reduction in subsidies and the possibility of liquidation, although the founding organ should first attempt a gradual programme of consolidation, direct administration for up to three years and merger or division ('Law', p. 14). In January 1989 38 enterprises, including Skoda Plzen, were declared insolvent and were thus subject to restructuring and stricter quality control.

Enterprises have to give at least six months' notice of changes in the labour force. They must try to redeploy affected workers in other jobs but, failing this, secure positions in other places in collaboration with relevant bodies. Greater use is to be made of the brigade system, a common trend as we have already seen. The norms imposed upon enterprises (such as for profit deductions into the obligatory rewards, development, socio-cultural, reserve, and foreign exchange funds; tax rates; and payments into the state budget) are to be uniform and stable. Encouragement is given to the establishment of direct links with enterprises in other CMEA countries, while a portion of any hard currency earnings may be retained by the enterprise.

Enterprise managers are to be elected. Normally the founding body organizes a competition from which a list of applicants is drawn up. The workers' collective elects the manager, although the founding organ has to confirm the decision. The 'self-management' bodies are the 'assembly' and the 'council', the former being the highest authority of the workers' collective and which must meet at least twice a year. At first glance their functions appear significant. They can, for example, approve the enterprise plan submitted by the manager. There are, however, constraints on this. For instance resolutions relating to deliveries concerned with defence, state security and the fulfilment of international obligations cannot be passed without the consent of the representative of the enterprise founder, while the manager may take a dispute with the council or assembly to the founder for a final decision (Resolution 1988: 76).

While the law on state enterprises is meant to come gradually into effect over the period 1 July 1988 to 1991, a reform of wholesale (but not retail) prices is to be implemented by 1 January 1989, taking account of socially necessary costs, demand, and world prices. The wholesale prices of fuels and raw materials will include a 50 per cent markup on total wages paid out and a 4.5 per cent profit markup on capital (Resolution 1988: 21). In certain cases and under specified conditions, 'contract prices' may be negotiated between enterprise and customer ('Law', p. 32). Credit policy is to pay greater attention to efficiency, thus not being used to cover up inefficiency, while a change in the banking arrangement is under consideration, with the possible creation of competing commercial banks, separate from the central bank.[3]

These reform measures have arisen, to a large extent, from the impact of Gorbachev on Czechoslovakia. There is disagreement within the country, with Lubomir Strougal (premier 1970 until October 1988, replaced by Ladislav Adamec) more enthusiastic than Central Committee Secretary in charge of ideology Jan Fojtik. Jaromir Matejka is secretary of the committee on economic reform. Husak himself, in early 1986, warned against any mechanical imitation of other countries' experiences and pronounced himself in favour of a creative use of those experiences in a search for answers best suited to Czechoslovakia's special needs and circumstances. Nevertheless, he criticized overcentralization and, while rejecting market-oriented reforms, accepted the need for greater decentralization of decision-making. After Gorbachev's visit in April 1987 a more positive attitude became discernible. Even conservative Central Committee member Vasil Bilak, who resigned from the Politburo in December 1988, supported the current proposals, this following a February 1987 attack on reform that he considered merely a convenient cover for anti-socialist tendencies. Milos Jakes, who was chairman of the National Economic Commission before he became General Secretary on 17 December 1987, seems likely to undertake a cautious implementation of the reform programme, warning against 'hurried' attempts at economic reform. He has rejected any analogy between the 1968 reforms and the present ones, stressing that the latter will preserve the leading roles for the party, social ownership of the means of production and the planned economy. The October 1988 change of government indicated a conservative approach to reform, Fojtik warning against weakening the role of the party and strengthening the private sector. At the end of 1988 both the GDR and Czechoslovakia decided to bring the next party congress forward a year to May 1990, arousing speculation about possible top leadership changes.

Since 15 November 1987 individuals have been allowed hard currency bank accounts for overseas travel, withdrawable without permission from the Ministry of Finance. Relatives and friends in the West are now able to pay for the necessary travel documents for Czech citizens.

Agriculture

When Czechoslovakia emerged as an independent state after the First World War nearly a third of agricultural holdings accounted for only 3 per cent of arable land, while 0.5 per cent of holdings farmed almost 20 per cent (Teichova 1988: 27). As a result of the land reforms of the 1920s 64 per cent of all agricultural land was taken up by holdings of five to twenty hectares (amounting to 95 per cent of all holdings), and only 1 per cent of all agricultural enterprises farmed more than fifty hectares each (accounting for around 20 per cent of agricultural land in total) (Teichova 1988: 12). The *1945–51 land reforms* took place in three stages, the final one fixing a ceiling of fifty hectares for private ownership (p. 104).

Agriculture currently employs 10 per cent of the labour force (*Abecor Country Report*, June 1988, p. 2). From the mid-1970s onwards emphasis was given to the establishment of agro-industrial enterprises combining farms and processing. Only four obligatory and thirty-one non-binding orientation indicators were set, although lower levels often added more (Cummings 1986: 112). In January 1982, as part of the New System of Planned Management of the National economy, decision-making in agriculture was decentralized to some extent, especially as regards day-to-day operations. The federal level issues only two obligatory targets, procurement of grain and the slaughter of animals, although up to three extra targets may be added by local officials (Cummings 1986: 113).

In the mid-1980s agricultural co-operatives had around 5,000 hectares on average and state farms 21,600 hectares. The figures for occupation of total farmland in 1986 were co-operatives, 64.5 per cent, and the state sector, 30.5 per cent (Matousek 1988: 47). An interesting variation is to be found in the Slusovice co-operative in south Moravia, now being imitated elsewhere in Czechoslovakia. This farm of 8,000 hectares and 3,500 employees produces, in addition to products such as cereals, milk, and potatoes, computers for agricultural and school use, biochemical products, agricultural machinery and microelectronics (*EEN*, 1987, vol. 1, no. 9, pp. 4–5). The co-operative is split into financially autonomous units called 'microstructures' (e.g. transport and milking) and managers are assessed at regular intervals in terms of criteria such as innovation and working conditions.

The September 1987 draft law on co-operative farming was to be implemented by 1989. Important aspects involve full cost-accounting, implying the phasing out of subsidies, and increased scope for decentralized decision-making after fulfilling state plan obligations (Matousek 1988: 47–58). For the agro-food complex as a whole, as of 1 January 1989, payments into the state budget are 50 per cent both from wages and bonuses and from profits (Cerny 1988: 52).

The private sector

The private sector, in 1985, accounted for only 3 per cent of arable land and 10 per cent of gross farm output, while the percentage figures for individual products were as follows: potatoes 14; vegetables 40; fruit 60; meat 15; eggs 40 (Cochrane 1988: 48). In addition to private plots there are still private farms, largely in hilly areas. The maximum size of private farm is set at one hectare (the average size is 0.4 hectares according to *EEN*, 1987, vol. 1, no. 9, p. 3), but grazing rights are allowed on some state lands. In 1980 they accounted for less than 2 per cent of the agricultural labour force (Cummings 1986: 113). The 1980s have seen encouragement given to the private sector. In 1982, for example, revenue from the sale of food produced by part-time individuals became taxfree (Cummings 1986: 114).

Foreign trade

Foreign trade accounts for a third of national income and is heavily oriented towards the socialist countries (78.6 per cent in 1986; around 75 per cent with Comecon), with the European Community taking 9.7 per cent and developing countries 5.3 per cent. Over the following year the socialist countries' share had risen to four-fifths, the Soviet Union and GDR accounting for 43 per cent and 7.0 per cent respectively of total foreign trade, while the developing countries' share had slipped to 3.5 per cent. The FRG and Austria were the most important Western trading partners (*Abecor Country Report*, June 1988, p. 2). Comecon trade has increased in importance during the 1980s (1960, 64 per cent; 1986, 74.6 per cent), the Soviet Union alone accounting for 44.4 per cent in 1986 (see *EIU Country Profile*, 1987–88, p. 31). Comecon specialization agreements have assigned, for example, trams to Czechoslovakia (although the Soviet Union and Poland make them for domestic use only) in return for relinquishing railway passenger cars. Engineering goods account for half of total exports.

Czechoslovakia has the lowest per capita net hard currency debt in Eastern Europe. A string of hard currency trade surpluses (1983, $1 billion; 1984, $850 million; 1985, $700 million), one of the results of an austerity programme aimed at reducing investment and imports, has helped reduce the size of the net hard currency debt ($2.3 billion at the end of 1984, though rising to $2.8 billion at the end of 1986, having been $3.1 billion at the end of 1974 and $3.6 billion in 1980; *EIU*, p. 37). The debt-service ratio was 20 per cent at the end of 1986, and gross debt rose from $4 billion in 1984 to $5.5 billion three years later (Leslie Colitt, *FT*, 8 November 1988, p. 2).

Although the planning and management of foreign trade remain highly centralized, there have been various experiments since 1981. Some individual enterprises have been given direct trading rights, retention of part of convertible currency earnings is allowed, and a number of producers (for example the Skoda and CKD engineering enterprises) have been merged with their competent foreign trade corporations. Since 1987 enterprises have been able to keep all the proceeds from the sale of export licences (*EEN*, 1988, vol. 2, no. 8, p. 5).

Joint equity ventures

Czechoslovakia became interested in joint equity ventures in 1985 and outlined the legal framework the following year. The main attraction was the prospect of obtaining advanced technology. Foreign ownership was originally limited to a ceiling of 49 per cent and the manager had to be a Czech national. The profit tax rate is 50 per cent (compared to 75 per cent for a native company); there is a social security tax of 25 per cent of the total salary bill and a 25 per cent tax on all dividends (*EEN*, 1987, vol. 1, no. 12, p. 2). Practical examples are few (eight by mid-1988; *EEN*, 1989, vol. 3, no. 3, p. 3); there are ventures set up in electronics, biotechnology, video production and hotels for instance. Since 1 January 1989 there has been no minimum start-up capital and no upper limit on the Western share in the joint venture; a foreign corporate body or person may hold shares and a Westerner may be director of a company or chairman of the board. The only excluded sectors are those 'important for defence and security' (Margie Lindsay, *FT Survey*, 13 December 1988, p. 39). Examples of joint ventures with the Soviet Union include the Robotics enterprise and the Elisa biotechnology company (*EEN*, 1988, vol. 2, no. 20, p. 4 and no. 23, p. 6).

The private non-agricultural sector

This sector has been severely repressed, even by East European standards. A savage economic elimination of self-employed craftsmen and industrial producers took place during 1948–53. Of the 383,000 small companies in 1948, only 47,000 remained by 1956, and sixteen years later only 2,000 self-employed craftsmen still functioned (Teichova 1988: 104).

In 1986 the sector was encouraged by things like tax reductions, after years of discouragement and heavy taxation. From January 1988 onwards small shops and restaurants may be leased from the state, although subject to strict controls on profit margins and to the condition that non-family members are not employed.

Table 6.2 Czechoslovakia: statistical survey

Average annual rate of growth of NMP (%)									
1951–55	1956–60	1961–65	1966–70	1971–75	1976–80	1981–85	1986	1987	1988
8.2	6.9	2.0	6.9	5.7	3.6	1.8	3.2	2.3	2.2

Private sector in agriculture (including some private farms) (%)	Arable land 3.0		Output 10.0	
Net hard currency debt ($ billion)	1974 3.1	1980 3.6	1986 2.8 (debt-service ratio, 20%)	
Population (1987)	15.6 million			

Sources: See Table 6.1 this volume; Cochrane (1988: 48); Economist Intelligence Unit, *Country Profile* (1987–88: 37).

Conclusion

Czechoslovakia was, untypically, an industrialized country on the eve of its socialist period, while the reforms associated with the Prague Spring would have transformed the economy and society. The 1968 Warsaw Pact invasion lead to a heavy mantle descending on the country, which persists to this day. Milos Jakes replaced Gustav Husak as General Secretary in December 1987, but the former only holds out the promise of a cautious implementation of modest reforms. Nevertheless, Czechoslovakia has one of the highest living standards in the socialist world and the lowest per capita net hard currency debt in Eastern Europe.

Notes

1. Justified by the 'Brezhnev doctrine'. *Pravda* 25 September 1968 provided an explanation for the invasion :

   The peoples of the socialist countries and the communist parties have and must have freedom....However, every decision of theirs must damage neither socialism in their own country nor the fundamental interests of other socialist countries nor the worldwide workers' movement.... Every communist party is responsible not only to its own people but also to all the socialist countries and the entire communist movement....A socialist state that is in a system of other states constituting a socialist commonwealth cannot be free of the common interests of that commonwealth.

2. See the Central Committee Resolution adopted at the Seventh Session, 17–18 December 1987, *Czechoslovak Economic Digest*, no. 1, (1988); Cervinka (1987); Rohlicek (1987); Kerner (1988); *FT Survey*, 9 October 1987.

3. The main sources of budgetary revenue are, as usual, profit transfers from economic organizations (43 per cent) and turnover tax (24 per cent) (*Abecor Country Report*, June 1988, p. 2).

Chapter seven

The German Democratic Republic

Introduction

The GDR has the highest standard of living among the socialist countries and, along with Czechoslovakia, was an advanced industrialized country before the socialist era. The *EIU* has made the following estimates for per capita GNP in 1986: GDR $8,130; Czechoslovakia $7,470; Hungary $4,300; Bulgaria $3,730; Soviet Union $3,560; Romania $2,080; Poland $1,900 (cited by Childs 1987: 17). Economic policy has been shaped by Soviet domination, especially in view of its position on the front line between East and West, and the continual comparisons it suffers to the Federal Republic of Germany, rather than its poorer socialist neighbours. One estimate puts the GDR's per capita GNP, in the mid-1980s and calculated according to Western methods, at two-thirds that of the FRG (Marer 1986c: 611). These comparisons, enhanced by the access of GDR citizens to West German TV and radio, make demonstrating the superiority of socialism and the quest for party legitimacy uphill tasks, even among those born after the Second World War and even though there is general awareness of the progress that has been made in the fields of economic and social policy. Legitimacy is largely sought in rising living standards, rather than liberal reforms or appeal to nationalism, although there is now increasing invocation of the past to provoke patriotism. Since socialism is the *raison d'être* of the regime, this puts close restraints on reform. Particular resentment is felt because of the inability of GDR citizens normally to travel to the West (the major exceptions being pensioners; this relaxation occurred since 1964), even though recent years have seen a significant increase in permissions given for 'urgent family visits'. These have been more liberally interpreted since February 1986 to include cousins and even friends instead of just close relatives like a parent or grandparent, although typically at least one very close relative has to stay behind in the GDR.[1] A new law was implemented on 1 January 1989 involving both people to be visited and acceptable occasions (for example, attendance at the funeral of an aunt, uncle, or in-law).

What is particularly fascinating at the moment is the impact of Gorbachev's ideas for economic and political reform on the GDR. Talk of *glas-*

nost', 'democratization' and *perestroika* and sweeping personnel changes, especially at the top, are naturally unsettling to a conservative leadership long used to proclaiming the virtues of its socialist system in the battle against capitalism and fearful of the possible consequences of political relaxation at home and of being exposed should events in the Soviet Union reverse course again. On 1 December 1988 Honecker attacked so-called influential people in the West who recommended that the GDR change course and march into 'anarchy', although he acknowledged difficulties in agriculture, the supply of consumer goods, investment and energy consumption.

The Soviet Union's attitude to events in Eastern Europe as a whole is not one-sided. While Gorbachev would no doubt like to see the more conservative regimes such as Czechoslovakia, Romania and the GDR broadly follow his vision of reform, there is a profound interest in political stability, especially at the coal face and given the past instability of Poland.

The Soviet Union has a natural interest in the economic diversification to be found within Comecon and the GDR's relative economic success has attracted attention. In May 1985 Gorbachev praised the GDR's endeavours to reach international standards in production and the following June what he called 'inter-industry associations'. Aganbegyan (1988a: 94) thinks positively about the incorporation of design and research organizations into large production enterprises, as has happened with the combine, and says that the Soviet Union is making use of the GDR's experience; many formerly independent institutes and construction departments are being turned into large productive concerns. The penchant for mergers and super-ministries, the nature of the Soviet foreign trade reforms, the idea of quality control, and the concessions to private and co-operative activity also suggest GDR influence. Gorbachev personally attended (as with the Polish, but in contrast to the Hungarian, Czechoslovak and Bulgarian congresses) the Eleventh Congress of the SED on 17–21 April 1986. That made him the first Soviet General Secretary to do so since 1971. The generally self-congratulatory tone of the conference contrasted markedly with that of the CPSU. Gorbachev again praised the GDR's success, describing the economic system as dynamic and flexible and its performance as high and smooth. He also complimented the work ethos of its citizens, although he did not specifically mention the combine. Honecker, General Secretary of the SED, indulged in some mild criticism, the need to improve service in shops for instance, but listed the GDR's economic achievements, in robotics for example. He stressed the importance of continued 'perfecting' of planning and management: 'We may not yet have reached a state of perfection, but we have made good headway'. Specific proposals were also forthcoming.[2]

Speaking at the Free German Trade Union Federation Congress in April 1987, Honecker again listed the GDR's successes since 1971, such as rising living standards and technical progress: 'We wish to continue this path with further success... the GDR has an efficiently functioning system of economic and social planning.' He spoke of the considerable changes that had taken place since he came to office and the open discussion that already existed in the party and trade unions. Since 1971 the SED had adapted Marxism-Leninism to fit the conditions prevailing in the GDR and had made use of the 'valuable experience' of other socialist countries. In an interview in *Stern* (9 April 1987) Kurt Hager (Central Committee Secretary in charge of ideology) said there would be no election of company directors, while in October he confirmed that the GDR would carry on with existing policies because it was on the sensitive dividing line between East and West. The overriding aims seem to be the maintenance of political control and the 'perfecting' of the present system. The former goal is a common one in socialist countries, of course, but the East German leadership is particularly sensitive to the issue.

Honecker visited the Federal Republic on 7–11 September 1987 as a guest of Chancellor Kohl (head of government). Apart from the immense importance in terms of political psychology, the specific results of the visit were as follows: agreements signed on scientific and technological co-operation, co-operation and exchange of information in nuclear energy, and co-operation on the environment; preliminary agreements for a joint economic commission, an inter-German electricity grid, including Berlin, and a fast rail link between Hanover and Berlin (inter-German rail fares were also to be reduced); and relaxation of cross-border regulations (e.g. from 1 November 1987 easier import controls).[3]

Table 7.1 shows official figures for rates of growth of produced national income.

Table 7.1 The GDR: official statistics for rates of growth of produced national income (%)

1950	22.0	1963	3.5	1976	3.5
1951	21.1	1964	4.9	1977	5.1
1952	13.7	1965	4.6	1978	3.7
1953	5.5	1966	4.9	1979	4.0
1954	8.7	1967	5.4	1980	4.4
1955	8.6	1968	5.1	1981	4.8
1956	4.4	1969	5.2	1982	2.6
1957	7.3	1970	5.6	1983	4.4
1958	10.7	1971	4.4	1984	5.5
1959	8.8	1972	5.7	1985	4.8
1960	4.5	1973	5.6	1986	4.3
1961	1.6	1974	6.5	1987	3.5
1962	2.7	1975	4.9	1988	3.0

Source: Statistical Yearbooks of the GDR.

Political background

Major early political events include the following: the split of Germany after the defeat of Hitler; the foundation of the GDR on 7 October 1949; Walter Ulbricht becomes General Secretary of the SED in July 1950, to be replaced by Erich Honecker in May 1971; the 17–18 June 1953 uprising; the building of the Berlin Wall in 1961; the June 1972 Quadripartite agreement (the United States, Britain, and France on the one side and the Soviet Union on the other) on transit rights between West Berlin and the FRG and the accompanying agreement signed by the West Berlin Senate and the GDR on travel between West and East Berlin.

Economic background

The end of the Second World War

Hitler's defeat led to the division of Germany and left the two parts at the front line between socialism and capitalism. The GDR started off in generally worse shape than the Federal Republic. What is now the Federal Republic suffered greater wartime destruction. The GDR's industrial production was only 10 to 15 per cent of its pre-war level. There was a loss of over 40 per cent of industrial capacity (Dennis 1988: 128) and the GDR fared relatively badly with respect to reparations paid from current production (until 1953) as well as the large scale dismantling and removal of plant to the Soviet Union. Reparations and occupation costs accounted for an estimated 25 per cent of social product between 1946 and 1948 (*DIW Handbuch*, 1985, p. 38). More than a quarter of industrial capital assets were dismantled by the Soviet Union (Dennis 1988: 128). In contrast, the Federal Republic fared much better in this respect and actually became a recipient of Marshall Plan aid after 1948.[4]

The economic structure of the GDR was unbalanced, in contrast to that of the Federal Republic. The GDR's industrial structure was relatively strong with respect to machine tools, office machines, textile machinery, optical equipment, electrical engineering, motor vehicles, light industry, textiles and aircraft. On the other hand, chemicals, iron and steel, heavy engineering and shipbuilding were weakly developed, the present area of the GDR producing only 1.3 per cent of the pre-war total of pig iron. In 1938 the share of iron ore was only 1.3 per cent and hard coal 1.9 per cent (Strassburger 1985: 114). In 1939 per capita industrial output was slightly higher than that of the present-day Federal Republic. In terms of total industrial output and population the present-day GDR accounted for 29 and 25 per cent respectively in 1944 (Childs 1987: 4). In the mid-1930s about 83 per cent of foreign trade was with the West. The GDR, like Czechoslovakia, was thus in the unusual position of being an advanced, industrialized (albeit unbalanced) country before the start of its socialist era.

Resource endowment

The GDR is generally poorly endowed with raw materials, with important exceptions such as brown coal and potash.[5] These two, however, are heavy polluters (potash, for example, exacerbates an already acute water supply problem), and brown coal extraction reduces the amount of already scarce land available for agricultural purposes (in 1985 only 0.37 hectares per capita, compared with 0.45 in Czechoslovakia, 0.53 in Poland, 0.62 in Hungary, 0.67 in Romania, 0.70 in Bulgaria and 2.15 in the Soviet Union (Merkel 1987: 213).[6] This poor resource endowment means that the GDR is heavily dependent on imports of fuels and raw materials, especially from the Soviet Union (the GDR imports some 60 per cent of its raw materials). Whenever the commodity terms of trade deteriorate, such as during the period following the 1973–74 oil shock albeit with a lag given the Comecon pricing system, particular attention is paid to increasing both domestic production to substitute for imports (although characterized by rising marginal costs) and the efficiency of resource utilization (reflected in economic reform measures).

Labour is also an acutely scarce factor of production in the GDR and this is reflected in economic policies such as the drive for 'intensification' (*Intensivierung*). The total population was 16.7 million in 1939 and reached a post-war peak of 19.1 million in 1947 (swollen by refugees). The present population is well below this figure (16,639,877 at the end of 1986).

Between 1949 and the building of the Berlin Wall (12–13 August 1961) almost 2.7 million migrants from the GDR were registered by the Federal and West Berlin authorities. They were mainly young (just below half less than 25 years of age), skilled workers, professionals and entrepreneurs.

GDR policy has been both to promote an increase in the birth rate (1974 saw an all time low of 10.6 per thousand) and in the participation of women in the work-force by measures such as the generous provision of crèches and kindergartens, maternity grants and reduced working hours. As a result, the present figure of 88 per cent of women of working age either at work or in training is the highest in the world (Edwards 1985: 10). In 1982 28 per cent of women in employment were in part-time work (p. 82). In 1983 females accounted for 49.5 per cent of persons employed, excluding apprentices (1950, 40.0 per cent; 1980, 49.9, per cent; *Statistical Pocket Book of the GDR*, 1984, p. 28).

The scarcity of labour as a factor of production has had a profound impact on both political (severe restrictions on movement to the West) and economic policy in the GDR. Incentives are needed to encourage a high level of commitment and productivity. Compensations for the acute shortage of labour include attempts to increase the amount of shift work and the GDR's (on the whole) successful efforts to maintain the tradition of a highly skilled work force, by a system of education having a strong vocational bent. Indeed, the German tradition in general has been of benefit: hard work, order, discipline, administrative efficiency, achievement orientation, and honesty. Apart from attitudes, corruption is less of a problem in the GDR because of a relatively good consumer supply situation, including gifts from the Federal Republic. This tradition encourages a relatively greater willingness to work with and within the rules and regulations of a command economy.

Planning

There is still a command economy. Real political power is exercised by the Politburo (Politbüro der SED) and the Secretariat of the Central Committee of the SED (Sozialistische Einheitspartei Deutschlands: Socialist Unity Party of Germany), whose members belong to the Politburo. Since 1976, the Order of Planning (Planungsordnung) has been the most important aspect of plan methodology, regulating the planning of the national economy and of its economic units, sectors and regions for both five year and annual planning (Tröder 1987: Chapter 6). It contains a list of plan indicators for the economic units and is designed to enhance the role of the five year plan as the chief form of state direction of the economy. Long term planning is described as the preparatory stage of five year planning, the latter being the 'main steering instrument' from which are derived 'annual slices'. The planning order realistically has to take account of deviations of annual plans from the guidelines, to allow for factors such as changes in demand, new technologies and altered world market circumstances, but the five year plan itself is now no longer redrawn. Note that five year and annual plans apply to all combines, but the former apply only to selected enterprises. Combines disaggregate the plan tasks received from ministries down to enterprises whose managements draw up detailed plan drafts and conclude preliminary inter-enterprise contracts. This is an important co-ordinating instrument of sub-plans because through them enterprise outputs can be legally guaranteed and bottlenecks identified at an early stage.

Trade unions and wage determination

Trade unions participate in planning, although their impact is marginal. Basic wage rates are formally agreed by the Council of Ministers and the FDGB: real power, however, lies in the former body. The limitations placed on the role of trade unions at the enterprise level is neatly summarized by Strassburger (1985: 468). The right to monitor, criticize and make proposals does not at heart affect the principle of individual management, democratic centralism and the political primacy of the SED at the enterprise level. It is true that pressure can be exerted upon enterprise management by means of discussion and criticism, but if these recommendations and proposals are not taken into account, there at best remains to the enterprise trade union executives the path of complaining to the relevant management organs. As Dennis (1988:

107, 160–61) puts it, the trade union only has 'co-operation' rights (which can be overridden by the manager) in the case of formulating the enterprise plan, while it has 'co-determination' rights in lesser areas such as allocation of bonuses and the setting of work norms. The procedure in the case of job rationalization is as follows: an enterprise has to draw up an 'alternative contract' (*Änderungsvertrag*) with the worker and the trade union representative, which includes the offer of a 'reasonable' alternative job. If similar work is not possible within the enterprise or if the worker rejects the alternative, a 'transfer contract' (*Überleitungsvertrag*) is concluded, involving another 'reasonable' job at another enterprise. A further rejection makes dismissal feasible, subject to appeal to the enterprise conflict commission, run by elected assessors proposed by the trade union to deal with labour disputes, or to a district court (Dennis 1988: 163). Loss of earnings in a new position or during retraining are made good for one year. A form of social welfare relief can be paid out to those adversely affected by structural unemployment; the number of people actually involved is probably very small. Social welfare is paid out in the case of dismissal without notice if no new employment follows immediately thereafter: otherwise unemployment is no longer a branch of the social security system (Vortmann 1985: 253–54). Dennis (1988: 164, quoting Belwe) cites workers' entitlement to a monthly rent allowance and a daily payment of eight marks between jobs.

The trade union leader is the deputy chairman of the enterprise 'production committee' (the chairman being the party secretary), although this committee only plays a consultative role. The annual 'enterprise collective contract' (*Betriebskollektivvertrag*), worked out by enterprise management and the trade union executive on the basis of the confirmed enterprise plan, constitutes an obligation to fulfil the enterprise production tasks and socio-cultural programme for the given plan period. It contains information about labour tasks, plans concerning qualifications, culture and training, the forms of wages to be applied, criteria for the allocation of bonuses and special measures for the promotion of women and youth (Strassburger 1985: 467–68). The right to strike featured in the 1949 constitution, but not that of 1968, the argument being that strikes make no sense in a workers' state since the workers would be striking against themselves.

There is a labour market in the GDR, so that the wage and salary system is used to allocate manpower and provide incentives to greater effort and qualifications. But during the 1960s and the first half of the 1970s only about 50 per cent of the actual earnings of most employees in the producing sectors were accounted for by basic wage rates. The 'extra-performance wage' (*Mehrleistungslohn*), that part of earnings linked to performance, originally introduced, as its name implies, as a means of increasing performance, came largely to lose that function. It came to be paid merely upon fulfilment of the prescribed norm – additions and deductions in cases of over- and underfulfilment were rare (Vortmann 1985: 258). Factors such as technical progress led to increased labour productivity, and enterprise management was reluctant to raise norms. With wage rates essentially remaining unchanged, increases in actual earnings were basically accounted for by increases in the 'extra-performance wage'. This led to distortion in the labour market, discriminating against those mainly reliant on basic wage rates, individuals like technicians, white collar workers, and master craftsmen and those working in sections such as trade and services.

After an announcement at the Eighth FDGB Congress in 1972 that the wage system was to be reformed, a 1976 resolution of the Central Committee affected production workers in industry, construction and other branches of the economy such as transport and communications over the course of the 1976–80 five-year plan. The 'basic wage' (*Grundlohn*), which comprised the set wage rate and a substantial proportion of the former 'extra-performance wage', was to constitute some 70 to 80 per cent of actual earnings. The 'basic wage' was to be paid on fulfilment of norms, underfulfilment being followed by deductions and overfulfilment by a real 'extra-performance wage' (Strassburger 1985: 849).

In 1982 the wage reform was essentially concluded, having involved around 1.8 million production workers and some 600,000 master craftsmen and employees who had completed college or technical college courses, for whom new, performance-dependent salaries were set (Strassburger 1985: 848, 850). Those involved in R&D and designing earn bonuses if a given task is solved within a certain time. There are still problems concerning differentials, however, such as cases where qualified engineers receive less pay than the workers being directed.

Besides wages and salaries (note there is a minimum wage of 400 marks per month for full-time work), employees also receive bonuses. These bonuses are intended to be paid according to performance, but in practice this is frequently not the case. In particular end-of-year bonuses are calculated more or less automatically and have developed de facto into a thirteenth month's salary. This bonus is by far the most important one for those who work in industrial enterprises (Vortmann 1985: 260).

The history of economic reform in the GDR

The New Economic System

The NES was the result of: (1) the 'growth crisis' (*Wachstumskrise*) – produced national income increased by only 1.6 per cent in 1961 and 2.7 per cent in 1962 and investment stagnated; (2) the particularly serious micro-economic problems of command planning in such a relatively advanced economy; and, arguably, (3) the Soviet need for a laboratory to observe the effects of reform.

The ambitious Second Five-year Plan (1956–60) was first revised downwards and then replaced by a seven-year plan (1959–65), following the Soviet lead. The '*main economic task*', adopted at the Fifth SED Congress in July 1958, was to catch up with and overtake the Federal Republic in per capita production of major foodstuffs and consumer goods by 1961 and in labour productivity by 1965. The reason was to staunch migration to the Federal Republic by holding out the promise of a much higher standard of living. By 1960 it was clear that this strategy was not going to be successful. The attempt to increase consumption rapidly, while maintaining the other items of expenditure, led to inconsistencies, stresses and strains. The seven year plan, which collapsed in reality in 1961, was formally annulled at the Sixth Congress of the SED in January 1963 with the announcement of a new plan for the period 1963 to 1970. This was the background to the building of the Berlin Wall in August 1961. When it was realized that the production of foodstuffs and consumer goods could not be increased fast enough to induce people to stay voluntarily, direct action was needed to staunch the labour haemorrhage. This meant that the aims of the 'main economic task' were, in a way, given up because they were unrealistic. The period 1961–63 was one of consolidation. 'Guidelines for the new economic system of planning and management of the national economy' followed the formal announcement at the Congress of the NES: this was renamed the 'Economic System of Socialism' in April 1967 – ironically to indicate permanency.

The NES did not represent a reform along Yugoslav, pre-1968 Czechoslovak, or post-1968 Hungarian lines, but an attempt to achieve state goals more effectively by means of a combination of traditional command planning (with its use of directives) and the greatest use to date of indirect steering of enterprises by means of mainly monetary instruments ('economic levers'). These included net profit deductions, taxes, prices, fund formation, and the cost and availability of credit. These levers were designed to induce enterprise behaviour in line with the state plan. The NES was the first comprehensive, post-Liberman reform and the most radical of its time among Comecon countries. Note, however, that the NES was only gradually introduced from 1964 onwards, the whole panoply of instruments only really operating by 1969–70. By this time the system was already amended by the introduction of 'structure determining tasks'. The hope was to bring about a scientific and technical revolution, a highly efficient, dynamic, innovative economy, which would prove the superiority of socialism and, at the same time, maintain effective party control.[8]

The VVB (*Vereinigung Volkseigener Betriebe*: association of nationally-owned enterprises) was an essentially administrative (in contrast to operational production) intermediate body between ministry and enterprise. The VVB declined in importance during the 1970s and finally disappeared during the 1980s.

The number of compulsory plan indicators imposed on enterprises was reduced, although still covering the main areas of activity: for example gross output, product groups, sales (home and abroad), fixed capital, science and technology and the wage fund (formerly there were also indicators for number of employees, average wage levels and labour productivity). Incentive funds were linked to net profit (*Nettogewinn*: gross profit minus the capital charge) and the other indicators – the bonus fund was reduced when the wage fund was overdrawn, for example. There was thus room for increased micro decision-making in areas such as investment, product and input mix, composition and organization of the labour force, contracts, and foreign trade. Enterprises were able, for example, to conclude short term foreign trade contracts not anticipated in the plan, provided they were approved by the foreign trade organ and did not adversely affect other planned export obligations and other plan targets. They received the right to employ convertible currencies for imports on overfulfilling export plans or underusing planned allowances by means of import substitution or cheaper purchasing. Hard currency credits were available for imports if future export sales were made possible. The decentralization of decision-making is particularly stressed by Granick, who describes the situation in mid-1970 as profit 'satisficing' (Granick 1975: 212). Keren also talks of lower bodies deciding on the more routine, operational matters, while major, strategic decisions remained with the state (Keren 1973: 557).

Indirect steering of decentralized activity was to be achieved via economic levers (*ökonomische Hebel*): thus, for example, decentralized investment was to be influenced by differentiated net profit deductions, the capital charge, and the availability and cost of credit. Parsons (1986: 36) notes that the NES saw an increase in negotiated credit conditions, while branch and district offices of the State Bank had the power to choose which projects to finance and each office was evaluated on the basis of its earnings in line with the self-financing principle – in and after the NES credit was granted to the enterprise as a whole, rather than for a particular product as previously (p. 37). The 'principle of earning one's own resources' (*das Prinzip der Eigenerwirtschaftung der Mittel*) meant that enterprises and VVBs should not only cover current expenditure from their own revenue, but that investment was no longer to be financed exclusively from budgetary grants (as previously), but out of profit, depreciation allowances, and interest-bearing credits. The 'unitary enterprise result' (*das einheitliche Betriebsergebnis*) for exporting enterprises involved the direct influence of foreign as opposed to domestic prices. The enterprise contract system was improved, violations involving price discounts and reimbursements for losses incurred.

The capital charge (*Produktionsfondsabgabe*: production fund levy) on the gross value of the fixed and working capital of an enterprise, to encourage greater efficiency, was introduced into industry from the beginning of 1967, with differentiated rates of 1, 4, and 6 per cent. With the exception of agricul-

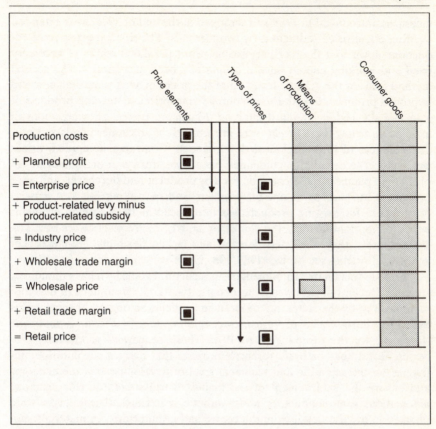

Figure 7.1 GDR: the price structure of producer and consumer goods

Source: Lexicon der Wirtschaft-Preise, East Berlin, 1979, p. 175; cited by Melzer in Jeffries *et al.* (1987: 145).

ture, it was made a uniform 6 per cent after 1971.

The period 1964–67 saw a three-stage *price reform*, moving time-wise from raw materials and materials, from semi-finished products to finished products, with prices rising by 70 per cent, 40 per cent and 4 per cent for each group respectively on average. These prices replaced the old system, largely based on 1944 prices. Figure 7.1 (relating to the late 1970s, strictly) shows the main price elements involved with producer and consumer goods, with wholesale price (still) based on an average cost plus markup basis.

In 1968 the 'capital-related price' (*fondsbezogener Preistyp*) was introduced. This involved a percentage profit markup (maximum 18 per cent) on the *necessary* (as opposed to actual) capital input (based on the experience of the most efficient enterprise in a product group).[9] This price type covered about a third of industrial production by the end of 1970. 'Price dynamization' measures, introduced in 1968 and scrapped at the end of 1970, were intended to bring about price reductions by two methods. The first expected price reductions down to a floor of permissible profit per 1,000 marks of necessary fixed and working capital once a ceiling had been exceeded.[10] The second method foresaw the gradual lowering of the prices of what were then new and improved products, in order to encourage enterprises to develop products of a technically higher standard later on. Maximum prices, allowing room to manoeuvre below these levels, were introduced for consumer goods and products subject to rapid technical development. 'Contractually agreed' prices were subject to calculation guidelines, but allowed for lower or higher rates of profit than planned; these could be fixed by producer and purchaser, and were prominent in spare parts, one-off products, and special machines. A general price freeze for existing products was introduced in 1971. Pricing problems were an important factor in the demise of the NES, since prices were based on average costs, they neglected demand and lacked flexibility. (For excellent analyses of pricing see Melzer 1983, 1987a, 1987b.)

The state was unable to implement its structural goals by means of indirect steering. Decentralized investment departed markedly from lines of development desired by the state, due to inefficient prices, among other things. This led to the introduction of *'structure-determining tasks'* (*strukturbestimmende Aufgaben*) for the period 1968 to 1970. These concerned production, processes, investment or basic research projects that exert a revolutionary influence on the scientific and technical level of development of the economy and ensure the achievement of the highest world standards (for example, automation, semi-conductors and synthetic materials). These tasks were planned in precise detail from the centre and given priority in materials supply. Not unexpectedly, the relative neglect of non-priority tasks led to bottlenecks and shortages, rebounded on the priority sectors, and thus aggravated an already acute supply problem.

The period of recentralization 1971-79

While lacking a new theoretical basis, the period saw a distinct shift back to the pre-NES situation, although significant elements remained, such as the capital charge, parts of fund formation and the principle of earning one's own resources. There was an increase in the degree of centralized decision-making, in the realm of product assortment and investment for example, and in the number of plan indicators, number of employees as well as the wage fund for example. The main role of profit was simply to satisfy the financial requirements of the plan.

On 3 May 1971 Erich Honecker replaced Walter Ulbricht as First Secretary of the SED and at the Eighth Congress of the SED (15-19 June 1971) three leading tasks were set:

1. The 'chief task' (*Hauptaufgabe*) was a quantitative and qualitative improvement in the supply of consumer goods.
2. The need for all-round 'intensification' (output increased mainly by means of the more efficient utilization of existing factors of production, especially through technical progress; the term was first used in the early 1960s).
3. An active social policy, which included a massive housing programme (1976–90), and numerous individual measures, such as increased pensions and reductions in working hours for shift workers.

There was a close linkage between these goals. The slogan 'unity of economic and social policy' was coined and awarded a prominent place in the party programme at the Ninth Congress of the SED in May 1976. This linkage helped compensate for the lack of a new theoretical basis and provided a central theme for the new Honecker era. The party leadership was careful to make the 'chief task' conditional upon the success of intensification, but the 'unity of economic and social policy' showed that the time had come to reward the relatively neglected consumer, provide incentives for increased effort and illustrate the virtues of socialism. Baylis (1986: 388) describes this idea as a sort of 'social contract' in which the state offers material benefits and other improvements in the quality of life in exchange for hard work and political loyalty. The disturbances in Poland in 1970 reinforced the importance of the present.

The raw material-poor GDR was battered by the increases in energy and raw material prices after the 1973–74 oil shock, though delayed by the Comecon pricing system. The GDR's response was to avoid any fundamental revision of the recentralized economic system. Domestic prices were increased in stages from 1976 onwards to reflect rising import prices, a lower priority was given to consumption and a slightly higher one to exports (although the 'chief task' was not formally abandoned), and resort was made to heavy borrowing from the West. The 1970s economic system did not overcome the fundamental problems afflicting the GDR economy and proved unable to provide the necessary 'intensification' of the economy.

The 1980s

The 1980s have seen the GDR coping with severe foreign trade and payments problems, with the enhanced need for 'intensification' pursued by means of the combine (*Kombinat*) and the 'perfecting' of the economic mechanism.[12]

The 1973–74 oil price shock was followed by that of 1979. The accumulated trade deficit for the years 1976–80 amounted to just under VM 29 billion, VM 25 billion with Western countries and VM 9 billion with the Soviet Union; there were surpluses with some East European countries. (Valuta Mark, foreign currency mark, is used in the presentation of the GDR's foreign trade results; currently 1 VM = 0.74 DM.) It took from the mid-1970s to 1984 for the GDR to restore an annual trade surplus with the Soviet Union, while indebtedness to the West rose from $6.76 billion in 1977 to a peak of $11.67 billion in 1981 (when the debt-service ratio was 35 per cent) and then fell to $6.83 billion in 1985 (Cornelsen 1987: 52).[13] In the early 1980s the GDR was also caught in the backwash of Poland and Romania's international debt problems, which led to Western banks' restrictions on credit, and suffered a 10 per cent fall in Soviet oil deliveries (down from around 19 to 17 million tonnes in 1982) coupled with lagged price rises. In 1984 the price of Soviet oil was 183 transferable roubles a tonne, compared with an average of 52 TR over the period 1976–80 (Klein 1987: 274). These foreign trade and payments problems enhanced the need for all-around intensification, in order to make more efficient use of factor inputs ('improving the relationship between expenditure and result'), for increased domestic output of energy and raw materials and a reduction in imports. Note that although producer prices of energy were raised after 1976, the GDR was the only CMEA country not to change its prices and rates for energy consumption to private households (Bethkenhagen 1987: 61).

The 1981–85 five year plan targets were set surprisingly high.[14] Furthermore, growth was to be achieved with no increase in inputs (i.e. achieved by means of intensification). Given the unwillingness to demote consumption seriously (note the rise of Solidarity in Poland) and to sacrifice defence spending, it was investment that suffered; 1982, 1983 and 1984 were years of negative growth. This stored up trouble for the future, hampering structural change and technical innovation.

In view of these ambitious targets, an 'economic strategy for the 1980s' was developed and expounded by Honecker at the party congress in April 1981, essentially revolving around intensification. The limited investment for expansion purposes was to be concentrated on a small number of priority projects in sectors involving key modern technologies: by 'key' technologies are meant micro-electronics, CAD/CAM (computer-aided-design and manufacturing), modern computer technology, automated production systems, industrial robots, biotechnology, laser technology, and new processes and materials. The emphasis, however, should be on the renovation and modernization of the existing capital stock. Along with the acceleration of scientific-technical progress (broad application of micro-electronics and robots, for example), stress was to be increasingly placed on the quality of and value added to products.

Given the deficiencies of the 1970s recentralized system and an unwillingness to return to an NES-type system (decentralization of decision-making without radical price reform would lead to serious divergences between the lines of development preferred by the state and those by the production units, for example), intensification was sought in a substitute model that eschewed radical price reform and decentralization worth talking about, but which would hopefully raise productivity. The answer was seen in making the combine the main production unit and in the 'perfecting' (*Vervollkommnung*) of the economic mechanism.

The combine

Combines[15] were not around in significant numbers until 1968–69; existing combines were used to help implement 'structure-determining tasks'. Acceleration during the third wave of combine formation (1978–80), however, saw it established as the basic production unit (combine decree of 1979). By 1981 combine formation was essentially completed, with 133 *Kombinate* in centrally directed industry and construction. These vary in size from 2,000 to 80,000 employees, with an average of 25,000, and constitute 20–40 enterprises (Bryson and Melzer, 1987: 52). According to Stahnke (1987: 29), the average in industry is 25,000 to 30,000 employees and 20 to 30 enterprises (in construction 10,000 and 15, respectively). By 1986 the number had fallen to 127; there were also 94 combines in regionally directed industry, with an average of some 2,000 employees and producing mainly consumer goods.

The combine is a horizontal and vertical amalgamation of enterprises, under the unified control of a director general. The 'parent enterprise' (*Stammbetrieb*: enterprises under the direction of a dominant parent enterprise) is increasingly the most important organizational type and is destined to be the sole one. Other types include enterprises under the direction of an independent management body; management carried out by a group of the leading enterprises in various product groups; and a single large enterprise.

The activities of a combine span the whole range from R&D, in order to encourage innovation, to marketing, so as to improve quality. The vertical element involves the incorporation of the most important supplier enterprises, with the aim of improving the acute supply problems that afflict command economies. The combine is seen as a means of streamlining the command economy, rather than replacing it, by, for example, reducing the number of production units to be centrally directed and allowing central bodies and ministries to concentrate on 'strategic' matters. For example, the director-general has to report each investment of more than 5 million marks, without a maximum value in the case of certain projects, to the SPC, which also specifies the contractors (Tröder 1987: 88). According to Cornelsen (1987: 46), the combines' share of total investment in equipment increased from 14 per cent in 1980 to 34 per cent in 1985. Note that major investment projects of national importance are in large measure centrally planned and major percentages of their finances are covered by budgetary grants (Parsons 1986: 33). Further advantages are seen in the following:

1. improving information relating to actual production processes, the combines having to submit their plan drafts not only to the competent

minister, but also to the SPC, the Ministry of Finance, and the State Bank;
2. the reaping of economies of scale;
3. concentrating production;
4. making a more rational use of materials;
5. encouraging innovation and the modernization of assets by the in-house manufacture of rationalization equipment and parts;
6. improving the supply of consumer goods by the combines ultimately having to devote at least 5 per cent of output to consumer goods;
7. improving foreign trade decision-making; and
8. aiding labour redeployment and retraining.

The broad targets passed down by ministries allow room for manoeuvre, but monitoring bodies keep a close and frequent check on plan fulfilment. Stahnke (1987: 31) lists the sort of limitations placed upon combines: no uni-lateral increases in investment or other inputs; requirements to increase the production of consumer goods, achieve product and process changeovers of the order of 30 per cent a year, reduce stocks, reduce transport costs and in-crease shift work.[16] There are ten industrial ministries, Coal and Energy hav-ing the most (22) combines and Machine Tools and Processing Equipment having the fewest (6) (Stahnke 1987: 29).

In 1981–82, in order to encourage exports and to improve knowledge about international markets, 24 foreign trade enterprises were placed under the joint jurisdiction of the Ministry of Foreign Trade (MFT) and the particular combine whose production profile matched that of the exports. Twenty with export ranges dissimilar to those of any combine were subject to the joint jurisdiction of the MFT and an appropriate industrial ministry. The situation in 1986 was that 64 foreign trade enterprises were divided into five groupings: 23 subject to the dual authority of the MFT and the particular combine; 12 subject to the dual authority of the MFT and the appropriate industrial min-istry; 12 also subject to the dual authority of the MFT and the industrial min-istry, but whose enterprises have been reorganized into 61 foreign trade units, without legal rights of their own, which are supposed to co-operate with com-bines; seven enterprises and combines empowered to engage directly in foreign trade transactions; and ten still subject to the direct and sole authority of the MFT. Note that although this arrangement erodes the strict separation of production and foreign trade, which is a feature of the traditional Soviet model, all foreign trade enterprises are still ultimately supervised by the MFT (Jacobsen 1987; Klein 1987).

The director-general of the combine is responsible for disaggregating the plan tasks received via the ministry to its own enterprises. The decision-mak-ing rights of the combine have increased with respect to both latter organiza-tions. Although the enterprise remains a legally independent unit and is able to draw up contracts with other enterprises both within and without the com-bine, the director-general of the combine is authorized to transfer tasks, functions and plant from one enterprise to another, to hire and fire enterprise managers, and to create new enterprise divisions.

Possible disadvantages of combine formation are: (1) the adverse effects on innovation of monopolies and the diminution of cross-branch co-operation; and (2) related to enterprise decision-making rights: the division of authority between enterprise and combine is not always clear, but the former has certainly lost out significantly; there is always the danger of a parent enterprise appropriating advantageous portions of a programme to itself.

Perfecting of the economic mechanism (direct and indirect steering)

Direct steering

The system of material balancing was further refined with the aim of increasing consistency and flexibility.[17] In 1982–83 roughly 76 per cent of production (and 87 per cent of foreign trade) was centrally determined in 2,136 balances, while a further 2,400 balances (some 24 per cent of production) were drawn up by the authorized combines and confirmed by the competent director-general. By 1986 the respective totals were 1,135 (451 state plan balances, dealing with goods described as of national economic importance, and 684 drawn up by ministries) and 3,400.

In 1982 the system of norms and normatives (upper limits for the use of specific materials in the shape of obligatory state targets), designed to reduce materials use, was reviewed, tightened and extended. The success indicator system was also amended (see Table 7.2).

On 1 January 1979 the 'final product' (*Endprodukt*) indicator was introduced for combines, equal to commodity production less deliveries of intermediate inputs between enterprises within a combine. This was done in order to reduce materials use and prevent commodity production being inflated by intra-combine transactions. But the problem of inefficient subcontracting outside the combine led to its replacement by a new indicator called 'net production' (commodity production minus all deliveries of intermediate inputs, including those from outside the combine: see Table 7.2 for details). At the same time another new indicator called 'basic materials costs per 100 marks of commodity production' was introduced. Since 1983 the following, designed to improve materials use and the relationship between expenditure and use, have been regarded as the main indicators: 'net production' (*Nettoproduktion*); 'net profit' (*Nettogewinn*: see Table 7.3); 'products and services for the population' (*Erzeugnisse und Leistungen für die Bevölkerung*) and 'exports' (*Export*). These replaced the former main indicators 'industrial commodity production' (*industrielle Warenproduktion*): a measure of gross output that tended to encourage production regardless of costs and sales) and 'basic materials costs per 100 Marks of commodity production' (*Grundmaterialkosten je 100 Mark Warenproduktion*). At present there are about 100 indicators in centrally directed industry. Table 7.2 shows the other important indicators now in operation, including the somewhat relegated cost indicators.

Table 7.2 The GDR: indicators of performance evaluation in industrial combines and enterprises

Regulation of June 1980	Regulation of April 1981	Regulation of March 1983
Basic indicators of perfor-mance evaluation	*Basic indicators of perfor-mance evaluation*	*Basic indicators of per-formance evaluation*
Industrial commodity production	Industrial commodity production	
Net production[a]	Net production[a]	Net production[a]
Basic materials cost per 100 marks of com-modity production[b]	Basic materials costs per 100 marks of com-modity production[b]	Net profit[c] Products and services for the population Exports
Further qualitative criteria	*Further qualitative in-dicators*	*Further important qualitative indicators*
Net profit[c]	Enterprise result	Labour productivity on the basis of net production
Increase in labour produc-tivity	Increase in labour produc-tivity	
Reduction in the cost of production	Reduction in the cost of production	Costs per 100 marks of commodity production
Proportion of products with quality labels	Proportion of products with quality labels	Production of products im-portant in national economic terms, espe-cially newly developed products and products with quality labels
Production meeting con-tractual obligations for domestic use and ex-ports	Production meeting con-tractual obligations for domestic use and ex-ports	
	Completion of investment projects/objects on time and meeting quality requirements	Materials costs per 100 marks of commodity production[b]

Sources: Scherzinger, A., 'Weiterentwicklung des Wirtschaftsmechanismus in der DDR', In *Wochenbericht des DIW* (1983): no. 41, p. 510; cited by Melzer, in Jeffries, Melzer, and Breuning (1987: 104).

Notes: a. 'Net production' (simplified) = commodity production *minus* consumption of materials (basic materials, energy, other materials), *minus* consumption of productive services (bought-in services, repairs, transport and warehousing costs, other productive services), *minus* rents and leases, *minus* depreciation.
b. In the GDR the concept 'basic materials' (*Grundmaterial*) comprises all the man-made objects that form the material substance of the product. It is thus only part of the wider concept 'materials', which comprises basic materials, energy, water, fuel, lubricants, and other materials.
c. 'Net profit' (simplified): unitary enterprise result of the enterprise or combine (i.e. including foreign trade profits and losses), *plus* subventions in accordance with statutory provisions, *minus* capital charge, *minus* profits not earned by own economic performance, *minus* profits from exceeding manpower plan, *minus* fines, transferred to state budget.

Indirect steering

If planned profit (note that impermissible profit, stemming from violations of price or quality regulations, is confiscated) is not achieved, there not only arise financing problems and adverse effects on fund formation, but access to funds such as those relating to performance and investment can be blocked altogether. In the event of overfulfilling profit targets, especially if connected with exports, a higher proportion than in the past can now flow into incentive funds. Planned 'net profit deductions' have now to be met in full even in the event of a profit shortfall, previously a part being remitted. Enterprises are, consequently, now obliged to draw on their funds or to turn to credits, although the quantity of credit is conditional upon proof of remedial action. If the net profit deductions are not realized promptly, and in full, the competent bank is authorized to deduct the sum due from the relevant account of the offending combine or enterprise. Incentive funds, linked to the success indicators, are designated for specific purposes and closely monitored.[18]

The capital charge is designed to encourage early completion of projects and to deter delays. With early commissioning of new plant, the charge has only to be paid from the date of the planned start, while an extra 6 per cent penalty is imposed in the event of not meeting plan deadlines, of excess stocks and of idle plant. Since 1986, the capital charge has been based on the net as opposed to gross value of fixed and working capital to encourage the retention in use of older capital assets. This has been accomplished by imposing a lower capital charge on older equipment.

Credit policy is also employed to achieve the desired state goals. The standard rate of interest is 5 per cent, but penalty rates of up to 12 per cent may be charged on overdue repayments, while the rate may be as low as 1.8 per cent, for credits used for the introduction of new key technologies for example (Buck 1987: 190).

An important innovation is the 'contribution for social funds' (*Beitrag für gesellschaftliche Fonds*), which was introduced in industry at the start of 1984, in construction, foodstuffs and water supply at the beginning of 1985 and in transport and forestry the following year. This is essentially a payroll tax of 70 per cent of the wage fund, designed to promote a more efficient use of labour by raising its cost and to contribute to the financing of social services such as education, housing and health. For new products this contribution is included in the fixing of their prices (not reduced if manpower is decreased, thus providing the incentive), but for existing products the previous prices continue to apply until subject to a general revision. In the meantime, a revenue supplement is allowed, but this covers only a part of the levy in order to retain some pressure for increased efficiency.

The increase in the number of regulations and in the power of combines has led to a corresponding enhancement of the role of monitoring bodies, in order to prevent departures from state goals.[19]

Price determination

Since 1976 there have been annual, staged price revisions, reflecting increases in the cost of energy and raw materials.[20] The pricing of new and improved products in accordance with the 'price-performance relationship' (*Preis-Leistungs-Verhältnis*), introduced in 1976, was abandoned in late 1983. This was a form of analogue pricing, relating to the improvement in use value characteristics compared with the most analogous existing product. Manufacturers were allowed to reflect 70 per cent of the improvement in price and consumers benefited to the tune of 30 per cent, while additional profit to manufacturers was only allowed for two years and removed over the following three. It was abandoned because of the lack of objective criteria for measuring use value, and, above all, the strong tendency of enterprises to overstate improvements. The prices of new products are at present determined on the basis of calculable costs, including the contribution for social funds, taking into account the price limit set in the development stage and the prevailing norms for input use. Since 1986 extra profits have been allowed for two years in order to stimulate innovation (previously it was three years), depending on efficiency criteria such as the level of export profitability. For commodities already in production, the position from 1976 onwards was that cost reductions achieved by manufacturers (via reductions in materials usage for example) within a five year plan period did not result in lower prices. Since 1984 they remain unchanged until a general, planned price revision. Goods with quality labels are allowed a 2 per cent markup. For goods sold in *exquisit* and *delikat* shops (special shops where quality GDR and Western goods are sold for GDR marks at relatively high prices) much higher profit supplements are allowed, and spare parts are also permitted higher supplements. On the other hand, price discounts penalize below-standard goods. During 1988 new regulations were introduced that are designed to encourage consumer goods production: combines that agree to manufacture goods in short supply are allowed a 20 per cent markup on the normal wholesale price; an extra 10 percent is added if the goods are delivered before the contract date, but failure to deliver seasonal goods on time results in a lower price; retail prices are unaffected (reported by Leslie Colitt in *FT*, 4 August 1988, p. 2; see also Jan Vanous in *Soviet Studies*, 1988, vol. 4, no. 3, p. 188). According to the 1985 regulations for new products, a portion of the cost reductions achieved during the first two years has to benefit users in the form of a price reduction. After this time extra profit has to be given up and prices may no longer exceed the price limit. After two years the price is to be fixed as the level of expenditure accepted by state bodies, including normal profit (Melzer 1987b: 15–6).

The GDR policy of preventing increases in retail prices was amended substantially in 1979. Basic foodstuffs (such as bread, potatoes, fish, meat and bakery products), children's clothing, housing rents and transport fares, remain immune from increases for political and distributional reasons. For example, bus and train fares have not changed since 1949, while rent takes only about 3 per cent of urban household income. But the prices of high quality industrial consumer goods, such as televisions, cars, refrigerators, washing machines, and cameras which are already heavily taxed, now have to cover costs and allow for a normal profit.

It is worth noting that on 1 January 1965 compensation became payable to owners and agricultural producers when land was used for non-agricultural purposes. This was followed in 1968 by the introduction of a charge for the use of land removed from agriculture and forestry, differentiated according to the quality of land and the subsequent use, and reflected in an increased capital charge. A charge for the use of water was also introduced in 1971. All these measures are aimed at increasing efficiency in resource utilization. In the event of emission norms being exceeded, charges for water and air pollution were introduced in 1971 and 1973 respectively. While payments for the use of land and water are included in the planned costs of production (unless norms are exceeded), the payments for excessive pollution are not, thereby reducing enterprise profit and incentive funds (Debardeleben 1985: 159).

Summary of the reforms

The present 'perfecting' strategy is clearly not based on any new theoretical blueprint, but judgements on its result have been varied. Hamel and Leipold (1987, Chapter 14), following Höhmann, succinctly lay out the opposing 'Popperian' and 'Krylov' theses. The Popperian thesis, following Karl Popper's reform strategy of piecemeal social engineering, holds that step-by-step improvements are possible in command economies (see, for example, Cornelsen, Melzer and Scherzinger). The Krylov thesis is based on the Russian poet's fable of four animal musicians who kept swapping seats but in vain as far as musical harmony was concerned. This doubts the possibility of an economically efficient amendment of a command economy, rather like Gertrude Schroeder's view of Soviet economic changes. She describes them as a 'treadmill' of reform, unable to solve basic problems because the system itself remains basically unchanged (Schroeder 1986).

Agriculture

Agriculture employs around 11 per cent of the labour force.[21] Co-operative farmers dominate GDR agriculture, in 1985 accounting for about 87 per cent of total LN (*Landwirtschaftliche Nutzfläche*: land used for agricultural purposes), 89 per cent of livestock and 80 per cent of the capital stock in agriculture (Merkel 1987: 218–19). Thus, the state farm (*Volkseigenes Gut*) plays a much smaller role in the GDR than in the Soviet Union, many state farms being involved in research and breeding.

The dominant production unit is the agricultural producer co-operative (*Landwirtschaftliche Produktionsgenossenschaft*). This large unit (in 1985 1,369 hectares of LN on average, 4,608 hectares in crop production) is modelled on the Soviet collective farm and is subject to state plans and procurement quotas. But there are differences. For example, while all land is owned by the state in the Soviet Union, the figure is only 30 per cent in the GDR. Land ownership in the GDR co-operative is a mixture of co-operative and private. Although the right to the use of land (with the exception of the private plot) belongs to the co-operative, individuals are compensated when land is used for industrial purposes and when land shares are paid off. As far as individual contributions in the form of machines, livestock and buildings were concerned, these became co-operative property, although there could be partial compensation if minimum levels were exceeded.

The basic form of labour organization is the brigade, subdivided into divisions and these, in turn, into 'work groups'. Remuneration is mainly based on the 'work unit'. The individual work unit is influenced by factors such as the degrees of responsibility and difficulty of the particular type of work. Its final value is not known until the end-of-year accounts are done, and the total number of work units is divided into net income. This residual form of income is ameliorated by the fact that advances are made to co-operative members. There have also been experiments to compensate members along state sector lines.

As far as pricing policy is concerned, in order to increase efficiency of resource use, the government has adopted a policy of increasing producer prices and reducing subsidies on agricultural inputs. This culminated in the 1 January 1984 price reform, which led to an average price increase of 60 per cent in product prices and the ending, more or less, of subsidies on factor inputs such as feedstuffs, machinery, fuels, mineral fertilizers and construction materials. The crop producing co-operative is now also subject to a fixed levy per hectare of LN, differentiated according to land quality, poor quality land being exempted and some farms even receiving a grant. Co-operatives also pay a progressive profit tax.

History

The *land reform* of 1945–52 confiscated about two-thirds of the land from those possessing more than 100 hectares, excluding the church, distributed in the shape of small farms, while a number of landed estates became state farms. There was also confiscation of the land owned by those described as Nazi activists and war criminals.

Collectivization took place from 1952 until the spring of 1960. Co-operatives accounted for 37 per cent of agricultural land at the end of 1958 and 84.2 per cent at the end of 1960 (Childs 1987: 7). Originally there were three types of agricultural co-operative (I, II and III), but Type III gradually replaced the others. In Type I members only contribute land, with livestock and the means of production remaining individually controlled. In Type II livestock, except draught animals, remains privately owned.

Reorganization began in the early 1970s, with the aim of applying industrial methods to agriculture. At present large, specialized (on crop production or animal husbandry) entities dominate. There are now, however, experiments with 'co-operation councils' to try to overcome the problems of such a division. These councils comprise representatives of the crop and animal husbandry entities and seek to co-ordinate their activities and have, since 1984, acted as a channel for the plans passed on by the district council. These entities evolved out of non-specialized production units. Inter-enterprise (co-operative and state) co-operation in various forms arose: e.g. the Co-operative Division for Crop Production: these were mainly transformed into specialized agricultural co-operatives during the latter half of the 1970s. There gradually emerged out of this the independent, specialized units of today. Inter-enterprise co-operation today takes the form of organizations like the agro-chemical centres. These supply and apply chemical fertilizers and plant pest control agents, and are also increasingly involved in seeding. In addition there are inter-enterprise organizations involved in livestock.

There are also other organizations of note. The district enterprises for rural technology maintain and repair agricultural machinery. The Machine Tractor Stations were abolished in 1963 and their machinery and equipment transferred to co-operatives. In addition there are factory farming combines under county control. These are mostly concerned with poultry and eggs, but some with pork and beef. After the Ninth Congress of the SED in 1976, eleven agro-industrial associations were set up (involving, for example, crop production, fodder plants, agro-chemical centres and land improvement enterprises) as a step on the way towards the formation of an agro-industrial complex.

Private production

In 1985 the private sector accounted for 9 per cent of arable land (Cochrane 1988: 48). Brezinski (1987: 87) reveals that there were 5,900 private farms in 1985 and some farms owned by the church. Individual farming accounted for 1.5 per cent of the agricultural labour force and 3.7 per cent of the net output of agriculture and forestry. In 1977 the private plot of individual members of agricultural co-operatives was fixed at 0.25 hectares (with a family maximum of 0.5 hectares) and restrictions were lifted on the amount of livestock: in 1983 these plots amounted to 3.8 per cent of total LN. There are also the small gardens of the members of the association of small gardeners, settlers and small animal-breeders (VKSK), accounting for 0.9 per cent of LN in 1985. Private plots and VKSK gardens (but not private farms) are entitled to a taxfree income of 7,000 marks annually (Brezinski 1987: 97). Private production is particularly important for certain commodities such as meat (more than 20 per cent of total output in 1985) and eggs and fruit (more than 50 per cent) (p. 88). According to the *DIW Handbuch* (1985: 188) private holdings account for approximately 5 per cent of total livestock: horses, 33 per cent; sheep, 15 per cent; pigs, 10 per cent; poultry, 25 per cent; and rabbits almost 100 per cent. About 30 per cent of fruit, 11 per cent of vegetables and 100 per cent of honey are privately produced.

International trade

GDR data are given in VMs and for total turnover only. Neither the rate of exchange between the VM and the domestic mark nor the one between the VM and the transferable rouble is made known officially.

In 1980 around 30 per cent of produced national income was exported (*DIW Handbuch* 1985: 294). Comecon accounts for about 63 per cent of GDR trade (the GDR some 16 per cent of intra-Comecon trade, second to the Soviet Union) and the Soviet Union alone about 39 per cent.[22] The GDR is a major supplier of relatively high-quality, high technology capital goods (e.g. machine tools,[23] robots and computers) to Comecon and is heavily dependent on imports of fuels and raw materials, especially from the Soviet Union. Of the approximately 23 million tonnes of GDR oil imports, 17 Mt come from the Soviet Union. Since domestic consumption is only about 10 Mt, GDR exports of oil and oil products to the West constitute an important source of hard currency earnings, especially given the difficulty of selling manufactured goods in Western markets. The exact amount of oil re-exported is the subject of controversy; it is significantly affected by the world price of oil and the value of the US dollar. Specialization agreements within Comecon have affected the GDR. In 1971, for example, the GDR agreed to cease production of trams in exchange for passenger cars.

The GDR has been granted valuable special concessions in its trade with the Federal Republic. Note that the latter refers to its exports to the GDR as 'deliveries' and its imports from the GDR as 'purchases'. Apart from the obvious ties of nationality, the FRG considers close economic links and increasing GDR living standards as important for Western security, while the GDR is a reluctant participant in Soviet plans to increase intra-Comecon links, providing the Soviet Union with top quality manufactures in return for stable supplies of energy and raw materials. Note, however, that the relative impact of inner-German trade varies, the GDR only accounting for 1.6 per cent of the FRG's foreign trade in 1986, while the FRG accounted for around 14 per cent of the GDR's foreign trade (Schäuble 1988: 213). GDR exports to the FRG are allowed in free of tariffs and levies and the GDR enjoys value added tax concessions, the West German importer being able to obtain a tax refund for the VAT on imports. The 'swing' provides an interest-free overdraft facility up to a certain limit, raised from DM 600 million to DM 800 million in July 1985, which thus allows a delay in repaying the deficit until the annual settlement. The government of the FRG guarantees West German bank credits to the GDR, while GDR exports of foodstuffs even escaped the post-Chernobyl restrictions. As Baylis points out, West German credits during the Western squeeze helped re-establish East German creditworthiness, while the FRG supplies vital producer goods, emergency materials and spare parts to help overcome shortages and bottlenecks (Baylis 1986: 418). The GDR also has valuable sources of hard currency earnings in the following: transit and road facilities to and services provided for West Berlin; the Genex-Geschenkdienst (handling gifts from the West to GDR citizens of goods and services produced in the GDR, Comecon or the West); Intertank (convertible currency service stations); 'intershops' (convertible currency shops); and the 'sale' of prisoners. (David Marsh, *FT Supplement*, 16 April 1988, p.I, provides the following information: the buying of prisoners began in 1963 and has cost the FRG more than DM 1 billion to date. The first exchange in 1963 involved eight persons costing DM 360,000. The number of releases was 880 in 1964, 1,160 in 1965 and then averaged around 1,500 annually up to 1987. The present price is DM 90,000–100,000 per head, with the proceeds placed in a special account in Stuttgart run by a charity belonging to the Protestant church, from which the GDR draws cash to pay for goods. Amnestied prisoners allowed to emigrate cost a few thousand DM per head.) It has been estimated that in the mid-1980s the total value of fees, concessions, gifts and so on from the FRG amounted to around 1.5 per cent of the GDR's GNP calculated on a Western basis (Marer 1986c: 613). The *Verrechnungseinheit* (VE; settlement unit) is the clearing unit of account used in trade between the two countries. Its value corresponds to that of the DM, but note that VEs earned by the GDR can only be used for purchases in the FRG.

The GDR seems to be reluctant to increase its involvement in direct links between enterprises within Comecon. In 1987 such an agreement was reached, for example, between a Soviet and an East German enterprise to develop a micro-electronic sewing machine, but GDR reluctance seems to stem from the failure of a joint project to develop a programmable washing machine (see Leslie Colitt, *FT*, 22 July 1987, p. 2).

The GDR is now isolated among the East European Comecon states in not allowing joint equity ventures with Western companies. This is possibly due to apprehension about the prospect of a sizeable influx of West German capital, technology and know-how, which may perhaps be seen as an admission of domestic economic failure. It is of interest to note that the GDR remains the only country not to have settled historical claims with Britain – the Soviet Union, China and Bulgaria, for example, have done so in recent years. Official policy is to finance imports from the West by means of exports, thus avoiding any general increase in borrowing. A joint venture with the Soviet Union to produce computer software was announced in March 1989.

The non-state, non-agricultural sector

Åslund (1985) has analysed the non-agricultural sector. He estimates that in 1979 the private sector contributed 3 per cent of net material product outside agriculture and employed 5.2 per cent of the non-agricultural labour force. Following the early nationalization measures there was a falling trend with cycles: a socialist offensive (1952–3), relatively late because of the uncertainty surrounding reunification; a liberal interlude (1953–7); a second socialist offensive (1958–60); a period of successful competition between the state and private sectors during the period of the New Economic System; a third socialist offensive (1971–5), in which the first half of 1972 was especially prominent. The period since 1976 has seen the granting of tax and credit concessions and many new licences for handicrafts, trade and catering. Excluding apprentices, employment in the private trades sector increased by 11,844 to 258,100 between 1980 and 1984. In 1985, 15,000 new licences were granted. The 1986–90 plan foresees further growth of the sector, encouraged by a tax-free two years and low-interest credit.

Brezinski provides figures for the share of private enterprises in national income (in per cent): 1950, 43.2; 1960, 12.5; 1970, 5.5; 1975, 3.4; 1980, 2.9; 1982, 2.8; 1983, 2.8; 1984, 2.8; 1985, 2.8. A sectoral breakdown of the 1985 net output figures show (in per cent): industry (including manufacturing handicrafts, but excluding construction), 2.3; construction, 5.9; agriculture and forestry (excluding household plots), 3.7; domestic trade, 2.7; and transportation, posts and telegraphs, 0.8 (1987: 86). In 1985 private production accounted for 58.9 per cent of handicrafts (manufacturing trades and the services are allowed to employ up to 10 people); retail trade, 5.1 per cent; restaurants, 3.1 per cent; and new houses, 15.1 per cent. Note that private construction enterprises account for around 6 per cent of construction output, but are mainly engaged in repair and renovation, since new private houses are mainly built by individual house owners (Brezinski 1987: 90). 'Groups of supply' are to be found in trades and services, in which a socialized enterprise guides a group of private enterprises with the aim of planning supply and allocating tasks. Chambers of Commerce and of trades (directed by district councils since 1985) are concerned with input supplies to the private sector, price control, quality, wages and the promotion of vocational training (Brezinski 1987: 99). 'After-work brigades' began operating in the 1970s and comprise employees of nationalized enterprises. Wages are legally determined and are exempt from income tax and social security contributions (p. 89). There are also 'DIY organizations' (training centres).

Mention should also be made of the existence of 1. production and trade co-operatives; and 2. semi-state enterprises: these were first set up in 1956, accounted for 10 per cent of industrial production in 1971, and were nationalized the following year (Childs 1987: 9).

Conclusion

The socialist, poorer half of a divided Germany, the GDR has, nevertheless, the highest standard of living in the socialist world. Like Czechoslovakia, the GDR was an industrialized country from the beginning, and the latter continues to benefit from substantial economic concessions granted by the FRG, such as the FRG allowing in East German goods free from tariffs or levies. Particularly important aspects to notice in the chapter are the 1960s New Economic System (the first systematic actual attempt at overall reform in Comecon) and the present stress on improving economic performance by means of the combine and the 'perfecting' of the economic mechanism. The present leadership rejects any radical reform of the economy, shares with Albania the distinction of having no prospective joint equity legislation, but has made a successful attempt at reducing the country's foreign debt. No major changes are likely until 1990 at the earliest, the probable end of the Honecker era. It may be significant that at the start of December 1988 it was announced that the next and Twelfth Party Congress would be brought forward from 1991 to May 1990.

Table 7.3 The GDR: statistical survey

Per capita GNP (1986)	$8,130			
Net hard currency debt ($ billions)	*1977*	*1981*	*1985*	*1986*
	6.8	12.5	6.5	7.9
Private enterprises, including private				
farms (1985) (% national income)	2.8			
Private farming, excluding private				
plots (1985) (% of net output for				
agriculture and forestry)	3.7			
Private sector (1985) (% arable land)	9.0			
Population (end 1986)	16.6 million			

Sources: Brezinski (1977: 86–87); Childs (1987: 17); Cochrane (1988: 448); Cornelsen (1987: 52); Economist Intelligence Unit, *Country Profile* (1987–8: 35).

Note: For rates of growth of produced national income, see Table 7.1, this volume.

Postscript

In May 1989 Hungary began to dismantle its border fence with Austria. This encouraged an additional emigration of East German citizens, mostly young and skilled. In the first eight months of 1989 around 77,000 in total left the GDR (59,320 legally), compared to 39,832 for the whole of 1988. An added stimulus came on 10 September when Hungary announced a suspension of the 1969 agreements with the GDR (which denied permission to each other's citizens to travel to a third country without the required documents). Refugees from the West German embassies in Prague and Warsaw increased the flow.

This emigration is an indication of the need for political and economic reform in the GDR. The leadership, already constrained by the need to maintain its own brand of socialism (as the basis of the very existence of the country), has used controlled emigration as a safety valve for dissent, but the scale of the present illegal outflow can only be deeply worrying to a conservative regime already facing a severe labour shortage.

Notes

1. In 1986 2.3 million East German citizens visited West Berlin and the Federal Republic, including 573,000 below retirement age on officially designated 'urgent family visits'. This latter figure was some 50,000 in 1982, 66,000 in 1985 and 1.2 million in 1987. Around 1.6 million pensioners visit each year, 2.2 million in 1987. The total number of trips may be more than 5 million in 1988, three-quarters by pensioners. In 1987 around 11,459 people were allowed to emigrate to the FRG (plus 5,964 without authority) and 25, 135 in the first 11 months of 1988 (8,388 without authority) (*FT*, 9 December 1988, p. 2). On 1 July 1987, however, the amount of money allowed to be exchanged into DMs before departure was reduced from 70 marks, on a one-for-one basis, to 15 marks. This was done to save on precious hard currency reserves, which is politically more acceptable than restricting the number of visits.
2. Examples include a paid year at home for working mothers after the birth of the first child, which became operative 1 May 1987 (in 1976 this applied to the second child only); higher-quality, non-essential goods to reflect the costs of producing them; increased support for private tradesmen; and more allotments for urban dwellers.
3. For details see *EEN*, 1987 (vol. 1, no. 8).
4. It should be noted, however, that the Federal Republic took in many refugees from the eastern provinces of the Third Reich and paid substantial compensation to Israel.
5. Primary energy consumption in 1984 was as follows: raw lignite, 71 per cent; oil, 11 per cent; natural gas, 10.0 per cent; and nuclear power, 3.0 per cent (Bethkenhagen 1987: 65).
6. The GDR and Czechoslovakia became the chief suppliers of uranium to the Soviet Union after the Second World War.
7. See Leptin and Melzer (1978); Jeffries, Melzer, and Breuning (1987: Chapter 3); Hamel and Leipold (1987).
8. In political terms, Ulbricht envisaged a special path for the GDR, involving a 'socialist human community', which would harness the technical revolution and help harmonize social classes and strata (Dennis 1988: 42).
9. Note that the capital charge was levied on the actual value of fixed and working capital.
10. According to the 1969–70 regulations, enterprises were initially allowed to deduct the full amount of profit loss from net payments due to the state, as an incentive to reduce costs.

11. See Melzer (1982).
12. See Jeffries, Melzer and Breuning (1987: Chapter 4).
13. The *EIU Country Profile* (1987–88, p. 35) estimates the GDR's net hard currency debt to be $12.5 billion in 1981, $6.5 billion in 1985 and $7.9 billion in 1986; this reached $8.7 billion by mid-1987 (*FT*, 4 February 1988, p. 2). It is worth noting Childs' point that by the second half of the 1970s priorities revolved around savings in energy and raw materials and boosting exports, a far more prudent investment policy than Poland's (1987: 63).
14. An annual average rate of growth of produced national income of 5.1–5.4 per cent, for example, compared to a planned figure of 5 per cent and an actual figure of 4.1 per cent over the period 1976–80.
15. See Melzer (1981); Bryson and Melzer (1987); and Stahnke (1987).
16. According to a report on the Textima combine by Leslie Colitt (*FT*, 28 May 1987, p. 2), 70 per cent of workers' wages is based on performance and the Director General is able to increase his salary by 20 per cent depending on results.
17. See Melzer (1987b, 1987c).
18. Combines and selected enterprises are able to finance specific imports from a hard currency fund financed from overfulfilment of export targets.
19. Some new, like the Inspectorate for Quality.
20. See Melzer (1983, 1987a, 1987b).
21. See Merkel (1987); *DIW Handbuch* (1985: Chapter 4.4); Thalheim (1981: Chapter 5).
22. See Jacobsen (1987); Klein (1987); Baylis (1986); UNCTAD (1987).
23. Jost Prescher (head of the GDR's export-import agency) gives the following information relating to machine tools. In 1987 the GDR ranked seventh in the world in terms of machine tools output and fourth in terms of exports. Sixty to seventy per cent of output is exported, although only 10 to 15 per cent of exports go to the West (reported by Nick Garnett in *FT*, 15 November 1988, p. 25).

Chapter eight

Hungary

Political and economic background

Hungary became an independent country in 1918 as a result of the disintegration of the Austro-Hungarian Empire. This country of 10.6 million people is endowed with good climate and soils (about 70 per cent of the land is cultivated), but is mainly poor in raw materials. There are important exceptions, such as bauxite, and coal, uranium and manganese. Oil production reached 2 Mt in 1986, about a fifth of the country's needs. In 1941 25 per cent of the labour force was employed in industry or mining; three years earlier nearly 50 per cent of those employed in industry were in handicrafts (Batt 1988: 51).

Imre Nagy, who was Prime Minister in 1956 until the Soviet invasion, was executed two years later. The trauma of the October-November 1956 revolution (until February 1989 officially described as a 'counterrevolution': the party now views the events as a 'popular uprising' which degenerated into a 'counterrevolution') and Hungary's heavy dependency on foreign trade led to the introduction of a unique economic mechanism. This has, despite difficulties, come under the close scrutiny of Gorbachev's Soviet Union. Immediate political repression was followed by economic reform to provide the material basis for molifying the population and by a process of relative political relaxation, which continues to this day.[1]

At the Thirteenth Party Congress,[2] 25–28 March 1985, Janos Kadar, who became General Secretary of the Hungarian Socialist Workers' Party in 1956, stressed the need to continue with a cautious fine-tuning of the economic reforms despite severe economic difficulties. The latter are illustrated in Table 8.1, which shows falling rates of economic growth,[3] rising inflation and an increasing net hard currency debt (the highest per capita in Eastern Europe). Kadar looked back on five years of hardship and worries since the last congress, during which the living standards of a third of the workers had fallen and those of the remaining two-thirds had stagnated, due to the need to repay the debt. A further round of austerity measures was adopted in September 1987, with consumption planned to fall by 6 to 8 per cent over the following three years and net hard currency indebtedness not to exceed $10 billion by 1990.

Table 8.1 Hungary: inflation, debt, and average annual rate of growth of NMP

Average annual rate of growth of NMP (%)

1951–55	1956–60	1961–65	1966–70	1971–75	1976	1977	1978	1979
13.2	7.6	7.5	6.2	6.4	4.6	6.6	4.9	3.0

1980	1981	1982	1983	1984	1985	1986	1987	1988
−1.6	2.5	2.6	0.4	2.7	−1.2	0.4	3.2	0.5

Inflation (average annual %)

1961	1962	1963	1964	1965	1966	1967	1968	1969	1970	1971	1972	1973
1.0	0.5	−0.7	0.5	1.1	1.8	0.6	0.0	1.3	1.3	2.2	2.8	3.4

1974–80	1987	1988
7.5	9.0	17.0(?)

Net hard currency debt ($ billions)

1970	1981	1982	1985	1986	1987	End September 1988
1.0	7.1	6.6	8.7	12.0	10.9	10.4

Sources: Smith (1983: p. 40); Economist Intelligence Unit *Country Profile* (1987–8: 11, 35); Marrese (1980) in *Economic Reforms in Eastern Europe,* Brussels: NATO, p. 187; *FT,* 16 February 1988, p. 2; *IHT,* 26–7, November 1988, p. 14; Kerpel and Young (1988: 96); *Abecor Country Report,* May 1989, p.1.

Kadar had successfully warded off threats to his position in late 1986 and in the summer of 1988, but he was finally ousted as General Secretary at the end of the special party conference held 20–22 May 1988 – special in the sense that it was the first to be held between the normal four-year conferences. Just short of his 76th birthday, he was nominally compensated with the new honorary post of Party President (losing even this in May 1989). Karoly Grosz (57) was appointed General Secretary, having been made Prime Minister only in June 1987. He remained as the latter until November 1988 when he was replaced by Miklos Nemeth. Rezso Nyers became Minister of State for Economic Affairs. In the new eleven-strong Politburo are liberals such as Imre Pozsgay (President of the People's Patriotic Front) and Rezso Nyers, architect of the original economic reform, who became the Central Committee Secretary in charge of economic affairs in 1962. Sweeping changes in the main party bodies meant substantial losses for the old guard.[4] Although Grosz is recognized as more of a pragmatist than a radical reformer, the future is sure to see moves toward economic and political liberalization, particularly the further withdrawing of the party from the day-to-day running of the economic and political life of the country. An indication of this is to be seen in the two bills passed by Parliament on 11 January 1989 concerning the rights of association and assembly. The former permits the establishment of independent organizations, including trade unions, provided they are not contrary to the constitution. This is to be followed by the submission of another draft bill dealing with the conditions enabling independent political parties to be set up, the formal acceptance of the principle of a multi-party system occurring in February.

The New Economic Mechanism

Although the New Economic Mechanism (NEM) was introduced en bloc on 1 January 1968, there were earlier changes of note. During the first half of the 1960s the number of state industrial enterprises was further reduced from the 1950s, from 1,368 to 840, in order to maintain central control as directive planning was relaxed (Marer 1986a: 244). In the late 1950s and early 1960s the (relatively modest) changes included employee profit sharing schemes, a reduction in the number of enterprise indicators (especially in light industry) and improvements in the determination of prices, to better reflect costs and world levels. In 1964 a 5 per cent charge on the value of fixed and working capital was introduced and treated as a component of costs – this was abolished in 1980.

The NEM has not transformed Hungary into a model of market socialism, where state-owned enterprises operate in a market environment. Although traditional command planning has been abandoned, the state still sets macro targets. There are no longer specific enterprise targets in the annual plan, which includes aggregate targets for magnitudes such as the growth of total output and investment. State enterprises draw up their own output and input plans on the basis of negotiated contracts, but the state employs a 'visible hand' to steer them mainly indirectly via informal pressures and economic levers such as prices, taxes, the cost and availability of credit, tariffs and import licenses. Kornai (1986) describes the system as a combination of certain elements of market co-ordination and, more importantly, indirect bureaucratic control. 'Regulator bargaining' has taken the place of plan bargaining in the sense that the enterprise is vertically dependent on a bureaucracy that makes innumerable micro interventions in areas such as investment, managerial appointments, firms' entry into and exit from industries, subsidies, prices, taxes and credits.

Direct methods include large investment projects in sectors such as energy, mining and infrastructure. The state also reserves the right to issue orders to enterprises as a last resort. Marer describes direct planning in the micro sphere as limited to infrastructural investment, large investments in priority productive sectors, central allocation of a few inputs, administrative regulation of the defence industries and the fulfilment of CMEA obligations. Taxes and subsidies are adjusted to ensure that the enterprise does not lose out financially (Marer 1986a: 240).

Until the mid-1980s state industrial enterprises worked within the constraint of their basic production profiles, although they were permitted to expand and modernize their plants to some degree,[5] to hold (since 1977) a share of the equity of small joint venture subsidiaries and (since 1982) to set up their own subsidiaries, although they are still legally responsible for them. Thus the state sets up large new enterprises and still effectively decides on the closing down of enterprises, control of investment in general being considered necessary to avoid 'capitalist business cycles' and to maintain full employment.[6]

The typical state industrial enterprise has always been relatively large, even though most state enterprises were freed from compulsory membership of trusts or associations in 1968 (Bauer 1988: 453). In 1968 there were only 840 industrial enterprises (Comisso and Marer 1986: 426). Kornai (citing Roman) states that in 1975 the three largest producers accounted for more than two-thirds of production in 508 of 637 industrial product aggregates (Kornai 1986: 1699). In a 1985 unpublished manuscript Kornai (quoted by Bechtold and Helfer 1987: 19) states that only 715 state-owned firms control 93 per cent of industrial output, with 37 per cent of them employing more than 500. Since 1980 many effective monopolies have been split up in order to encourage competition.[7] In the period 1980–85 the number of trusts fell from twenty-four to nine and more than 400 new and independent organizations were created out of this process and out of the division of enterprises (von Czege 1987: 133).

In 1980 the three industrial ministries were merged into a single *Ministry of Industry* in order to reduce ministerial interference and resistence to reform. In December 1987 a ministerial change was announced, including the merger of the Ministry of Trade and the Ministry of Foreign Trade into a new Ministry of Commerce (under Jozsef Marjai), the setting up of the first Environment Ministry, the establishment of the Planning and Economic Commission under Peter Medgessy (combining the functions of the Ministry of Finance and the planning, prices and wages and labour commissions) and the setting up of a new Ministry of Health and Social Affairs under Judit Csehak.

There is some dispute about how important a role *profit* plays in industrial enterprise decision-making, this generally being considered much stronger in agriculture and in the co-operative and private sectors. The introduction of a profits tax in 1968 gave an incentive to increase profits since the enterprise would gain a share (rather than all exceeding incentive funds being transferred to the state budget). Kornai (1986: 1726), however, considers the profit incentive to be weakened by the 'soft budget constraint' and the importance of vertical dependence on the bureaucracy.[8] Crane, on the other hand, has assessed the results of interviews conducted in mid-1982. Rewards for managers are based on the formula $\frac{P}{(W+K)}$ (where P is profits, W is the total wage bill, and K is the enterprise's fixed assets); this determines between a half and three-quarters of bonus income (which itself equals a third to one-half of base salary). On the other hand, superiors' recognition affects career and salary, while a 'complex evaluation' by superiors, involving factors such as plant safety, increasing hard currency exports and decreasing energy use, is also important (Crane 1986: 440). The main aim is to avoid a loss, with its adverse effects on bonuses and possible dismissal (Crane 1986: 442). It is also worth noting that the tax regime that existed before 1 January 1988 meant a sharp difference between gross and net profit, the lack of value-added tax and of a personal income tax placing a large budgetary burden on enterprise profit.

The trend over time has been towards greater refinement of the NEM despite some setbacks. *The period 1972–78*, for example, was one of retrenchment, due to a deteriorating trade and payments situation and the superior performance of small and medium enterprises relative to larger ones. In November 1972, fifty of the largest enterprises (accounting for 50 per cent of industrial output) were subjected to special ministerial supervision and benefited from special concessions. These large enterprises were not happy with smaller ones adversely affecting their supplies of labour and materials. The activities of smaller enterprises were more tightly controlled and some even merged into the larger ones. 'Plan juries' (interministerial, functional and sectoral advisory committees on enterprise plans) were introduced, and emphasis was placed on 'complex evaluation'. This involved such criteria as technological progress and other aspects of long-term development. Other measures included a greater isolation of domestic from world prices and increased use of quantitative regulations such as purchase quotas and central allocations. Macro policy following the 1973–74 oil shock involved increased investment and growth and a switch to CMEA trade, which was to lead to the severe trade and debt problems afflicting Hungary today (Marer 1986a: 246). On the other hand, some individual measures were taken that enriched the reforms. In 1976, for example, the obligatory division of net profit into the enterprise reserve, development, bonus and housing funds was abandoned and replaced by tax regulation (Marer 1986a: 263).

Despite growing external economic problems and others involving inflation, declining growth rates, and living standards for much of the population, and the considerable income and wealth differentials attributable to the operation of the extensive 'second economy',[9] the period since 1979 has seen a return to the path of reform (such as the splitting up of large enterprises and the encouragement given to the private sector) as well as the introduction of austerity measures.

January 1985 marked the start of a two-year *managerial reform*. The largest enterprises, such as those in electric power generation, oil, aluminium, armaments, and transport, are unaffected. Here managers and management staff are still hired or fired by the minister. In medium and certain large enterprises (employing more than 500 workers), however, 'enterprise councils' are formed, comprising representatives of workers and management (employees form at least a half of the membership) and the secretaries of the party, the trade union, and the Communist Youth League. The council elects the managers and staff, but the ministry or local authority (the founding body in other words) has the right to veto the candidacy of aspiring directors and to dismiss any elected director. Formally, the manager is in charge of day-to-day operations, while the council makes 'strategic' decisions. The new management structure is able to decide on such factors as the issue of bonds, asset transfer and mergers with other enterprises (Adam 1987: 612). In enterprises with a work-force of less than 500, the employees themselves (the general assembly or delegated representatives) hire and fire the manager and staff without ministerial interference. In reality, of course, the usual party and state pressures make themselves felt, but it is still worth noting that one of the motivating forces of this reform is to enhance enterprises' independence from ministries.

Since January 1982 *private work partnerships* ('enterprise contract work associations') have been allowed in state enterprises, groups of workers are able to rent equipment at negotiated rates for work after normal hours to fulfil contracts with their own enterprise or, with permission, outside enterprises. A maximum of thirty is placed on the membership (fifteen is usual), which can undertake extra production or provide services such as cleaning and maintenance (Noti 1987: 72). Problems encountered include resentment of higher earnings felt by the other workers and a temptation by those involved to slack during regular working hours.

As in all other socialist countries there is a general reluctance to close down 'uneconomic' enterprises (despite the associated problems of the 'soft budget constraint'), not only to avoid unemployment ('temporary restructuring of manpower'), but also to avoid having to import substitute commodities. On 1 September 1986, however, a *bankruptcy law* was introduced, the first in Eastern Europe. Courts are now able to declare an enterprise bankrupt and company managements or creditors, including banks, can take proceedings. Until 1 January 1989 there were only specific examples of 'job-finding support' for workers, but still not a general system of unemployment benefit. There were retraining schemes and early retirement programmes, and 'relocation benefits' (especially to help with the severe housing difficulties), usually paid for six months in lieu of notice, have been available since 1986 for workers made redundant in groups of at least ten (Susan Greenberg, *FT*, 5 January 1988, p. 2). Even so, the first half of 1987 saw only three companies liquidated and in September of that year Karoly Grosz, who had held the premiership since June, stated that in 1986 30 per cent of budgetary expenditure went in support of unprofitable enterprises. In November 1987 it was proposed to close down four large iron and steel works. In 1979 about 800 workers were made redundant at the Raba works, the first and, until recently, the only case on a mass scale (Greenberg, *FT*, p. 2). Under the new system unemployment pay is available for one year, with a higher rate paid to those made compulsorily redundant. School-leavers are not eligible, but are offered training instead, while strikes are now fully legal (Imre Karacs, *The Independent*, 27 October 1988, p. 13).

Manpower allocation and wage determination

There is a labour market in Hungary and 'full employment'.[10] This has led to problems such as a high labour turnover and the frequency of second and more jobs, with adverse effects on the state sector.[11] Ranges of basic wage and salary rates are set centrally (the ranges tending to increase over time), dependent on factors such as the level of skill, the degree of responsibility and working conditions. Total pay is the sum of these plus profit share. Until 1 January 1988, however, wage control was mainly exercised by subjecting above-norm pay increases to highly progressive taxation. In 1968 the tax base was average pay increases, designed to avoid unemployment among unskilled and low-skilled workers as productivity rose. In 1983–84, however, there was a switch to increases in total wage bill in order to avoid distortions in manpower allocation. In more extreme circumstances wage freezes have been introduced.[12]

In 1980 an average of 63.9 per cent of the gross profit of enterprises was taxed away (Heinrich 1986: 157), and by 1985 this had risen to 80 per cent (Adam 1987: 614, quoting Gado). *The tax reforms introduced on 1 January 1988* were designed to help shift part of the burden from successful enterprises to consumers in the shape of a value-added tax on all but basic goods and services. The maximum rate is 35 per cent on, for example, luxury durable consumer goods; the basic rate is 25 per cent. The other advantage is that the tax system is uniform, in contrast to the previous individual bargaining between enterprise and state. The other element of the new system is a progressive income tax system: 20 per cent up to 60 per cent at first, currently 17 per cent up to 56 per cent; there is to be no tax deduction for the first two children. The tax is paid by employers or the self-employed, partly as an attempt to trap more second economy earnings and thus moderate growing income disparities. Take-home pay allegedly remains the same because of increases in pre-tax basic money wage rates. Local councils will capture a share of personal income tax. Various criticisms led to concessions to modify the effects on certain low-income groups. In September 1987 approval was given to pension increases and increased family, child, and maternity allowances.

The financial system

The banking system and monetary policy

The NEM system originally involved the state, which determined credit tranches for designated sectors. Enterprises were allowed to compete within those totals, and greater use was made of interest rates and forecasted rates of return.

On 1 January 1987 the banking system was reorganized, with the National

Bank of Hungary becoming more like a conventional central bank, exercising indirect control over five commercial banks. This control is exercised via the following: reserve requirements;[13] facility for refinancing of preferred credits such as exports; the rediscounting of bills of exchange; and a current account facility subject to ceilings related to each bank's capital subscribed by the state. This is a facility destined to decline and to be substituted by a system involving the rediscounting of commercial bills. Since 1988 a system of open market operations has developed, based on the purchase by firms, via banks, of treasury bills issued to cover a portion of the budget deficit (Jones 1988: 19–20). Around 60 per cent of all bank credit is currently refinanced by the central bank (p. 20). Of the five, three were new, namely the Hungarian Credit Bank, the Commercial and Credit Bank, and the Budapest Bank,[14] and two, established in the 1950s, changed their status, namely the Hungarian Foreign Trade Bank and the General Banking and Trust Company.[15] The commercial banks are joint stock companies. The state has majority ownership in all but the Hungarian Credit Bank, and state and co-operative enterprises the remainder (individuals are debarred at present). The National Bank of Hungary retains its monopoly of foreign exchange, foreign borrowing and the issue of forints. The commercial banks are now able to compete for customers (during the first six months they were assigned) and to develop according to commercial success (starting-up capital was provided by the state). The main aim is to improve the efficiency of credit allocation (credit is mainly allocated on a commercial basis) and to increase financial responsibility. Commercial criteria are employed, the banks as creditors are able to instigate bankruptcy proceedings in court against defaulting enterprises, and each bank's revenue is dependent on the profitability of transactions. Commercial banks are able to issue shares for the purpose of capital raising for enterprises.

There are now rudimentary inter-bank and inter-enterprise markets in short-term credit. Since the idea was first mooted in 1982, subsequent legislation has made it possible for foreigners to open convertible currency accounts encouraged by competitive interest rates and Swiss-style secrecy rules.

The first bonds were issued in 1981 by the National Savings Bank on behalf of local authorities. Since 1 January 1983 not only scrutinized local authorities (for public utilities and so on) but also enterprises (including co-operatives and, since 1987, the new commercial banks) have been able to sell bonds to other enterprises or individuals.[16] The bonds are fixed term, with some offering a variable element in the interest rate linked to profitability. Until 1 January 1988 bonds sold by enterprises to individuals had to be guaranteed by the Ministry of Finance; since then the commercial bank handling the issue has taken over responsibility. From 1988 onwards enterprises have been able to issue bonds without permission and to fix the interest rate, and there a 20 per cent tax on bond earnings (*EEN*, 1987, vol. 1, no. 12, p. 5).

In October 1987 the first joint stock company was set up since 1948, the

Gallakarbon transport company (a joint venture between the Budapest Bank and Tatabanya Coalmines), with freely marketable shares. Private citizens are allowed to hold a maximum of only a quarter of the share capital and to trade shares within the enterprise.

A new company law was introduced from the start of 1989, allowing the general establishment of joint stock companies whose shares could be offered to the general public and to foreigners (*EEN*, 1988, vol. 2, no. 3, p. 3). Among the small number of previous such companies was the Tungsram lightbulb manufacturer, whose shareholding was restricted to company employees (the 14 October 1987 decree legalized employee shareholding). The enterprise decides the size of dividends. Employees are able to cash in their shares and sell shares to fellow employees, although this applies only to shares purchased – those given by the company are not transferable (*EEN*, 1987, vol. 1, no. 12, p. 5). The aim is to create a competitive capital market, encouraging enterprises and individuals (individuals will be able to have a majority holding in state enterprises) to utilize their spare funds more productively than at present. Share ownership will be available to all, including foreigners (up to 100 per cent) and there are six types of companies: (1) 'joint incomes' company: formed by at least two individuals, who have unlimited liability; (2) 'deposit' company: formed by at least two individuals, but with differing sorts of partners, internal with unlimited and external with limited liability; (3) 'joint stock' company: liability is proportional to shareholding; (4) 'limited liability' company: the same, but intended primarily for subsidiaries of existing companies; (5) 'joint venture': involves foreigners, liability being in proportion to shareholding; and (6) 'association': formed only by institutional shareholders, who have unlimited liability. There is no requirement for worker representation in a company's management, but it is not ruled out, and they may retain up to a third of total voting power at any rate. The one-person business was originally meant to be unaffected by these changes, but is, in fact, covered by the limited liability legislation. Co-operatives will be allowed to buy shares in other companies (see *EEN*, 1988, vol. 2, no. 11, pp. 3–4, and vol. 2, no. 20, p. 7). Firms of lesser importance are allowed a majority of privately owned shares; this majority permits them to employ up to 500 people (Leslie Colitt, *FT*, 7 October 1988, p. 2). In large state enterprises a 30 per cent ceiling is imposed (William Underhill, *The Daily Telegraph*, 5 October 1988, p. 12). Problems arise in the form of compulsory minimum amounts of starting capital and the stipulation that a government institution owning a third of the shares automatically controls 51 per cent of the company (*The Economist*, 15–21 October 1988, p. 61). The Budapest stock exchange opened on 1 January 1989, although it is restricted to members only, under the new regulations. Note that a stock market had been operating since July of the previous year, dealing with the stocks of 40 state enterprises and clients in the shape of state enterprises and co-operatives (*The Economist*, 5–11 November 1988, p. 130).

Prices

One of the major problems that arose over time was the narrowing of the levels of producer and consumer prices. This was due to the increase in producer prices and, via subsidization, the holding down of consumer prices. This effect was so pronounced that the two were roughly equal by the mid-1970s and the latter, for a short time afterwards, was actually higher than the former. The absence of a two-tier price system means a low taxation of consumption. Subsequent price increases at the retail level and the new taxation systems beginning on 1 January 1988 were designed to remedy this. The aim was to make the consumer price level, with specific exceptions, approximately higher than the producer level, in order to reflect costs of production.

The 1968 reform introduced a four-tier pricing system of fixed, ceiling, range and free categories. Since 1980 most prices have not been state determined in a formal sense. 'Competitive pricing', designed to act as a substitute for the lack of competitive pressures in the domestic economy, means that the prices of products like important raw materials and energy approximate world levels, while various other rules affect other commodities, such as regard for world price changes, similar profit margins as on hard currency exports (to lessen the attractiveness of domestic sales and thus stimulate exports), hypothetical hard currency import prices and 'fair' profit margins.[17] Marer estimates that the set of competitive rules for determining industrial producer prices introduced on 1 January 1980 accounted for 70 per cent of industrial output, while about 20 per cent is determined purely by domestic market forces (Marer 1986a: 258; about 10–20 per cent of combined agricultural and industrial output, p. 260). Free prices accounted for 58 per cent of consumer purchases in 1987 (Adam 1989: 141).[18] In non-competitive branches, agricultural product and construction producer prices are set on the basis of average cost plus profit markup (Adam 1987: 618). The prices of basic foodstuffs such as bread are still controlled, while fruit and vegetable prices are market determined. The 1985 reform stressed the principle of supply and demand, providing that costs were 'justifiable' (Swain 1987: 24). In that year provision was made for the profit margin in hard currency markets and there have since been only two categories in manufacturing industry, the one concerning the price ruling in hard currency markets and the other concerning the 'Price Club', where proof of competitive conditions allows free prices (Adam 1987: 619). Since 1 April 1988 the aim has been to decontrol consumer prices, with the exception of staple commodities and a number of public services.[19]

Agriculture

The 1935 census revealed that 0.8 per cent of landowners owned 46.4 per cent of agricultural land, while 76.1 per cent owned 12.0 per cent (Batt 1988: 51). *The 1945 land reform* involved the confiscation and redistribution of all holdings of more than 57 hectares (Heinrich 1986: 159). Forced *collectivization* took place during 1949–56. The 1956 revolution led to two-thirds of members leaving the collective farms, but recollectivization took place in 1958–62, although this mainly relied on persuasion and incentives (e.g. land and other assets contributed being compensated and the chairman directly elected by members; Marer 1986a: 237). In 1957 compulsory delivery targets were abandoned and replaced by voluntary contracts at (more generous) state-determined prices[20]. Economic reforms were generally introduced in agriculture before industry; mandatory plans were scrapped for the former in 1966. In 1967 co-operatives were permitted to pay a guaranteed annual wage, with the residual 10 to 15 per cent constituting a dividend dependent on net profit (Marer 1986a: 135). The following year non-agricultural activities were allowed, such as food processing, electronic products, construction, component parts and repair shops (diversification out of agricultural production entirely if desired; Swain 1987: 28), and two years later the limits on small-scale livestock holdings were deemed to be the prerogative of co-operatives themselves (Batt 1988: 265). Even today the market mechanism is most effective in agriculture (and in retail trade), although the state has considerable monopsony power in the case of many products.

According to Vankai (1986: 343), collective and state farms have to draw up a five year plan in accordance with the broad national economic objectives relayed by the Ministry of Agriculture. The plan must be approved by the Ministry, which has the task of summing all the individual plans. If national objectives do not seem likely to be met, changes in economic levers are used indirectly to steer farms in the desired direction.

Since the late 1950s most farm prices have been set annually on the basis of national average production costs, with account being taken of production incentives and the aim of raising farm incomes (Marer 1986a: 260). Purchase prices are determined so that a farm on average land would be able to cover average costs plus a small (normal) profit margin, with rent being taxed away from farms occupying above average quality land (Marrese 1986a: 335). In 1981 state determined prices affected nearly 40 per cent of agricultural output, covering such products as maize, wheat, and beef. The producer prices of those products that heavily employ hard currency imports, are used for hard currency exports, or are hard currency import substitutes, are based on world market prices (Hartford 1985: 131). The income of co-operative members depends not only on work performed, but also rental payments for land ceded by individuals.

Agricultural co-operatives dominate the scene, although they only own half of the land they farm, the remainder belonging to the state and individuals, mainly their own members (Hartford 1985: 124). In the mid-1980s they accounted for just over 50 per cent of the gross output of agriculture and some 75 per cent of the agricultural work-force, and occupied 82 per cent of arable land and 4,000 hectares on average. The respective approximate figures for state farms (involved in a great deal of experimental work) are 15 per cent, 16 per cent, 15 per cent and 7,700 hectares.

The private sector

The private sector in 1985 contributed 34 per cent of gross farm output (crop 26 per cent and livestock 42 per cent) from 13 per cent of arable land (Cochrane 1988: 48–49), over half of this from farm household plots and under half from private farms (which only account for about 1 per cent of agricultural land) and the auxiliary holdings of the non-agricultural population. In the same year personal plots accounted for 5.99 and auxiliary holdings 5.7 per cent of the area farmed, while the private farms (average size 3.6 hectares) covered 1.3 per cent of cultivated land (Lang, Csete, and Harnos 1988: 232). The private sector (figures for 1985) is especially important in products such as meat (51 per cent), fruit (60 per cent), vegetables (65 per cent) and eggs (61 per cent) (Cochrane 1988: 48–49). In addition to private plots of 0.30 to 0.60 hectares per member (where there are now no restrictions on keeping animals or owning machinery), co-operatives are permitted to rent land to individuals and to provide them with inputs, advice and marketing channels. Policy during the 1970s and 1980s was and still is geared to integrating private agriculture into the socialist economy, with co-operatives providing services for household plots and loaning out funds to construct buildings housing animals raised under contract to the co-operatives (Swain 1987: 28). In 1980 permission was given to purchase tractors of up to 30 HP (Cochrane 1988: 49). Experiments have begun involving the fixed-term hiring of land, equipment, and/or buildings by co-operatives to individuals for activities such as grazing or workshops (*EIU Country Profile*, 1987–88, p. 17).

In 1985 state farms followed the practice, already instituted in co-operatives, of employee election of the farm director and management committee. 'Agrocomplexes' are joint undertakings providing a range of inputs such as feedstuffs, or stock and construction services, or involved in processing agricultural commodities. 'Technically operated production systems' come in two forms, namely 'proprietory' and 'technological transfer'. The former is owned by co-operative and state farms and leases out automated technology packages to participating farms, while the latter provides member farms with technical training, introduction to new technology, and assistance in obtaining the credit needed to purchase their own equipment (Hartford 1987: 198–200).

In the early 1980s there was a resurgence in some state and co-operative farms of decentralized work groups, which act as sub-contractors to the farm, which provides administrative services (Swain 1987: 30).

In the 1985 reform farms were given the choice of three methods of wage regulation, the growth in gross income (value added) per worker, the growth

147

of the average wage or a tax on each individual employee's income.

Foreign trade and debt

Hungary is highly dependent on foreign trade, exporting about 50 per cent of net material product (*EIU Country Profile*, 1987–88, p. 29). In the mid-1980s about 53 per cent of trade was conducted with Comecon (the share has shown a falling trend since 1968), with the Soviet Union alone accounting for 32 per cent of total trade. The Soviet Union supplies Hungary with energy and raw materials and takes delivery of Hungarian foodstuffs and manufactures such as computers and buses. The OECD countries accounted for 35 per cent of trade and developing countries 12 per cent. The 1987 figures for Hungarian exports were Comecon 51 per cent and the Soviet Union 32 per cent, and for imports 47.5 per cent and 28.5 per cent respectively (Emma Klein, *Guardian Survey*, 5 May 1988, p. 12).

Hungary has the most liberal foreign trade system within Comecon. Industrial enterprises either have their own trading rights (270 by the start of 1986; von Czege 1987: 134) or are allowed to choose a foreign trade corporation to act on their behalf, on a commission or on a risk-taking partnership basis (most trade is carried out by trade corporations). A few foreign trade corporations are now able to trade in any commodity, while in other cases the product lines assigned to the corporations overlap in order to increase competition (Marer 1986a: 253). Since 1 January 1988 any state-owned enterprise or co-operative has been able to trade with the West on condition that, for example, it has qualified staff and registers with the Ministry of Trade (Kerpel and Young 1988: 69). Until 1976 exchange rates were called 'foreign trade multipliers'. Five years later a uniform exchange rate for hard currencies was introduced, formerly one for foreign trade and the second for other transactions) . The value of the exchange rate is based on the average producer-price-based cost of producing a unit of convertible foreign exchange in exports; the rate changes with the fluctuations in the exchange rate of a basket of hard currencies (Adam 1987: 622). The *Economist Survey* (1988: 15) describes 'domestic convertibility' for the forint as the situation where Hungarian enterprises are able to buy and sell hard currencies at a unified exchange rate; Aganbegyan (1988a: 15) describes this as 'internal convertibility'. Within Comecon Hungary has been the most persistent advocate of the reforms needed to make possible currency and goods convertibility and thus stimulate multilateral trade, while it plays an important role in Comecon's plans for science and technology in areas such as computers/software and biotechnology.

Table 8.1 traces Hungary's net hard currency debt position (gross debt minus foreign assets). The debt-service ratio (interest and repayment of principal as a proportion of hard currency exports) was 60 per cent in 1986, compared to 20 per cent in 1975. The National Bank of Hungary provided the following figures for the end of September 1988: net debt $10.4 billion (gross $17.3 billion minus foreign assets of $6.9 billion); but if non-interest-bearing foreign assets are excluded (mostly trade credits and soft loans to developing countries), the net figure rises to $13.4 billion (reported in *IHT*, 26–27 November 1988, p. 14). The aim is to limit net debt to $10 billion by 1990.

This situation is partly the result of policies adopted in the 1970s and partly the parallel retrenchment in the reform process. The 1973–74 oil price shock produced increased energy and raw material prices and recession in the industrialized West. The Hungarian response up to 1979 was to accelerate the growth of total output, investment and consumption (the last for incentives), financed by foreign credits, which were supposed to lead to the increase in exports needed for repayment. The domestic economy was increasingly isolated from world markets and CMEA trade became more important (Marer 1986b).

In 1979 policy changed on both fronts with an austerity drive to reduce imports, investment and consumption, and to boost exports, and a return to the path of economic reform. Batt (1988: 277) sees late 1978 as marking a major shift in long term economic strategy, from import substitution to one of export promotion, the whole policy signalling a resuscitation of the reform. In 1982, however, Hungary came close to debt rescheduling as it was caught in the backwash of the Polish and Romanian crises, having already been subjected to rising interest rates and facing declining markets after 1980 because of the restrictive monetary policies adopted by the advanced Western countries. It was avoided by a combination of intensified austerity measures, especially severe constraints on imports (there is a licensing system for imports and exports), and credits provided by the IMF and the World Bank, which Hungary joined in May 1982.[21] The 'consolidation programme' agreed upon in 1987 combines new reform measures with an austerity programme for 1988–90.

The July 1988 extraordinary Central Committee meeting passed the more severe of two austerity programmes for further discussion and for approval at the October Central Committee meeting. It was envisaged that unemployment would rise from around 30,000 to 100,000, inflation would increase to more than 15 per cent as subsidies on consumer goods were reduced, and the forint would be further devalued.

It is of interest to note that the first hard currency state lottery draw took place on 2 October 1988 (the prizes were luxury consumer goods), and four days later it was announced that the first free-trade zone in Eastern Europe was to be set up around Sopron, with a special economic zone a more distant possibility.

Joint equity ventures

In 1972 a decree on '*economic associations with foreign participation*' was published, with several amendments thereafter, as occurred at the beginning of 1986. It is now possible for foreign ownership to exceed 50 per cent,[22] and the concessions have become more generous over time, especially for reinvestment.[23] Since 1 January 1989 100 per cent foreign ownership has been possible, while no licence is needed for joint ventures with minority foreign ownership; only registration is required. By the end of 1985 fewer than 60 ventures were operating, but between the start of 1986 and September 1987 40 new ventures had been formed (*EIU Country Profile* 1987–88: 38). By the end of 1987 there were 111 (*FT*, 14 April 1988, p. 3, quoting the UN Economic Commission for Europe's *Economic, Business, Financial and Legal Aspects of East-West Joint Ventures*, Geneva, 1988). By mid-1988 about 140 were operating (Kerpel and Young 1988: 69).

Joint ventures have been extended to banking. The Central European International Bank (CIB), founded in 1979, has its headquarters in Budapest, but it is the only 'offshore' organization – the National Bank of Hungary owns 34 per cent, with each of two banks from Japan and one each from France, West Germany, Austria, and Italy owning 11 per cent. It transacts business only in convertible currencies, providing credits to and accepting deposits from foreign as well as Hungarian firms, although it now has a subsidiary dealing in domestic currency transactions. In 1986 the CIB also began to lease Western equipment to Hungarian enterprises. It is not subject to Hungarian foreign exchange laws or regulations issued by the Hungarian National Bank. The Citibank-Budapest Bank, which began operations in January 1986, is a joint venture between Citibank of New York (which has an 80 per cent share) and the Central Exchange and Credit Bank. It does not deal with individuals, but provides investment and trade credits to Hungarian and Western enterprises and accepts deposits in forints and convertible currencies. Interest rates are fixed independently of the National Bank.

In January 1987 the Unicbank was established. It is a venture bank jointly owned by the World Bank's International Finance Corporation and two Western banks (with 15 per cent each) and six Hungarian institutions (owning 55 per cent). Later in 1987 the International Investment Agency (involving the Hungarian Foreign Trade Bank and two Austrian banks) was set up to provide financial services for joint ventures, while in March of that year the Hungarian Foreign Trade Bank formed a joint venture brokerage firm with a Liechtenstein holding company and an Austrian Bank.

The International Training Centre, due to open in February 1989, is a joint Hungarian-Italian venture, substantially backed by US capital. Trainee managers are to come from other socialist countries and perhaps even from the West.

The non-agricultural private and co-operative sector

The 'first economy' consists of state enterprises, co-operatives, government agencies and officially registered non-profit institutions, while the 'second economy' comprises the formal (officially licensed) and informal private sectors.[24] In 1984 the following contributed to net material product: the state sector, 65.2 per cent; the non-state sector, 34.8 per cent (co-operatives, 20.6 per cent; household farming, 2.8 per cent; auxiliary production of employees, 5.9 per cent; and the formal private sector, 5.5 per cent) (Kornai 1986: 1692). The private sector accounts for 20 per cent of total investment (*Abecor Country Report*, May 1988, p. 1). At the July 1988 extraordinary Central Committee meeting, Miklos Nemeth (Central Committee Secretary responsible for the economy) stated that there should be no fear of the idea of the private sector eventually accounting for 25 to 30 per cent of national output.

Bauer (1988: 455) makes the interesting point that concessions to the private sector encounter less resistance from vested interests than those made to the state sector. Hungary has a flourishing private sector, and there is the prospect of legislation formally putting the private, co-operative and state sectors on an equal footing. An already relatively generous limit of seven non-family members and twelve inclusive of family members in private firms was raised to thirty on 1 January 1988 (*EEN*, 1988, vol. 2, no. 3, p. 3).[25] Since 1981 it has been possible to lease state property to individuals. Private guesthouses are permitted to have up to thirty guests. (See section on the new company law for recent changes, p. 144.)

The health of the co-operative sector is indicated by the production of 6 per cent of total industrial output (*Abecor Country Report*, May 1988, p. 2) and by Skala-Coop, the largest retail organization. It was formed in 1973 by 200 consumer co-operatives to compete with the state retail organizations, but has since expanded into wholesale trade, industrial production and international trade. It has its own import-export organization and undertakes joint ventures with Western companies (Table 8.2). It has also issued bonds to individuals and other enterprises.

The first private insurance company was set up in 1986.

Conclusion

Hungary overcame the trauma of the 1956 revolution to introduce overnight on 1 January 1968 the most radical reform in Eastern Europe outside of Yugoslavia. While the New Economic Mechanism has not made Hungary into a model of market socialism, the state achieves its aggregate plan targets overwhelmingly indirectly, via the use of economic levers, leaving the enterprise typically free from the need to fulfil the success indicators associated with the traditional Soviet economic system. Informal pressures are also important. There has been pioneering work in elected management, while the 'second economy' is large and flourishing. Nevertheless, Hungary faces current problems of considerable magnitude, especially a severe foreign debt problem and worries about inflation. Although General Secretary Karoly Grosz (who replaced Janos Kadar in May 1988) is recognized as more of a pragmatist than a radical reformer, further market-oriented reforms are in the pipeline and progress towards political liberalization has been marked. Grosz maintains that in a July 1988 conversation in Moscow, Gorbachev said, 'It is probably the Hungarian endeavours and Hungarian perceptions that are the closest now to those of the Soviet Union' (reported by James Markham in IHT, 11 July 1988, p. 1).

Table 8.2 Hungary: statistical survey

Joint equity ventures (end 1987)	111		
Private sector in agriculture (1985)		*Agricultural output*	*Arable land*
(including private farms) (%)		34	13

Contributions to NMP (1984) (%)			*Auxiliary*	*Formal*
		Household	*production of*	*private*
State sector	*Co-operatives*	*farming*	*employees*	*sector*
65.2	20.6	2.8	5.9	5.5

Population (1987)	10.6 million

Sources: Cochrane (1988: 48–9); *FT*, 14 April 1988, p. 3; Kornai (1986: 1692).
For figures on growth rates, inflation, and net hard currency debt, see Table 8.1.

Postscript

On 24 June 1989 the powers of Grosz as General Secretary were diluted by the setting up of a four-strong party presidium headed by Nyers (as party president) and including Pozsgay and Nemeth. One of the tasks of the new body was to prepare a party programme for the forthcoming freely-contested, national election in March 1990. At the Fourteenth Party Congress, held 6–9 October 1989, the Hungarian Socialist Workers' Party was renamed the Hungarian Socialist Party (HSP), committed to a multi-party, democratic political system and a welfare state / market-based economy. Rezso Nyers was elected party president. The presidium included Poszgay (the HSP's candidate in the election for state president to be held in November) and Nemeth. The moves towards greater democracy have been rewarded by Western aid and trade concessions.

Notes

1. For example, 1983 legislation allowed multi-candidate elections, including non-party candidates. The independent Democratic Union of Scientific Workers was set up

on 14 May 1988, followed by the Motion Picture Democratic Trade Union and (in February 1989) by the first blue-collar union (the Solidarity Workers' Trade Union Federation).

2. Important political changes at the Congress included limiting the tenure of a future General Secretary to two terms of office totalling ten years.

3. Using the growth-accounting methodology developed by Edward Denison, Robert Jerome evaluates the economic growth of Hungary in the period 1950–85, with estimated post-reform average annual rates of growth of 3.5 per cent for 1970–75, 2.0 per cent for 1975–80, and 1.1 per cent for 1980–85. Jerome found a marked decline in productivity growth, with increases in factors (mostly capital, and specifically plant and equipment) accounting for nearly all of total growth in the post-reform period. He concludes that this is similar to other socialist countries like Bulgaria and that the reforms did little to improve the performance of the Hungarian economy over what it likely would have been (Jerome 1988: 112–13).

4. Eight of 13 of the previous Politburo and not far short of a third of the Central Committee lost their positions.

5. At the start of the 1980s enterprises were allowed to determine up to 30 per cent of turnover without special permission (von Czege 1987: 134). Since 1985 they have been able to change their sphere of economic activity, providing they inform their founding organ and the appropriate branch ministry (Swain 1987: 34).

6. According to Schüller (1988: 32), about 50 per cent of investment is directly determined by the centre, while decisions regarding the remainder (excluding self-financed maintenance, rationalization and small expansion investment) are influenced by credit policy.

7. Technical economies of scale have not been sacrificed, since plant size is generally small. Where these economies are significant some trusts remain, such as in aluminium. On 1 January 1988 the Ganz Mavag engineering concern was divided into seven enterprises.

8. State financial support in the form of subsidies, price increases or tax reductions is forthcoming to cover any losses. This ensures the survival of inefficient enterprises, but does not encourage financial discipline.

9. Essentially the non-regulated sector, involving both legal and illegal private activity, which expanded rapidly during the 1970s because of the restrictions placed upon the small and medium-sized enterprises.

10. In mid-1987 10,000 were officially estimated to be 'seeking work'; some 400 unemployment offices have been set up.

11. Causing wide income disparities; those working full time in the 'first economy' were especially disadvantaged.

12. In the first quarter of 1986 and the four months to March 1987 for instance.

13. Two per cent of short term deposits (less than a year) and 10 per cent of all time deposits to be placed in an interest free reserve account at the central bank.

14. In 1987 the Budapest Bank absorbed the State Development Bank, which operated the secondary bond market after 1984. This market is currently largely concentrated in the new bank. Budapest's first stockbroking house, Co-Nexus, opened on 20 January 1988 (*EEN*, 1988, vol. 2, no. 3, p. 3).

15. The three new banks are not allowed to handle foreign exchange transactions, while the former of the two previously existing banks, for example, deals with the financing of foreign trade in both forints and hard currencies.

16. Note that it is the National Savings Bank that handles the accounts of individuals and that banks themselves are only able to issue bonds to enterprises. Individuals have been allowed to trade bonds freely since 1984.

17. 'Financial bridges' are the taxes and subsidies that span the divide between domestic

and world prices.
18. The so-called 'free' category of prices may still be subject to delays and profit margin restrictions.
19. A temporary price freeze ended 31 March 1988.
20. Although until 1968 local government procurement recommendations, reflecting the state plan, tended to carry the force of orders (Hartford 1987: 130). Quotas for bread grains were imposed until 1969 (Bleaney 1988: 103).
21. Hungary has been a member of GATT since 1973 and has benefited from MFN concessions in its trade with the United States since 1978.
22. First conceded to the financial and service sector and, since 1985, to manufacturing; up to 99 per cent generally and in cases like hotels even 100 per cent.
23. There is a maximum corporate tax on profits of 40 per cent for the foreign partner and 20 per cent in the first five years in areas like electronics, hotel construction, and packaging technology. It is possible for individual firms to be awarded a five year tax holiday.
24. Second jobs are attractive because of the possibility of pilfering materials from the state sector.
25. In addition, limited liability was given to private individuals when in partnership with state enterprises or co-operatives (*EEN*, 1988, vol. 2, no. 3, p. 3).

Chapter nine

Poland

Political and economic background

Poland is the largest country in Eastern Europe in terms of population (37.8 million at the end of 1987) and area, with good agricultural land (about 60 per cent of land is used for agricultural purposes) and minerals such as coal,[1] copper, silver, natural gas, lead, zinc, and sulphur.

Poland lies in a vulnerable geographical position on the north European plain and has a history of dismemberment.[2] In 1772 Russia, Prussia, and Austria devoured a third of the country, and by 1795 Poland ceased to exist. Re-emerging as an independent country only in 1918, Poland in the inter-war years was caught up in war against the Soviet Union in 1919–20 and a military coup in 1926. The Nazi-Soviet pact of 1939 included a secret agreement to partition Poland. Twenty per cent of the population died during the Second World War amid massive destruction.

Wladyslaw Gomulka was restored to power in 1956 (he was prime minister from 1945 to 1948) and replaced by Edward Gierek after the 1970 disturbances. Gierek was removed in September 1980 and replaced by Stanislaw Kania. Wojciech Jaruzelski became General Secretary of the United Workers' Party in October 1981, later became President (Chairman of the Council of State), but resigned his post of Prime Minister, assumed in February 1981, in favour of Zbigniew Messner (November 1985). There were riots in Poznan in 1956 against depressed living standards and anti-price-increase protests in 1970, 1976 and 1980. Solidarity was born August 1980, suspended December 1981, formally banned the following October and relegalized in April 1989.

Economic strategy in the 1970s

Poland was a key player in import-led growth during the 1970s (see Chapter 3).[3] Edward Gierek replaced Wladyslaw Gomulka as First Secretary in December 1970, following rioting over increases in the price of food. These were the climax of a switch in emphasis away from consumption and towards investment, which itself was the result of an attempt to reverse the worrying slowdown in growth rates that had occurred by the mid-1960s (see Table 9.1). Gierek's remedy involved increasing consumption to provide incentives for increased output while borrowing massively from the West in order not only to import capital, technology and, know-how (to boost the convertible currency exports needed to pay off the debt by the end of the 1970s), but also to import consumer goods, raw materials (including grain to feed livestock), semi-fabricates, components and spare parts. Thus investment and consumption rose in tandem. This import-led strategy of the first half of the 1970s was seen as a substitute for radical economic reform, but the reforms actually undertaken were meant to improve management and to encourage innovation in order to take advantage of and to further the new techniques and know-how.

Table 9.1 Poland: inflation, debt, and average annual rate of growth of produced national income.

Average annual rate of growth of produced national income (%)

1951–55	1956–60	1961–65	1966–70	1971–75	1976	1977	1978	1979
8.6	6.6	6.2	6.0	9.4	6.8	5.3	2.8	–2.3

1980	1981	1982	1983	1984	1985	1986	1987	1988
–6.0	–12.0	–5.5	6.0	5.6	3.4	4.9	1.9	4.7 *(estimate)*

Inflation (%)	1980	1981	1982	1983	1984	1985	1986	1987	1988
	8.5	18.4	109.4	21.9	15.0	15.1	17.7	26.0	60.0

Net hard currency debt *($ billions)*	1971	1981	1985
	0.8	25.5	27.6

Gross hard currency debt *($ billions)*	1986	1987	1988
	33.5	36.3	39.2

Sources: Blazyca (1986: 19, 26, 76–7; Economist Intelligence Unit, *Country Profile,* (1987–88: 17, 21) and *Country Report* (1989, no. 3, p. 2); *IHT,* 23 December 1988, p. 15; Kolankiewicz and Lewis (1988: xiv); *IHT,* 25 April 1989, p. 6.

Although the period 1971–75 witnessed an annual average rate of growth of 9.4 per cent, the economy soon ran into trouble (see Table 9.1). In 1979 produced national income fell by 2.3 per cent and there were chronic balance of payments and foreign debt problems. By the end of 1981, Poland's net hard currency debt had reached $25.5 billion, mainly short and medium term. The debt-service ratio rose to 101 per cent in 1980 (see Blazyca 1986: 19, 76–77). In March 1981 Poland suspended repayments on the principal of the debt, which led to a drying up of fresh Western credits.

There was also severe macro disequilibrium, with money wages increasing faster than planned,[4] 40 per cent over the 1971–75 period, compared to Gierek's target range of 17–18 per cent. Open and repressed inflation were also at significant levels. Investment climbed to 35.7 per cent of national income by 1975, compared with some 25 per cent on average during the 1960s. Investment plans were exceeded, due to such factors as pressure both (1) from enterprises: the lack of penalty for failure encouraged irresponsibility, while 'hooking on to the plan' implied that it was easier to obtain resources to finish projects already under way; and (2) from Western banks anxious to recycle OPEC surpluses. The absorptive capacity of the economy was exceeded, the system was still incapable of making use of and developing the new technologies, and a broad spread of projects was adopted, which meant exaggeration of the normal problems of the 'scattering of resources' (ever longer gestation periods often resulted in product obsolescence). Priority was given to enlarging the capital stock rather than modernizing the existing one and to sectors such as ferrous metallurgy, petrochemicals and engineering (shipbuilding and cars, for instance) which were import-intensive and badly hit by the world recession. Infrastructural investments, such as energy and transport, as well as agriculture and consumer goods were relatively neglected; the result was bottlenecks. There were large cost overruns in projects like the giant steelworks at Huty Katowice, and foreign machinery and technologies were often unable to be utilized effectively. Other problems included the following: (1) many investment projects that were import-substituting rather than export-promoting; (2) the poor project decision-making process, ignorance of export potential, and future dependence on imported inputs; (3) insufficient awareness of the need to meet world market demands in terms of price, quality, and delivery times; and (4) the attempt to insulate the economy from world inflation (Fallenbuchl 1986: 363–9). Blazyca (1986: 31) describes the leadership as losing control of the economy amid the wage push of the workers and the investment push of the powerful ministries. Kolankiewicz and Lewis (1988: 104) talk about investment policy responding to various lobbies and pressure groups.

The mounting difficulties resulted in a sharp reversal in the latter half of the 1970s. The mid-1970s *economic manoeuvre* involved recentralization of decision-making in 1976, an attempt to link wage increases with productivity, a drastic decline in both imports and investment,[5] and an increase in exports (with the aim of achieving a hard currency trade surplus by 1979). The attempt to divert foodstuffs to exports and the associated rise in domestic prices led to the strikes of summer 1980 and the rise of Solidarity.

Table 9.1 shows the negative growth rates associated with the period 1979–82. In 1981 exports to non-socialist countries fell by 22.1 per cent, and imports from them decreased by 31.5 per cent (Kolankiewicz and Lewis 1988: 23). Over the period 1978–82 national output fell by nearly a quarter, investment halved and consumption declined by about 15 per cent (*World Bank Report* 1988: 29). In 1986 national output was at the same level as a decade earlier (Bleaney 1988: 96). Martial law was imposed on 13 December 1981 (ended 21 July 1983) with the aim of stabilizing the economic and political situation, and Solidarity was banned, despite the 31 August 1980 Gdansk agreement. Consumer goods shortages became severe, rationing was widespread, and the state felt secure enough to impose food price increases without the disturbances that characterized the previous attempts in 1970, 1976 and, 1980. Vital industries were militarized and 'operational programmes' instituted. Positive growth resumed in 1983 (see Table 9.1).

Financial policy has been aimed at restoring macro-economic equilibrium. Wage and salary increases during the 1980s have been far in excess of plan and of productivity increases (partly deliberate in order to avoid industrial unrest), but regular increases in retail prices have been achieved, without political disturbances, in order to reduce both subsidies and the extent of rationing. Meat is still partially rationed, and petrol was rationed from the beginning of 1982 to that of 1989. Table 9.1 provides the record for inflation. In 1985, in order to combat the black market, individuals were allowed to put hard currency into interest-bearing accounts with no questions asked. After 1 April 'undocumented' earnings (those not earned or presented as gifts from abroad) were placed in a non-interest-bearing account for a year.[6]

Poland's net hard currency debt has mounted steadily, as Table 9.1 illustrates.[7] The debt-service ratio of 67 per cent in 1986 was the highest in Eastern Europe. There have been regular reschedulings, and austerity policies have been heavily oriented towards increasing exports. Convertible currency trade surpluses were attained in 1983–86 despite obstacles such as US retaliation for the imposition of martial law and the banning of Solidarity.[8] Poland rejoined the IMF in June 1986, having withdrawn in 1950 even though a founding member, and joined the World Bank in the same year. In November 1988 the World Bank made its first loan to Poland.

In June 1987 the decision was taken to cover interest obligations on the hard currency debt to the West by 1991 (two years earlier than had originally been planned) and to achieve a current account surplus by the same date.

Industrial reform

Significant economic reforms were implemented as early as 1956–57; enterprise decision-making powers were increased (the number of compulsory indicators was reduced to eight), and workers' councils formed spontaneously and were legalized. The director was supposedly subject to the dual authority of the workers' council and the ministry. But recentralization soon began in 1958. The number of plan indicators was increased, the powers of workers' councils were curtailed (in December 1958 they were incorporated into state run 'workers' self-management conferences'), and 'associations' were established. These associations behaved essentially as administrative links between enterprise and ministry, allocating disaggregated plan tasks in traditional fashion and were endowed with research, marketing and project design functions.

The period between 1958 and 1972 was one in which a command economy was subjected to relatively insignificant administrative changes and experiments, such as the use of 'leading enterprises', involving a loose form of association, 'patron enterprises', where a technological leader benefits whole groups, and the setting up of vertically integrated *kombinats* in 1969 (Blazyca, 1980b).

The 1972 blueprint led to the 1973–75 experiment involving the use of WOGs (*wielkie organizacje gospodarcze*: large economic organizations).[9] These operated on a *khozraschyot* basis and were given enhanced powers of decision-making at the expense of both enterprise and ministry. WOGs were able to decide for themselves how to manage their internal affairs and had varying degrees of independent decision-making as regards product mix, depending on product scarcity. These powers extended to employment, wage policy, price fixing (especially for new products), investment, and output assortment. Obligatory indicators still remained, however, and included sales, exports, in some cases the level of production in physical or value terms, investment, inputs, and financial norms. These indicators were conditional with respect to incentives, but the basic incentive scheme involved value added and profit. The traditional wage fund limit was abandoned and replaced by a link between the wage fund and value added and by a 20 per cent tax on the wage fund. Basic managerial salaries were tied to the growth of wage and salary scales, but depended on the growth of value added being greater than that of employment. Managerial bonuses were related to the level of or increase in net profit and were conditional both on fulfilment of the other plan indicators and on wage payments not exceeding the disposable wage fund. A link was to be forged between domestic and international prices by means of various 'multipliers' (exchange rates effectively) and exports encouraged by WOGs, which were to be allowed a share of foreign currency earnings and greater involvement in export promotion and price regulations, with the foreign trade corporation acting as an agent.

By mid-1974 approximately 100 pilot units accounted for nearly 50 per cent of socialized industry, but the latter half of the decade witnessed a recentralization process, due to deteriorating world and domestic conditions and to the excess demand caused by an ambitious growth strategy. *Recentralization after 1976* involved controls on employment, wages linked to productivity increases, the imposition of investment limits, the strengthening of ministerial powers, an increase in the number of enterprise indicators, an excess profits tax on windfall profits from exports, and a progressive tax on unplanned growth of the wage fund.

The industrial reform of 1 January 1982

On paper this was a Hungarian-type reform that was intended to be applied only gradually over a period of three to five years. In reality so little of the reform was actually carried out that it was only at the Tenth Party Congress of 29 June–3 July 1986 that a firm resolution was made to implement it.

The reform, in principle, laid stress on indirect steering of the economy via the use of economic levers. The state would still be responsible for infrastructual investment and large investments in key sectors. The enterprise was to be: 1. free of most state-imposed targets: there were exceptions related to goods of national importance such as armaments, basic consumer goods and exports needed to meet trade agreements; 2. 'self-financing', that is normally operating without subsidies, bankruptcy thus becoming a possibility; pay was to be tied to enterprise performance (enterprises were to be free to set wage scales, subject to central guidelines on relative rates) and controlled indirectly via taxes on average pay increases before 1983 and total pay increases afterwards; and 3. 'self-managed': workers, either directly or via workers' councils, were to be given significantly enhanced decision-making powers, including consultation about management decisions relating to output, employment and prices, and to have the final say in the spending of social welfare funds.

Gomulka and Rostowski (1984: 389) consider that the main aim of the enterprise under such a scheme would seem to be the maximization of after-tax wages and bonuses, including retained profits, per employee, similar to the system in Yugoslavia. Brodzka (1987: 30) summarizes the purpose of the reform as: 1. the introduction of an economic system based primarily on economic, financial and market mechanisms rather than central administrative regulation, with a decisive increase in the autonomy of enterprises and the general application of profit as the criterion of choice of output in place of quantitatively determined targets (enterprises freely determine the distribution of most of their profits); 2. the state is to influence the economy through policy and financial instruments; 3. a decline in the role of ministries and an enhanced one for banks; and 4. the eventual emergence of a capital market. Blazyca sees the essence of the reform as the abandonment of short-term central planning, with enterprises drawing up their own plans on the basis of negotiated contracts at (eventually) free prices.

There is a *three tier system of prices*: state determined ('administered' prices for energy for example) ; 'regulated', based on a cost-plus formula; and 'contractual' or freely negotiated. Prices are to be more closely linked with world levels (especially for raw materials) and are increasingly to reflect domestic supply and demand forces.[10] According to Kaczurba (1988: 25), until the early 1980s the domestic price system was largely isolated from world prices. Since then 'transaction prices' have been introduced, accounting for about 85 per cent of trade turnover by the end of 1987. These are effectively export and import prices converted through the current exchange rate, set by comparing domestic and foreign production costs in foreign trade prices).

Some enterprises were to be given *direct trading rights* (349 at the end of 1985; Blazyca 1986: 100) and others were to have the option of entering into commission contracts with foreign trade corporations. Enterprises producing goods for export were allowed to retain a percentage of hard currency earnings, hard currency bank credits were to be available and there were to be foreign exchange auctions. The current situation is that enterprises are permitted to export independently if exports constitute at least 5 per cent of the value of their production (rather than 25 per cent previously), while in future foreign exchange allocation will depend on the degree of processing of the exported products (*Abecor Country Report*, April 1988, p. 2). There was to be a single exchange rate, with convertibility as the ultimate aim. The exchange rate is set against the dollar to make most enterprises profit from exporting to the West, but subsidies still protect domestic industry (*EIU Country Profile* 1987–88: 16).[11]

The ministries were reduced in number from twelve to six and were supposed to be endowed with reduced powers. The 'associations' of enterprises (*zjednoczenia*), channels for relaying detailed central plan targets and exercising close supervision, were scrapped in mid-1982, but ministries (responsible for structural change and technological progress) then began to encourage enterprises to join together in new 'amalgamations' (*zrzeszenia*) by means of improved input and foreign exchange supply. At present there are 616 'amalgamations', of which only 31 are compulsory, and they embrace almost all the 6,065 state enterprises; there are also *kombinats* (Kolankiewicz and Lewis 1988: 111). In 1987 there was continued resistance from the Ministry of Finance, fearing a powerful lobby, and from workers' councils, fearing a diminution of their powers, to the formation of an electronics trust. Nevertheless, ELPOL (Elektronika Polska) is to be set up, 10 per cent of whose shares will be bought by the Treasury and the remainder by participating enterprises (*Polish Perspectives*, 1987, vol. XXX, no. 4, p. 52).

In the event, many aspects of the reform were not carried out. *Martial law* was in operation from 13 December 1981 to 21 July 1983. Military commissars were made superior to enterprise managers in large enterprises, coal miners were enlisted and general labour direction was introduced. Unjustified absenteeism became a criminal offence. The 42 hour week agreed upon in December 1981 for most workers (i.e. three of every four Saturdays were work free) was rescinded in February 1986. Crucial workers like coal miners have been affected since the introduction of martial law. Solidarity was outlawed in October 1982 and replaced with new official trade unions.[12] Workers' councils were introduced in 1981, while workers' self-management did not begin to operate until two years later. Although self-management bodies are elected by the work-force, they are strictly plant based and are not very influential (although they resist enterprise amalgamations). After the martial law period, self-management was allowed to operate in 5,230 enterprises (out of 6,580), although in 1,371 of the former figure the power to nominate and dismiss the director was not allowed (these 1,371 are described as being of 'fundamental significance for the economy' and employ 80 per cent of the work-force). Their number was reduced to 400 in 1987–88 (Kolankiewicz and Lewis 1988: 114). The law does not, to varying degrees, apply in certain cases, such as banks, railways and defence establishments (Kolankiewicz 1987: 61–2). Apart from the usual bureaucratic resistance to reform, supply difficulties emanating from negative rates of growth and a crippling foreign debt (see Table 9.1) have left the materials allocation system essentially intact; here the ministries are the chief channel. Central allocation applies to half of fuels and major materials, especially imports (for which a licensing system exists) and government contracts confer privileged access to supplies (*World Bank Report* 1988: 30).

Even as late as April 1987 the bankruptcy law had been applied to only nine enterprises (a large construction enterprise was also made bankrupt in the summer of 1987), and subsidization was still on a massive scale and selective basis.[13] Former deputy premier Zdzislaw Sadowski (who had chief responsibility for the reform programme until he lost his position in the government in September 1988), emphasized the alternatives to bankruptcy in the form of reorganization, such as changes in the product mix and the splitting up of big enterprises into smaller units (*Polish Perspectives*, 1988, vol. XXXI, no. 1, pp. 10–11). Nevertheless, in June 1988 it was decided to close 21 medium and small enterprises, and 140 in total faced liquidation.

Severe restrictions were placed on enterprises' use of hard currency earnings; 80 to 85 per cent of foreign exchange remained centrally allocated in 1986 (Blazyca 1986: 42). According to the *EIU Country Profile* 1987–88: 39), in 1985 the share of hard currency imports financed through enterprise foreign exchange accounts was 14.9 per cent, falling to 13.9 per cent in 1986. In 1987 ROD balances (convertible currency retention quotas) were held by 2,500 enterprises, and about a quarter of hard currency expenditures was financed in this way. By the early 1990s at least half of all export earnings is to be accounted for in this fashion (Kaczurba 1988: 26). Since the first half of 1987 there has been a fortnightly auction of US dollars by the Export Development Bank,[14] where enterprises are able to sell surplus foreign currency to other enterprises needing to buy. The target is for more than one third of hard currency imports to be financed via state auctions in 1989 (Christopher Bobinski, *FT*, 22 November 1988, p. 3). According to Peter Montagnon, an envisaged increase in foreign exchange retentions by enterprises plus state auctions means that in 1989 the state will dispose of only around 30 per cent of total foreign exchange, compared to 70 per cent in 1988 (*FT*, 25 November 1988, p. 2). Since 15 March 1989 there has been a free market in foreign exchange for private individuals. Individuals may also apply for a licence to operate retail exchange bureaus.

In March 1985 two types of hard currency accounts for individuals were opened, one for approved earnings yielding interest and the other only able to be converted into the former after one year (*EIU Country Profile* 1987–88: 16). In July 1987 this was changed into a system whereby the central bank issues savings certificates for fixed terms of one, two and three years at interest rates of 3, 8 and 9 per cent respectively, with a premium after three years if the interest is allowed to accumulate (*Polish Perspectives*, 1988, vol. XXXI, no. 1, p. 54). In the following November the National Savings Bank was turned into an independent commercial bank, which, from 1 June of the following year, entered the market for the purchase and sale of dollar-denominated coupons for use in hard currency shops.

Tax reliefs and subsidies have, in reality, been granted on a discretionary basis, showing the influence of relative bargaining strengths. Blazyca (1987: 49) provides a splendid example of how vested interests can undermine reform. In 1982 a tax was placed on increases in average wages over a certain percentage; firms' complaints of rigidity brought about a tax linked to wage growth exceeding 0.5 times the growth in the volume of enterprise output. This shifted firms' attention to output volume, while special pleading arose from those firms whose favourable output record in the previous year now penalized them. There followed discriminatory degrees of tax relief. A great obstacle to reform, however, is provided by the powerful ministries. Direct intervention took the form, for example, of 'operational programmes', the command planning of particular areas. In 1983 'government contracts' were introduced, and enterprises were induced by input and foreign exchange supplies to fulfil orders for goods. The former is being phased out and the latter increased. In the same year employment offices began to assign people to enterprises (Kurakowski 1988: 17), and the state budget now claims most enterprise depreciation allowances and enterprises forfeit the required percentage of any sum invested, which they have to deposit in banks, due to the failure to fulfil criteria such as deadlines and payback (Kurakowski 1988: 28).

The Tenth Congress in 1986 was attended by Gorbachev personally. Jaruzelski was critical of many aspects of the Polish economy, such as bureaucracy, reluctance of managers to accept responsibility and low levels of productivity. He promised, however, a better implementation of the reform, designated as the 'second stage' of the reform. The 1986–90 five-year plan revolves around energy and materials savings, increased exports to the West and restoring domestic equilibrium.

The October 1987 'second stage' of the reform

Aspects of the 'second stage' include the following:

1. *A three-year programme to restore macro equilibrium*, reducing inflation to 9 per cent by 1990, eliminating balance of payments deficits by 1991 and achieving zloty convertibility by the mid-1990s. Reducing subsidies implies steep rises in the prices of fuel and energy to bring them into line

with world levels and a 40 per cent increase in the prices of consumer goods and services (matched by income rises). Full employment was to be seen as the right to 'effective' work.[15]

2. *A streamlining of the institutional framework.* This not only involves a reduction in the number of central administrators, but also an integration of the enterprises in sectors such as coal, steel, petrochemicals, paper and electronics in order to centralize sales and purchasing programmes at home and abroad.[16] At the ministerial level it is envisaged that 'super-ministries' would be created in industry, energy and transport. The new ministries include the Ministry of Industry (superseding the ministries of energy and power, chemical and light industry, metallurgy and engineering, and materials and fuel management) ; the Ministry of Development and Construction; the Ministry of Transport, Shipping and Communications; and the Ministry of External Economic Relations (Chelstowski 1988: 13–4). There is also to be an increase in the powers of regional and local government bodies, including the transfer to them of a number of enterprises (p. 15).

3. Even so an *anti-monopoly law* was planned and has been operational since 1 January 1988. According to Brodzka (1987: 32), the rule whereby it is necessary to get prior permission for any business undertaking is to be abandoned and in the future a statement of intent will suffice. A list of 'large monopolist structures' will be drawn up that should be divided into smaller autonomous units, making it possible for enterprises to split if justified on efficiency grounds (Chelstowski 1988: 17). A competitive banking system, comprising nine state-owned 'credit' banks, was to be created by 1 January 1989. Enterprises are free to choose a bank, while banks are allowed to set differential charges and interest rates. The state monopoly in the procurement and wholesale distribution of food was to be ended, while the private and co-operative sectors of the economy were to be treated on a par with the state sector (e.g. given access to hard currency loans). State enterprises were to be permitted to sell bonds and shares,[17] to invest their earnings in partnerships or joint ventures, and to choose their own banks (Brodzka 1987: 32). There was talk of possible joint state-(domestic) private ventures (the terms of joint ventures with foreign companies were to be improved). There is also talk of 'benefits for persons temporarily without employment' (Brodzka 1987: 32).

In the *29 November 1987 referendum*, however, the government failed to get the required 51 per cent of eligible voters necessary to secure approval for its economic and political programme. Of the 67 per cent of the electorate who voted, 66 per cent approved the economic aspect and 69 per cent the political aspect, but these only constituted 44 per cent and 46 per cent respectively of the total potential electorate. As a result, the government planned to implement parts of the economic programme more slowly. Specifically, food price increases planned for 1988 would take place over a three-year period; prices would increase by an average of 40 per cent in 1988 instead of 110 per cent and retail prices as a whole would go up by 27 per cent on average as opposed to 40 per cent. On 1 February 1988 there was an average increase in prices of 27 per cent, with food prices rising by 40 per cent, accompanied by some protest marches and a 20 per cent increase in average pay, and on 1 March 1988 there were increases in the cost of bus and tram fares (66 per cent), and newspapers and nursery school charges. On 1 April 1988 coal prices were raised by 200 per cent and gas, heating fuel and electricity by 100 per cent. There would be no further price increases for the remainder of the year, meat rationing would remain during 1988, and there would be a lessening in enterprise profit tax reductions planned for that year, budget deficit reductions, and the rate of decentralization of raw materials distribution.

The end of April 1988 saw the start of over two weeks of isolated but significant labour unrest, the first since the introduction of martial law. The economic causes included the high inflation rate,[18] and political factors included the quest to relegalize Solidarity and protests against the detaining of its supporters. The government's response was a mixture of force, concessions, and the taking of special powers. There were wage concessions, accompanied by adjustments to the enterprise tax system. Special powers legislation (first mentioned in March) was passed, valid to the end of the year, which provided the government with the following powers: (1) labour disputes were only to be sanctioned if supported by the official National Trade Union Alliance (an outright ban was mooted at first); (2) to delay or reverse wage and price increases or even to impose freezes; to impose new taxes on individuals and enterprises; (3) to control spending decisions, including investment; (4) to liquidate and merge/divide enterprises more quickly; (5) to order redundancies; and (6) to dismiss management (see *Polish Perspectives*, 1988, vol. XXXI, no. 3, p. 56). This interference with the rights of enterprises and labour was deemed necessary to ensure the success of the economic reforms (ironically) and to combat inflation.

Despite these special measures, further strikes broke out in mid-August in which the demand for Solidarity's recognition figured much more prominently. Lech Walesa met Interior Minister General Czeslaw Kiszczak on a number of occasions, the first on the last day of the month, and the government agreed to broad talks beginning in mid-October. After a critical report from a parliamentary commission, which claimed, among other things, that actual economic reforms had been minimal, Prime Minister Messner and his government resigned on 19 September. He was replaced shortly afterwards by Mieczyslaw Rakowski. October saw the new Industry Minister Mieczyslaw Wilczek (a successful private businessman) preparing to draw up a 'hit list' of 150 unprofitable enterprises, followed by the announcement of the 'progressive liquidation', over the period up to the end of 1990, of the Gdansk shipyard (over

10,000 workers). The government stressed the losses made by the shipyard, with one eye on the international lenders, while the opposition attributed political reasons, since Gdansk was the birthplace of Solidarity. The October talks failed to materialize, but the following January the Polish leadership accepted the principle of trade union pluralism, subject to conditions such as abiding by the constitution, working within the law, and supporting economic reform. Solidarity agreed to enter into discussions, these beginning on 6 February 1989. The Roundtable Agreement was reached on 5 April. Solidarity was relegalized. In the following June election, the lower house (*Sejm*) was to have 65 per cent of its seats reserved for the Polish United Workers' Party and its allies, with the remaining 35 per cent contested by the opposition alone. All the seats in the new upper house (*Senate*) were to be freely contested. Both houses elect a new executive President. Solidarity and the government agreed on 80 per cent indexation of wages. There were also promises to decontrol farm prices and land sales.

Agriculture

After the 1944 land reforms the average size of landholding was still only 6.4 hectares (Kolankiewicz and Lewis 1988: 33). The collectivization process was reversed in 1956. At the end of 1986 land tenure as a percentage of arable land was as follows: individual land holdings, 72.0; state farms, 18.5; collective farms and agricultural circles, 3.9; others (e.g. State Land Fund), 5.6 (p. xv). The private sector is also dominant in respect of agricultural output, contributing 78 per cent in 1985. In 1970 the figure for output was 85 per cent, and 81 per cent for agricultural land.[19] In the early 1950s the maximum private holding was set at 15 hectares, but this was increased during the 1970s, to reach 50 hectares by the end of the decade (CIA 1986: 454). The average private farm, sometimes not even in one piece, however, is very small. In 1982 this was only 6.6 hectares, excluding farms of under two hectares, and 5.0 hectares including them (Cook 1986b: 474). In 1986 the farm structure, in hectares, was as follows: 0.51–2, 29.6 per cent; 2–5, 28.09 per cent; 5–7, 12.2 per cent; 7–10, 12.9 per cent; 10–15, 10.6 per cent; and over 15, 6.7 per cent (Cochrane 1988: 53). Technology is typically backward (horses are more typical than tractors), while farmers rely mainly on inputs from the state sector (e.g. the state exercises monopoly power over the supply of machines, chemicals, and building materials and monopsony power over the purchase of the product). By contrast, in 1984 the average state farm was 3, 169 hectares in size (Blazyca 1986: 5).[20]

After 1956 private farmers were still required to meet state obligatory delivery quotas for products such as grain, potatoes, meat, and milk. In January 1972, however, this system was substituted for one of voluntary contracts, although, of course, the state could still use its considerable monopoly and monopsony powers: prices and input supplies were also improved. On 1 January 1989 the state monopoly in the purchasing of agricultural products came to an end (with exceptions such as tobacco, poppyseed, and hemp). The monopoly in respect of fruit and vegetables had been ended some years earlier *(Polish Perspectives*, 1989, vol. XXXII, no. 1, p. 57).

Cook (1984 and 1986b) describes agricultural policy during the 1970s as guided by a belief that the socialized sector could be strengthened by bureaucratic intervention without injuring the private sector. Thus, for example, agricultural circles (co-operative bodies providing services) were taken into state control in 1973; crop and cultivation schedules were also imposed by local administrators during the 1970s (Kurakowski 1988: 23). Land sales were prohibited if the result would have been farms of less than eight hectares (Cochrane 1988: 50).

The Solidarity era[21] saw the start of a period of encouragement given to private agriculture, with promises of permanent status and improved input supplies, credit, prices and opportunities to purchase land from the State Land Fund.

The impact of free market prices varies between commodities. While only 5 to 8 per cent of grain is thus priced, the figure for the marketed output of fruit, vegetables, flowers and eggs is over 60 per cent (Quaisser 1986: 566). Government price determination is affected by factors such as the state of the consumer good market and the cost of farm inputs. Since 1983–84 there has been an annual adjustment in purchase prices to take account of rising input prices; previously, purchase prices were based on factors such as the average cost of production (Quaisser 1986: 276).

The Polish Roman Catholic Church's 1982 plan to aid private agriculture with Western funds has had a chequered history. The plan mainly involves sales of Western commodities such as machines to private farmers to provide the zlotys to finance schemes such as water supply, storage, and repair facilities, and the equipping of farming colleges. The original sum was envisaged to be $2 billion to $3 billion, but this was drastically reduced to $25 million. Cardinal Jozef Glemp abandoned the scheme altogether in September 1986 on the grounds of the state's desire to exercise control. In July of the following year the Polish government approved a $10 million US government scheme, and on 18 September the Church Agricultural Committee was formally set up, which was exempt from taxes and customs duties and free from state control.

The Foundation for the Development of Polish Agriculture was set up, with government approval, on 20 February 1988. This is a non-profit-making organization backed by the Rockefeller Foundation and managed by a council including agronomists and businessmen from the United States and Western European countries and a minority of experts from Poland itself, although permission is needed from the Polish Ministry of Agriculture for specific activities. The aim is to promote agricultural exports in particular and to improve agriculture in general. For example, the first loan from Western banks, for $2.4 million over three years, was used to import high protein pig feed in order to stimulate exports of ham to the United States, the proceeds going to improve educational, technical, and commercial projects in agriculture.

Joint equity ventures

Since 1985 Poland has allowed joint equity ventures with Western companies, originally on the following conditions: a normal maximum 49 per cent foreign ownership (exceptions being possible); the head to be a Polish citizen; repatriated hard currency profits to be earned by exports (the other possibility is for foreign partners to buy Polish goods with zloty earnings for resale in the West); a proportion of foreign exchange earnings must be sold to the state; and the profit tax is to be reduced as the proportion of output exported rises. Few ventures have actually been set up. In 1986 the Polish National Airline entered into one with an Austrian construction company and a US hotel chain to refurbish a terminal-hotel complex. By the end of 1987 there were sixteen ventures in operation (*Polish Perspectives*, 1988, vol. XXXI, no. 1, p. 51). A new law, operational after 1 January 1989, allows the following: wholly foreign-owned enterprises; joint foreign-private Polish ventures; top management to be foreign; an extension of the normal tax holiday from two to three years (up to six years for priority sectors); a reduction in the basic profit tax from 50 to 40 per cent (lower rates, in proportion to output exported, apply, down to 10 per cent for 100 per cent exports); and only 15 per cent (instead of 25) of hard currency earnings is to be sold to the state at the official rate (Peter Montagnon, *FT*, 17 November 1988, p. 9). Repatriated hard currency dividends are taxed at a rate of 30 per cent, while foreign partner dividends retained in Poland avoid this (Margie Lindsay, *FT Survey*, 13 December 1988, p. 39). The 'Polonia' companies are discussed in the following section.

The private non-agricultural sector of the economy

According to Åslund (1984, 1985), the sector reached its nadir in 1955, and from that point onwards the state recognized the value of the private sector, albeit restricted, to complement the state sector. A process of cyclical recovery after 1956 resulted in a 1982 private sector figure of 5.9 per cent of the non-agricultural labour force (1984: 428). The employment maximum for a handicraft enterprise was raised from one employee in 1955 to six (eight in construction) in March 1966, and then 15. On average handicraft firms employ only about two people and the figure is lower for other private firms (1984: 429). The limit was subsequently raised to fifty (*FT*, 24 December 1988, p. 2). According to Kurakowski (1988: 15) the non-nationalized, non-agricultural sector of the economy employs nearly 10 per cent of the non-agricultural labour force, and Dobija (*The Independent*, 26 November 1987, p. 11) reports that private enterprise accounts for seven per cent of industrial output and that in the Lomianki district just outside Warsaw private firms employ between two and ten people on average (several employ up to 100). At the Thirteenth Congress of the Democratic Party in 1986 there was a call for an increase in the private sector's share of national income from the current 7 per cent to perhaps 25 per cent (Kolankiewicz and Lewis 1988: 127). The leasing of state property was allowed in 1964, and twelve years later it was made possible for foreigners who were once Polish citizens (and later on others) to set up sizeable private companies in Poland – the 'Polonia' companies, which are owned by former Polish citizens, pay no tax for three years and can repatriate 50 per cent of hard currency earnings; Kolankiewicz and Lewis (1988: 127) give a figure of 683 firms. Bobinski (*FT*, 16 December 1987, p. 5) states that their association, called Interpolcom, now represents only 660 Western-owned companies (compared with 695 at the end of 1986), due to stricter hard currency regulations and tax increases. They employ 60,000 and account for about 1 per cent of national income.

During 1987 and 1988 further encouragement was given to the private sector as part of the new round of reforms. As of 1 January 1989, the private sector is, theoretically, treated on a par with the state and co-operative sectors as regards taxation, number of employees, access to credit and input supply. Instead of needing authorization as before, private enterprises are able to register without licences, except in certain defined activities such as explosives and drugs. In September 1987 the first meeting took place of the independent Economic Society of Warsaw, even though it took some time afterwards to actually get registered. The aims of this organization and the Industrial Society of Krakow, comprising private businessmen and economists, are to encourage the private sector and the market economy in general. The advice given to start up private enterprises is envisaged to bring in revenue in the form of a fee and a share of future profits.

Rostowski (1989: 194–95) estimates that in 1986 the private sector as a whole (including agriculture) accounted for almost one-third of the total labour force, and between 38 per cent and 45.2 per cent of personal money incomes (compared with an official figure of 24.5 per cent). He considers the official figure of 18.2 per cent (of which agriculture 10.2 per cent) of produced national income to be a considerable underestimation, although the true share is probably considerably smaller than the share in personal money incomes.

Conclusion

Poland has a history of political dismemberment. World attention was focused on the country during the 'Solidarity era'. A whole series of industrial reforms has been undertaken, the most recent being the January 1982 version, largely thwarted by factors such as severe supply bottlenecks, and its 'second stage' version of October 1987. On paper this reform is along Hungarian lines, but it remains to be seen whether it will be translated into reality. According to legislation operative as of 1 January 1989, the private sector is, in theory, treated on a par with the state and co-operative sectors. Poland has, like Yugoslavia, a largely private agriculture and shares problems such as high foreign indebtedness and inflationary tendencies. Poland shows quite clearly the need for political reforms to accompany the economic, involving society more in decision-making in return for shouldering the burden of austerity. The Roundtable Agreement of 5 April 1989 was a good start.

Table 9.2 Poland: statistical survey

Arable land (%)	Individual holdings	State farms	Collective farms and agricultural circles	Others
	72	18.5	3.9	5.6

Private sector contribution to total agricultural output (1975)	78%
Private non-agricultural sector share of national income (1987)	7.0%
Joint equity ventures (end 1987)	16
Population (1987)	37.8 million

Sources: Kolankiewicz and Lewis (1988: xv, 127); Polish Perspectives, 1988, vol. xxxi, no. 1, p. 51. For figures on growth, inflation, and debt, see Table 9.1.

Postscript

In the election of 4 June 1989 and the run-off of the 18th, with turnouts of 62 and 25 per cent respectively, Solidarity won all the opposition seats in the Sejm and 99 out of the 100 Senate seats (one going to an independent). Only 2 of the 35 (unopposed) candidates on the Government's National List gained the necessary majority of votes in the first round. Jaruzelsky was elected President on 19 July 1989 by a margin of only one vote. Rakowski replaced Jaruzelsky as General Secretary on 29 July. Czeslaw Kisczak became Prime Minister on 2 August, but resigned only 15 days later unable to form a government.

The new premier, confirmed on 24 August, is Tadeusz Mazowiecki (formerly editor of Solidarity's weekly newspaper). Solidarity (winning all the contested 161 seats) came to an agreement with the United Peasants' Party (UPP) (allocated 76 seats in the 460 member Sejm) and the Democratic Party (DP) (27 seats), both formerly subservient to the Polish United Workers' Party (PUWP) (173 seats: another 23 seats are occupied by its Catholic allies). Continued respect for the Warsaw Pact helped ensure a positive Soviet response to the new premier, a significant reflection on the status of the Brezhnev Doctrine. Mazowiecki did not present a detailed economic programme during his acceptance speech, but made several proposals: 'Those institutions which have been blocked, such as the market, must be set free. The role of the state should be similar to that in Western countries'. More specifically, he promised an anti-inflation policy and an end to the state monopoly over food procurement. A request was made for more generous debt rescheduling and Western aid ('He who helps early helps twice'). Allocation of the 23 seats in the government is as follows: Solidarity (11, inluding finance, industry, construction, labour and social policy, Central Planning Office and Economic Council), the PUWP (4, namely defence, interior, transport, and foreign trade), the UPP (4, including agriculture), the DP (3, namely scientific development, domestic trade, and communications), and one independent (foreign ministry). The new finance minister, Leszek Balcerowicz, has pronounced in favour of deflation (tempered by unemployment benefit), competition, privatization, and the market: what Poland needs is a 'normal Western market economy'.

These moves toward greater democracy have been rewarded by the Western trade concessions, debt rescheduling and aid (this includes a US scheme to support the private sector, and an EC co-ordinated food programme – the proceeds from zloty sales are to go into a jointly administered fund for the development of agriculture and food distribution). On 25 July the European Community and Poland initialled a trade and economic co-operation accord; most quotas on Polish industrial imports are to be phased out by 1995, and even tariffs on a few Polish agricultural products are to be lowered.

On 1 August 1989 meat rationing and price controls on most foodstuffs were ended. This gave a big boost to inflation (already 85 per cent over the first seven months of 1989 compared to the same period of the previous year: *FT*, 31 August 1989, p. 16).

Notes

1. Coal accounted for nearly 70 per cent of primary energy consumption in 1980. Hard coal output in 1987 was 193 Mt, of which 31 Mt was exported, making Poland the world's fourth largest producer. The first nuclear reactor is not due to be operational until 1991.
2. See especially Kolankiewicz and Lewis (1988: Chapter 1).
3. See Blazyca (1980b); Nuti (1981a, 1981b); and Brus (1982).
4. One reason for this was the linkage of wages to value added, the latter being boosted by price increases resulting from the manipulation of 'new' products.
5. Investment fell to 26 per cent of national income in 1979. Blazyca (1986: 17) shows that the annual average rates of growth of investment and import volume respectively were 17.8 per cent and 27.3 per cent for 1971–75; 1.0 per cent and 11.4 per cent for 1976; and –0.9 per cent and –5.8 per cent in 1977–79. Investment fell by 12.3 per cent in 1980, 22.3 per cent in 1981 and 12.1 per cent in 1982 (p. 25): this extended completion times and enlarged bottlenecks.
6. Note that Pewex stores supply scarce goods for convertible currencies.

7. Poland also owes 6.5 billion roubles, mainly to the Soviet Union (Kolankiewicz and Lewis 1988: 98).
8. In 1984 fishing and aircraft landing rights were restored, but it was not until February 1987 that US credits and MFN treatment were reinstated.
9. See Nuti (1977, 1981a); Wanless (1980); Brus (1982); and Blazyca (1980b).
10. The *EIU (Country Profile* 1987–88: 16) suggests that in the setting of the prices of such products as cigarettes, vodka, and cars, black market prices are used.
11. Kurakowski (1988: 36) describes the exchange rate as fixed to cover the domestic cost of 80 per cent of all exports.
12. A membership figure of around 7 million is usually given for 1987–88. Membership was a little over half the eligible work-force at the start of 1987, compared with a peak of over 80 per cent for Solidarity.
13. In 1985 subsidies in total, including those for final consumption, amounted to 39.2 per cent of total state expenditure (*EIU Country Profile*, 1987–88: 33). *EEN* (1988, vol. 2, no. 6, p. 5) estimates that subsidies have amounted to around a half of state expenditure in recent years.
14. Set up in January 1987 to encourage exports, with shares owned by the state, banks and other state and co-operative enterprises.
15. Note that the restoration of living standards is now not envisaged to take place until 1995 at the earliest (Kolankiewicz and Lewis 1988: 100).
16. Enterprises are encouraged to join by funding, tax concessions and increases in retained foreign exchange earnings.
17. A stock exchange is a future possibility. In 1987 an experiment was begun in a textile factory in Lodz to sell stocks to its employees.
18. Forty-five per cent in the first quarter of 1988, compared with the same period in the previous year.
19. Until 1981 socialized agriculture had priority purchase rights from the State Land Fund. Retiring private farmers only received a pension if their landholdings were handed over to this organization.
20. For an analysis of the performance of private and state agriculture see Boyd (1988).
21. The organizations banned in 1982 were Rural Solidarity, Solidarity of Individual Farmers, and Farmers' Solidarity.

Chapter ten

Romania

Background

Walachia in the late fourteenth century and Moldavia in 1455 were absorbed
into the Ottoman Empire. Russia annexed Bessarabia (south-east Moldavia)
in 1812. Under the terms of the Treaty of Paris of 1856, following Russia's
defeat in the Crimean War, the Principalities of Walachia and Moldavia were
placed under the joint protection of the European Great Powers, Turkey retaining only formal sovereignty. In 1959 a single prince was elected who, two
years later, gained international recognition of his administrative unification.
This *de facto* statehood was internationally recognized by the 1878 Treaty of
Berlin. A royal dictatorship was established in 1938, the monarch forming his
own fascist organization (the Front of National Rebirth), and increasingly
closer economic links helped lead to alliance with Germany during the Second World War, until 1945, when Romania switched sides.

President Nicolae Ceausescu, who became First Secretary of the Romanian Communist Party in 1965 after the death of Gheorghe Gheorghiu-Dej,
party leader since 1944, and who has effectively introduced a form of family
rule in Romania, has exercised a relatively high degree of foreign policy and
economic independence from the Soviet Union. Severe debt problems have
moderated this stance in the 1980s, however, and there is the argument that
the impression of independence has been deliberately exaggerated in order to
gain access to Western capital and technology. Soviet troops were withdrawn
in 1958, and 1962 saw both the last Warsaw Pact troop exercise on Romanian
soil and the rejection of Khrushchev's plans to make Comecon a supranational planning agency and Romania mainly a primary producer. Romania
has boycotted Warsaw Pact troop manoeuvres in other countries since August
1967 (staff still participate), did not break off diplomatic relations with Israel
after the 1967 Arab-Israeli War, sent an ambassador back to Albania as early
as January 1963, was the first Comecon country to recognize the European
Community, and spoke out against the invasion of Czechoslovakia in 1968,
although on the grounds of political sovereignty and not support for liberal
reforms.

Brezhnev, in 1976, was the last Soviet leader to visit Romania before Gorbachev did so in 1987. Romania was the last East European Comecon state to be visited by Gorbachev.

Before the Second World War Romania was one of the poorest of the European countries, a mainly agricultural country, with 75 per cent of the population classified as rural and a similar proportion of the labour force working in agriculture. Per capita national income in 1937 was less than half that of Czechoslovakia (Crowther 1988: 55, 175, based on Berend and Ranki). Large estates predominated, despite spasmodic and limited attempts at land reform; agriculture provided a subsistence living to most of the agricultural population and export crops to Western Europe. Only 8 per cent of the labour force was employed in industry in 1938. Industry was overwhelmingly oriented towards consumer goods and the processing of raw materials; only oil production was large-scale and modern (see Tsantis and Pepper 1979: 1; Gilberg 1975: 9). Agricultural products accounted for 65 per cent of exports, and manufactures only 2 per cent (Crowther 1988: 55, quoting Spulber). Even by 1950 agriculture employed about three-quarters of the work-force and contributed nearly 40 per cent to the national product (Shafir 1985: 139, 109). The population is currently some 23 million[2] and the country is well endowed with agricultural land, energy, and raw materials.

Table 10.1 shows net hard currency debt and official figures for rates of growth of NMP. Note that there is particular concern about the meaningfulness of official Romanian statistics.

Table 10.1 Romania: debt and average annual rate of growth of NMP

Average annual rate of growth of NMP (%)

1951–5	1956–60	1961–65	1966–70	1971–75	1976–80	1981	1982	1983
14.2	6.6	9.0	7.8	11.3	7.3	2.2	2.6	3.4

1984	1985	1986	1987	1988
7.7	5.9	7.3	4.8	3.2

Net hard currency debt	*1981*	*1986*
($ billions)	9.8	5.8

Sources: Economist Intelligence Unit, *Country Profile* (1987–8: 13, 34); Shafir (1985: 110); Smith (1983: 40); *The Economist* (15 April 1989, p.122); Abecor Country Report, October 1988, p. 1.

Industrial reform

The pre-1967 Romanian economy seems to have been even more highly centralized than its pre-1965 counterpart in the Soviet Union; targets were imposed on industrial enterprises with little consultation. After a series of experiments, the *blueprint of industrial reform ('Directives') appeared in December 1967*, although the first stage of implementation actually ran from 1969 to about 1972 (Granick 1975; Smith 1980, 1981; Spigler 1973).

The basic production unit was to be the 'Central' (*Centrala*), usually the result of a country-wide horizontal integration of one large enterprise with smaller ones, with location of headquarters at the site of the former. The first Central was not set up until 1969, due mainly to ministerial resistance to loss of power. Plan targets were of the traditional type, such as output and assortment, sales, exports, imports, cost reduction, material inputs and financial aspects: these remained obligatory, but the degree of consultation was stepped up. According to Granick, there was little real decision-making below the level of the ministry. The role of the enterprise involved little more than enhancing technical efficiency. For example while ministries could reallocate individual enterprise tasks within aggregate central targets, enterprises could administer only the details of previously concluded contracts. Managerial behaviour could not in any sense be explained by bonus maximization, since bonuses were easily obtained – the targets were not only slack but were frequently changed, partly to fit in with ministerial assessment of managers. This was more important in determining managerial rewards than plan fulfilment. Romanian industry remained even more tightly controlled than its Soviet counterpart (Granick 1975). The Central was responsible for imposing disaggregated plan targets on constituent enterprises, including gross output, assortment of key products in physical terms, material supplies, labour productivity, wage fund, investment, and payments to the state budget.

The Directives stressed financial discipline, showing a greater concern for cost and profit and the need to increase the role played by interest-bearing credits in the financing of state-determined investments. There were some limited concessions to decentralized investment, and credit policy in general included the use of penal interest rates if credit conditions were not met. The incentive system involved reducing the impact of bonuses by integrating most of them into basic wage and salary scales and introducing penalties for non-fulfilment of plan targets. A distinction was made between above-plan profit due to the enterprise's 'own activities' (a part of which was to finance bonuses and socio-cultural activities, with the rest going into the state budget) and that due to external circumstances, which was to be surrendered to the state budget.

A novel innovation was the replacement of 'one-man management' by 'collective management', involving a board of management at the enterprise level (called a 'workers' committee' after 1971) and an 'administrative council' at the level of the Central, later called a 'council of the working people'. Until 1971 the *de facto* powers of management boards were not great and enterprise autonomy between 1971 and 1978 was negligible.

During the *second stage of implementation* (1973–78) the number of Centrals was approximately halved, each constituting about 15 enterprises and 32,000 employees. The declared aim was to reduce ministerial power and move management closer to production. Consequently, Centrals were to deal with intra-Central material balancing and materials and labour transfer between constituent enterprises. The number of centrally allocated products, however, actually increased from 180 to 720 in 1974. Centrals were to co-ordinate their plans with functional ministries (such as labour and finance) and with local authorities, while substantial numbers of engineering personnel were transferred to enterprises to concentrate on technical matters. The desirability of enhancing the importance of credits as opposed to grants was confirmed, although from 1973 onwards state approval was needed for all investment. In 1971 the profit markup on average cost was shifted from costs to capital employed.

A wholesale price revision in the period 1974–76 aimed at reducing subsidies and the considerable differences in profitability between branches. Capital and rental (land tax) charges were introduced in 1971, although in 1977 the former was replaced by a progressive tax on planned profit in excess of 15 per cent: turnover tax was reduced in part compensation. Personal income tax on public sector earnings was replaced by a tax on the wage fund.

The *third stage of the Romanian reform* was announced in March 1978 and put into operation from the start of 1979. The *'New Economic-Financial Mechanism'* is theoretically based on the principle of workers' self-management and has as its main aim financial discipline. Economic and financial self-management involves the covering of costs, including socio-cultural services and investment, out of revenue (the latter is also to be financed by credits rather than grants). A prime stimulus was the damage caused by rising world prices of raw materials and energy, and this pressure to economize on raw materials and other inputs also caused net output to be the replacement for gross output as the main enterprise indicator and increased emphasis to be given to cost reduction and export indicators. Other remaining indicators include gross output, investment and labour productivity. Compulsory payments to the state budget (such as taxes on profits, net output and the wage fund) and repayment of bank credit have priority over the enterprise's own funds in the distribution of planned profits, but over-plan profits are divided up according to set rules. Monthly wages and salaries are affected by bonuses and penalties for over- and underfulfilment of gross output, labour productivity, exports or material consumption targets, while funds for personal bonuses and socio-cultural activities are fed by over-plan profits caused by overfulfilling targets such as cost reduction, physical output and exports. Bonuses from planned profits are reduced if the net production indicator and delivery contracts for physical output are not fulfilled. Despite the complexity of the scheme, bonuses account for only about 5 per cent of earnings. There is now a single rate of exchange between the leu and the dollar and the transferable rouble with respect to enterprise accounting. This forging of a direct link between domestic and world prices helps to identify profitable and loss-making enterprises.

'Self-management' in Romanian industry is not equivalent to its Yugoslav

counterpart (see especially Smith 1980, 1981). Workers are actually in a minority on 'workers' committees', compared with managerial-technical staff and representatives of the party and the trade unions. Although there appears to be a degree of real consultation in plan setting, the committees seem to be mainly a means of achieving centrally determined goals by going over the heads of management in questions such as the search for hidden reserves. It is also worth noting that large production units also perform social functions such as the provision of housing and education.

The New Economic-Financial Mechanism (NEFM) has undergone changes, but Romania has always retained a command economy. In 1981 the minimum wage was abolished, while pay has subsequently been tied to enterprise performance, especially in export and mining activities. On 1 September 1983 a new piece rate system was introduced, which meant the end of the former guarantee of a monthly income equal to 80 per cent of an employee's regular pay and of the 20 per cent limit on extra income dependent on plan fulfilment (Shafir 1985: 124). Thus wages are related to output without upper or lower limits as an incentive to increase production (Turnock 1986: 275). A new employee has to sign a contract with an enterprise to work there for at least five years. During this time the employee is given only half of profit share entitlement, with the remainder placed in a bank account. Premature quitting of the job results in forfeiture of both this sum and the years counting towards pension rights (Shafir 1985: 124–25). In addition to the practice of school-children, students, teachers and clerical workers donating a number of days of free labour at harvest time, the September 1985 draft law required everyone over 18 years of age to contribute an unpaid six days each year in public works or an equivalent monetary compensation. A new poll tax was introduced and the proceeds paid over to local and regional councils. The normal 1–2 May holiday was rescinded in 1987 for those working in enterprises not fulfilling their output plans. In August 1987 workers were granted bonuses for overfulfilling export targets.

The harsh winter aggravated power shortages to such an extent that in October 1985 the military took control of coal-fired and hydroelectric power plants,[3] with the civilian director subordinated to an army officer and workers subjected to army regulations. Absenteeism was treated as absence without leave or desertion. In 1987 there were rumours of possible military takeovers of larger industrial enterprises and mines, in response to worker unrest and strikes due to the austerity measures. In October a state of emergency was declared in energy before the onset of winter, thus militarizing the sector. Several ministers for mining and energy were also dismissed in that month. Sweeping personnel changes in general may perhaps be seen as a substitute for economic and political reform.

In a January 1987 speech Ceausescu called for a more effective application of the NEFM and the system of 'self-management' and 'self-financing', rejecting moves towards market socialism and private enterprise as incompatible with socialism. On 5 May he stated that one cannot speak about the reform of socialism through the so-called development of small private property; capitalist property, small or large, is capitalist property. Ceausescu thinks it inconceivable that production units and sectors of the economy should become 'independent'. This demonstrates the conservative way in which 'self-management' and 'self-financing' are interpreted in Romania.

In June 1987 Ceausescu, as chairman, announced that the Supreme Council on Socio-Economic Development (SCSD) was to be placed in 'supreme command' of the economy, the State Planning Commission functioning as Secretariat of the Supreme Council. The SCSD was to be responsible for both drafting and implementing economic policy and was to play a more important role in drawing up plans. Departments in charge of economic and social policy were to be represented on the SCSD's new standing board. This move, together with others (such as the merging of the ministries of chemicals and petrochemicals and the creation of new ministries for mining and oil) may be seen as an assertion of party control over a more streamlined planning system, in an attempt to avoid radical economic reforms. By any standards the Romanian economy remains highly centralized.

Agriculture

In 1945 a *land reform* took place. The decision to *collectivize agriculture* was taken four years later and the process was completed by 1962. Note, however, that some independent private farms still exist even today in mountainous regions, although no person outside the family is allowed to be employed and a progressive tax is levied. In 1985 co-operatives accounted for 61 per cent of cultivated area, state farms and other state institutions 30 per cent and private agriculture 9 per cent (*EIU Country Profile*, 1987–88, p. 17). In 1971 co-operative farmers were allowed minimum monthly advances, although two years later these became dependent on the fulfilment of plan targets (state farms were also affected by this). Since 1982 peasants have had to work at least 300 days for the co-operative or at other specified places. Compulsory livestock quotas were introduced in 1984, and it was also decreed that every farmstead that did not meet the (raised) obligatory procurement deliveries could be deprived of the use of *private plots* or, as far as individuals are concerned, the plots could be transferred to the co-operative or into state ownership. Only those peasants meeting the quotas may sell any surplus on the open market, where maximum prices are actually state determined (Shafir 1985: 117). According to Turnock (1986: 185), in 1983 local authority certificates were needed for individuals who wished to sell their own fruit and vegetables on the open market at maximum prices set by the state. Individual and co-operative farmers must register all their animals and must breed animals under contract to the state.

As a result of the 1970s measures, individuals or groups were able to sign contracts with co-operative farms to work at piece-rate pay or in share-cropping arrangements, while more land was made available for family use if plans were fulfilled (Shafir 1985: 109). Since 1979 there have been experiments with agro-industrial associations, concerned with processing agricultural products (Turnock 1986: 185).

At the end of March 1988 an actual timetable was announced for a highly controversial scheme of so-called *systemization* (*sistematizare*). This had already begun and was originally made law in 1978. The idea is to destroy 7,000 to 8,000 of the 13,000 villages (villages of less than 3,000 residents are the ones affected), creating instead 550 'agro-industrial centres' by the year 2000. This deadline was extended a short while later. The aims are as follows: originally to increase cultivable land by up to 300,000 hectares, but Ceausescu conceded, in November 1988, that this was not feasible (*EEN*, 1988, vol. 2, no. 25, p. 5); reduce the costs of providing rural infrastructure and 'improve' services and housing (in the form of blocks of flats); enhance police surveillance (*EEN*, 1988, vol. 2, no. 7, p. 7; no. 10, p. 5; no. 22, p. 3); remove the remaining differences between urban and rural life, including living standards; take account of the replacement of people by machines in agriculture; and reduce ethnic differences. The Hungarian government is openly concerned that this last point may be a way of further suppressing the Hungarian minority in Romania. As Ceausescu put it in a 2 June 1988 speech, the programme 'would eliminate essential differences between villages and towns, increasingly draw working, living, and cultural conditions in villages and towns closer to each other and create the necessary prerequisites for a homogeneous society' (reported in *FT* 21 June 1988, p. 2).[4] In a 28 November speech he hinted at some possible policy amelioration in saying that a considerable number of villages could already be rated as 'genuine agro-industrial towns'. Each family with a farming background was initially deemed to be entitled to a private plot of up to 250 square metres; this was reduced to 80 for others (*EEN*, 1988, vol. 2, no. 22, p. 3). In November 1988, however, a general figure of 300 square metres was announced (*EEN*, 1988, vol. 2, no. 25, p. 5).

The private sector

In 1980, as a percentage of agricultural land, individual farms accounted for 9.4 per cent, the private plots of co-operative farmers 6.2 per cent, co-operatives 54.4 per cent, state farms 13.6 per cent and other state lands 16.4 per cent (Turnock 1986: 184). The following year the first two accounted for nearly 14 per cent of cereal output, more than 22 per cent of maize, over 60 per cent of potatoes, more than 40 per cent of vegetables, 93.9 per cent of fruit, nearly 44 per cent of meat, almost 60 per cent of milk and eggs, and over 46 per cent of wool (Shafir 1985: 45). In 1985 the private sector occupied 14 per cent of arable land and was responsible for 59 per cent of potatoes, 40 per cent of vegetables, 63 per cent of fruit, 48 per cent of meat, 59 per cent of milk, and 57 per cent of eggs (Cochrane 1988: 48). Obligatory elements persist. For example there are mandatory quotas for products such as potatoes, milk, and eggs and since 1986 plotholders are required to devote 500 square metres to wheat. This is to be delivered to the collective farm in return for the lower yield from an equivalent area on the collective farm (Cochrane 1988: 49). There is a theoretical maximum limit of 0.15 of a hectare for private plots, but in practice this is often restricted to 250 square metres (*EEN*, 1988, vol. 2, no. 15, p. 4).

Foreign trade and payments

Romania's more independent role in foreign policy cost it dearly in terms of the lack of access to cheap Soviet oil (due to the Moscow price formula) following the 1973–74 and 1979 OPEC price hikes. The cost was especially high in view of the massive expansion of the petrochemical industry and of oil-refining capacity with exports to the West in mind. This capacity increased from 16 Mt in 1970 to 34 Mt in 1987. Romania became a net oil importer in the mid-1970s. Domestic production fell from 14.7 Mt in 1976 to 11.5 Mt in 1984 when 9 Mt was re-exported in the form of refined and processed products; 10.5 Mt was re-exported in 1986. It was not until December 1985 that an agreement was reached with the Soviet Union to increase oil deliveries by 250 per cent over the following five years, up to five Mt annually from two Mt in 1985; in 1986 6.3 Mt were actually delivered. World oil prices started to fall in November 1985.

Romania continued to stress all-around, rapid industrialization, especially heavy industry, despite Khrushchev's plea for Comecon specialization. Crowther (1988: 132) traces the origins of the desire for autonomous industrialization back to a pre-socialist history of economic subordination to powerful neighbours. Ferrous and non-ferrous metallurgy, petrochemicals (even though domestic oil production was declining) and engineering were priority sectors during the 1970s, since these were badly hit by the world recession. The energy-intensive strategy of expanding petrochemical industry, oil refining capacity, and engineering was based on the expectation that exports of machinery and equipment would pay for oil imports and for other raw materials, and that these would be processed with the aid of Western capital goods bought with borrowed funds to provide hard currency exports.

In late 1981, following Poland, Romania asked to reschedule its hard currency debt, by which time the debt-service ratio was 35 per cent. Service payments were suspended in early 1982 and rescheduling took place in 1982, 1983 and 1986, the last partly due to the effects of Chernobyl on exports of foodstuffs. Romania's response has been a severe austerity programme, mainly affecting imports, defence, and domestic consumption, in order to try to repay the debt by 1990.[5] The idea is to avoid such overdependence again. Hard currency trade surpluses were achieved in 1983, 1984, 1985 and 1986 as a result of a drastic reduction in imports and a fall in domestic consumption, and the net hard currency debt fell to $5.8 billion by the end of 1986 from a peak of $9.8 billion in 1981 (*EIU Country Profile*, 1987–88, p. 34). Borrowing, however, was to resume in the mid-1980s. The gross hard currency debt was $10.2 billion in 1981, $5.5 billion six years later, and an estimated $3.2 billion (net debt $1.7 billion) by the end of 1988 (Judy Dempsey, *FT*, 15 February 1989, p. 6, and 14 April 1989, p. 4). In April Ceausescu announced that Romania had fully paid off its foreign debt by the end of March 1989, and did not intend to borrow again.

In November 1987 there were serious protests against economic conditions in Brasov and other places, especially pay reductions linked to the non-fulfilment of performance targets, redundancies, price increases, serious food shortages and fuel restrictions. These constituted the most serious disturbances since the three-day Jiu Valley miners' strike in 1977 (although unrest and strikes have punctuated the 1980s). Forced labour direction was also rumoured to be a factor elsewhere. State reaction included promises of short-term bonus payments, pay increases from mid-1988 onwards and increased food supplies, but the general strategy of rapid debt repayment and aversion to market reforms was confirmed. There was to be a change to a district-based production and distribution system, with each district allowed to retain output in excess of planned quotas. The harsh winters of 1984–85 and 1985–86 greatly aggravated supply problems and drastic measures were taken to restrict power usage by households. Rationing of basic commodities, especially foodstuffs such as bread, sugar and cooking oil, has increased since 1981, when bread rationing was introduced after a gap of 27 years. The general public is not legally allowed to possess hard currencies, and Kent cigarettes have become a means of exchange in black markets.

Romania joined GATT in 1971 and the IMF and the World Bank the following year. Hungary, Poland and Yugoslavia are granted MFN treatment by the United States. This was given to Romania in 1975 on the basis of a relatively independent foreign policy and a liberal stance on Jewish emigration. Human rights abuses, however, have caused second thoughts in the United States, and on 26 June 1987 the US Senate voted to suspend MFN status for six months while a review was carried out. The Reagan administration actually extended MFN for another year on 2 June 1987. But before the renewal date Romania 'renounced' MFN status and other trade benefits, such as US government-supported credits, because of its unwillingness to make concessions in this regard.

The share of foreign trade turnover with Comecon has varied with the political climate. Between 1960 and 1980, for example, Comecon's share fell from 66.8 to 33.7 per cent, and that of the Western countries rose from 22.1 to 32.8 per cent. Since then, however, it has increased once more (Shafir 1985: 49).

Joint equity ventures

Romania was actually the first Comecon country to introduce a joint equity venture law relating to Western companies in 1971, the Western contribution not to exceed 49 per cent. Ventures have been few since early successes in areas such as textiles, electronics and engineering (five were in operation at the end of 1987; *FT*, 14 April 1988, p. 3) (Table 10.2). In May 1987 approval was given to direct links between Soviet and Romanian enterprises.

Table 10.2 Romania: statistical survey

Cultivated area (1985) (%)	Co-operatives	State farms and other state institutions	Private sector (including some private farms)
	61	30	9.0
Joint equity ventures (end 1987)	5		
Population (1987)		23 million	

Sources: Economist Intelligence Unit, *Country Profile* (1987–88: 17); *FT*, 14 April 1988, p. 3.
For rates of growth of NMP and for net hard currency debt, see Table 10.1, this volume.

Conclusion

Romania has distinguished itself politically by adopting a relatively independent foreign policy and currently stands out because of its draconian domestic economic policies established to eliminate its large foreign debt (fully paid off by the end of March 1989 according to Ceausescu). These have caused civil disturbances even in one of the most tightly controlled political regimes, where power is mainly in the hands of the Ceausescu extended family. The 'systematization' programme has aroused general condemnation. The economy remains highly centralized, with very little prospect of change in the foreseeable future. Nevertheless, Romania has introduced some novel ideas, such as a pale imitation of a self-management system, and was actually the first Comecon country to pass joint venture legislation as far back as 1971.

Notes

1. See Crowther (1988: Chapter 2).
2. The goal is a population of 30 million by the year 2000. Birth control and abortion are illegal, and childless people and married couples have to pay 10 per cent of their salaries to the state (Nick Seden, *FT*, 3 December 1988, p.xvi).

3. In normal circumstances coal accounts for about 40 per cent of electricity, hydroelectric power 20 per cent, and oil and gas 40 per cent, the long-delayed nuclear programme will probably not contribute until the early 1990s.
4. According to Janet Heller, owners of private homes in general which are appropriated by the state are compensated by no more than 25 per cent of their real value. The aim in converting owners into tenants is to create a collective rather than an individual mentality (*EEN*, 13 December 1988, p. 4).
5. The strategy of very broad industrialization and constructing grandiose infrastructural projects, such as the Danube-Black Sea Canal, has continued.

Chapter eleven

Yugoslavia

Background

Yugoslavia became an independent state in December 1918 (although the name only emerged in 1929, at first it was known as the Kingdom of Serbs, Croats and Slovenes), following the defeat of Austria-Hungary and Turkey in the First World War. The new state centred on Serbia, which had achieved its independence from Turkey in 1878. The assassination by Gavrilo Princip of Archduke Francis Ferdinand, heir to the Habsburg throne, at Sarajevo on 28 June 1914 sparked off the First World War. During the inter-war period a parliamentary democracy turned into a monarchical dictatorship. Maintaining the unity of this quarrelsome region has remained a perennial problem.

The Socialist Federal Republic of Yugoslavia was proclaimed in 1945 under Josip Broz Tito, who led the partisans to victory, both against the Axis Powers and in the civil war. McFarlane (1988: 6) notes that in September 1944 an agreement was signed with the Soviet Command before Soviet troops actually crossed into Yugoslav territory. Tito died in May 1980 and bequeathed an annually rotating presidency, among eight from the republics and autonomous provinces, plus the President of the Presidium. The major features of Yugoslav politics are:

1. Its non-aligned status. Tito broke with Stalin in 1948 over the question of sovereignty and Yugoslavia was expelled from the Cominform.[1] The Comecon blockade (1949–53) helped push Yugoslavia into increased trade with the West and into a different economic system.
2. Its regional diversity and decentralization of decision-making. Yugoslavia is composed of the republics of Slovenia, Croatia, Bosnia and Hercegovina, Montenegro, Macedonia and Serbia. Within Serbia there are the autonomous provinces of Vojvodina (with people of Magyar stock) and Kosovo (of Albanian stock): their autonomy was substantially reduced in March 1989.

Besides the great linguistic, cultural and ethnic differences, there are also economic extremes in terms of per capita income and levels of unemployment, despite regional aid, with wealthy Slovenia at one end of the spectrum and poor Kosovo at the other. McFarlane (1988: 60) gives some illuminating statistics for 1981, comparing the respective figures for the unemployment rate (the Yugoslav average is 12.6 per cent) and for social product per inhabitant (the Yugoslav average being equal to 100): 1.3 per cent and 205.8 for Slovenia, and 27.3 per cent and 26.8 for Kosovo. Federal decision-making in this country of over 23 million is often delayed or thwarted altogether by the veto power exercised by self-interested republics, with economic consequences in the form of wasteful duplication of capacities and the lack of national product and capital markets.

The Thirteenth Congress of the League of Communists of Yugoslavia (the Yugoslav Communist Party was renamed in November 1952) took place on 25–28 June 1986, soon after the rotating premiership went to Branko Mikulic. He replaced Mrs Milka Planinc on 6 May 1986, but resigned on 30 December 1988. He, in turn, was replaced by Ante Markovic in the following month. During Gorbachev's March 1988 visit to Yugoslavia, the joint declaration went beyond the 1955 and 1956 Khrushchev-Tito agreements, recognizing that no one had a monopoly of truth and that the Soviet Union could benefit from the experience of the Yugoslav system of self-management. Countries had a right to choose their own ways of social development and the threat or use of force to interfere in the internal affairs of other states should be ruled out.[2] Gorbachev conceded Soviet blame for the 1948 split and viewed non-alignment in a positive light.

The Yugoslav Communist Party inherited a country in which three-quarters of the population were rural and the same proportion of the labour force was employed in agriculture. In 1931 68 per cent of peasant families owned only 30 per cent of the land, and there were many landless labourers (McFarlane 1988: 5). Primary commodities accounted for more than 80 per cent of exports before the Second World War. There was good arable land for crops like grain and a variety of raw materials such as copper and bauxite.[3] The former Habsburg territories in the north (Croatia, Slovenia and Vojvodina) were relatively industrialized, in contrast to the subsistence agriculture that characterized the South.

Table 11.1 summarizes the principal statistics for growth, inflation, and debt.

Market socialism in Yugoslavia

A traditional planning system was voluntarily adopted initially. Yugoslavia, since the proclamation of the Basic Law in June 1950, however, has developed a unique system of market socialism based on the principle of 'self-management' of the socially-owned[4] industrial enterprise via an elected workers' council.

Table 11.1 Yugoslavia: debt, inflation, and average annual rate of growth of GDP

Average annual rate of growth of GDP (%)

1946–52	1952–62	1957–61	1961–65	1966–70	1971–75	1976–80	1981–85
2.3	8.3	10.4	6.8	5.7	5.9	5.2	1.1

1986	1987	1988
–	0.5	–1.5

Annual average inflation (%)

1952–62	1963–73	1974–79	1980–85	1985	1986	1987	1988
3.6	13.0	33.3	48.7	76.0	88.0	167.4	251.0

	1981	1986
Gross hard currency debt ($ billions)	18.3	19.4
Debt-service ratio (%)	21	45

Sources: Mencinger (1987: 107–110); Economist Intelligence Unit, *Country Profile* (1987–88: 34); *IHT*, 9 February 1989, p. 4; *FT Survey*, 29 June 1989, p.1.

An enterprise can be set up by the state, existing enterprises, banks, or groups of individuals. The principle of self-management arose from a desire to achieve Yugoslavia's own brand of socialism through decentralization, to further mass participation, to stress independence (neither Soviet-type nor capitalist), to defend the country, to overcome the nationalities problem (and reduce regional disparities), and to avoid class distinctions between workers, managers, and owners. The essential feature is that enterprises do not have state targets imposed upon them, but the state steers the economy both indirectly via economic levers and directly through measures such as temporary wage and price freezes. It is also possible for temporary management boards ('enforced management', which overrides the principle of self-management) to be set up to restructure heavy loss-making enterprises (e.g. the MKS steelworks in Serbia; reported in the article by Judy Dempsey in *FT*, 28 October, 1987, p. 6).

The basic organization of associated labour

According to Estrin (1983: 103), the bottom 20 per cent of firms produced some 1 per cent of industrial net output in 1966 and the bottom 30 per cent only 2 per cent in 1972, while the top 5 per cent of firms accounted for 41.2 per cent of industrial net output in 1966 and the top 1.7 per cent accounted for over 30 per cent in 1972. In 1970 the largest ten companies produced 22.8 per cent of industrial output. Sacks (1983: 30, 33) maintains that in 1969 the fifty largest industrial firms were responsible for 26 per cent of total industrial sales and in 1981 for 53 per cent, the year when the 130 largest accounted for three-quarters of sales. The large size of many industrial enterprises (the market structure is highly imperfectly competitive) gave rise to a concern that the notion of self-management would be compromised by the power of management and state administration. In consequence, the 1971 constitutional amendments, which were later incorporated into the 1974 constitution, meant that the Basic Organisation of Associated Labour (BOAL) replaced the enterprise as the basic legal and economic unit (the enterprise now being a 'working organization of associated labour'; in some cases working organizations are grouped into 'complex organizations of associated labour'; Lydall 1989: 13) as the basic legal and economic unit. Each BOAL represented a stage in the production process, the smallest unit producing a marketed or marketable product. An enterprise constitutes a BOAL or a group of BOALs in voluntary association. Each BOAL may become independent or join another enterprise provided no contract is broken, and is represented on the enterprise workers' council and management board (Prout 1985: 65; Marer 1986c: 625).

The manager is elected by the workers' council from a list drawn up by a nominating committee. At present half of the members (compared to two-thirds at first in 1953) are politically appointed, including representatives of local government. A majority of two-thirds of all members is needed for decisions. There is controversy about the distribution of the decision-taking powers between the workers' council and the manager and the danger, too, of over-generalizing. In theory managers are responsible for 'day to day' operations, but, in reality, their role is larger, due to greater technical expertise and more information at their disposal and the ability to present ensuing alternative policies,[5] and the fact that they also often exercise greater political influence. Workers, on the other hand, tend to be more interested in matters of immediate personal concern such as remuneration and the allocation of tasks, and socio-cultural benefits such as housing. It is also difficult to pinpoint an enterprise maximand, since managers are influenced by such factors as growth, prestige, and political favour, but most observers point to 'net income' (wages and profits, i.e. gross income minus the cost of non-labour inputs, depreciation, capital charges and taxes) and perhaps 'net income per employee' (this would help explain the relative aversion to employing extra workers). If managers do indeed take the lion's share of decisions, this would tip the balance towards profit.

Planning

In 1951 the Federal Planning Commission was scrapped, as was command planning. Today the federal government does have the right to intervene directly, by imposing a wage freeze for example, but only temporarily and only to preserve the unity of the market. Of the economic levers, fiscal policy was weakened by the 1965 measures, which confined federal responsibility to areas like defence, foreign debt management, pensions, and the regional fund (currently only about 25 per cent of total government expenditure is controlled by the federal government: Lydall 1989: 65), and the 1971 measures, which deprived the federal government of most of its revenues. The turnover tax, the main previous source of federal revenue, went to the republics, leaving such items as customs duties. Even monetary policy has been weakened by negative interest rates (monetary control is exercised via credit directives and changes in reserve requirements); the unwillingness to see large-scale bankruptcy; and the avoidance of credit restrictions by enterprises that provide credit to each other. Foreign trade is steered by means of tariffs, quotas, and foreign exchange regulations. The intention over time has generally been to move towards the market and the 1982–83 Kraigher Commission report suggested the creation of a more unified market economy and further reforms to increase efficiency.

Scholars have tended to identify sub-periods. Estrin (1983), for example, describes 1952–65 as the 'visible hand' period (involving, for instance, tight state control over investment) and 1965–72/4 as the 'market self-management' period. Mencinger (1987: 102) sees 1974–82 as a distinct move away from market socialism, a period characterized by 'social compacts' and 'self-management agreements' (Estrin's term is 'social planning'). Contractual planning, which acts with the market, involves information exchange and agreements between government authorities ('socio-political communities'), trade unions, and Economic Chambers (representing enterprises), which eventually leads to a plan. Social compacts are not legally binding and mainly cover broad policy objectives such as prices and pay (principles determining the proportional division of enterprise net income between personal income, fringe benefits, and accumulation: Lydall 1989: 60) at a republic or inter-republic level. Social 'contracts', as Schüller (1988: 41) calls them, are concluded between territorial authorities, economic chambers, trade unions, and the party. Self-management agreements, on the other hand, are legally binding contracts, dealing with investment and the delivery of goods and so on, between economic agents such as enterprises and BOALs (see Estrin 1983: 72–77; Prout 1985: 71–72).

Prices

Prices were mainly centrally determined in the earlier periods. It was the intention of the 1965 reforms largely to replace price controls with market determined prices, but since fiscal and monetary policies were inadequate to deal with inflation, administered prices were retained (including temporary price freezes). Control was tightened after 1965 and by the end of the decade covered 70 per cent of products (Estrin 1983: 70). Until 1973 the prices of basic products such as electricity, sugar and oil were set at the federal level, and a number of other basic services and food set by communes. Wholesale trade margins were worked out by republics and retail margins by communes.

Federally fixed maxima were set for important products such as steel and coal, while others were subject to notification and delays when seeking increases (Prout 1985: 165). Price controls did not cease after 1973. In October 1980 federal and republic 'communities of price' were established. These contained sectoral representatives of both producers and consumers and set prices after consulting the particular socio-political communities, Economic Chambers and trade unions, using criteria such as market conditions and world market prices (Prout 1985: 168). According to the *EIU* (*Country Profile*, 1987–88, p. 14), by November 1986, 39 per cent of goods prices were freely determined. As a result of liberalization this figure had risen to 70 per cent by August 1988 (Aleksandar Lebl, *FT*, 12 August 1988, p. 2).

In November 1987 there were hefty price increases (to last until 1 July 1988) in goods and services such as electricity, coal, railways, postal and telecommunications charges, agricultural chemicals and oil products, while other prices were frozen at the 1 October 1987 level until June 1988. Wages and salaries were to rise according to social compacts. In ten industries where above-norm wages had been paid, increases were to be limited to 90 per cent of compact agreements. Banks and insurance companies were to fix pay at the average level of the third quarter of 1987, while loss-making enterprises were to set pay increases at 90 to 95 per cent of the 1986 cost of living increase (Aleksandar Lebl, *FT*, 16 November 1987, p. 6). Taxes were also imposed on income from second jobs and value added tax was to be introduced (*IHT*, 16 November 1987, p. 1). Strikes immediately began to undermine the wage controls.

Remuneration

Yugoslavia is prone to inflationary pressures. One element in this is the strong proclivity of workers' councils to favour wages at the expense of re-investment when allocating net revenue, due to such factors as the workers' time horizon being limited to their span of employment, itself due to such factors as the lack of property rights. Pay policy has, therefore, reflected such problems (Prout 1985).[6]

By the end of 1957 wages ceased to be a contractual element in cost. Until 1965 strict legal controls were placed on the distribution of enterprise net revenue (after non-labour costs and taxes) for remuneration, investment, socio-cultural expenditures and reserves. An important reason for this was to limit the growth of personal income, in order to generate the savings needed for the higher rates of growth of investment and national product. In that year, however, all such legal restrictions on the allocation of net revenue were lifted. Before 1955 taxes were levied on the size of the wage bill, but then, because of the increasing degree of monopoly, there was a change to net revenue: specifically, if net revenue was 25 to 40 per cent of the total wage bill, a tax from zero to 9.4 per cent was payable, while a 60 per cent proportion meant a rate of 37.3 per cent (McFarlane 1988: 152). In 1965 the net revenue tax was scrapped and taxes were thus imposed solely on personal income funds. Seven years later pay control switched to the social compact system, while there have also been periodic temporary wage freezes, for example in 1983 and 1987. The constant concern about money wage rises greatly exceeding productivity increases culminated in the 'intervention law' (operative 1 March 1987) which reduced wages to the average level of the final quarter of 1986, froze them until June 1987 and linked future increases to the growth of productivity. Adverse reactions included strikes: official figures show 851 strikes involving 88,000 workers in 1986, and 1,570 and 365,000 respectively in 1987. This led to qualifying measures: the prices of products increasing more than 20 per cent were to be pegged at the 31 December 1986 level (20 March 1987), and wage regulations were not to apply to tourism, construction, education and health and industries with 'long-running production cycles'.

The role of *trade unions* has been reduced to what McFarlane (1988: 197) describes as something little different from that of advisory bodies or social welfare agencies. Specific functions after 1952 included ensuring that legal minimum wages were paid and fulfilling an educational-cultural role, while the 1974 constitutional changes left each republic's government to deal with its own union movement (p. 53). Trade unions are officially responsible for nominating the members of the workers' council (Lydall 1989: 20).

Although actual *bankruptcies* have been few, unemployment is a serious problem: the average rate is around 17 per cent, despite the fact that more than 500,000 Yugoslavs work abroad. Regional variations are considerable, ranging from over 40 per cent in Kosovo to around 2 per cent in Slovenia. There is no federal or uniform system of unemployment benefit; only 3 per cent of the jobless are given financial compensation while unemployed (*FT Survey*, 22 June 1988, p.iv). A new law operative since 1 January 1987 gives loss-making enterprises six months to recoup the previous year's losses, during which wages are reduced to the minimum level.[7] Failure to respond allegedly results in bankruptcy. August of the same year saw the closure of a construction company and a lead and zinc mine, while officials estimated 7,000 enterprises, employing 1.5 million workers to be in debt. In November it was announced that the Agrokomerc company was to be declared bankrupt.

Estrin, Moore, and Svejnar (1988: 465–77) point out that the widening of inter-firm and inter-industry income differentials since the late 1950s has been a major problem. Their conclusion is that the main reasons are to be found in labour allocation factors (such as immobility) and monopoly power rather than in capital market imperfections which permit capital rents to be appropriated as workers' income.

Investment planning

The social investment system was in operation until the end of 1963 (Prout 1985). Essentially this involved the centre deciding upon aggregate investment and its sectoral allocation. The banking system supposedly granted branch credits to enterprises on the basis of such criteria as expected rate of return, the degree of self-financing and foreign trade implications. Estrin (1983: 65), however, considers that, in reality, political and regional factors predominated. After that date the Federal Investment Fund was scrapped and its assets distributed to three banks (for investment, foreign trade and agriculture). A new investment fund to aid the less developed areas was established in 1966, however, financed from enterprise contributions. Under the contractual agreement system, social compacts include investment targets, which firms compete for and ultimately incorporate into self-management agreements (Prout 1985: 74; see also Marer 1986c: 627). By the end of the 1960s investment was financed in the following ways: approximately 10 per cent budgetary, 45 per cent bank credit, and 45 per cent enterprises (Bleaney 1988: 136).

Major problems in the field of investment include substantial duplication between republics (typically plants are too small to reap all the economies of scale), general over-investment due to this duplication, the growth motivation of managers and local leaders, and the existence of negative interest rates (which themselves enhanced the desire to use funds locally; note also that there is now no capital charge imposed by the state on an enterprise's capital stock). There is also a strong incentive to invest using bank credits, because failure is unlikely given the state's unwillingness to allow bankruptcies. In any case, it is difficult to attach blame. All of this encourages irresponsibility. The unwillingness of banks and government authorities to bankrupt enterprises is an important cause of the growth of credit which fuels increases in the money supply and hence inflation; this reached 290 per cent by January 1989 (see Table 11.1). Lydall (1989: 3) cites a report by Bajt which found that the productivity of Yugoslav fixed investment was only 70–75 per cent of the average of that of Portugal, Spain, Greece and Turkey over the period 1960–80.

It is now possible for one enterprise to invest in another at an agreed rate of return or for a share in profits, but the former is not entitled to management rights and is unable to sell its holding (Bleaney 1988: 142).

Banking

The process of consolidation that began in 1946 ended in two banks, the National Bank and the Investment Bank, the latter exercising control over investments and foreign borrowing. By the 1950s six regional State Banks, mainly serving agriculture, and 90 communal banks had been established, although the latter were scrapped in 1952. A Foreign Trade Bank and an Agricultural Bank were also set up (McFarlane 1988: 89–90). In 1961 the National Bank renounced its commercial functions, while communal banks were reintroduced: two-thirds of their management boards were to be nominated by workers' councils located in the territory (p. 90). 'Basic' banks are controlled by their 'founders' (usually local enterprises) and most belong to an 'associated' bank whose principal role is to arrange finance for large projects and to undertake foreign exchange transactions (Lydall 1989: 155).

The slackness of monetary control has been highlighted by the 1987 *Agrokomerc scandal* (*EEN*, 1987, vol. 1, no. 8, p. 4–5). Agrokomerc is a multi-product company in Bosnia-Hercegovina (originally employing more than 13,000 people), which was ultimately unable to honour the vast number of promissary notes it had issued to cover its grandiose, partly politically driven investment programme. These notes were automatically underwritten by the Bihac Bank in the same republic (the bank's chairman was Agrokomerc's deputy chairman) and purchased by other banks, which subsequently ran into financial losses. This was only the tip of the iceberg. The promissary note system was introduced in 1975 to facilitate inter-enterprise transactions. Agrokomerc's issue of uncovered notes (i.e. not backed by sufficient assets) began in late 1986 when the firm's subsidiaries started to issue notes to themselves and to cash them in banks. Bankruptcy was avoided by creditors agreeing to write off nearly 50 per cent of the debt, with repayments of the rest spread over five years.

Some novel financial innovations in 1987 include the sale of negotiable debentures by the electric power industry of Serbia, and investment funds provided by Investbanka of Belgrade on a risk-sharing basis (rather than charging fixed interest).

Agriculture

The drive for collectivization started in 1949, but was made voluntary the following year, by which time a fifth of the arable area was affected. The compulsory sale of foodstuffs to the state at fixed prices was suspended and the Machine Tractor Stations were abolished. In 1952 the peasants were given the option of liquidating work co-operatives (McFarlane 1988: 99). The private sector dominates Yugoslav agriculture, owning, in 1985, 80 per cent of arable land and accounting for 69 per cent of gross farm output (Cochrane 1988: 48) and 85 per cent of livestock. The original 10 hectare limit to private farm size was fixed in May 1953 (with a 15 hectare ceiling in less fertile areas), but this was modified in two respects: (1) in hilly and mountainous regions republic authorities had the right to exceed this maximum or to reduce it in fertile regions (in Croatia, for example, the lowland maximum was 20 hectares and the hill maximum 40 hectares); and (2) in practice, land can be rented from other individuals. The average holding, however, is only 3.2 hectares and can be fragmented into as many as nine separate plots (Cochrane 1988: 50). In late 1988 it was agreed to raise the maximum from 10 to 30 hectares (*The Economist*, 29 October–4 November 1988: 60). Private farmers are encouraged to join co-operatives, but this has not been very successful in production, although more so in marketing (Cochrane 1988: 50). The socialized sector includes agro-industrial combines (usually spanning the range from primary activity to sales of processed products), state farms and co-operatives (Cochrane 1988: 577). Socialized organizations account for most of the purchasing, processing, and distribution of agricultural products (p. 584).

Although the 1965 and later decrees stressed the prime role of the market in price determination, in reality the state exercised control over the prices of major agricultural products such as wheat, meat, and rice. Prior to 1978 there were support prices: (1) 'guarantee' prices – intervention prices at which purchasing organizations or local authorities were obliged to buy if prices fell below the fixed level; and (2) 'minimum' prices – applying mainly to industrial crops; the purchasing organizations, mainly manufacturing enterprises, are not allowed to pay less than these. In 1978 'producer guide' prices were set at the federal level as guidelines for the price determination of major products. Support prices, for example, could fall below the guide only to certain (varying) extents. The prices of other products, such as fruit and vegetables, are largely market determined, but even here the republic authorities are able to set and guarantee prices. From 1 January 1985 onwards only guarantee prices were set centrally for 'products of particular social interest', as the major products are called (Loncarevic 1987: 631).

An event worthy of note was the creation, in May 1988, of the Slovene Farmers' Union, an independent organization, albeit under the umbrella of the Socialist Alliance. Non-political, its aim is to further agricultural reform.

Foreign trade and payments

The foreign trade system

Until 1961 export and import price coefficients were used to steer foreign trade, but served to shield the domestic economy. In that year these coefficients were scrapped and tariffs were gradually to replace quantitative restrictions (Prout 1985: 21, 26). Trade liberalization ensued:

1. zero protection for agriculture and timber; 10–40 per cent tariff rates for consumer goods and 17–60 per cent rates for industrial goods; in 1965 nominal tariffs were reduced from an average of 23.3 per cent to 10.5 per cent;
2. a single exchange rate was introduced;
3. National Bank foreign exchange allocations and import quotas

determined the flow of imports: the aim was integration into the world economy and ultimate full convertibility of the dinar, but subsequent balance-of-payments problems put an end to this (McFarlane 1988: 121–22).

The allocation of foreign exchange

By the end of 1955 exporters had to sell all their foreign exchange earnings to the National Bank, while in 1967 a share of foreign exchange earnings could be retained by exporters. Six years later an inter-bank foreign exchange market was introduced, and the central bank bought and sold to influence the exchange rate (Prout 1985). On 1 January 1986 a new scheme relating to foreign exchange was introduced. This replaced the system introduced in July 1984 whereby enterprises transferred 54 per cent of hard currency export earnings to federal government (allowed a share of enterprise foreign exchange earnings in 1963) and local authorities, with that part of the remainder not needed for their own use supposedly sold on the inter-bank foreign exchange market. In reality, however, very little found its way onto this official market, since more profitable transactions could be negotiated privately. The new scheme required all foreign exchange to be sold within 60 days to banks, which then resold. Enterprises no longer had foreign currency accounts, although individuals still did. The aim was to restore the foreign exchange market (and ultimately full convertibility of the dinar) and to reduce imports – the continual devaluation of the dinar made repurchase increasingly expensive. The scheme provided the federal government with a means of influencing the use to which the scarce foreign exchange was put. In the first quarter of 1988, as a temporary solution, net exporters were given priority in the repurchase of some of their foreign exchange earnings.

Yugoslavia and the IMF

Yugoslavia has been a member of the IMF since its foundation and a full member of GATT since 1966. Standby agreements with the IMF meant that conditions had to be laid down in the period 1981 to 16 May 1986, when these agreements were replaced by 'enhanced monitoring'. This involves twice yearly checks on performance for the benefit of creditors, conceded after Western banks agreed to multi-year rescheduling. There has been friction over some of the policy measures, the IMF (unlike Yugoslavia) consistently favouring positive real interest rates, the relaxation of price controls, free trade, a depreciating dinar, financial discipline, wages strictly linked to productivity and free markets for goods and factors of production. A new agreement over interest rates was concluded for 1 April 1985. The old one fixed rises in interest rates on three month deposits to 1 percentage point above the average of the rise in producers' prices over the previous three months by 1 April and after that to keep in line with inflation. The new agreement involved both interest rate rises based on the average of the rise in producers' prices over the previous quarter and estimated inflation over the next quarter, and dinar depreciation by the difference between world and Yugoslav inflation rates. In fact, in December 1985, against IMF advice, Yugoslavia froze interest rates for the following month.

Fresh standby financing was agreed with the IMF in April 1988 and in the middle of May a programme was put into operation that involved deflationary reductions in the money supply and in public expenditure, the lessening of price controls, wage moderation, import liberation and measures to increase exports. Specifically, the following measures were to be introduced:

1. 40 per cent of prices to be freed on 15 May (plus a further 20 per cent on 'advance notification'), 60 per cent by the end of 1988, 70 per cent by the end of 1989, and 90 per cent by 1990;
2. a gradual liberation of imports in order to end most restrictions by 1990;
3. an end to the present foreign exchange system;
4. a devaluation of the dinar on 15 May followed by floating and the re-establishment of the domestic foreign exchange market; and
5. federal expenditure to be kept constant in real terms and other expenditure to be kept 10 per cent below inflation; bank lending to be restricted to 28 per cent below the inflation rate, provided the latter does not exceed the 90–95 target (see, for example, *EEN*, 1988, vol. 2, no. 8, pp. 3–4).

On 16 May 1988 ceilings were imposed on wage increases. Compared with a year earlier, wages and salaries were to be no more than 139 per cent higher by 30 June, no more than 132 per cent higher by the end of September, and no more than 119 per cent higher by the end of 1988. The whole package was to be operational by 31 May, the aim being to reduce inflation, then at an annual rate of 152 per cent, to 90 to 95 per cent by the end of the year. Unrest led to concessions in October, such as additional food imports and pay increases in the more successful enterprises and in social services like health and education. The Central Committee meeting in the same month charted a future course of progress towards a market economy, a clearer distinction between party and state and an enhanced federal role in economic policy making.

The national party conference (29–31 May 1988) saw much criticism of the failure to implement reforms and of unacceptable aspects of party life such as corruption. Short-term remedies included price increases (petrol, 32.2 per cent; rail fares, 38.5 per cent; coal, 30.3 per cent; electricity, 31 per cent; postal services, 28 per cent), while longer-term remedies revolved around deregulating the goods, money and labour markets. In November greater substance was given to reform ideas. The 'enterprise' was to replace the BOAL as the basic unit, with profit as the main objective; socially owned enterprises were to be permitted to issue shares and bonds, partly in order to tap the hard currency deposits owned by Yugoslav citizens at home or abroad,[8] estimated at some $10 billion and $10 billion to $20 billion respectively (Cavoski 1988: 47); 100 per cent foreign ownership was to become possible; banks were to become independent financial units and the National Bank was to act more like a central bank in a Western economy; price controls were to be exceptional (controls were to remain over certain basic foodstuffs; policy included raising the relative price of capital to labour); the private sector was to be encouraged and new forms of ownership were to include mixed state-private and state-co-operative.

The path to indebtedness

The path of Yugoslavia towards serious foreign payments and debt problems is a familiar one (Babić and Primorac 1986). The basic strategy after the Second World War was to industrialize Yugoslavia as quickly as possible, with a relative neglect of traditional exports. Rapid rates of growth of gross material product were achieved (see Table 11.1). During the 1970s more rapid rates of growth of consumption, investment, and imports (also induced by overvaluation of the dinar) than total output led to rising trade deficits. Institutional changes encouraged external borrowing. Specifically, from 1967 onwards large enterprises and authorized commercial banks were able to borrow abroad directly, while this concession was made general in 1972.

Heavy borrowing from the West during the 1970s as well as the recessionary effects following the 1973–74 and 1979 oil shocks brought about severe foreign trade and payments difficulties for Yugoslavia. Yugoslavia's total gross debt increased somewhat from $19.9 billion in 1981 to $20.7 billion in 1986; of this $18.3 billion and $19.4 billion was for hard currency debt alone. The hard currency debt-service ratio rose from 21 per cent to 45 per cent (*EIU Country Profile*, 1987–88, p. 34). In the 1985 arrangements with the IMF Yugoslavia agreed to begin serious repayments three years later, but this was subject to a maximum 25 per cent of annual hard currency earnings (McFarlane 1988: 94). Premier Mikulic reported in October 1987 that the hard currency debt-service ratio over the previous year had been 46.5 per cent (19 per cent in 1975). Deflationary measures have been taken since 1978 and debt reschedulings made since 1983. Particular emphasis was placed on reducing imports at first, but increasing exports have since been given more equal attention, and hard currency current account deficits in the early 1980s have been transformed into surpluses over 1983–86. The October 1987 programme was more liberal in using imports and foreign capital to try to increase productivity levels and product quality in the drive to increase exports.

On 30 December 1988 the government resigned, the first time this had happened since 1945. Failure to win approval for the federal budget was the immediate cause. Three weeks later Premier Mikulic was replaced by Ante Markovic, a firm believer in the market economy.

Joint equity ventures

There have been many changes since joint equity ventures were first allowed in 1967, relaxing the conditions of operation in the urgent search for high technology, capital and know-how. In November 1984, for example, majority ownership was allowed (up to 99 per cent), excluded fields were narrowed down to insurance, retail trade and social services (other than in health recreation), and on completion the foreign partner would be able to repatriate the full value of the original investment. It was announced in October 1987 that conditions were to be further relaxed, allowing equal rights for both partners, extending the scheme to all sectors except social services, education, and insurance (although in the small number of customs-free zones insurance and reinsurance will be allowed), promoting small and medium-sized enterprises and allowing individuals in Yugoslavia to buy stocks. There were then 275 ventures in operation. Further concessions announced the following year included joint power to choose management and to hire and fire workers, although the foreign partner must contribute at least a 30 per cent share of the equity. One hundred per cent foreign ownership as of 1989 is envisaged, although this will be restricted to hotels and road concessions and to the free trade zones (19 in late 1988).

The private non-agricultural sector

In 1946 a maximum of five workers, including family members, could be employed in handicrafts, and in hotels three employees outside the family could be taken on. The maximum today varies between republics. Ten were allowed in Slovenia up to 1987, when the ceiling was raised to 20. The republic also deals with licence applications far more speedily than others. Misha Glenny gives a figure of 7.5 per cent of Slovenian GNP accounted for by private businesses and discusses further legislation that will open up all manufacturing and service enterprises, including parts of the health service, and raise the employment ceiling to a possible 125 (*Guardian Survey*, 16 May 1988, p. 13). Treatment of the sector has varied over time depending on the political situation, but currently it is being encouraged. In 1986, according to Judy Dempsey (*FT*, 22 December 1987, p. 12), the sector accounted for 5.7 per cent of total production.

Conclusion

Socialist Yugoslavia did not owe its existence to the Red Army, and soon after the Tito-Stalin quarrel of 1948 Yugoslavia launched itself into developing a unique system of market socialism based on 'self-management' by workers' councils of 'socially owned' enterprises. Private agriculture is dominant and the private non-agricultural sector is treated in a relatively relaxed fashion (Table 11.2). Current problems are immense, especially a massive foreign debt, rapid inflation, a high unemployment rate, and centrifugal forces operating through powerful republics. Serious trouble flared up once again in Kosovo when its autonomy was greatly reduced. The future points firmly in the direction of the market.[9]

Table 11.2 Yugoslavia: statistical survey

Private sector in agriculture (%) (1985)	Arable land	Output
	80	69
Joint equity ventures (October 1987)	275	
Private non-agricultural sector (1986) (% total production)	5.7	
Population (1986)	23 million	

For growth, inflation, and debt figures see Table 11.1, this volume.
Sources: See Table 11.1, this volume; Cochrane (1988: 48).

Postscript

Inflation has rapidly accelerated. The 1989 rate is likely to be over 1,000 per cent.

Notes

1. The Communist International Bureau, set up in 1947 to promote international communism and Soviet control over the movement, was dissolved in 1956.
2. Gorbachev first opined the rights of countries to choose their 'different paths' to socialism in December 1986 and it is of interest to reflect on how far this rejects the 1970 'Brezhnev doctrine', which justified intervention, as in Czechoslovakia in 1968, to prevent socialism in any particular country and in the socialist community as a whole being threatened.
3. Energy resources were not well exploited, however. It is also worth noting that in 1987 Yugoslavia decided not to build any more nuclear power stations, there being one already in operation.
4. The industrial enterprise is owned by society and not by the state; thus the workers' co-operative is able to use but not sell the enterprise's capital stock (Mirkovic 1987).
5. McFarlane (1988: xiii) cites workers' complaints that managers resubmit proposals until they are accepted. On the other hand, note should be taken of managers' complaints that the decision-making process under self-management is extremely slow.

6. Inflationary pressure is also caused by the following: the operation of the soft-budget constraint; envy of earnings in profitable concerns; and the existence of several factors that encourage investment, namely the difficulty of pinpointing responsibility, regional duplication and negative interest rates. Bleaney (1988: 150) attaches importance to the devolution of price controls to the 'communities of price' as an inflationary spur because of local pressure to gain resources at the expense of others.

7. The law does not apply to certain enterprises, such as those supplying weapons and electric power. According to McFarlane (1988: 89), a 1984 law forced loss-makers to pay only the minimum wage. He also mentions the December 1986 legislation that enforced realistic depreciation rates, in order to make the tax base more efficient, and which required enterprises to repay creditors *before* deciding on the distribution of net revenue (p. 143).

8. A novel scheme to attract the hard currency capital of Yugoslavs abroad was proposed in 1985. Three year loans to Yugoslav companies would secure a job for the person concerned (or a nominated alternative) as well as interest.

9. There are two chambers at the federal level. The first is elected directly by communes in each republic or province, while the second (the Chamber of Republics and Provinces) is elected by a joint session of the chambers of the particular republic or province. This delegate system plus the unanimity practice of the latter chamber (which decides major economic issues) helps explain the difficulty of reaching federal decisions (Bleaney 1988: 139).

Part three

Asia and the Caribbean

Chapter twelve

The People's Republic of China

China is the largest country in the world in terms of population (1.085 billion at the end of 1987). The 1986 growth rate was 1.41 per cent, the birth rate 2.08 per cent, and the death rate 0.67 per cent: 92 per cent of the population consisted of Hans. China is third largest in terms of land area, after the Soviet Union and Canada. Approximately 22 per cent of the world's population is sustained on less than 8 per cent of the world's arable area. In 1979 only 11 per cent of the total land area of China was cultivated, with just 0.12 hectares per capita of the agricultural population, compared to India's 0.42 (World Bank 1984: 35). Table 12.1 shows rates of growth of NMP and agricultural output.[1]

Table 12.1 China: average annual rate of growth of NMP and agricultural output

Average annual rate of growth of NMP (%)	1953–57	1957–65	1965–76	1976–85		
	6.61	2.09	5.11	8.78		

Average annual rate of growth of the gross value of agricultural output						
	1952–57	1957–65	1965–75	1971–78	1980–82	1982–86
(%)	4.7	1.2	4.0	4.3	7.5	13.0

Sources: Perkins (1980) 'The central features of China's economic development', in Dermberger, R. (ed.) China's Development Experience in Comparative Perspective, Cambridge, MA: Harvard University Press; Perkins (1988: 612, 628); Riskin (1987: 185).

*See note 10 for later figures.

China is an ancient and continuous civilization. Notable dates include the foundation of the first centralized Chinese state during the Qin dynasty (221–206 BC) and the ending of the Qing or Manchu dynasty (1644–1911) by Sun Yat-Sen. The Kuomintang Party (founded in 1924 by Sun Yat-Sen) and the Communist Party of China (founded in 1921) co-operated in the drive to break the power of warring landlords, but in 1927, following the earlier death of Sun Yat-Sen and under the new leader Chiang Kai-Shek, the former party turned on the latter. Mao emerged as leader of the CCP, now based on the peasantry. The Japanese annexed Manchuria in 1931 and waged general war in 1937. The two parties again collaborated in the fight against the invader, but in the civil war that followed Japan's defeat, Mao emerged victorious and Chiang Kai-Shek fled to Taiwan. Mao Tse-Tung (Mao Zedong) established the People's Republic on 1 October 1949 and died in 1976.

Although there were pockets of modern industry in the Treaty Ports and a commercial and monetary tradition, at the start of its socialist period China was, in other respects, a classically poor country. Eighty five per cent of the population was rural; average life expectancy was 35 years. The 1953 rate of population growth was 2.3 per cent, with a birth rate and death rate of 3.7 per cent and 1.4 per cent respectively. The literacy rate was 20 per cent. The commodity structure of foreign trade was characterized by mainly primary product exports and manufactured imports. In the period 1931–36, net investment was only about 3 per cent of net domestic product (Riskin 1987: 33), while the socialist regime also faced a hyperinflation on taking control.

In 1952, by which time the economy had largely recovered from decades of foreign and civil war, per capita GNP was only \$50,[2] while agriculture employed 84 per cent of the work-force and contributed 60 per cent to net material product (Riskin 1987: 269). The 1953 census revealed a 1952 population of 575 million and shocked the party into a population control programme[3] after 1956. Previously, exclusive blame for poverty was based on capitalism and imperialism – Mao opposing birth control as a 'bourgeois Malthusian doctrine' (Fang Lizhi 1989: 19). By 1986 life expectancy had risen to a remarkable 66.9 years for men and 70.9 for women, while the 1981–2000 plan envisages a rise in real per capita income from \$300 to \$800.

Early socialist developmental aims put greater stress on equality in the distribution of income and saw international trade, even with other socialist countries, as a last resort to fill gaps between supply and demand (exports were seen simply as a means of financing unavoidable imports) and as a means of providing the capital goods needed to attain ultimate self-sufficiency. China has also made significant departures from the traditional Soviet economic system in a number of ways, even during the first five year plan (1953–57) when the greatest similarities can be found. For example, much more frequent use has been made of rationing (of basic commodities, such as grain, cotton cloth, edible oils, sugar and meat), not only for ideological reasons, but also as a means of controlling population movements. These departures provide a theme for the following sections on agriculture, central planning, manpower and industrial management.

Agriculture

Agriculture has been subject to great policy swings. The land reform (1950–53) involved a massive redistribution of land and property to poorer peasants, while the subsequent strategy was geared to avoiding the calamity experienced in Soviet collectivization. There was a progression through varying degrees of co-operation, as 'mutual aid teams' and elementary and advanced agricultural producer co-operatives were formed before 1954, with the first accounting for some 60 per cent of peasant households in that year and the latter two rapidly increasing in number in 1955 (the elementary type accounting for 59 per cent of peasant households by the end of that year). The advanced type increased dramatically in 1956 (accounting for 88 per cent of households by the end of that year). According to Putterman (1988: 42), the elementary type recruited peasants on a substantially voluntary basis, but there was no real choice about joining the advanced co-operative.

Mutual aid teams

Involving 5 to 15 households on average usually, these varied from simple labour exchange to the co-operative use of implements and draught animals. Compensation was in the form of proportionate rental payments for these two inputs.

Elementary agricultural producer co-operatives

Typically 20 to 25 households, these pooled land as well as draught animals and large implements, with remuneration based on a combination of rental payments for these contributions and remuneration for work performed.

Advanced agricultural producer co-operatives

These co-operatives involved 150 to 200 households (constituting a large village or a number of smaller villages). Land, draught animals, and larger implements became co-operative property, with compensation payments spread over a period of up to five years. Private plots were allowed, though they were not to exceed 5 per cent of the average per capita cultivated area (Riskin 1987: 91). Collective remuneration, however, was entirely dependent on labour input – that is, the workday system. In November 1953 private trade in cotton cloth, grain and edible oil was declared illegal, and other commodities were included the following year.

The Great Leap Forward, 1958–60

This dramatic policy swing saw the ascent of politics in and decentralization of decision-making to the countryside (provinces and communes) in order to accelerate economic development and the transition to communism. In 1958 Mao vowed to overtake Britain in the production of iron and steel and other major industrial products within 15 years. National output was to double in one year (Xu Dixin, quoted by Johnson 1988: 226). Extreme technological dualism ('walking on two legs') led to centrally controlled, large-scale, modern, capital-intensive enterprises accompanied by locally controlled, small-scale, technologically backward, labour-intensive plants such as the familiar 'backyard steel furnaces'. Local industrialization was meant to mobilize all unused resources (including surplus labour), supply consumer goods to the surrounding population and supply inputs to and process the output of agriculture. Surplus labour in agriculture (having a low or zero marginal product), it was assumed, could be redeployed at virtually zero opportunity cost, especially when accompanied by deep ploughing and close planting. The idea was that this could be used to operate the small enterprises needed to increase the degree of rural industrial independence and to build up the agricultural infrastructure, such as dams and irrigation schemes.

The 'people's commune', whose origins lay in large-scale water conservancy systems, was the key instutution, with a unified management of land and distribution of income. It was meant to release the huge human potential that Mao believed existed and to erode the differences between worker and peasant, town and countryside, and mental and physical labour. The commune was an administrative (dealing with education, health, and public security, for example), as well as an economic unit, dealing with taxation, the assignment of production plans and procurement quotas, manpower allocation, and income distribution. It was divided into brigades and teams. Initially, the accounting unit was the commune or the brigade, while the team was the actual production unit (Johnson 1988: 226). The first commune was set up in April 1958, but by September 1958, 90.4 per cent of peasant households were communized; the average size was 4,550 households. Rural markets were abolished in the Autumn of 1958. Private plots were reclaimed at the same time, only to be restored with a maximum of five per cent of local arable land in May 1959 (Skinner 1985: 400). Trees, large farm implements, and draught animals were communized: a small number of other animals could be retained in theory. A varying proportion of income was distributed free in such forms as meals taken in communal (team) dining rooms, need ranked equally with work as a criterion for food distribution, and communal nurseries were intended to release women for work.

This pronounced move towards egalitarianism and distribution according to need as opposed to labour had a catastrophic effect on work incentives and effort. The quality of industrial products was generally very low. The demise of an objective statistical system led to hopelessly optimistic harvest forecasts (such as 1958 grain production doubling), blinding planners to the adverse effects of withdrawing labour from agriculture at peak periods when its opportunity cost was high and too rapid consumption of grain in the early post-harvest months. Official figures subsequently showed the fall in agricultural output: the grain harvest totalled 170 Mt in 1959, 143.5 Mt in 1960, and

147.5 Mt in 1961.[4] Famine stalked the countryside in 1960, optimistic reports caused the government to increase grain procurements, while output, in reality, was falling. Official statistics show a rise in the death rate from 11.98 to 38 per thousand between 1957 and 1960. Using official demographic statistics, Penny Kane concludes that at least an extra 14 million deaths occurred in the officially designated 'three difficult years' between 1959 and 1961 (review by John Gittings of her book *Famine in China 1959–61* (Macmillan), in the *Guardian*, 17 December 1988, p. 7).

The period between the GLF and the 'household responsibility system'

The GLF debacle led to the reinstatement of centralized control and economic orthodoxy. At the end of 1959 the brigade (the pre-GLF advanced producer co-operative) became the basic unit of account and in 1961–62 the production team was re-established as the basic unit for production and income distribution. In 1960 private plots, generally 5 to 7 per cent of cultivated land and rural markets were restored, although subject to considerable restrictions. The government decreed that 90 per cent of the work-force was to be employed in agriculture proper (Riskin 1987: 128), and in 1962–65 the contracting out by the team of certain functions (such as fish and stock breeding, the tending of draught animals and the maintenance of farm equipment) and even land in some areas to individuals or small groups was permitted, foreshadowing the present household responsibility system (HRS) (Riskin 1987: 171). The number of communes was increased and the institution itself was retained as an administrative and planning body to transmit and carry out central decisions. In 1961 agriculture was termed the 'foundation' and industry the 'leading factor'. The following year sectoral priorities were ranked as agriculture, light industry, and heavy industry.

The pre-responsibility system organization of agriculture was as follows:

1. The production team (20–50 households, usually a small village or parts of a larger one) was the basic unit of production and income distribution and owner of land. It negotiated the fixing of compulsory state procurement quotas; the state set prices at levels below those needed to produce those sales on a voluntary basis (Perkins 1988: 609). Individual income distribution depended on a workday system – points were based on the quantity and quality of work contributed and advances were obtainable before the end-of-year reckoning. Lin (1988: 200) argues that, in general, peasants received fixed work points for a day's work regardless of work effort, with predictable effects on incentives. Putterman (1988: 431) too, argues that from 1964 to the late 1970s there were strong tendencies to use time-based work points, with little linkage to work effort in either a quantitative or qualitative sense. The team itself owned enterprises, but points also accrued to the team (and to individuals in

later years) as a result of work performed in brigade and commune industrial enterprises and collective infrastructure projects. Minimum food needs were met, however, regardless of work effort. This weakened incentives, especially in poorer areas where such minima took up a large proportion of output. Private plots provided income in kind and cash from the sale of products such as fruit and vegetables and meat (pork and poultry mainly) on free markets.

2. The production brigade, usually a large village or several smaller ones and consisting of 7 to 8 teams, was involved with the following: work needing the co-operation of a number of teams (power and irrigation schemes, for example, and their output distribution); the renting out of large machinery; primary education; health clinics; and the running of industrial and other enterprises, such as brick works.

3. The commune (12–15 brigades) acted as a channel for the transmission of central plan orders and for materials allocation. It also provided secondary education and health services, disseminated political and technological information, operated industrial and other enterprises (canneries, electronics, textiles, and furniture, for example), collected taxes and procured farm quotas (at state determined prices) on behalf of the state. The commune was the lowest level of state administration (also dealing with public security), and organized major irrigation and water conservancy schemes, using labour voluntarily donated by teams, which either directly benefited or were compensated in work points. A commune member required permission to leave.

State farms today play a relatively minor role overall, although they are not insignificant as a means of developing and reclaiming land in border regions (a role that was more important in the past).

The household responsibility system

Johnson (1988: 229) provides some very useful information on the situation in 1978: 294 million employed in agriculture; 52,780 communes, with an average of 13 production brigades per commune and each brigade with 7 to 10 teams; 800 million total commune population, with an average of 15,000 per commune; each team had an average of 60 workers and 35 households.

In 1982 the commune lost its political and administrative functions to the resurrected county township (*xiang*). After that communes virtually disappeared, losing their enterprises and their powers to mobilize labour for capital construction projects (Riskin 1987: 299). The brigade has now been replaced by the village. The rural enterprises owned by the teams and villages operate in a market environment and can be leased out to individuals.

In 1987 rural industry produced more than 30 per cent of total gross industrial output (*EIU Country Report*, 1988, no. 1, p. 5); there is some dispute about the year when the value of rural non-agricultural output overtook agricultural output; Tam (1988: 63; referring to rural industrial output only) gives 1985; Wong (1988: 3), 1986; and Dowdle (*FEER*, 24 March 1988, p. 76), 1987. The administrative restrictions on rural enterprise, except for cigarettes, were lifted in 1984, and by the end of that year private enterprise accounted for 14.2 per cent of the gross value of output in the rural enterprise sector (Wong 1988: 11, 26).

It is no coincidence that of the 'four modernizations' it is agriculture that comes first, since the population is still overwhelmingly rural. Perkins (1988: 613) makes the important point that reforms in agriculture were easier to implement than in urban areas because significant use was already made of markets. In 1964 and again in 1975 Zhou Enlai announced the aim of attaining the modernization of agriculture, industry, defence and science and technology by the year 2000, but later more realistic goals were adopted, such as the quadrupling of gross agricultural output and industrial output between 1980 and the year 2000 (Lockett 1987).

The Third Plenum of the Eleventh Central Committee in December 1978 was the watershed as far as economic reform in general is concerned, but agriculture was given priority. Sicular's differentiation of two stages in policy regarding agricultural trade is useful:

1. 1977–82. The old system of state procurement quotas was maintained, but quota prices were raised (by more than 20 per cent in 1979), premia on above-quota prices were increased (by between 30 and 50 per cent for grain and oil-bearing crops), and a new 30 per cent price bonus for above-quota deliveries was introduced for cotton. Private markets (including urban) were encouraged, and by the early 1980s market trade was permitted in all products except cotton, which occurred later on. By 1984 18.1 per cent of all purchases of agricultural products took place at market prices, compared with 5.6 per cent in 1978. 'Negotiated' state trade was introduced for above-quota deliveries to the state, at negotiated prices which were in general not to exceed market prices (Sicular 1988: 286–88). Further encouragement was given to agriculture in the following forms: an increase in investment; a decrease in the amount of grain sold to the state, above local consumption needs, from 90 to 70 per cent (Johnson 1988: 231); a green light to private plots, which accounted for 5.7 per cent of arable area in 1978 and 7.1 per cent in 1980; and increases in product diversification and sideline production.
2. The design of commercial policy. This was subsequently modified, as we shall see, with the introduction of a single price for oil seeds (1983), cotton (1984) and grain (1985), and a contract system.

It is important to note that the HRS arose from below in the form of local experiments. These were endorsed centrally only later on, and only in poorer areas until late 1981, as a result of their obvious success. The official position in September 1978 was that the production team was to be the basic unit of production, distribution, and accounting (Lin 1988: 201; Johnson 1988: 231–2), and that the important thing was to link effort and reward (Perkins 1988: 607). By July 1983 the HRS affected 93 per cent of production teams (Hartford 1987: 213). Initially, the reforms amounted to 'production responsibility systems', involving small groups and individuals, but the 'household responsibility system' became overwhelmingly dominant by 1983–84 (Hartford 1987: 212). By December 1980 47.1 per cent of production teams operated reponsibility systems, and about 30 per cent of teams implementing household contracts (Ash 1988: 534, 538).

The HRS has a 'limited' and a 'comprehensive' form. Under the 'limited' form, the team devolves day-to-day management decisions to individual households, providing inputs, setting output targets and awarding work points to households for contract fulfilment (this determines household income). This type predominated in the first half of 1981, but thereafter the 'comprehensive' form rapidly became the norm (Hartford 1987: 213). Under the 'comprehensive system', the household is now typically leased land[6] and after meeting the sales quotas for specified basic products contracted with the team at state determined prices, tax obligations, and payments for collective services provided by the team (irrigation, large machines, welfare, etc.), it is free to determine output, to consume output itself, and to sell to the state at the higher above-quota prices, at negotiated prices or in free markets.[7] The household also makes its own decisions regarding inputs and is able to apply directly for bank loans. There is a (legal) maximum placed on the number of 'helpers'.[8]

Households are now effectively allowed to sub-lease land among themselves (land does not formally belong to the individual, being in public ownership), with the official stipulation that freely negotiated compensation can be made for improvements made to the land, although the village authority has to be informed of the whole arrangement. It was during the September 1987 visit of World Bank officials that the intention was revealed of openly allowing leasing, on a general basis, of smaller plots to form larger units that are better able to employ modern machinery and technology, while allowing the lessor to concentrate on more specialized aspects of farming or leave the land altogether. Cheung notes that the transfer of responsibility contracts (in effect a form of land sale) arose in the grey market as early as 1982 and was formally permitted in 1983 (Cheung 1986: 66).[9] In 1984 contract duration, three to five years initially, was extended beyond 15 years, and today 30 years and even longer is possible (perhaps effectively indefinitely), to encourage a long view among peasants towards the health of the land. Land use can be passed on to children. The optimistic announcement in December 1984 gradually to end obligatory quotas and state-determined prices for all products except grain and cotton, has been superseded by concern over the grain harvest and the generally more restrictive atmosphere from 1985 onwards.

There have been changes in the grain procurement system, following the ending of price bonuses for above-quota deliveries of oilseeds in 1983 and of cotton the year afterwards (Sicular 1988a: 471). After 1978 a compulsory grain quota was purchased by the state, which also promised to purchase further sales at a higher price (the farmer also had the option of the free market for above-quota sales). Delfs (*FEER*, 18 February 1988, p. 68) describes how this system broke down under the strains of subsidization, storage and transport imposed by the record 1984 grain harvest of 407 Mt, when the state effectively reneged on its promise to purchase all the surplus grain. The two-tier pricing system, in general, encouraged evasion of basic quotas in a situation where the state's ability to enforce deliveries had been weakened (Sicular 1988b: 691). Under the new 'contract purchase system', introduced in early 1985, farmers sign contracts. These are still effectively obligatory, it seems – inducements are the uncertainty of future market prices, ensured supplies of chemical fertilizers, credit priority (Ash 1988: 549), and the ultimate threat of loss of land (Prybyla 1987: 18). Contracts involve an agreement to supply agreed amounts of grain to the state at a price based on 30 per cent of the contracted amount at the old base price and 70 per cent at the old surplus price, and the state no longer promises to buy grain beyond the grain contract (Watson 1988: 7). Sicular (1988b: 694) notes, however, that if market prices of grain fall below the old quota prices, the state promises to purchase any amount at the old quota prices.

Watson (1988: 11) adds that the number of categories subject to price controls has been reduced from 111 (accounting for 90 per cent of total social purchases) to some 17 (30 per cent of purchases), while another 11 categories, representing a further 10 per cent of purchases, are subject to state guidance prices. About 50 Mt of grain is purchased annually by the state and sold to urban residents, who receive grain ration coupons, at subsidized retail prices. Farmers sell another 50 Mt in further negotiated sales to the state and in free (mainly rural) markets. The remainder is retained by farmers for their own use. The system means that the state controls some 18 to 20 per cent of total grain production, 75 per cent of market supply and nearly all the urban grain trade (Delfs, *FEER*, 18 February 1988, p. 68). Do Rosario estimates that the free market in grain typically accounts for some 10 per cent of output (*FEER*, 3 November 1988, p. 99).

Note that private plots remain and have been expanded, and the maximum proportion of cultivated area allocated has increased from 7 per cent in 1978 to 15 per cent in March 1981 (Skinner 1985: 406). Agricultural performance under the HRS has been impressive; the gross value of agricultural output (which includes sidelines production) has been increasing at an annual average rate of 10.1 per cent in the period 1978–85.[10] Johnson estimates that the real income of farm people doubled during 1978–86 (1988: 234). Nevertheless, a number of problems have arisen that have caused concern to the state:

1. The responsibility system and sideline activities have made labour a valuable asset and thus helped undermine the population control programme.
2. Land use has not always coincided with state preferences. The switch from grain to other more profitable crops and sideline activities contributed to a fall in the grain harvest from 407 Mt in 1984 (a record) to 380 Mt in 1985, 390 Mt in 1986, 401 Mt in 1987, and 394 Mt in 1988. In early 1987 the state took various measures to try to attain the 1987 plan target of 400 Mt (410 Mt in 1988, 450 Mt by 1990 and 480 Mt by the year 2000). These included increased state prices, reduced quotas to allow more free market sales, improved supply of subsidized inputs and levies on land used for other crops. The construction of houses and graves on farmland was banned in 1982. Concern about the cotton harvest led in December 1987 to incentives in the form of ensured supplies of low cost fertilizer.
3. The responsibility system benefited from the existence of an extensive rural infrastructure, but there are signs that the concentration of activities on the household has led to deficiencies in the provision of collective works (such as drainage, flood control, and irrigation schemes) and the underutilization of the larger pieces of equipment such as tractors. In November 1987 village committees were given increased powers to try to overcome these problems. Agricultural investment took only 3.4 per cent of the state budget in 1987 compared with 12 per cent in 1985 (*The Economist*, 26 March – 1 April 1988, p. 48), while as a proportion of total investment there was a fall from around 10 per cent in the 1970s to only 3 per cent in 1986 (Delfs, *FEER*, 18 February 1988, p. 66). A new body, called the China Agricultural Investment and Development Corporation, was set up in 1988 to reverse the fall in investment (*EIU Country Report*, 1988, no. 1, p. 14).
4. Delfs (*FEER*, p. 67) describes the farming sector as consisting of 180 million household producers, each working small plots of land averaging 0.6 hectares; Johnson (1988: 237) puts the figure at less than two acres of cropland. The increasing fragmentation of land makes it increasingly unsuitable for crops such as grain or the use of large machinery. In September 1987 experiments started in which local authorities leased out larger plots of land to private individuals for grain production on contract, the plots being formed out of the merger of smaller unused or underutilized plots. According to *The Daily Telegraph* (9 January 1988, p.IX) each family is allowed to rent up to seven acres of land from the township.
5. There is concern about land being left idle as people move into subsidiary production, retaining it for family use in the event of a change in the

political atmosphere (Colina MacDougall, *FT*, 30 September 1988, p. 6).

Central planning

There have been enormous policy swings in this as with other aspects of the Chinese economy, with seemingly self-sustaining cyclical movements revolving around 'economics versus politics' and 'centralization versus decentralization'. This phenomenon is caused by centrally induced rigidities and inertia and decentrally induced disorder. Some indication of the swings can be seen in the changing number of centrally determined material balances of category I and II goods over time; these are widely used and specialized materials allocated by the State Planning Commission and the central branch ministries: 1952, 28; 1953, 96; 1957, 532; 1958, 132; 1963, 522; 1964, 592; 1966, 579; 1970s, low 200s; 1978, 210; 1981, 67 (Prybyla 1985: 569).[11] The lack of effective medium term (five years) and long term planning during the period 1958–76 has been reflected in a number of problems facing China today. There are severe bottlenecks in the provision of infrastructure (especially energy, transport and communications), while the development of planning techniques, including input-output analysis, has been retarded.

The First Five-year Plan (1953–57)

During the First Five-year Plan familiar Soviet-type institutions were set up, material balancing was employed and economic calculation was dominant. The State Planning Commission was founded in 1952, although annual and even shorter term planning was later taken over by the State Economic Commission, established in 1956. In 1954 the State Investment Commission was established and two years later the Materials Supply Office and the State Technology Commission. The plan was only approved midway through. Regional decision-making was more important than in the traditional Soviet model, but the economy was highly centralized. The centre controlled the output targets of the most important industrial and agricultural goods, total investment, sectoral allocation, and large projects; material balancing of the most important commodities and their inter-provincial flows; foreign trade turnover and commodity structure; total employment, total wages, labour allocation at national level, and allocation of scientific and technical workers (Donnithorne 1967: 462). The number of centrally allocated commodities increased from 28 in 1952 to 235 in 1956, with the centre directing those enterprises producing these goods (the centre's share of industrial output rose to nearly 50 per cent by 1957; Riskin 1987: 101). The provinces and localities managed those enterprises under their direction, producing those commodities mainly used internally.

The Great Leap Forward 1958–60

The GLF brought extreme administrative decentralization and politics in ascendancy over economics. There was a disdain for the idea of economic efficiency. The 1958 reform concerned the following:

1. It considerably enhanced the decision-making powers of local government over investment and the supply of raw materials.
2. Most central enterprises were transferred to local control. The exceptions were large operations in strategically important sectors, although even these came under dual leadership.
3. The system of unified material balancing was changed into one based on regional planning and 'bottom-to-top' balancing.
4. The number of products controlled by the State Planning Commission was substantially reduced.
5. Local authorities were able to reallocate centrally rationed materials held by all enterprises in their regions.

One result of all this was that sectors expanded without regard to intersectoral relationships. The statistical network collapsed and targets became unrealistic. Provinces gained increased revenue when they were allowed 20 per cent of the profits of the newly decentralized plants, and local authorities were also permitted to alter tax rates and to decide on credit policy. Enterprises in the state-owned sector were also given increased autonomy, with reduced plan targets. The system of unified retained earnings became enterprise-specific (especially Wu and Reynolds 1988: 461–62.) The centre still attempted to control key variables such as total investment, inter-regional allocation, and major projects, and the output of the most important commodities.

The period between the Great Leap Forward and the Cultural Revolution

This period saw the reinstatement of central command planning and the primacy of economic calculation. Central control over most of the enterprises and commodities that had been passed down was reinstated, although the power of local authorities continued to be relatively great compared with other socialist countries. Many decisions were taken by substantially self-sufficient provinces (and, later, even counties), with the centre concentrating on intra-provincial flows and the larger enterprises in strategic sectors (Perkins 1988: 607).

The Cultural Revolution

Prybyla (1985: 563) describes central planning during the 1961–65 period as being largely on an *ad hoc*, emergency basis, turning into a shambles by the late 1960s. The Cultural Revolution is normally dated 1966–76, but the most extreme aspects had ended by 1969. The reversal to more pragmatic policies and the attempts to diminish Mao's power, led by Liu Shaoqi, resulted in a backlash. Following Mao's call for 'continuous revolution', Red Guards attacked 'old' ideas and 'capitalist roaders', research and higher educational programmes were decimated, professionals and critical party members (including Deng Xiaoping) were given menial jobs to perform and many intellectuals were persecuted. Mao used the army to restore control.

The decade was by no means homogeneous as regards the economic system, but, in general, there was a decentralization of decision-making, to local authorities in 1970, for example. The need for this and for increasing the amount of revenue retained by enterprises was stressed in 1978, and after 1979 there was greater emphasis laid on expanding the decision-making powers of enterprises (Wu and Reynolds 1988: 462). Politics took command once again, and self-reliance and egalitarianism became the keynotes. Central command planning largely collapsed, to be replaced not by a market economy, but by a system whereby provinces, localities and enterprises were to be as self-reliant as possible in order to minimize the need for central coordination. The central bureaucracy, which Mao was averse to, could be reduced to a size commensurate with this restricted role. Centrally issued economic criteria were reduced to highly generalized forms such as the need for a high degree of local self-sufficiency in industry and agriculture. The number of centrally determined material balances was reduced, and central control concentrated on the modern, large-scale enterprises producing these goods. The notion of 'self-reliance' was also applied at the national level and found one of its reflections domestically in the 'grain first' slogan; this stressed provincial self-sufficiency in grain production.

The general aim today is to create a 'planned socialist commodity economy'; the term 'planned commodity economy based on public ownership' being introduced in 1984. Bergson (1985: 76–77) describes the reform as a greater emphasis on what the Chinese call 'guidance' planning as opposed to 'mandatory' planning, involving increased decision-making autonomy for enterprises and provincial/local authorities, and greater emphasis on economic levers. What specifically these concepts and others such as 'socialism with Chinese characteristics' mean in reality will be explored in the following pages.

The allocation of manpower

Do Rosario presents some basic statistics: China's total work-force is 500 million (350 million in the countryside and 120 million in the cities); 85 per cent of urban workers are employed by state-run enterprises; urban unemployment is officially given as 5.9 per cent in 1978 and 2 per cent in 1987 (*FEER*,

12 May 1988, pp. 72–73). White (1988: 181) puts the state industrial and non-industrial work-force at 18.1 per cent of the total work force and 70 per cent of the urban.

Manpower is an area where China made an early departure from the traditional Soviet economic system. The situation generally is that there has been no labour market, on the grounds that labour is not a commodity and for purposes of state control over population movements. Manpower has typically been allocated to enterprises by institutions such as the school or area assignment office, and workers stay for their working lives. The 'iron rice bowl' mentality ensures a job and a wage (literally, everyone eats from the same pot regardless of work effort). Promotion and increased pay have been dependent more on factors such as seniority. Workers' housing[12] and medical insurance are also subsidized by the work unit (Hu, Li, and Shi 1988: 77). Workers need permission to change jobs and are almost impossible to sack, however unsatisfactory. The enterprise 'congress' of workers and staff, which includes the party representative, has the final say. Since 1979, in Beijing and elsewhere, enterprises have been given a greater say in selecting individual workers within the manpower quota, while job seekers have been able to apply via the local labour bureaus, directly to enterprises or through one of the new 'labour service companies'. These companies are sponsored by government bureaus or enterprises and are able to provide training and, in some cases, actual jobs in their own enterprises (White 1988: 194–95).

Wage and salary differentials have been small by Soviet and East European standards, and piecework payments have been rare since 1956; then 42 per cent of industrial workers were so rewarded (Richman 1969: 314). Bonuses have been based more on factors such as tradition and seniority than on performance and skill and in any event are normally more equally dispersed. Hu, Li and Shi describe the present wage set-up as originating in the Soviet-type system introduced in 1956. Wages for workers in enterprises have three components: technical skill (determined by type and years of work experience), the wage grade level (determined by job requirements and responsibilities) and basic wages. There are eight grades of wages for workers, ranging from Grade 1 for an inexperienced new worker to Grade 8 for a foreman. During the late 1970s and the 1980s bonuses were made available, but were seldom based on productivity. Wages for cadres and professional staff (in administration, schools, hospitals, etc.) have four components: basic wage, job responsibility, supplemental wage for years of work, and bonuses (Hu, Li, and Shi 1988: 78). A small number of enterprises have recently been subjected to experiments where total wage bills have been determined by output or profit (p. 79). Their empirical findings are that wages are greatly influenced by the years of work experience, affiliation to a state-owned enterprise, and by occupation (especially for cadres). The wage system has not placed a great deal of emphasis on educational attainment or industrial affiliation; there is not much wage incentive for productive workers (p. 93).

Contract labour of some form has been around since the 1950s. During the GLF the percentage of non-permanent workers in the state economy rose to about 30 per cent, but declined during the Cultural Revolution to some 6 per cent (Korzec 1988: 120–1). There have been experiments with contracts since 1979, especially in construction. Early experiments took place in Shanghai and the SEZs. In Shenzhen all workers were on contracts of limited durationm (Korzec 1988: 121). In 1983, however, 96.8 per cent of state workers were still 'fixed' (White 1987b: 366, 1988: 183). According to Rosen, in the year to October 1986 more than 80 per cent of all new state sector employees had signed labour contracts (White 1987b: 44). By the end of 1986 only 5.6 per cent of state workers were on contracts (White 1988: 196), and 7.8 per cent of the work-force in state-owned industry by the end of March 1988 (*EIU Country Report*, 1988, no. 3, p. 16). From 1 October 1986 a more general contract system was introduced for new workers.[13] New prospective employees undergo tests and a trial period before negotiating the length of the fixed-term work contract with their employers.[14] There have also been recent moves to loosen the extraordinarily tight restrictions on sacking, such as in cases of gross violation of work rules and rudeness towards customers so persistent as to threaten the loss of sales.

The right to strike was removed from the 1982 constitution, but strikes were not made illegal.

There have also been experimental relaxations of the rigid labour allocation system to provide a measure of choice for graduates and skilled workers on the one hand and employers on the other. Increasingly, enterprises are making specific requests to universities for graduates. Daniel Southerland (*IHT*, 20–21 February 1988, p. 14) reports that the state assigns jobs to 70 per cent of university graduates; the aim is to require most students to pay for their own tuition and to find their own jobs. In April 1989, however, it was announced (as part of the retrenchment process) that graduates would only be permitted to contact potential employers for information, and would not be allowed to find their own positions.

1987 saw the start of a new pensions scheme. State enterprises will no longer be directly responsible for pensions, but contribute instead 11.5 per cent of their wage bill (supplemented by contract workers paying 3 per cent of their monthly earnings) to a state insurance fund (do Rosario, *FEER*, 12 May 1988, p. 74). On 28 February 1988 Beijing's first labour market was opened to help those registered (for a 1 yuan fee) to receive help finding another job.

Wage reforms involve a greater linkage between effort and reward, especially the increased use of piece rates and bonuses tied to performance. It is now also possible to send workers to the 'second front' (labour reserve team) of the enterprise on basic pay only. In 1985 government workers salary increases began to be based mainly on performance and responsibility rather than longevity of service.

The tax system has also been employed to try to curb pay increases. The scheme introduced in 1986 stated that if bonuses paid to employees exceeded the value of the wage bill for five months, the enterprise had to pay a 30 per cent tax, rising to 100 per cent for six months, and 300 per cent for over six months. On 1 January the following year the income tax system was revamped, the minimum taxable level was reduced to four times the average wage (half the previous level), and the maximum rate reached 60 per cent.

August 1986 was noteworthy since it marked the first state enterprise *bankruptcy* in China since 1949, after being warned in 1985 to return to profitability within a year. The assets of the Shenyang Explosion-proof Equipment plant were auctioned off; this was followed on 13 October 1988 by the opening of China's first labour exchange. Despite a number of other enterprises being placed under threat and the closure of the Nanchang Underground Department Store in November 1987, the proposed bankruptcy law was shelved. In the more conservative atmosphere prevailing, preference shifted towards merging failing enterprises with more efficient organizations. Inefficient army plants producing civilian goods can now be brought under civilian control, the first example occurring in January 1988 when CITIC took over a vehicle works (*EIU Country Report*, 1988, no. 1, p. 17). Approval for legislation to implement a bankruptcy law (for a trial one year period starting November 1988) was finally given at the Seventh National People's Congress (25 March – 13 April 1988), having awaited the passing of the law on the state industrial enterprise. An early problem that has emerged is that there are cases of directors inviting threat of closure in order to take advantage of concessions in the form of tax relief, low interest loans and the abolition of debt repayment (Graham Hutchings, *The Daily Telegraph*, 11 November 1988, p. 17). There is the prospect of the sale of inefficient small or medium sized enterprises to foreigners (reported in *FT*, 2 August 1988, p. 4).

Prior to 1978 it was claimed that urban unemployment was not a problem, but events such as the return of many school leavers and students sent to the countryside during the Cultural Revolution has brought about its open recognition. A form of unemployment pay has been available since 1986, however, for those workers who have been dismissed or lost their jobs through bankruptcy, or whose contracts have expired. Payments, financed by a 1 per cent levy on enterprise wage bills, will be available for up to two years for those employed for five years or more and for up to a year for less than five years. Seventy-five per cent of the previous wage is payable for the first six months and a fixed sum amounting to something less than a third of the average industrial wage for the remainder.

The financial system

Pricing

Pre-1949 prices had a long-term influence because of the concern for stability in price determination, most industrial prices remaining stable for a quarter of a century after the mid-1950s and there were only limited price changes during 1979–83 (Perkins 1988: 620). However, the subsequent basis used by the state (centre, province, or county) of branch average planned cost plus a profit markup (large enough to permit most or all enterprises to operate profitably in each important production area) for industrial wholesale prices still largely applies today (see Prybyla 1987). New product prices have also long taken import prices into consideration to a lesser extent. China has been slow to introduce a capital charge. Traditionally, enterprises have been provided with fixed and working capital in the shape of a grant, but the 1980s have seen a change. In the early years of the decade experiments were begun, generally involving a small capital charge of 1 to 2 per cent, and in 1984 it was announced that there was to be a move away from grants to interest-bearing credits (3 to 6 per cent). In 1982 enterprises favourably located or favourably endowed were subject to a rental charge ('adjustment tax'). The October 1984 reform proposals included a charge on fixed and working capital and a rental charge for extractive industries.

Prices have tended to remain fixed for long periods of time and reform has been slow, despite the professed aim in October 1984 to restrict fixed prices to 'major' products and allowing considerably increased scope for range and freely negotiated prices. At the end of 1985 market prices accounted for more than 30 per cent of the value of industrial and agricultural output, while range prices covered 20 to 30 per cent (Chan 1986: 30). After some experiments in 1979 the present decade has seen increasing use made of range prices (plus or minus a percentage around the state price) and, to a lesser extent, market determined prices ('negotiated' prices). According to do Rosario, 65 per cent of agricultural products, 55 per cent of industrial consumer goods and 40 per cent of industrial raw materials are no longer subject to fixed state prices (do Rosario 1987: 70). She estimates that a third of the prices of all agricultural and retail goods are now freely determined (*FEER*, 30 June 1988, p. 50). Ishihara (1987: 304–5) states that of the 47 per cent of total agricultural and sidelines production sold from rural to urban areas in 1985, 32.1 per cent involved purchases at state listed prices and 51.2 per cent involved 'negotiated' (which sometimes involves supervisory state organs in the negotiating process) or 'floating' (with upper, lower, or upper and lower limits) prices; the respective 1978 figures were 84.7 per cent, 1.8 per cent and 5.6 per cent. In 1984 there was offical acknowledgement that industrial enterprises could sell a percentage of their production on the market at range prices. In January of the following year they were permitted to charge a price a shade below local market prices; these new prices were termed 'market floating' prices (Chan 1986: 26–7). Thus a noticeable feature is multiple pricing for the same product. In January 1988 price ceilings were imposed on basic fuels and materials, such as oil, gas, coal, electricity, steel and timber, and on transport charges. In his speech opening the Thirteenth Party Congress in 1987, Zhao Ziyang referred to the need to move gradually to a situation where the state sets the prices of only a few vital commodities and labour services, while leaving the remainder to be determined by the market.

In order to reduce the high level of subsidies paid out to stabilize the prices of staple consumer goods,[15] attempts have been made since 1985 to raise retail prices. These have often been rescinded, however, in the face of public unrest and fears of inflation. Efforts with respect to luxury goods have been more successful. A general twelve month price freeze was introduced in January 1987. In August, due to the ineffectiveness of the price freeze, retail prices of consumer goods under state control were to be unchanged for the remainder of the year, in view of the 6.3 per cent increase in the national retail price index in the first half of the year compared with the same period of 1986. In July 1988 a partial price freeze was implemented because of the inflation rate of 13 per cent in the first six months, with exceptions such as the better brands of alcohol and tobacco, which were to be sold at market prices. In September it was announced that further major price changes were to be shelved during a two year 'rectification' period. Yao Yilin (Chairman of the State Planning Commission) said that price controls would remain for products such as grain, edible oils, cotton and steel, and that the multiple pricing system may last for two decades, officially until most goods are in excess supply. The following month price controls were actually reimposed on some basic commodities; for example, the prices of vegetables in northern cities were to be frozen for the winter period. A freeze was applied to state controlled prices of essentials.

In December 1987 the city of Beijing extended rationing for grain and cooking oil to other products like pork (due to factors such as a shortage of feed grain), eggs and sugar. Other cities are also affected, for example Shanghai and Tianjin in the case of pork.[16] At the Seventh National People's Congress in 1988, it was announced that the World Bank (for the first time anywhere) was giving a policy-linked loan. Specifically, part of the $300 million is to be used for an experiment, to run in two areas (counties in Henan and Guangxi), to replace grain subsidies with income supplements. In fact this became a more general policy when, in the same year, urban residents began to be paid income supplements to compensate for food price increases, thus switching subsidies from products to incomes. Hangzhou became the first city to introduce the new income subsidy scheme in mid-January 1988 (do Rosario, *FEER*, 26 May 1988, p. 72).

Banking

The banking system in China is now quite complex and includes joint ventures with and branches of foreign banks, and independent credit co-operatives (see the report on credit co-operatives by Edward Gargan, *IHT*, 8 August 1988, pp. 11, 13).[17] At the apex of the domestic system is the People's Bank of China which, since 1984, has acted more like a Western central bank. The People's Bank is responsible for controlling the total volume of credit in line with the plan as well as that granted by individual banks. It fixes the discount rate at which the commercial banks are able to borrow from and the ratio of reserves to be deposited at the People's Bank and issues directives and imposes credit rationing. For example, on 1 September 1988, because of concern about inflation, the interest rate on one-year deposits was raised from 7.2 to 8.6 per cent (up to 12.42 per cent for eight year deposits) and that on bank loans from 7.9 to 9.0 per cent, while the reserve ratio went from 12 to 13 per cent. The People's Bank also declared its intention to index-link the three-, five-, and eight-year savings deposits of individuals, in addition to paying interest. Since 1984 the then newly established Industrial and Commercial Bank of China has provided short- and medium-term loans to urban industry and commerce and has taken over the function of accepting deposits from the general public from the People's Bank. The Agricultural Bank (re-established in 1979) mobilizes the savings of and provides credit to the rural economy as a whole: the People's Construction Bank deals in long term funds for specific capital projects; the Investment Bank of China is concerned with investment credits and foreign capital; and the Bank of China handles foreign exchange transactions and dealings with foreign banks and governments. The People's Bank publishes credit targets and sectoral priorities, issues plan instructions, and allocates state funds to commercial banks to meet part of their planned expenditures (they are consulted during the drawing up of the credit plan). The remainder and above-plan loans are covered by attracting deposits.

A notable event took place in April 1987 with the opening of the Shanghai Bank of Communications. Fifty per cent of its shares are owned by the central government, 25 per cent by the Shanghai municipal government, about 20 per cent by other institutions and a maximum of five per cent by individuals. It has no state capital allocation and thus makes loans on the basis of the deposits it succeeds in attracting. The aim is to provide competition to totally state owned banks in terms of both domestic and foreign business; it has overseas branches and branches in other cities in China. Domestic interest rates can be fixed within a range set by the People's Bank.

The banking reforms, which began in 1979, have three major goals (White and Bowles 1988: 28–36): (1) to encourage savings sufficient to match the investment rate of some 30 per cent; (2) to establish methods of monetary control; and (3) to increase the efficiency of credit allocation by enhancing the role of profitability – banks are able to retain 10 per cent of profits. According to White and Bowles, the first aim has been met relatively successfully, the other two less so because banks are still ultimately subservient to the state plan. Thus, monetary targets have been continually exceeded, while the commercial banks have rarely used their theoretically draconian powers over loss-making enterprises to restrict credit to, restructure, reorganize management in, merge or even bankrupt enterprises.

Other interesting experiments include some local 'foreign exchange adjustment centres', which allow enterprises to trade their surpluses and deficits in foreign exchange, a number of bank branches to buy and sell promissary notes issued by enterprises short of funds, and local cases (such as in Shanghai) of direct interbank borrowing. Private citizens have been allowed to hold foreign exchange since 1985 (Baum 1986: 46). Rural and urban credit co-operatives have also increased in importance.

The first experiments with stock issues took place in 1981. Since 1986 the People's Bank has been authorized to approve the issuing of shares and bonds by companies to government, other enterprises, employees and outside individuals, which can be traded on a few rudimentary 'stock exchanges' in Shanghai, Shenyang, Tianjin, and Beijing.[18] Shares normally consist of a basic fixed interest equal to that on bank deposits, or sometimes coupons giving the right to a scarce good or lottery ticket from such goods, plus a regulated element dependent on company profitability. In some cases the larger shareholders have a vote at a conference that elects the company board which, in turn, elects the manager. The ownership rights associated with Western equities are absent, and Goldman and Goldman (1988: 558) point out that stocks are limited to a maximum 30 per cent of the value of the capital stock of an enterprise. Since early 1987 state enterprises have, in general, only been able to issue bonds: exceptions include shareholding among enterprises for forging horizontal links (*China Briefing*, December 1988, no. 31, p. 9). In October 1988 a Shenjang bus and truck manufacturer began issuing freely tradeable shares in foreign exchange (Jasper Becker, *The Guardian*, 14 October 1988, p. 11). Progress towards large-scale stock issuing by state enterprises subsequently became another victim of the 'rectification process'.

The first bank-enterprise joint venture (the Anshan Trust and Investment Corporation, owned by the Industrial and Commercial bank of China and the Anshan Iron and Steel Company) was set up in early 1988 (*EIU Country Report*, 1988, no. 1, p. 22).

In November 1987 it was announced that in the following year 'house banks' (in effect building societies involved in selling house and land leases) would be set up and individual estate agents allowed, as well as four new investment corporations to take over most investment finance from the Ministry of Finance, moving away from the interest-free funding of large national projects. In order to reduce investment spending, a 15 per cent construction tax and a 20 per cent of cost compulsory donation to finance their purchase of government bonds were also to be imposed on construction projects considered unnecessary (Robin Pauley and Colina Macdougall, *FT*, 28 November 1987, p. 20). Each tier of government will be responsible for raising the taxes necessary to cover its own expenditure.

Budgetary policy

The increasing activation of money is also reflected in budgetary policy. Adopting conventional Western practice and ignoring the curious Chinese one of counting borrowed funds (both foreign loans and treasury bond sales) in with revenue, China suffered a string of budget deficits over the period 1979 to 1987, with the exception of 1985. This has caused concern because of the printing of money to finance the deficit and the consequent implications for inflation. The government began issuing bonds in 1981 to cover the deficit, as well as for capital investment projects and started to redeem them five years later (*The Times*, 28 March 1988, p. 26).

A noticeable feature of budgetary revenue, in contrast to the Soviet Union, is the historically more important role played by enterprise profit deductions as opposed to turnover tax. In the late 1970s some 50 per cent of revenue derived from the former and a large proportion of the remainder from the latter, but between 1978 and 1980 the former had fallen by nearly 25 per cent (Ellman 1986: 434). In recent years a falling share of budgetary expenditure has gone to defence: in 1979, 20 per cent; in 1984, 15 per cent; in 1985, 12 per cent; in 1986, 10 per cent; and in 1987, 8.2 per cent. Goldman and Goldman (1988: 566) estimate that the proportion of GNP devoted to defence has declined from 13 per cent in 1973 to 8.6 per cent in 1983 and to 6 to 7 per cent currently. *The Economist* quotes a current CIA figure of around 4 per cent (14–20 May 1988, p. 66). Budgetary financing of investment in capital construction has also fallen from 80 per cent in 1979 to 54.4 per cent in 1984, the remainder financed from credits and plough-back profits (Kosta 1987: 153). Another distinctive feature according to Robin Pauley (*FT Survey*, 18 December 1987, p.VI), is that the central government receives only slightly more than a quarter of total tax revenue.

Industrial management

The Chinese state industrial enterprise (varying considerably in size) is still usually a plant, although there are also specialized integrated corporations and industrial associations with a nation-wide network of branches in existence. Enterprises are vertically integrating, as in the car industry, and horizontally integrating, as in textiles (Ling 1988: 522). Plant consolidation took place in and after the late 1970s to reap economies of scale and to increase efficiency in the use of inputs (Perkins 1988: 630).

Even during the First Five-year Plan (1953–57), when the organization of the larger state industrial enterprises most resembled the traditional Soviet model, there were divergences: (1) the lack of control over manpower allocation; (2) virtually all profits and the depreciation fund were transferred to the state budget; (3) the *danwei* or workplace was an important provider of housing and the chief supplier of welfare services such as pensions and sickness and disability benefits; (4) management incentives were much less oriented towards bonuses and, instead, party praise or criticism, promotion or demotion, and measures of the general contribution to socialism and party goals were more important; and (5) income differentials between managers and workers were less prominent.

From 1958 to 1978 the departures from the Soviet model became much more pronounced, especially during the GLF and the Cultural Revolution. The principle of one-man responsibility and control was thrown out at the end of the First Five-year Plan. During the GLF Mao's idea of involving management in labour and workers in management was implemented. Groups of workers became responsible for formerly specialized management functions such as quality control, repair and maintenance, and workers, administrative personnel and technicians formed work teams. Managerial bonuses were largely abolished and group bonuses replaced individual worker ones. Non-material incentives became more important, as did model workers, praise and criticism, and emulation campaigns. Between 1962 and 1965 'workers' congresses' were reintroduced, made up of elected representatives of workers and staff. In theory these were able to approve leadership reports on enterprise affairs and to sack management, but in reality confined themselves to plan targets and welfare (Riskin 1987: 160). The number of obligatory indicators was reduced from twelve to four, namely quantities of important products, total employment, total wage bill, and total profit. During the Cultural Revolution workers took over many enterprises. In response, 'revolutionary committees' were established by the state, whose members were representatives of mass organizations, the party and the army (Riskin 1987: 186). These committees were, in effect, means of exercising party control over enterprise management.

The Cultural Revolution was followed by the reintroduction of a more traditional system of industrial organization. Industrial reform after 1978 aimed to change the relationship between state and enterprise, rather than just affecting the relative decision-making powers of centre and region. Reform experiments were first started in October 1978 in Sichuan province under Zhao Ziyang and widened after the following year. Halpern (1985) discusses the nature of the early experiments, including the ability of some of the experimental enterprises to determine above-plan production and sales and to increase decentralized investment. Wong (1986) attributes the reason for the failure of the 1979–83 reforms to the soft budget constraint generating quantity drives and supply problems, which brought about administrative interventions. Ellman (1986: 433) estimates that by the end of 1980 the experiment covered 60 per cent of the output of state industrial enterprises. The 1981 'economic responsibility system' involved a profit sharing contract between state and enterprise – if the volume of profit exceeded target there was a division in fixed proportion between the two, and underfulfilment meant a part of the sum had to be paid out of enterprise funds (p. 434).

In general, enterprises, now subjected to a profits tax rather than simple profit remission, were allowed to retain a part of profit, and a minority of enterprises simply paid over stipulated taxes. Profit retention was dependent on fulfilment of a limited number of success indicators, namely output in terms of quantity, quality, and assortment; contract fulfilment; materials, fuel, and power consumption; labour productivity; cost; use of working capital; and profit. Retained profit was used to feed an 'enterprise fund', determined by a certain percentage of planned profit and a higher percentage of above-plan profit and could be used for decentralized investment, socio-cultural expenditures (such as housing) and personal bonuses. By 1980–84 only 27.5 per cent of total gross investment went through the state budget, compared with 54.5 per cent during 1953–57 (Perkins 1988: 617). Part of the depreciation fund could also be retained, as well as the additional profit (for two years) earned by self-financed innovation. Enterprises were able to apply for bank credit to finance capital investment. In 1983 there was a general switch to a system of defined taxes: the capital charge; the rental charge (called a 'resource tax' in extractive industries, and an 'adjustment tax' in industry), a negotiated percentage of enterprise profit increases; a sales (so-called product) tax; and a profits tax. The state then claimed a share of after-tax profits (Riskin 1987: 344–46). The share of profits retained by state enterprises increased from 3.7 per cent in 1978 to 42.4 per cent in 1986 (Prybyla 1987: 16). Other important changes in 1983–84 included the switch from gross to net value as the main output indicator, the ability of enterprises to sell most above-quota output direct to users, and the ending of working capital grants (Field 1984: 758).[19]

The May 1984 provisions and the Central Committee announcement of 20 October heralded a general extension of reforms to the state-owned industrial sector, to be introduced gradually over the following five years.[20] In the May provisions state-owned enterprises were permitted to determine production plans after meeting state targets and to sell the resulting products at market prices. Unused assets could be sold; power was given to rearrange staff, to appoint middle-level administrative staff and to dispose of the bonus fund (Wu and Reynolds 1988: 463). The aim of the October 1984 measures (a 'planned commodity economy under public ownership') seemed to be: (1) to retain central control over key industrial and agricultural products, such as coal, oil, steel, armaments, heavy machinery, electrical equipment, cotton, and cereals; (2) allowing 60 of the 120 industrial products and 19 of the 29 agricultural products currently assigned by the state, though representing a lower percentage of the value of output, to be produced within the context of general state guidelines or even the market (such as consumer goods, textiles, fruit and vegetables). Increasing stress is to be placed on indirect steering by means of economic levers such as prices, taxes, interest rates, and credits. The key financial element involved a gradual end of state claims to a share of after-tax profit and, thus, a move towards a purely tax-based system.

After meeting targets set by the state, which also guarantees the necessary inputs at state determined prices, enterprises are now allowed to produce and sell (at negotiated prices, usually within a range, directly to buyers or at fairs, and via their own retail outlets in some cases) whatever they like and wherever they choose. This is the so-called self-disposal system. There is thus now some scope for purchase of non-labour inputs outside the materials allocation system. For example, although in 1987 China was the world's fourth largest producer of steel, demand greatly exceeded supply. The distribution system is also inefficient, and in 1984 direct sales to final customers was allowed, with prices negotiated within a set range. At the start of 1987 53 per cent of steel was allocated on quota (although another 40 per cent of production capacity is affected by quotas determined by local authorities) (Colina Macdougall gives the market price of rolled steel as at least twice the state price; *FT*, 16 December 1988, p. 4). At the same time, while the entire output of oil was on quota and subject to state-determined prices, only 42 per cent of coal, 30 per cent of timber and 16 per cent of cement was thus affected. There are now no quotas for production of heavy industrial manufactures (producer durables), and prices are fixed by supply and demand. Previously there existed a range 20 per cent above and below the official price. Only 20 per cent of consumer durables and processed food are on quota and sold at official prices, while 40 per cent are on quota and sold at a price within a range 20 per cent above or below the state price, with the remainder sold at free prices (Kaser 1987: 407). Ishihara states that half of total coal production is left out of the central government distribution system; 50 per cent of this is produced by locally administered state coal mines, and the other 50 per cent is produced by collectively or individually managed mines and sold at market prices. Citing Li Wenzhong (1985), Ishihara gives the following figures for the percentage of total production outside the central government distribution plan: coal, 50 per cent; steel materials, 40 per cent; lumber, 60 per cent; cement, 75 per cent. These are distributed at market prices. An example of over-target production sold by enterprises at freely negotiated prices, the percentage of the output of steel materials sold in this way, increased from 23.5 per cent in 1980 to 30.2 per cent in 1985 (Ishihara 1987: 34). Between 1978 and 1986 the central government reduced the number of major commodities distributed exclusively within the state commercial network from 256 to 20 (do Rosario 1987: 70).[21]

Earlier experiments were widened in 1985 to make research institute revenue more dependent on negotiated contracts with industrial clients. Discussion on the 'enterprise law', which defined the legal responsibilities of an enterprise and strengthened the role of the director at the expense of the party, was postponed at the Sixth National People's Congress (26 March – 13 April 1987). The implementation of the January 1987 'bankruptcy law' depended on its passage. Experiments with 'management contracts' have also been carried out, which involve enterprises competing for contracts, albeit at fixed prices. Surpassing of profit targets (the contracted profit being handed over to the state) means bonuses for management and workers, but managerial income is reduced in the event of losses. According to do Rosario, there has been a widespread application of the contract management system since April 1987 (*FEER*, 14 April 1988, p. 55). The 'management contract' or 'contracted managerial responsibility' system now applies to most state enterprises; these sign one- to five-year contracts with the supervising state body (do Rosario, *FEER*, 8 September 1988, p. 132).

Chamberlain (1987) considers *party-management relations* in large and medium-sized enterprises. The Soviet-type principle of 'one-man management', adopted in the early 1950s, was replaced in 1956 by that of 'factory director responsibility under party committee leadership', in order to re-establish party control. In reality, however, the party committee secretary was in control (Chamberlain 1987: 632). In the late 1960s there were widespread experiments involving collective management by workers and cadres in 'revolutionary committees', but by the early 1970s the secretary had regained control. In 1976 the principle of 'factory director under party leadership' was formally reinstated (p. 633). Since May 1984 there has been a gradual application of the 'factory director responsibility system', which is not a return to the Soviet-type principle, but involves, in theory, the party committee and its secretary 'advising' the director and 'supervising' enterprise operations to ensure compliance with central party policies (pp. 645–46). The director is also meant to consult with the 'staff-workers congress', which disappeared during the Cultural Revolution and reappeared in 1975, and whose role is to 'deliberate' over policies, although it seems to have a decisive say over the use of funds for bonuses, welfare, and safety. The 'management committee', chaired by the director and staffed by key individuals such as the chief engineer, accountant and economist, also plays a solely advisory role (p. 649). In reality, however, Chamberlain considers that the party secretary is still in charge, especially since the state enterprise law had been in circulation since late 1984 awaiting ratification, with reluctance being shown over the inclusion of a clause to direct party officials to support the director in the discharge of their managerial powers (p. 651). A draft law on state-owned industrial enterprises was in fact published on 12 January 1988, and the so-called Industrial Enterprise Bill was subsequently approved at the Seventh National People's Congress in 1988. In it the party's function is to 'guarantee and supervise the implementation of party principles and policies', leaving the director to assume responsibility for running the enterprise. The legislation was made effective in August 1988 and applies to state industrial enterprises accounting for 70 per cent of gross industrial production, but not to state commercial and financial enterprises. Colina MacDougall expresses concern at a 10 December party circular, which emphasizes that politics and ideology are an 'indispensable part' of management and proposes that the enterprise manager or his deputy could be the party secretary (*FT*, 31 December 1988, p. 3).

As far as *regional decentralization* is concerned, Shanghai, for example, was allowed in 1985 to retain 23.7 per cent of revenue instead of 10 per cent, and 25 per cent of foreign exchange earnings instead of 6 per cent (Jasper Becker, *Guardian Survey on Shanghai*, 19 November 1987, p. 27). Over the period 1988–92 a fixed sum only has to be paid to the central government, and any excess revenue is thus retained (do Rosario, *FEER*, 21 April 1988, p. 71). The current trend is to reduce regional powers, especially due to concern over inflation. Even in 1985 ceilings were fixed for provincial and municipal investment projects, ranging from a typical $5 million to a maximum $30 million (e.g. for Shanghai). Ten cities (e.g. Dalian) have 'separately listed plans', economic development plans are submitted directly to the central government rather than passing through the provincial government en route (*China Briefing*, 1988, no. 30, p. 2).

The non-state, non-agricultural sector

The Chinese economy is mixed ('double tracked'). Do Rosario presents the following figures for 1987: 7.53 million industrial enterprises in total; around 98,000 state enterprises accounted for 60 per cent of total industrial output; 1.85 million collectives (34.6 per cent of output, compared with 19.2 per cent in 1978); and 5.58 million individually operated enterprises (3.6 per cent of output); the remainder comprised mainly joint ventures with foreign companies (*FEER*, 8 September 1988, p. 130). At the Eleventh National People's Congress in 1988 the following figures were revealed for the end of 1987: there were 13.7 million private businesses, employing more than 21.6 million people and accounting for nearly 13 per cent of all retail sales; there were 115,000 private enterprises employing eight people or more and in total over 1.8 million.[22] Private employment was 3.5 per cent of urban employment in 1985 (Johnson, 1988: 240). *The Economist* (9–15 January 1988, p. 87) places private sector employment at something less than 4 per cent, while a CIA report gives a figure of less than 3 per cent of the industrial labour force (*IHT*, 2 May 1988, p. 7). Private and co-operative rural non-agricultural employment now accounts for over 80 million jobs out of a total labour force of 370 million (Wu and Reynolds 1988: 463).

The private and independent co-operative sector has been flourishing since 1979 in China, after experiencing a long-run downward trend. This suppression was especially marked in 1956 and during the GLF and the Cultural Revolution, with only a mild respite in the first half of the 1960s. Under the new regulations, private businessmen are subject to a 35 per cent tax on net profit. There are also provisions for an adjustment tax on the individual income of the private investor (A. H. Hermann, *FT*, 4 August 1988, p. 18). Since 1986 it has been possible for local authorities to lease out failing enterprises to individuals (Goldman and Goldman 1988: 556) trace the leasing of industrial enterprises back to 1982). Some private enterprises and co-operatives today are descendants of the 'state capitalist' enterprises, in which owners became employees and between January 1956 and September 1966 were paid compensation in the form of interest payments normally equal to 5 per cent of the value of the shares (Goldman and Goldman 1988: 97). The first national law concerning the private sector went into operation on 1 September 1987, and at the Seventh NPC in 1988 the constitution was amended thus: 'The state permits the private sector of the economy to exist and develop within the limits prescribed by law. The private sector is a complement to the socialist public economy'.

The 'open door' policy

In 1978 the policy was announced of opening up the economy to foreign trade, capital, technology and know-how in order to modernize and speed up the growth of the economy. An important event in the run-up to this announcement was President Nixon's visit to China in February 1972. Fangui (1987: 579–80) notes that after 1979 there was a policy switch from both (1) the importation of complete sets of plant and equipment to greater diversification, involving such forms as joint ventures, total foreign ownership, co-operation ventures, licence trade, and compensation trade; and (2) the creation of new enterprises to expanding and technically transforming existing ones. There was also a decentralization of decision-making in 1980. For example Guangdong and Fujian provinces were able to transact economic business below 100 million renminbi, Shanghai and Tianjin below RMB 30 million, Beijing, Liaoyang, Dalian and Guangzhou below RMB 10 million and the other provinces below RMB 5 million (Fangui 1987: 580). On 23 January 1988 Zhao Ziyang gave a boost to the open door policy by stressing the need for all the coastal regions, especially Guangdong and Hainan, to establish closer links with overseas investors and with the world market, encouraging export-led growth and a greater role for solely foreign owned enterprises. Zhao seems to wish to take advantage of the shift of labour-intensive industries away from economies like South Korea and Taiwan to countries like China, where wage levels are lower.

Foreign trade

In recent years China has accounted for 1.5 per cent of total world trade (Anthony Rowley, *FEER*, 10 March 1988, p. 78), and foreign trade turnover as a proportion of national income has generally varied between roughly 13 and 18 per cent. *The Economist* (12–18 March 1988, p. 71) estimates that total trade is now 23 per cent of GDP; the ratio increased from 6 per cent in 1952 to 9 per cent in 1959, but fell during the 'self-reliance' strategy of the Cultural Revolution.

The distribution of trade by country has changed dramatically over time, with the socialist countries' share falling from two-thirds in 1960, to 23 per cent in 1970, and 15 per cent by the mid-1980s (with the developed capitalist countries taking more than 70 per cent). The 1950s were a period of deep involvement with the Soviet Union in particular. The heart of the First Five-year Plan (1953–57) industrial programme was 156 Soviet aid projects, especially in heavy industry such as iron and steel, heavy engineering, vehicles, petroleum, mining and electric power. Soviet credits, know-how, and technicians (only technical documents, licences and blueprints were provided free of charge) were involved, with interest rates of only 1 to 2 per cent, but short- to medium-term repayment periods. The Sino-Soviet quarrel, in addition to general aspects such as territorial disputes and leadership of the world socialist movement, involved Mao's objections to the denunciation of Stalin at the Twentieth Congress of the CPSU in 1956, the 1959 Soviet abrogation of an agreement to pass on technology relating to the atomic bomb and Khrushchev's policy of peaceful coexistence with the United States. Khrushchev himself denounced the GLF and its premature attempt to hasten the attainment of communism. In 1960 the Soviet Union withdrew its aid personnel, and China paid off its debt within the next five years, earlier than planned. Sino-Soviet trade subsequently fell to virtually zero, and it was only in the mid-1980s that agreement was reached for Soviet experts to update seventeen of the old plants (including the Anshan Iron and Steel Works), collaborate on seven new projects, and provide much needed extra electrical generating capacity.

China is currently showing more interest in counter-trade due to concern over the hard currency reserves. China is treated more leniently by COCOM, has had observer status at GATT since November 1984[23] and is a member of the IMF, the World Bank (since May 1980), and the Asian Development Bank (since 1986).

There is now considerable diversity in the institutional structure of foreign trade in China, with the degree of decentralized decision-making dependent on broad economic circumstances. The Ministry of Foreign Economic Relations and Trade (MOFERT) acts as an umbrella organization. It was set up in March 1982 as a merger of the Ministry of Foreign Trade, the Import-Export Commission and the Foreign Investment Control Commission (established in

1979 to control the use of foreign exchange), with the aim of overcoming the considerable overlapping of decision-making authority among the old and new bodies.

The exact situation varies with circumstances, but there is greater emphasis today on indirect steering of trade by the centre via the exchange rate,[24] tariffs, taxes and subsidies, the cost and availability of credit, the amount of foreign exchange earnings allowed to be retained by local authorities and enterprises, and import licences. For example, balance of payments problems and declining foreign exchange reserves have led to a recent tightening of state controls on the use of retained foreign exchange earnings, export licences, foreign borrowing and joint venture deals, and tariffs were raised throughout China on consumer goods such as cars and television sets in July 1985. The exchange rate is operational in the sense that in principle exporters receive and importers pay the world price, but a comprehensive subsidy system for exports still shields the domestic producer and trader from the full effect of international competition. There are, for example, subsidies for some imported raw materials to reduce the cost to users, and each producer of exported goods negotiates individually with the particular foreign trade corporation that bears the difference between the cost of production and the export price. Export subsidies are designed to overcome the strong inclination to deal in the easier domestic market.

Cheng believes moves in 1988 are intended to make the provincial foreign trade corporations under MOFERT financially independent and to allow them a share of some 30 per cent of retained foreign exchange earnings. Exporting production enterprises are to be allowed to retain a varying proportion of foreign exchange earnings – in light industry, where the experiment is to start, up to 70 per cent; machine-building and electrical equipment, up to 50 per cent; and even up to 100 per cent in electronics (Cheng, *FEER*, 24 March 1988, p. 74). The People's Liberation Army may now be allowed to keep up to 85 per cent of revenue from arms sales abroad (*The Economist*, 14–20 May 1988, p. 67). It was in 1979 that enterprises were generally allowed to retain a percentage of export earnings (normally 7.8 per cent), in a credit account with the State Administration of Foreign Exchange Control (*SAFEC*), which controlled its use. The following year inter-enterprise sales were permitted, but the Bank of China set the rate of exchange and charged commission. In 1985 most provinces were allowed to retain 25 per cent of foreign exchange earnings, which were split equally with the exporting enterprise, but exceptions included the SEZs (100 per cent), Guangdong and Fujian (30 per cent), the electrical and machinery industry (50 per cent) and the tourist industry (30 per cent). Since January 1988 the following have applied: for light industry, arts and crafts, and garments, the province and raw materials suppliers retain 38.5 and enterprises 31.5 per cent, leaving only 30 per cent for the central government. Certain provinces sign new contracts with the central government; export targets are based on past export achievements. If not achieved, 1985 retention percentages apply; if overachieved, the province retains 80 per cent. Sales of foreign exchange are organized via a complicated system of 'foreign exchange adjustment centres'. For example in Shenzhen rates are negotiated between buyers and sellers, although under the supervision of the SAFEC, while official rates are set in centres organized by local governments (for details see *China Briefing*, no. 29, May 1988, pp. 6–7, and no. 30, October 1988, p. 3).

The renminbi is still not a convertible currency, but the traditional system of the Ministry of Foreign Trade, operating through its foreign trade corporations, has been scrapped and replaced by a complicated set-up. The traditional central foreign trade corporations tend to specialize on standardized products such as grain and coal. There are now foreign trade corporations at the ministerial (industry), regional (including provincial and municipal levels, such as Guangdong, Fujian, and the three main municipalities), and even at the enterprise level. The China National Native Products and Animal By-products Import and Export Corporation is a state-owned, specialized foreign trade organization under the direct jurisdication of MOFERT, with 64 branches in municipalities, provinces and autonomous regions. The China National Machinery and Equipment Import and Export Corporation operates under the Ministry of Machine Building (servicing the machinery and technology export and import needs of its industrial enterprises). Certain large enterprises have been allowed direct links with foreign companies – the National Chemical Fibres Corporation and the China National Petroleum Corporation for example. However, decision-making was recentralized in the hands of MOFERT, with the power of approval over trade agreements.

Foreign capital

In addition to Western credits, the open door policy involves direct foreign investment. When the law on joint equity ventures was promulgated on 14 July 1979, foreign ownership was limited to a maximum of 49 per cent and the lifespan to a maximum of 30 years, at which time there would be reversion back to full Chinese ownership. Subsequent amendments have allowed the following: (1) up to 100 per cent foreign ownership, in the case of advanced technology and/or export orientation. By the end of 1985 there were 120 solely foreign-owned enterprises (Kosta 1987: 158; *The Economist* gives a later figure of 225; 13–19 August 1988, p. 68); and (2) a lifespan of 50 years and even more in certain cases. In May 1988 Shanghai Volkswagen became the first joint venture to receive permission to issue bonds to individuals and enterprises in China. A particular national institution should be noted in this context.

The China International Trust and Investment Corporation (CITIC) was set up in July 1979 to 'introduce, absorb, and apply foreign investment, advanced technology and equipment for China's construction'. It has become a vast 'socialist conglomerate' dealing in banking (including bond issues in Hong Kong, Japan and West Germany), trade (including arms), consulting and legal services, investment (including abroad, in order, among other things, to secure vital materials such as aluminium and timber), travel, property, and joint ventures with foreign partners at home and abroad. Its subsidiary, CITIC Industrial Bank (formally opened in September 1987, but actually operating since May of that year) deals in foreign exchange. It is a competitor, like the Shanghai Bank of Communications, to the Bank of China. Another subsidiary, a consultancy agency, was set up in November 1987 to provide assistance to joint ventures in trouble. At the same time CITIC Industrial Bank was given permission to set up retail branches throughout China and to collaborate with the Ka Wah Bank of Hong Kong: note that no foreign bank has access to China's retail banking market. CITIC at present consists of sixteen separate enterprises, three of them abroad, and is to be renamed CI (Holdings) (*EIU Country Report*, 1988, no. 1, p. 12).

There have been a number of problems associated with joint ventures reflected in declining interest by Western companies and subsequent concessions by China. The value of joint venture contracts signed fell by 40 per cent in 1986; contracted foreign investment as a whole fell 48 per cent in 1986, but increased by 30 per cent in 1987. Utilized investment increased by 1.3 per cent in 1987 (*FT*, 23 January 1988, p. 2). The causes lie in the conflicting interests of the host country and guest investors:

1. China is especially interested in foreign investment projects which embody the latest technology and which increase exports to hard currency markets. In contrast, Western companies are mainly interested in penetrating the domestic Chinese market. Joint ventures are generally expected to be self-sufficient in terms of hard currency expenditure and revenue, and repatriated profits have to be financed by hard currency exports earnings. The limitations imposed on the use of hard currencies and credit restrictions in 1985, resulting from balance of payments deficits and declining exchange reserves, led to increased difficulties.
2. The inadequate infrastructure (especially energy supplies, 72 per cent of which was generated by coal in 1987, and transport and communications) have caused perennial problems. According to Max Wilkinson (*FT Survey*, 18 December 1987, p.IX), more than 20 per cent of industrial capacity is unused because of a shortage of electric power or, as Edward Gargan (*IHT*, 29 March 1988, p. 2) puts it, Chinese industry is idle for an average of one day in five because of the lack of power supplies.
3. Manpower is mainly supplied by the Foreign Enterprises Service Corporation at wage rates above domestic levels. Since the Chinese workers and managers only receive approximately the prevailing

domestic rate, the state imposes a sort of tax. Dismissals have been possible since 1981, but difficult to achieve in reality, needing the approval of the enterprise workers' committee or the relevant trade union. Other costs, such as housing and office rents for foreigners, are also very high.

4. Foreign companies are often not allowed to write detailed contracts and there is often Chinese insistence on signed contracts being renegotiated and imposition of new conditions by local government. The backward legal system relating to aspects such as patents or copyright is also a serious problem.

5. There is less of a tradition of hard work and less concern with quality among Chinese industrial workers, compared with those in Hong Kong.

Concern over declining foreign interest has led to concessions over time. In 1983–84 some were made that related to profit and other taxes and to tariffs, and other stimulatory factors such as the introduction of patent law and the possibility of marketing part of the output domestically; 22 further concessions were granted in October 1986. Foreign enterprises designated as 'export oriented' (more than 70 per cent of production) or 'technically advanced' were provided with additional incentives: lower land rent and lower costs of raw materials and power; priorities in the supply of water, electricity, transport and communications, which were charged at the same rate as local state companies; easier hard currency loans; hard currency payments for designated import substitutes; tax concessions; and permission for ventures to swap foreign exchange surpluses and deficits among themselves – the same foreign investor involved in two or more ventures can be treated as a single unit for self-financing purposes. At the Seventh National People's Congress in 1988 it was confirmed that the foreign partner could provide the board chairman and that the remittance of profit and capital funds on termination of the project were assured. Disappointing off-shore oil exploration has also led to both extra concessions and permissions for on-shore drilling. In November 1987 it was revealed that only about one-third of the 4,000 joint ventures established in recent years were making foreign exchange profits, another third were profitable only in renminbi terms, and the remaining third were sustaining losses (Robert Thomson, *FT*, 26 November 1987, p. 7). In March of the following year China announced that discussions about joint investments were taking place with the Soviet Union and other East European countries.

In May 1987 China raised its first loan in the United States since 1949. In June agreement was also reached with Britain on claims arising from pre-revolution debts, leaving the door open to bond issues in the London market, the first of which took place in September 1987.

The Special Economic Zones

Special foreign trade status was bestowed upon Guangdong and Fujian provinces in 1979, but the Special Economic Zones (SEZs) were not formally designated until the following year. It is no coincidence that three of the SEZs (Shenzhen, Zhuhai and Shantou) are in Guandong province, adjacent to Hong Kong and Macao, and Xiamen is in Fujian province, opposite Taiwan. Special status (e.g. permission to decide on foreign investment projects up to $30 million dollars, and tax concessions) was also awarded to Hainan Island in April 1983 and it became both a separate province and a SEZ in 1988. That status was also given to 14 coastal cities in April 1984 (thus spreading the concessions northwards).[25] In July 1985 attention was focused on only four coastal cities (Guangzhou, Shanghai, Tianjin and Dalian) with a better endowed infrastructure and superior record in attracting foreign capital. In January 1987 the first National Programme for Overall Land Development was announced to be in the process of being drawn up, designating areas selected for comprehensive development. The areas are strong in industry, foreign trade and natural resources, and both state and foreign capital will be channelled to them.

Shenzhen dominates, attracting nearly 70 per cent of the combined foreign capital investment of the original four zones by the mid-1980s. The exact nature of the concessions granted to these areas has varied between themselves and over time. These include profit tax concessions, increased local decision-making powers over foreign trade decisions and the spending of convertible currency earnings (since the beginning of 1989 the SEZs' right to retain their foreign exchange earnings has been reduced from 100 per cent to 80 per cent, while that of some inland provinces has been increased; Cheng, *FEER*, 12 January 1989, p. 45), reduction in or even elimination of tariffs, and greater control over the hiring and firing of workers.

Problems have arisen in the operation of this policy, so much so that in 1985 Deng described Shenzhen as 'an experiment that remains to be proved'. The SEZs as a whole were downgraded and greater attention was paid to cities like Shanghai and Tianjin, and there were general restrictions resulting from balance of payments and foreign exchange reserves problems. Particularly disappointing were factors such as: (1) the SEZs' failure to reach the roughly 60 per cent export-total output target set (only about 20 per cent was actually achieved in Shenzhen; foreign exchange earnings were less than foreign exchange expenditure even by the mid-1980s); and (2) the fact that foreign capital (mainly from Hong Kong)[26] has favoured sectors such as tourism (hotels etc.), retailing, construction (such as offices), and low-tech manufacturing rather than high-tech manufacturing and critical infrastructure projects in power and transport. There has also been a relative failure to attract small-scale but profitable work involving the finishing of goods, especially those brought in from Hong Kong.

Corruption, too, has caused alarm. For example, in 1985 officials on Hainan Island were revealed to have resold vast quantities of consumer durables (paid for, in part, by purchases of foreign currency on the black market), such as cars and television sets. These were imported tariff free, supposedly for use on the island itself, but then resold on the mainland at substantial markups. There was a subsequent ban on the diversion of imports from one province to another. Convicted officials, however, claimed that the resources were used to further development and social welfare, rather than for personal gain. Black markets have inevitably sprung up for convertible currencies and 'foreign exchange certificates' (FECs, introduced in April 1980). FECs were meant to control the black market in convertible currencies, thus preventing unauthorized use by Chinese citizens. The aim is to phase out the FECs sometime in the future. Increasing income differentials within the zones and between the zones and the non-favoured areas have also caused concern.

Wong (1987) points out the inherent difficulties of achieving the aims of the SEZs, especially the development of new, remote, isolated areas, with no industrial tradition and with their need for massive infrastructural investment.

Problems and economic reform

The Chinese economy has become a fascinating field of study since Deng has talked about 'socialism with Chinese characteristics' and quoted the old proverb, 'It does not matter whether a cat is black or white as long as it catches the mouse.' Restrictions have been imposed since the mid-1980s, however, in response to a number of problems (see Table 12.2).

The growth of national income has been so rapid that infrastructural bot-

Table 12.2 China: foreign exchange reserves and average annual rate of growth of national income and retail prices

Average annual rate of growth of national income (%)					
1981–85	1984	1985	1986	1987	1988
10.0	13.0	16.0	7.8	9.4	11.2

Foreign exchange reserves ($ billions)	Oct. 1984	Sept. 1986	End 1987	July 1988
	16.7	10.4	15.2	19.0

Average annual rate of growth of retail prices (%)								
1950–59	1959–62	1962–65	1965–79	1980	1981	1982	1983	1984
2.3	7.5	−4.1	0.2	6.0	2.4	3.3	1.5	2.8

	1985	1986	1987	1988
	8.8	6.0	7.3	18.5

Sources: Hong Kong Bank, China (June 1985) and China Briefing (1987), no. 27; Financial Times, 16 June 1988, p. 36, 19 January 1989, p. 4 and 25 January 1989, p. 4; Perkins (1988: 623); Economist Intelligence Unit, Country Profile (1987–88); Do Rosario, FEER, 17 November 1988, p. 90.

tlenecks have become exacerbated. The current account balance of payments, according to IMF figures, went into deficit to the tune of $11.4 billion in 1985, and foreign exchange reserves fell from a peak of $16.7 billion in October 1984 to $10.4 billion by the end of September 1986, subsequently rising. Official figures for the balance of trade, it should be noted, vary. The Ministry of Foreign Economic Relations and Trade (which does not take account of imports by foreign funded projects) provided figures indicating a trade deficit of $9.1 billion in 1986 and a surplus of $1.9 billion in 1987. Customs (which includes foreign donations and barter trade with other socialist economies, but excludes gold sales) estimated a deficit of $12 billion in 1986 and a deficit of $3.5 billion in 1987. The State Statistical Bureau's figures are for deficits of $12.8 billion and $3.7 billion respectively. Gross foreign debt was $20.5 billion in 1985, $27 billion in 1986, and $32 billion at the end of 1987, when the debt-service ratio was some 10 per cent (Robert Thomson, *FT*, 22 February 1988, p. 4). Later figures provided by the China News Service reveal a short-term debt of $10 billion and $30 billion of a year or more (Colina MacDougall, *FT*, 19 November 1988, p. 2). According to *The Economist* (19–25 March 1988, p. 92), foreign debt was negligible in 1981 and the debt-service ratio was 20 per cent in mid-1987. Since 27 August 1987 companies have needed permission from the State Administration of Foreign Exchange Control (which now registers all foreign loans) to borrow abroad, and it is possible that a new body will be set up to approve all new borrowing. Table 12.2 shows the record for inflation according to official figures. The rising trend has caused the regime considerable anxiety.

The first two years of the Seventh Five-year Plan 1986–90 were to be years of consolidation. This involved: (1) reducing state expenditure, especially keeping fixed investment at the 1985 level in real terms to check over-plan capital expenditure; local authorities are required to keep within centrally determined limits; and (2) controlling consumption levels. The average annual rate of growth of national product was to be kept to 7.5 per cent. Note that over the period 1981–2000 it is still planned to quadruple industrial and agricultural output (raising per capita income from $300 to $800 in 1980 dollars), with priority sectors including energy, transport and communications, agriculture, light industry and tourism.

Deng (who made comebacks in 1975 and 1977) has met increasing opposition from powerful figures like Peng Zhen (former Chairman of the National People's Congress) and Li Xiannan (former President), who are disturbed at the ideological implications of reform and specific problems such as the decline in grain output. In 1983 there was a short-lived 'spiritual campaign' against Western ideas. Student demonstrations in December 1986 and January 1987, calling for greater democracy and freedom, led to a political clampdown and the dismissal of Hu Yaobang (General Secretary for seven years) in January 1987 for not doing enough to resist 'bourgeois liberalism'[27] and for other errors such as allowing consumption to increase too rapidly. The party was particularly disturbed at the threat to its control and to 'unity and stability'.

It is likely, however, that there will be no major retreat from the overall course of economic reform, especially in light of the agreements reached with Britain and Portugal over Hong Kong (19 December 1984) and Macao (1987) respectively. The idea is to maintain their capitalist systems ('one country, two systems' – to become Special Administrative Regions) for fifty years after the handing over of power to China on 30 June 1997 and 20 December 1999 respectively. Deng has talked of a possible 100 years for Hong Kong. The big prize is Taiwan and the lure of a peaceful reunification is an enormous incentive to rule out any lurch to the left. The survival of the economic reforms is also helped by the limited actual experience with traditional central planning, the discrediting of left utopian policies by the GLF and Cultural Revolution (and the consequent change in leadership and weakening of the bureaucracy), the relatively less pressing demands of the defence sector as a result of detente in foreign policy, and the intellectual theory of the 'initial stage of socialism'. This stresses the importance of current economic conditions rather than pure Marxist theory and the development of productive forces (see below). The aim is to draw a clearer distinction between party and state, to reduce the former's role in the implementation of policies.

During the September 1987 visit of World Bank officials, the intention was disclosed of furthering the reforms during the 1990s, including tendering for the management of state-owned enterprises, conventional share issues (although the state will hold a majority), the general sub-leasing of land in order to form larger units better able to employ modern technology and less emphasis on domestic production of grain. On 1 October 1987 the People's Daily declared 'leftism' to be the main threat to progress.

At the Thirteenth Party Congress (25 October – 1 November 1987) Zhao Ziyang was confirmed as General Secretary and made first Vice-chairman of the party Central Military Commission; he became Vice-chairman of the state counterpart at the Seventh National People's Congress the following year. In his opening address to the 1,936 delegates at the Party Congress (representing 46 million party members) he confirmed that the reform programme was to continue despite problems such as corruption, inflation, and concern over the grain harvest. Zhao stated that the role of the state was not to exercise direct control over enterprises, but to determine macro-economic policies, with the state regulating the market and the market guiding the enterprises. A high priority was attached to education to ease the skilled labour bottleneck. The ideological justification is to be found in the theory of the 'initial or primary stage of socialism', a process of gradually moving towards a modern industrial economy (which took place under capitalism in Western countries),[28] and a stage that started in the 1950s and which could last until beyond the mid-twenty first century, by which time China would be a 'first rank power'.

During the 29 October 1987 conversation with the general director of GATT Arthur Dunkel, Zhao Ziyang forecast that only 30 per cent of the economy would remain centrally planned in two or three years' time, compared with 100 per cent nine years ago and 50 per cent currently. Of course one must bear in mind that there is an incentive on China's part to stress market orientation, given the application to join GATT. This contrasts with the views of conservative leaders such as Chen Yun, who believes that change must be confined by the (albeit expanding) 'cage' of central planning. Specific measures included the confirmation that Hainan Island was to become China's thirtieth province and latest special economic zone in April 1988.[29] The scheme allowing even foreigners to lease land for up to 70 years is to apply to all SEZs and the main coastal cities initially and generally later on.[30] Constitutional approval for the purchase and sale of land-use rights was given at the Seventh National People's Congress in 1988: 'The right to the use of land may be transferred according to law.' Foreign enterprises and joint ventures producing technically advanced goods are allowed to sell some on the domestic market. It should be noted, however, that the problems of the bankruptcy law and the role of the party at enterprise level were not tackled then. As has already been discussed, the Industrial Enterprise Bill was approved at the Seventh National People's Congress.

Major political events have included the stepping down of Deng Xiaoping from both the Standing Committee and the Politburo itself (the intention being to separate party and state) and the election of a new Central Committee from candidates whose numbers exceeded the (reduced) number of places available. There were sweeping reductions in the numbers of old guard members, and the intention was expressed of distinguishing between the categories of administrators, the 'political affairs' personnel (selected by the party for a fixed term of office to determine policies) and the 'professional work' personnel (on permanent tenure and selected through competitive examinations) to administer these policies. The new system is expected to be fully operational by 1992. As expected, Li Peng became acting Prime Minister on 24 November 1987.

At the Seventh National People's Congress (NPC: 2,970 delegates met 25 March – 13 April 1988) Li Peng was confirmed as Premier. More cautious than Zhao Ziyang, he nevertheless supported the reform programme as a whole, adding, however, that he thought inflation to be 'the outstanding problem in our economic and social life' and to be caused by an excessive use of currency, overinvestment (especially by provinces), the rapid growth of consumption funds, and aggregate demand exceeding aggregate supply. In early September it was announced that Zhao Ziyang had lost overall control of economic decision-making, thus strengthening Li Peng's conservative influence. This was closely followed by the announcement of a two-year 'rectification' process, 'restoring control of the economic environment and rectifying economic order'. This included a shelving of further major price reforms, the reimposition of price controls on some basic goods, a slowing down of industrial growth and a reduction in public expenditure, and was due to inflation in particular. The party leadership was concerned about recent panic buying in shops and a rapid run down of bank deposits.

The NPC is formally described as the 'supreme organ of state power', although it is in reality more of a rubber stamp for party decisions already taken. In an attempt to alter this image, open debates were held, many resolutions were not passed unanimously and secret ballots for officials were held. Nevertheless, the Congress was used to approve both the legislative and constitutional basis of the reform programme (for example, the private sector, the transferral of use-of-land rights, joint ventures and bankruptcy) and the appointment of new officials. A number of specific aspects have already been discussed. Following the rural and urban reforms, plans were outlined for the streamlining of government administration. The purpose was to support the reform process in general and especially to tackle the problem sectors of energy, transport, and raw materials supply. Specifically, there was to be a 20 per cent reduction in central government personnel and the creation of new bodies. A revamped State Planning Commission was set up (the State Economic Commission was scrapped and some staff were transferred); the aim was to strengthen the tendency away from direct control of enterprise management, which will be responsible for micro decision-making. New ministries were created for Energy (taking over the responsibilities of the Ministries of Coal, Petroleum, and Nuclear Power) and Materials. The aim is to improve the distribution of raw materials, particularly to end hoarding by ministries. The new ministry will gradually reduce the number of production materials subject to restrictions from over 200 to about 50 (*China Briefing*, no. 29, May 1988, p. 2). The Labour and Personnel Ministry was split into the Labour Ministry (to oversee labour market reforms) and the Personnel Ministry (to oversee the new civil service system).

The National People's Congress held 20 March–4 April 1989 promised a few more years of austerity and reform retrenchment. Proposed measures included the use of the price and tax system to encourage agriculture at the expense of rural enterprises and grain at the expense of non-staple foodstuffs.

Conclusion

A general introduction has sketched the political and economic background to a country accounting for 22 per cent of the entire world population. Attention was given in the first place to agriculture, on the grounds that China is still a basically agrarian economy and this sector headed the reform procession in 1978. The reader should particularly note the dramatic policy swings over time, from the convulsions of the Great Leap Forward and Cultural Revolution to the present market orientation of the 'household responsibility system'. Another key point to grasp is the nature of the departures, from the beginning, from the traditional economic system. Until the current reforms there has been virtually no labour market and rationing of consumer goods has been much more prevalent. Planning has been much less centralized, even during the First Five-year Plan 1953–57. The changes in the nature of planning and in the role of the industrial enterprise over time were analysed, ending with application of the urban reforms first outlined in October 1984 and the passing of the state enterprise legislation in April 1988. The economy has gone a significant distance down the market road. Political reform, in contrast, has lagged behind, and this raises an interesting general question as to the extent to which political reform is a precondition of successful economic reform. The Chinese leadership points to capitalist examples like Taiwan and South Korea, which developed rapidly under authoritarian regimes. In this regard it is important to stress again that the Chinese economy has typically been less centralized than the other command economies.

The non-state sector has been rapidly expanded. The 'open door' policy was highlighted, with its implications for foreign trade and capital, and particularly emphasis was given to the 'special economic zones' and the other coastal areas. The chapter ended with a discussion of current preoccupations (such as inflation) and vital political events like the Thirteenth Party Congress in late 1987 and the Seventh National People's Congress in the spring of 1988, the latter giving constitutional backing to the reforms. The traumatic episodes in recent Chinese history have actually helped the reforms by discrediting ultra-leftism and ultra-leftists. The conclusion is that truly remarkable changes have taken place in the Chinese economy, changes which, in general, seem likely to stick in the light of the agreements over Hong Kong and Macao and the aspirations about Taiwan. Current problems, especially inflation (views on which are coloured by the experience of hyperinflation in the late 1940s), however, have led to austerity and retrenchment, as has been seen in the 'rectification'

Table 12.3 China: statistical survey

Contribution to industrial output (1987) (%)

State sector	Co-operatives	Individually operated enterprises	Others (mainly joint ventures with foreigners)
60.0	34.6	3.6	1.8

Contribution to retail sales made by private businesses (1987)	Nearly 13.0%
Joint equity ventures	Numerous
Solely foreign-owned enterprises (mid-1988)	225
Population (End 1987)	1.085 billion

Sources: Do Rosario, *FEER*, 8 September 1988, p. 130; *The Economist*, 13–19 August 1988, p. 68. See Tables 12.1 and 12.2 for growth of national income and agricultural output, inflation and foreign exchange reserves.

process and the playing down of the idea of developing all the coastal areas.

Postscript

The death of Hu Yaobang on 15 April 1989 sparked off the student pro-democracy demonstrations in Beijing that were brutally suppressed in the early hours of 4 June. Zhao Ziyang lost his position as General Secretary on the 24th, being replaced by Jiang Zemin. At the end of July an anti-corruption and anti-privilege programme was announced (a concern that featured strongly in the students' demands). For example, 'high officials' (members of the Politburo, Party Secretariat and State Council) and their families were to be banned from business activities as of 1 September, and China's leaders were to be deprived of special allocations of food.

Despite official statements proclaiming continuity of economic policy, domestic political repression and adverse Western reaction are sure to have some negative consequences. On 2 July 1989 an inspection of 'individual businesses' (employing fewer than 8) was announced, to combat activities such as tax evasion, pornography, smuggling and profiteering. The following month Li Peng promised a two-year extension to the 'economic rectification' programme (originally due to end in late 1990).

Notes

1. Fifty per cent of India's land is arable (*The Economist*, 18–24 June 1988, p. 59).
2. Compared with $240 (in 1952 dollars) for the Soviet Union in 1928 (World Bank, 1984, vol. 1, p. 43).
3. It was not until the early 1970s, however, that the programme really took off, with the aim, since 1980, of restricting the total population to 1.2 billion by the year 2000 (officially admitted to be unlikely in 1988). A mixture of financial and non-pecuniary incentives and penalties have been applied especially to try to attain the goal of one child per family, formally adopted in 1979. This was relaxed somewhat in 1984–85 and tightened in 1987. After mid-1988 a surprising switch in policy took place, allowing families in rural areas to have a second child if the first was a girl, due to the difficulty of enforcing policy. But policy was maintained for urban areas and tightened up generally for larger families. Amid contentious allegations of coerced sterilization and abortion, the United States withdrew its $25 million contribution to the United Nations Fund for Population Activities in August 1986 (after withholding $10 million in September 1985).
4. Poor weather was partly responsible. The 1958 grain harvest was actually somewhat larger than the previous record attained the year before.
5. Currently, local bodies below the provinces (22, including Hainan Island: there are also five autonomous regions, including Inner Mongolia and Tibet, and the three municipalities of Beijing, Tianjin and Shanghai) are the prefecture, county, town and village.
6. Split up into plots of varying quality and distributed more or less equally among households, although the team may permit consolidation.
7. The quotas and the tax calculations are based on the land area and the average yield

of the last three years, although there is now emphasis on stable quotas (Quaisser 1987: 178).

8. Cheung (1986: 67) places this at seven, but this number has, in reality, been substantially exceeded at times.

9. All lands in Hong Kong are 'owned' by the Crown.

10. Fourteen and a half per cent in 1984, 13 per cent in 1985, and 12 per cent in 1987. Excluding the output produced by rural industries, the figures are only 3.0 per cent for 1985, 3.5 per cent for 1986, 3.0 per cent for 1987, and 3.2 per cent for 1988.

11. There is a general distinction to be made between central state enterprises, with priority access to inputs at state-determined prices, and local state enterprises which have to purchase many of their inputs at market prices (Wong 1986: 375).

12. Monthly housing rental payments amount to only 3 to 5 per cent of a worker's money wage. By 1982 the value of urban subsidies exceeded the average wage paid (Johnson 1988, p. 235, quoting Lardy). The range of benefits provided by the traditional enterprise includes medical and labour insurance, child care facilities, pensions and guaranteed jobs for workers' children (White 1988: 184).

13. A notable exception is demobilized members of the armed forces. This is significant given the July 1986 plan to reduce the People's Liberation Army from 4 million to 3 million people (it is worth noting here the 1987 decree that civilian goods must eventually be produced in all armaments establishments). Further exceptions are professionals, office workers, and cadres.

14. The contract system is often less effective than might be imagined, with cases of 30- to 50-year contracts. Contracts are often routinely extended, and workers often fail to give notice before quitting (do Rosario, *FEER*, 12 May 1988, p. 74).

15. Total subsidies, thus including these, amounted to a quarter of government spending in 1987 (*FT*, 24 March 1988, p. 3).

16. Pork accounts for 88 per cent of meat production (Delfs, *FEER*, 17 December 1987, p. 100).

17. The currency unit is the yuan (renminbi: 'people's currency').

18. A purpose-built exchange is due to open in 1990.

19. For a detailed analysis of the 1978–83 reforms see Lee (1986) and S. Jackson (1986).

20. About 43 per cent of state-owned industrial enterprises were subject to the management responsibility system by 1986 (Salem 1987: 77).

21. Light industrial enterprises are mainly under the control of provincial authorities.

22. In April 1988 the NPC voted to permit private businesses to take on more than 7 employees outside the family (Gold 1989: 194). In reality, however, examples were to be found, prior to this date, where the number of employees could be counted in hundreds.

23. China was a founder member in 1947, left in 1950 and applied to rejoin in July 1986. Since GATT encourages the use of GNP as a measure of national output, China subsequently adopted it as an important indicator.

24. The official rate is set every day by the State Administration of Exchange Control, but there are in fact a number of unpublished rates in operation.

25. Zhanjiang, Beihai, Guangzhou, Fuzhou, Wenzhou, Ningbo, Shanghai, Nantong, Lianyungang, Qingdao, Yantai, Tianjin, Qinhuangdao and Dalian. Note Sit's (1988) use of the term 'Open Areas' to describe these, the SEZs, and other areas.

26. Hong Kong provides nearly 80 per cent of China's foreign capital as a whole (Japan, in contrast, provided only 8.7 per cent at the end of 1987) and 90 per cent of Shenzhen's.

27. Western ideas such as free elections and freedom of assembly, speech, and publication which threaten both socialism and the traditional view that, in reality,

243

these merely cover up the bourgeoisie's domination of society.

28. At the Thirteenth Congress Zhao said, 'During this stage we shall accomplish industrialization and the commercialization, socialization and modernization which many other countries have achieved under capitalist conditions.' Schram (1988: 177–78) points out that the term 'underdeveloped socialism' was used in 1979 and 'primary stage' in June 1981, although the implications of the latter have only now been spelled out.

29. The Hong Kong dollar will be allowed to circulate as a second currency, as in Shenzhen; land leases up to 70 years, with possible extensions and with lease transference permitted; and a maximum tax of 15 per cent plus an optional 10 per cent local tax (Cheng, *FEER*, 26 May 1988, p. 96).

30. In September-December 1987 Shenzhen sold off 50-year land leases to domestic companies (the first in China since 1949), followed in March 1988 by auctions open to foreigners as well. Shanghai, for example, has also held land lease auctions, the first to domestic enterprises in March and the first to foreigners in July 1988 (*China Briefing*, 1988, no. 30, p. 7). Note that leasing refers to the use and not the ownership of land, although rights to the use of the land can be resold. Land in China is in 'socialist public ownership', which is of two types: (1) state ownership ('ownership of the whole people') or (2) collective ownership ('ownership by the working masses' or the peasantry at large, in practice the commune in the past or village and township organizations today). Urban land is state owned, while suburban and rural land is collectively owned (Stephen Morgan, *FEER*, 14 July 1988, pp. 22–6).

Chapter thirteen

Cuba

Political and economic background

Cuba was discovered by Columbus on 27 October 1492, but the conquest by Diego Velazquez did not take place until 1511. The first shipment of African slaves arrived in 1526, and a plantation-based economy subsequently developed. Slavery was not abolished until 1886. The third and final war of independence against Spain (1895–98; the others were in 1868–78 and 1879–80), in which the United States finally intervened, was followed by four years of US military government, until an independent republic was declared on 20 May 1902. Even after this date the United States exercised a dominant direct and indirect influence, respectively: (1) there were actual interventions in 1906–9, 1912, and 1917; the Platt Amendment was added to the 1901 constitution, allowing the United States to intervene 'for the preservation of life, property and individual liberty'; (2) economic links involved considerable investment and commercial treaties, such as the one in 1903, which provided preferential treatment for Cuban sugar imports into the United States and opened up the Cuban market to US imports. The new treaty in 1934 extended the range of products affected.

Fulgencio Batista led a military coup in 1934, was elected President for a term in 1940, and led another coup on 10 March 1952. On 1 January 1959 the guerrillas of the 26 July Movement under Fidel Castro came to power, having overthrown Batista's dictatorship after a two-year struggle. Full diplomatic relations were established with the Soviet Union in 1960, which led, together with the expropriation of US property, to the United States breaking off such relations with Cuba in January 1961. In this year (17 April) the Bay of Pigs invasion by 1,500 Cuban *émigrés* was defeated and socialism formally embraced. The Cuban Communist Party was founded in 1965. The 1962 Cuban missile crisis was defused when the Soviet Union agreed to remove the missiles and the USA promised never to invade Cuba. Cuba was a founding member of the Non-Aligned Movement (see especially Azicri 1988).

In 1959 the population of Cuba was nearly 7 million (10.36 million in 1988), of which an unusually high (for a developing country) percentage of 53 per cent was urbanized (70 per cent today).[1] Even so, agriculture dominated the economy, with industry, intimately linked to the former, only employing 17.4 per cent of the labour force in 1953, compared with agriculture's more than 40 per cent. In 1970 industry still accounted for only 20 per cent (Eckstein 1981: 135); in 1986 industry contributed nearly 45 per cent of gross social product (*Abecor Country Report*, March 1988, p. 1). The sugar industry alone accounted for 5 per cent of national product, 25 per cent of manufacturing industry, and 75 to 80 per cent of exports. In 1957–58 73.3 per cent of imports were consumer goods and only 17 per cent were machinery and industrial supplies (Azicri 1988: 121). Large estates dominated the land area as well as sugar and cattle rearing, and crops like tobacco, food and coffee were mainly produced by small farmers (MacEwan 1981: 3–4). During the early 1950s Cuba was the main producer and exporter of sugar in the world (and is still the world's leading exporter of raw sugar). In 1960 the United States withdrew Cuba's sugar import quota and the following year imposed a trade embargo, later even including products from any third country that embodied Cuban inputs. Before the revolution the United States and Canada accounted for 70 per cent of Cuba's foreign trade, and Western Europe took a further 15 per cent (*EIU Country Report*, 1987–88, p. 23).

Mineral resources include nickel (the fourth largest reserves in the world), estimated at 19 Mt. Nickel and cobalt production was over 40,000 tonnes in 1981, 33,500 tonnes in 1985 and 35,800 tonnes in 1987 (*FT*, 18 May 1988, p. 34). Alumina, chromium, cobalt, and iron ore are also significant. Domestic crude oil output was some 259,000 tonnes in 1981 and 868,000 tonnes in 1985 (Zimbalist 1988b: 25). The current output of 1 million tonnes supplies 10 per cent of the country's needs (Tim Coone, *FT Survey*, 17 February 1989, p. 35). The country's first nuclear reactor is due to begin operating in 1990, the aim being to reduce dependence on oil.

Agriculture

In 1959 land ownership was very unequal with 9.4 per cent of owners controlling 73.3 per cent of the land, and 66.1 per cent of owners holding only 7.4 per cent (Rodriguez 1987: 24). Wage labour, mainly seasonal, was common – this made up 60.6 per cent of the rural work-force in 1953 (Ghai, Kay, and Peek 1988: 6). A significant proportion of agricultural wage workers had access to a plot of land of between 0.25 and 1.0 hectares (Kay 1988: 1240). The *17 May 1959 land reform* affected 70 per cent of agricultural land: a general ceiling of 402.6 hectares per owner was fixed (1,342 hectares in exceptional cases). Free tracts of 26.8 hectares were given to tenant farmers and squatters, with a possible maximum holding of 67.1 hectares. Even the additional land was not usually paid for; expropriated landowners typically forfeited compensation by emigrating (Ghai, Kay, and Peek, 1988: 9). As a result of the reform state farms occupied 51.5 per cent of total farmland (p. 11). Of the land affected, 60 per cent went to individual peasants. Sharecropping was abolished, as were rents in money terms and in kind for tenants. Large estates were at first given over to co-operatives, but from the middle of 1961 these were replaced by state farms (MacEwan 1981: 50).

The *second land reform* of 1963 saw the 67 hectare limit made general for all private farms, with the result that the state held 76 per cent of all land and 63 per cent of cultivated land (MacEwan 1981: 73). According to Zimbalist (1988: 14), the private farmer today typically owns 20 to 60 hectares of land. The state sector contributed 37 per cent of agricultural output in 1961 and 70 per cent within two years (MacEwan 1981: 70). At present state farms account for 83 per cent of land ownership (Table 13.1), 80 per cent of the agricultural labour force, 75 per cent of livestock, and 77.5 per cent of agricultural and livestock output (Kay 1988: 1246). In 1983 the *non-state farm sector* (collectives and individual peasant farms) accounted for 22.5 per cent of output (compared with 42.3 per cent in 1964 and 20.6 per cent in 1980) and owned 16.6 per cent of land (Kay 1988: 1260). The private sector's share of cultivated land continued to fall from 37 per cent in 1963 to 30 per cent in 1975, when Castro declared that private farming, although destined for ultimate elimination, was indispensable for the foreseeable future (Zimbalist 1988: 197–98).

Table 13.1 Cuba: land tenure, debt, and average annual rate of growth of social product

Average annual rate of growth of general social product (%)							
1962–65	*1966–70*	*1971–75*	*1976–80*	*1981–85*	*1986*	*1987*	*1988*
3.7	0.4	7.5	4.0	7.3	1.4	–3.5	2.3

Debt owed to the West ($ billions)	*1974*	*1982*	*1986*	*1987*	*June 1988*
	0.66	2.86	3.87	5.7	6.4

Land tenure (Azicri) (%)	*Government property*	*Co-operative property*	*Individual private property*
	80.0	12.0	8.0

Sources: Azicri (1988: xvi); Zimbalist and Eckstein (1987: 8); Zimbalist (1987: 15–16); *Abecor Country Report* (March 1988), p. 1; Economist Intelligence Unit, *Country Profile*, (1987–88: 7; *The Economist*, 27 August 1988, p. 60, and 17 December 1988, p. 65; *IHT*, 17 January 1989, p. 3; *FT*, 17 February 1989, p. 35.

A *'revolutionary offensive'* began in 1968 to increase state ownership, but the failure to achieve the 10 Mt sugar harvest brought about a change of mind in the early 1970s. In 1967 state farm workers lost their private household plots and the state began to interfere with the crop planting decisions of private farmers. The following year they were obliged to sell their produce to the National Agrarian Reform Institute at relatively state-determined prices (Roca 1981: 86). Private plots were reintroduced in the 1970s, but at the start of the next decade the individual plots of state and co-operative farms were merged into collective plots for own consumption purposes (Gey 1987: 87).

The early 1970s saw the start of a dual policy of amalgamating state farms and decentralizing administrative and work systems within each farm. By 1983 there were 422 state farms (a decade earlier there were about three times as many), with an average size of 14,255 hectares and an average labour force of 1,390 (Kay 1988: 1246). While the revolutionary offensive of 1968 saw a switch from piece to time rates and a narrowing of earnings differentials, the SDPE (see p. 250) involved the use of accounting methods and the calculation of indices such as cost per unit value of production (Kay 1988: 1247). Since 1981 'permanent production brigades' have been very gradually introduced into state farms. These brigades are on an economic accounting basis – they are assigned production targets and inputs, they are able to distribute a portion of profits to workers, they have a stable labour force and sometimes they are tied to a particular land area (Kay 1988: 1251). By mid-1985 73 of 406 state farms under the Ministry of Agriculture were affected (Ghai, Kay, and Peek 1988: 58). By 1986 120 were involved, with an average of 75 workers per brigade (Zimbalist 1989: 87). Small private plots were reintroduced in state farms in 1982 (Zimbalist, Sherman, and Brown 1989: 374). State farms supply most domestically consumed foodstuffs (such as meat, eggs and milk) as well as ex-portables such as sugar and citrus fruits (Ghai, Kay, and Peek 1988: 71). Agro-industrial complexes now account for practically all the sugar cane state farms (only four in 1981); these are vertically merged with the mills (p. 34).

A state agricultural purchasing organization was set up in the early 1960s, and so too were various types of co-operatives; credit-service, mutual aid teams, and co-operatives in which land, livestock and equipment were collectively owned. The Credit and Service Co-operatives were the most successful – some 66 per cent of peasant farmers belonged to them by 1970 and 77 per cent a decade later. Most early production co-operatives faded away (Kay 1988: 1255). *Collectivization*, put forward at the first congress of the party in 1975 on a voluntary basis, was slow until 1981–83 and then slowed again. The percentage of non-state-sector land collectivized rose from 13 per cent in 1980 to nearly 58 per cent within three years and around 61 per cent at the start of 1986 (Gey 1987: 86), although in terms of the percentage of peasant farms belonging to production co-operatives, the figure was well below 50 per cent (Kay 1988: 1255). The average size of collective farm was 144 hectares and 23 members in 1979 and 732 hectares and 51 members six years later (pp. 1256–57). Peasants were encouraged to join co-operatives by factors such as the provision of old-age pensions, the lack of a private land market, the unwillingness of children to stay on farms and the inability to hire permanent as opposed to seasonal wage labour (p. 1255). Co-operatives are subject to negotiated procurement quotas and benefit from state supplies and the ability to hire labour at peak periods. All sugar, coffee, tobacco and beef production is subject to state procurement (Ghai, Kay, and Peek 1988: 47).

Co-operative and individual farms concentrate on specialized exportable crops, such as tobacco and coffee. In 1977 they accounted for 80 per cent of tobacco, 50 per cent of coffee, 50 per cent of fruit and vegetables, 16 per cent of sugar and 32 per cent of cattle (Ghai, Kay, and Peek 1988: 129, quoting Mesa-Lago). Only family members who directly cultivate farmland are permitted to inherit it, and the state has first refusal when land is sold. Private farmers have to sell a certain percentage of their crops to the state at official prices and, in return, have access to credit and inputs. The state uses subsidies and regulations to induce private farmers into state-owned projects (Azicri 1988: 113–4). Individual private farms are responsible for less than 10 per cent of both area and production.

In 1980 a *free farmers' market* was introduced where, in addition to artisan products, above-procurement quota sales by individual farmers and co-operatives, if not sold to the state at above-quota prices, could be transacted. The free peasant markets accounted for 1 per cent of retail trade turnover in 1985 (Gey 1987: 90) and over 5 per cent of the value of food sales to the population (Zimbalist 1988: 13). This market was taken over by the state on 15 May 1986. Since then all farm produce, including that from private plots, has to pass through the hands of the state. Reasons included the appearance of middlemen, excessive profits, and the illegal use of state resources such as lorries. Kay (1988: 1262) lists other factors, such as the reluctance of some farmers to sell to state maketing agencies and the idea that the co-operative movement was being hindered. The National Association of Small Farmers (set up in May 1961) represents the interests of co-operative members and private farmers in negotiations with government bodies.

Central planning and the industrial enterprise

The advice of Czechoslovak planners was particularly sought in the early 1960s. The period 1963–65 was one of debate on theoretical alternatives. Azicri (1988: 130–31) describes the 1964–66 stage of development as one in which new economic models were tested as well, with a centralized system used in industry (such as enterprises were financed through the state budget) and a more decentralized model used in agriculture. This was followed by the so-called *moral economy stage* 1966–70. During this period certain departures from the traditional Soviet model were pronounced, such as the strong emphasis on moral incentives. These were inspired by the perceived need to stress independence. Then came the introduction of reformed Soviet-type measures during the 1970s.

The 1962–65 four year plan was abandoned prematurely in 1964. Two years later the powers of the Central Planning Board (Juceplan: *Junta Central de Planificatión*) were substantially reduced and those of the political leadership correspondingly enhanced. Annual plans were probably discontinued during

1965–70, and a number of special 'mini-plans' relating to particularly important regions or sectors were introduced, with the subsequent lack of national co-ordination associated with command planning. Note, however, that in 1968 a crude computerized input-output table of the industrial sector was compiled (Mesa-Lago 1981: 12). Zimbalist (1988: 77) points out that before 1976 Cuba did not have a five-year plan or the basic institutions of planning. State enterprises (including those in agriculture) were tightly controlled and lost most of their financial independence by the imposition of budgetary finance and their inability to receive bank credits. Their plants were not the subject of close cost accounting. In 1967 personal taxes, including income and property taxes, were scrapped.

The 1970s saw the implantation of reformed Soviet-type measures, the result of a disappointing economic performance during the 'moral economy' period (see Table 13.1), the subsequent greater reliance on Soviet aid and advice, and the greater integration with the rest of Comecon (1976–80), having become a member in 1972. The first Congress of the Cuban Communist Party took place in December 1975, at which the *System of Economic Management and Planning* (*Sistema de Dirección de la Economía*: SDPE) was outlined, a system heavily influenced by the 1965 Soviet reforms and to be introduced gradually from 1976 onwards. Annual plans were drawn up, starting in 1973, with five-year plans and a perspective plan for 1980–2000 following.

The SDPE acknowledged the importance of economic levers such as interest rates, prices, and taxes. Enterprises were put on an economic accounting basis, and management was given greater decision-making powers over matters such as manpower and investment. Profitability was given an enhanced role as an indicator, alongside output, quality, productivity and costs. A portion of profit, dependent on the fulfilment of plan indicators, could be retained for personal bonuses, investment and social projects. Zimbalist (1988: 77) notes that until the SDPE material rewards to motivate management did not exist, but afterwards received a share of the bonus funds roughly in line with the proportion of managerial salaries in the enterprise's total wage fund. Interest-bearing credits were available from the National Bank. Wages were tied to performance – by 1982 this affected 1.2 million out 2.9 million workers in the state sector (Pérez-López 1986: 32). Stimulation funds in enterprises were started in 1979 on an experimental basis (usually linked to indicators such as productivity, costs, output, and exports) and by 1985 affected around 52 per cent of enterprises (Zimbalist 1988: 77). Individual work norms apply to more than 50 per cent of the workforce (p. 77). In 1985, however, total bonuses (from the incentive funds and from meeting specific tasks such as savings on inputs) and overtime totalled only 10.6 per cent of basic wages on average (Zimbalist 1989: 80–81). Since 1980 workers have been able to make direct contact with enterprises instead of having to go through the local labour office. Nevertheless, enterprises still have to comply with their labour force plan; this is the result of negotiations with the planning authorities who have to be kept informed of hirings (Ghai, Kay, and Peek 1988: 35–36). It is worth noting that redundant workers are eligible for 70 per cent of their former wages while waiting to be re-employed and are allowed to work part time without affecting this benefit. Short-term work is now permitted in all state enterprises and not just in the sugar industry (*EIU Country Profile*, 1987–88: 9).

The State Price Committee (*Comite Estatal de Precios*) was established in 1976 and fixes the *prices* of over 1 million products. Local governments set the prices of locally produced and consumed goods such as those produced by artisans, and some prices are freely determined (e.g. perishable consumer goods towards the end of the marketing period) (Zimbalist 1988a: 38). Before the 1981 comprehensive price reform, prices in the material production sectors were either those of 1965 or, for new products, were based on the first-year-of-production price. The 1981 reform (in which new wholesale prices were introduced in January and retail in December) was based on 1978 prices, costs, and structures, while the next comprehensive reform was meant to use those of the year 1985 (Zimbalist 1988a: 38). Wholesale prices are set on the principle of estimated branch average cost of production plus a profit markup sufficient for the typical enterprise to pay a profits and a social security tax and to finance the incentive fund. At present the markup varies according to plan priorities, but the intention is for a uniform markup in 1989 (Zimbalist 1988a: 39). The Price Commission allows price surcharges for higher quality, new product designs and new styles (p. 39). The general rule is for retail prices to include a turnover tax aimed at balancing supply and demand (Mesa-Lago 1981: 18), and luxury or health-impairing goods such as tobacco, alcohol and cars to bear heavy rates (Zimbalist 1988a: 41). Import prices are either converted into domestic currency terms with the addition of the internal trade margins or based on an average converted price for the previous three years, with state subsidies or turnover taxes making up the difference with respect to the latter (Zimbalist 1988a: p. 47). According to Gey (1987: 92), the range of surplus products sold at market prices was increased during the 1970s and the number of rationed non-foodstuffs declined from 150 in 1980 to 68 in 1985.

Production or service units of local importance were subjected to the dual subordination of elected Assemblies of People's Power. Set up in 1975, these could, for example, appoint and dismiss enterprise managers. The assemblies were also to 'take an interest in' the units still directly subordinate to the central bodies (Roca 1981: 99). The general increase in local participation and consultation in the processes of economic planning via these Assemblies was complemented by attempts to enhance the role of workers and their organizations in the management of enterprises (White 1987a: 154). One-man management was replaced by a Management Council (comprising the director and other managerial personnel, and elected representatives of the party, the trade union, and communist youth), there are monthly assemblies of workers in production sections, and elected workshop delegates attend a quarterly meeting with the Management Council (Zimbalist, Sherman, and Brown 1989: 370).

After 1980 retrenchment took place. In February 1982 Castro criticized the SDPE, and the task of 'revitalizing' it went to a new body called the National Commission for the System of Economic Management, with ministerial rank. Rather than destroy the SDPE Castro stressed the need to eliminate incipient capitalism and consumerism and to restore moral values (Pérez-López 1986: 32).

In December 1984 the role of the pro-SDPE Juceplan was reduced by the creation of a new 'Central Group', composed of the vice presidents of the Council of Ministers, ministers with economic responsibility, and powerful party representatives. This group reviewed the 1985 and 1986–90 plans (p. 31). Zimbalist (1988: 78) interprets this move as an attempt to reduce the powers of ministries, to facilitate lines of communication and command, and to deal with a deteriorating foreign exchange situation. (Note that as of 1983 about 600 products or product groups were centrally planned, amounting to 70–80 per cent of GSP: Zimbalist 1989: 74.) According to Gey (1987: 91), self-financing (i.e. the end of automatic budgetary coverage of losses) is part of current plans.

White (1987a: 154–60) describes the economy in the mid-1980s as being highly centralized, administrative and directive. Only marginal use was made of economic levers, although repayable interest-bearing credits were increasingly used instead of budgetary grants to finance enterprise working capital and, after 1985, fixed capital needs. According to the *EIU* (1987–88: 21), interest rates, ranging from 4 to 12 per cent, have been charged on credits since 1978, and interest (from 0.5 to 2 per cent) has been earned on personal savings accounts since 1983. Only very limited independent decision-making was enjoyed by enterprises. For example, the 200 or so horizontally or vertically integrated 'combines' or the greater number of medium to small enterprises were allowed only a small amount of retained profit to feed the stimulation, socio-cultural, and investment funds. In addition, only a marginal impact on planning decisions was made by the consulted Assemblies of Popular Power and enterprise work-forces, although the degree of consultation was high by Eastern European standards. It is worth noting, however, the formation of work brigades in enterprises since 1980, which are able to elect their own directors. These (1) form an accounting unit; (2) organize their own plans, although in conformity with the state plan via the contract made with the enterprise and constrained by allotted inputs; and (3) depend significantly on final result (Zimbalist and Eckstein 1987: 12; Jiménez 1987: 135). Gey (1987: 84, 95) estimates that in September 1985 only 5 to 6 per cent of workers in the productive sphere were in brigades, while the average number of workers per brigade was 59 in 1985.

Zimbalist (1988: 12–13) views the 1986 measures to limit private activities and enhance the importance of moral incentives not as representing a reversal of direction or a repudiation of SDPE and material incentives, but rather a moratorium on the liberalization trend and a correction of excesses. His reasoning is that (1) while more activities have returned to the public sphere and there is greater control over foreign exchange, direct inter-enterprise contracting for inputs is being encouraged ('resource fairs', in operation since 1979, allow enterprises to trade unused inputs directly, and the 1980s has seen encouragement given to above-plan production: Zimbalist 1989: 74); (2) there is less reporting by enterprises to ministries; (3) there is a pruning going on of administrative personnel involved in planning; (4) there is increased enterprise self-financing of investment; (5) the role of enterprise brigades is being extended; and (6) parallel markets are multiplying.

Castro's position seems to be that while there is a need for strict cost accounting and economic calculation, there is to be no move towards the market mechanism, which he perceives to be taking place in several other socialist countries. At the Third Party Congress Castro stated that enterprise efficiency and profitability would not be meaningful if achieved simply by raising prices. While 'we still have a lot to learn in the field of efficiency,... becoming the sorcerer's apprentice [i.e. apprentice capitalists], is not the solution' (quoted in Dominguez 1986: 123). In an anniversary speech on 26 July 1988, his message was that effort should be concentrated on improving central planning; both capitalist methods and other countries' solutions are to be rejected. 'We must guard the ideological purity of our revolution. We will use nothing of any method that smells of capitalism' (quote taken from Julia Preston's report in *IHT*, 16 August 1988, p. 1). In a December interview Castro insisted that Cuba was undertaking its own changes and its own self-criticism. He much admired Gorbachev, but considered that the Soviet President has some political advisers who are enraptured with capitalism, and if they continue as they are they could do great damage to the Soviet people (reported by Geoffrey Matthews in *The Times*, 24 December 1988, p. 7).

Manpower and remuneration

In 1962 wages were made to vary with the degree of underfulfilment or overfulfilment of work norms. An eight-group wage scale (of approximately a 3-to-1 range) was set up, taking account of factors such as qualification and complexity. Time rates were dominant, with hourly tariffs taking into consideration other factors such as dangerous conditions. Wage differentials were meant to achieve goals such as incentives to improved qualifications, but in the first half of the 1960s political mobilization to achieve specific economic goals was also important (see Jiménez 1987: 128–130).

During the *'moral economy' stage 1966–70* emphasis was placed on moral incentives and collective (group) interests rather than individual material incentives, for ideological reasons and because of repressed inflation. Norming more or less came to an end, overtime payments were ended (overtime was expected to be donated free), and pay ceased to reflect the complexity of work. Wages were either frozen or reduced. For a while even time rates in many industrial workplaces were replaced by 'conscience time', with attendance depending on revolutionary consciousness (Ghai, Kay, and Peek 1988: 21). This policy was supplemented by appeals for voluntary labour, although some groups were paid. For example 'microbrigades' were released by enterprises, while remaining on the payroll, to work on housing and other social infrastructure projects. The remaining work-force was expected to work harder or donate overtime free. The microbrigades were phased out because of the adverse effects on enterprise payrolls at a time when financial accountability was given enhanced importance, but were re-established in May 1986 (Pérez-López 1986: 34).

The adverse effects on incentives led to serious problems such as increasing absenteeism in the late 1960s. In consequence, policy switched, in 1970, to greater emphasis on personal material incentives. From that date the Soviet-type worker norms, which were introduced 1963–65 but poorly enforced after 1966, were gradually reintroduced (Mesa-Lago 1981: 19). In 1971 consumer durables such as cars and colour television sets and building materials were allocated to enterprises, with distribution mainly determined by work attitude and performance but also to a lesser extent, by need. Similar criteria were applied to the allocation of housing, including that put up by the voluntary microbrigades, and vacations (Mesa-Lago 1981: 27–28). In the same year it became compulsory for men to work, absenteeism leading to exclusion from vacations and benefits such as the works canteen and, in extreme cases, periods in work camps (Zimbalist and Eckstein 1987: 11). The 1981 reform spread the wage range from 4.67 to 1 to 5.29 to 1. By the end of 1985 37.2 per cent of the labour force had pay tied to output (Zimbalist 1989: 75, 79). Over the period 1979–81 greater use was made of piece rates, by September 1979 affecting 36 per cent of the total working in production (Ghai, Kay, and Peek 1988: 37). Bonus schemes were introduced, linked to criteria such as the fulfilment of work norms, increased quality, input savings and repair and maintenance tasks (Kay 1988: 1248–49). The introduction of 'free or direct labour contracting' in 1980 gave managers permission to hire and fire workers under certain conditions (p. 1449). In general workers are only sacked for misconduct (Ghai, Kay, and Peek 1988: 37).

In 1986 major criticisms were levelled at many aspects of the existing economic system, and there was a sharp reversal of many policies. Bonus payments were to be related to the quantity and quality of performance and work norms revised upwards. Great emphasis was to be placed on non-material incentives, while a new government commission was set up to monitor management techniques and suggest improvements. At the Third Congress of the Cuban Communist Party on 4–8 February 1986 and its December 1986 follow-up Castro catalogued a whole series of problems: bureaucracy, apathy, corruption, incompetence, irresponsibility, self-seeking, laziness, negligence, inefficiencies, profiteering, theft, absenteeism, waste, poor quality, unearned bonuses, low productivity, poor motivation, and lack of accountability. He singled out people like high-earning artists, peasants charging high prices on the free market, and state managers who both overcharged and put the enterprise profit above the interests of the country as a whole. A *'rectification' process* and an austerity programme were set in motion. Castro considered it more important to protect the moral sense of the workers by honest behaviour than merely to meet the enterprise plan at any cost. In Castro's view 'the first thing a socialist, a revolutionary, a communist cadre must ask himself is not if his firm is making more money, but how the country makes more'. He criticized managers 'who want their enterprises to be profitable by increasing prices and distributing bonuses by charging the earth for anything' (quoted in Dominguez 1986: 123). 'Although we recognize that there is room for bonuses under socialism, if there is too much talk of bonuses they will corrupt workers' (p. 124). 'Socialism must be built through political work. These market mechanisms only build capitalism.' The glories of the revolution were 'not based on money' (p. 124).

The allocation of consumer goods and services

Rationing has been a more common and persistent feature of the Cuban economy than of the traditional Soviet system. On equity grounds and because of severe repressed inflation, the state introduced widespread rationing of staple foodstuffs and consumer goods in 1962 and made this general thereafter – in 1963 price controls were imposed on all goods and services. By 1968 there was free provision of education, medical care, social security, and even services such as local telephone calls and water supply. Free meals at works canteens were made available to many workers and housing rent could not exceed 10 per cent of family income (Roca 1981: 86–7). Note that in 1960 the state took over the houses and flats belonging to landlords and those who had left the country.

In line with the new overall economic policy in the 1970s, policy changes included: (1) the introduction of a water charge in 1971; (2) the December 1970 decision not to fulfil the promise made a decade earlier to scrap housing rents generally – only some low-income workers benefited (Roca 1981: 101); (3) some raised consumer price – a dual pricing system was introduced in 1972 for certain commodities (this 'parallel market' was made more general in 1980), whereby extra-ration purchases in 'free shops' could be made at higher prices and some commodities were entirely derationed. According to the *EIU*

(1987–88: 10), rationing now accounts for 26 per cent of individual consumption, while the number of non-food lines subject to rationing fell from 150 to 68 between 1980 and 1985 (ibid., p. 10).

From January 1985 onwards individuals were able to purchase outright their own homes from the state, or continue with rental (effectively mortgage) repayments, with past rent credited to the account. Individuals were also allowed to rent out accommodation at the full market price, but ownership was limited to one home and they took responsibility for repairs and maintenance.

The year 1986 was generally one of reform retrogression. The policy of individual home ownership was halted by the 'rectification' process and private sales were banned because of alleged profiteering. Restrictions were placed on the drinking of alcohol in bars. The austerity programme (the 28 measures were dubbed Castro's 'commandments') put into operation at the beginning of 1987 involved sharp increases in electricity prices and transport fares and reductions in canteen subsidies, television broadcasting hours, many ration allowances, petrol allocation, and a limit on the number of cars available for state bodies. Note that many retail prices were revised in December 1981, including some staple foodstuffs, in order to reduce the high level of subsidies.

Mention should be made of a scheme, introduced in 1987 in order to boost foreign exchange reserves, whereby Cuban citizens are able to trade jewels and precious metals for certificates providing access to scarce consumer goods.

Economic strategy

Sectoral strategy in the 1960s and 1970s

In the early years after the revolution there was a strong reaction to the dominance of sugar in the economy. Consequently, agricultural diversification became a key policy, although agriculture itself was allocated a declining share of state investment as industrialization received increased emphasis. Growth problems during 1962–64 and the willingness of the Soviet Union to enter into a long-term agreement in 1964 to purchase sugar at generous and stable prices (although payment was in the form of Soviet goods) led to a change in strategy. The price paid by the Soviet Union for Cuban sugar was approximately double the world market level during 1964–70 (MacEwan 1981: 97), while the former took over 40 per cent of the latter's sugar crop in some years during the 1960s (p. 217). Agriculture, especially sugar, was given priority, and industrialization was largely based on agriculture (refining, canning and shoe production etc.), although it was also partly resource based (nickel and cement production, for example). The ambitious 1970 sugar harvest target of 10 Mt was set in 1963; the actual crop-year harvest was 8.5 Mt. The agriculture-based strategy in general (especially, in addition to sugar, cattle, tobacco, citrus fruits and coffee) was meant to save on imports and stimulate exports, thus increasing the foreign exchange available for imported capital goods. In the early 1970s sugar and its derivatives alone accounted for three-quarters of export earnings, reaching 86.4 per cent in 1974 (Hagelberg 1981: 141). Even today the sugar industry accounts for 12 per cent of the work-force and 10 per cent of GSP (Azicri 1988: 169).

During the 1970s industrialization, similarly linked with agriculture (e.g. equipment such as mechanical cane cutters) and natural resource endowment, and with an emphasis on consumer goods, was given priority, attaining first priority in the late 1970s.

'Debt-led growth' in the latter half of the 1970s

Cuba took advantage of the recycled OPEC funds to indulge in 'debt-led growth' (Turits' term, 1987: 163), hoping that the resulting increase in exports and decrease in imports would service the foreign debt. Initially Cuba had a good record of repaying its hard currency debt (see Table 13.1), but was forced to start rescheduling in March 1983. The debt-service ratio over the period 1981–85 was 58.7 per cent on average (Zimbalist 1988: 152). Of the $4.68 billion hard currency debt at the end of September 1986, 57 per cent was owed to private credit institutions, while the debt to the Soviet Union amounted to 7.5 billion roubles (Zimbalist 1988b: 38). Debt repayments to the Soviet Union were suspended in 1972 and were to resume in 1986, but a further delay to 1990 at least was agreed upon (p. 39). Dominguez (1986: 135) estimates that Soviet bloc subsidies, excluding military aid, have run to at least a tenth of Cuba's gross national product since the mid-1970s. According to a report by Clyde Farnsworth (*IHT*, 17 March 1988, p. 3), Soviet subsidies, principally oil and sugar prices favourable to Cuba, run between $4 billion and $5 billion annually.[2] The *EIU* (1987–88: 25) estimates that by the end of 1987 the total debt to Western governments and banks was $5.2 billion. The *IHT* (17 March 1988, p. 3) splits this into $2.4 billion owed to Western governments and $3.1 billion to Western banks and suppliers. *The Economist* summarizes the picture as follows: most Western estimates put Soviet aid at around $4 billion annually; the latest US estimate gives $6.8 billion for 1986, $4.7 billion in subsidies associated with purchases and sales, $1.5 billion for armaments and $600 million for aid projects (17 December 1988, p. 65). In July 1986 Cuba temporarily suspended most principal and interest payments to the West. Note that Cuba has had no dealings with the IMF since the early 1960s.

In 1985 the value of exports plus imports constituted 50.1 per cent of net material product and 26 per cent of gross social product (Zimbalist 1988b: 21). In the mid-1980s the foreign trade of Cuba was dominated by the socialist countries (which took about 85 per cent), though Cuba's aim is to reduce this to about 80 per cent. This compares to an average of 65.2 per cent for 1971–75 and 73.3 per cent for 1976–80 (Fitzgerald 1988: 140). The Soviet Union alone accounts for around two-thirds, although imports from the Soviet Union fell during the first nine months of 1987 for the first time in nearly 30 years (Fitzgerald 1988: 3).[3] As a result of an agreement reached in 1976, following a similar nickel arrangement four years earlier, the Soviet Union pays above-world prices for sugar. For example in 1982 the price paid by the Soviet Union was 29.9 centavos per pound, compared with 28.9 by the other CMEA countries and only 7.7 by the capitalist countries (Pérez-López 1986: 20).[4] Cuba also benefits from oil re-exports: this has been allowed by the Soviet Union since 1980 on the basis of consumption savings and aided by extensive substitution of oil by the waste product *bagasse* in the sugar industry. In 1985 these re-exports constituted the most important source of hard currency earnings (42 per cent, falling to 26 per cent in 1986), although the fall in oil prices after November 1985 had a devastating effect. This was aggravated by a depreciating US dollar, with imports mainly priced in other currencies because of the US embargo. The situation was made worse by a prolonged drought, which reduced the sugar harvest[5] (see Table 13.2) and by the fall in the value of the US dollar, in which its exports are mostly denominated.[6] The austerity programme since 1984 has involved a switch from domestic consumption and welfare spending to exports, in contrast to the earlier programme.

The commodity structure of Cuba's exports in the mid-1980s was still dominated by primary products: (1) Food (overwhelmingly sugar, but also citrus fruits, fish products and live animals) – 80 per cent of total exports in all, with sugar alone making up some 75 per cent; in 1986 sugar provided 78 per cent of total exports (*Abecor Country Report*, 1988, p. 2). This compares to an average of 84.1 per cent for 1948–58 and 85.9 per cent in 1979 (Zimbalist 1988: 6–7). (2) Other products like nickel and oil re-exports, which had risen sharply from only 0.1 per cent in 1975 to some 10 per cent. Cuba imports mainly fuels (around 30 per cent), machinery and transport equipment (roughly the same), and manufactured products (around 13 per cent) (Pérez-López 1986: 22).

Joint ventures

The February 1982 law allowed up to 49 per cent foreign equity, with the aim of either exporting output or saving on imports. Production, pricing, and manpower decisions are within the sphere of the venture. Priority projects in tourism, for example pay a maximum net profit tax of only 30 per cent (Turits 1987: 172). There are few examples to date, but these include an agreement with Spain to recycle and export scrap metal (Pérez-López 1986; 20), with Japan in shipping, with Mexico in agricultural machine-building marketing, with Panama in finance and sugar refining (Zimbalist 1987: 17) and Argentina in hotel construction (Turits 1987: 172).

The private, non-agricultural sector

By 1961 the state sector accounted for 85 per cent of industrial output and 95 per cent two years later (MacEwan 1981: 70). During the 'revolutionary offensive' of 1968 the remaining rump of the private non-agricultural sector was eliminated, even the relatively more important retail trade (Roca 1981: 85). In 1976 licensed private businesses were permitted in activities such as car, plumbing and appliance repairs, but the self-employed were not allowed to employ others or to resell products. The period 1976–85 was a relatively liberal one, but late 1988 saw arrests being made of 'speculators' (including those who sell their places in queues) and those producing consumer goods illegally.

Table 13.2 Cuba: statistical survey

Non-state farm sector (1983)			*Output*	*Land*
(Co-operatives and individual peasant farms)			22.5	16.6
(% contribution to agricultural output and land)				
Sugar industry today (% of work-force and			*Work-force*	*GSP*
Gross Social Product)			12.0	10.0
Sugar harvest (Mt) *1970*		*1985*	*1986*	*1987*
8.5 (Target, 10)		8.1	7.4	7.1
Joint ventures	Very few			
Private non-agricultural sector	Very small			
Population (1988)	10.2 million			

Sources: Kay (1988: 1260); Azicri (1988: 169).
For figures on rates of growth and Western debt, see Table 13.1, this volume.

Conclusion

Cuba was a Spanish colony for some four centuries and remained under US influence for around 60 years. Fidel Castro came to power in 1959 and made Cuba the centre of world attention during the 1962 missile crisis. Despite industrialization, mainly linked to agriculture, the Cuban economy is still substantially agrarian in nature, with sugar remaining vitally important (Table 13.2). The country is heavily in debt despite generous Soviet support. Particular points worth noting in this chapter are: (1) the early departures from the traditional system, such as the greater use of both consumer goods rationing and of moral incentives, the latter characterizing the so-called moral economy stage of development (1966–70); and (2) Cuba retrenching and even retrogressing in some respects. Thus, while the 1970s saw implementation of 1965-style Soviet reforms, in particular the 1975 System of Economic Management and Planning, the period after 1980 has been one of retrenchment, leaving the economy today highly centralized, administrative and directive. There is increasing stress, once again, on moral as opposed to material incentives, and some of the concessions made to private activity have been taken back. For example the 1980 free farmers' market for above-quota sales was monopolized by the state six years later. The outlook for reform of the Cuban economy does not seem rosy.

Notes

1. In 1984 life expectancy was 73, compared with 61.8 in 1959 (Rodriguez 1988: 98); in 1965 infant mortality was 16.5 per thousand, compared with 34.7 in 1959 (Santana 1988: 113).
2. The problems of calculating the value of aid include the relatively poor quality of many Soviet manufactured goods. Note that Cuba itself runs an extensive foreign aid programme (for details see Zimbalist 1988b: 37–38).
3. National product also declined by 3.5 per cent and investment by more than 20 per cent.
4. Note, however, the argument that the world price of sugar is not a good guide since only some 14 per cent of world sugar is sold at free market prices (Zimbalist 1988: 7). The remainder is sold under preferential agreements at prices above the world market level, encouraging supply and discouraging demand and thus having a depressing effect on the world price (Zimbalist 1988b: 32). Fitzgerald (1988: 139) notes that, beginning with the First Five-year Plan (1976–80), the price of Cuban sugar exports to the Soviet Union was indexed to the price of Cuban imports, especially petroleum.
5. Cuba has even had to buy in world markets in order to meet Comecon commitments.
6. Cuba's imports, on the other hand, are largely denominated in other Western currencies, due to the US trade embargo, which was made fully operational in 1962 (the United States invoked the 1917 Trading with the Enemy Act). Since 1975, however, US companies have been able to trade legally with Cuba, although only indirectly via subsidiaries in third countries and only then with a licence obtained from the US Treasury (Jones, K. and Rich, D. (1988) *Opportunities for US-Cuban Trade*, Baltimore, MD: John Hopkins University Press).

Chapter fourteen

Democratic People's Republic of Korea

Political background

A unified state from AD 668 to 1945, Korea was liberated (and divided at the 38th parallel) in 1945, having been part of the Japanese Empire from 1910 to 1945. An isolated state, it was known as the 'hermit Kingdom'. The North was occupied by Soviet forces in August 1945 and the United States occupied the South. At the 1943 Cairo Conference the allies had envisaged an independent and unified Korea. In the Korean War (1950–53),[1] UN forces backed the South, the Soviet Union having absented itself from the Security Council, and China the North; the Soviet air force also took part. The DPR was proclaimed on 9 September 1948 and became a member of the Non-Aligned Conference in 1975. Cumings (1988: 14) sees Korea as a civil war that started in 1945 with the Soviet and US occupations and then became enmeshed in the Cold War.

The Korean Workers' Party has been led since 1948 by Kim Il Sung ('the great leader', who also became President in 1972), 77 years of age in April 1989, who has groomed his son Kim Jong Il ('the dear leader') as heir. A neutral stance is taken in relations with China and the Soviet Union. After the 9 October 1983 assassination, through bombing, of 17 South Korean members of President Chun Doo Hwan's delegation, including three ministers, in Rangoon (Burma), North Korea performed the unlikely act the following year of providing aid relief (chiefly rice, clothing, cement and medicine) to the September flood victims in the South. In 1985 the first family exchange visits took place, specifically 30 North Koreans and 35 South Koreans. The Democratic People's Republic did not participate in the Seoul Olympics, which opened 17 September 1988. The aim had been to co-host the games, but only five sports were offered. The only other non-participants were Albania, Cuba, Ethiopia, Nicaragua, and the Seychelles.

North Korea is concerned at the expanding links between socialist countries and South Korea. In February 1989 South Korea and Hungary established full diplomatic relations. Indirect trade with China, via Hong Kong and Japan especially, started in 1979 and there has been something of a history of joint ventures since 1985 (Jae Ho Chung 1988: 1034, 1042). This trade has been estimated at $1.5 billion in 1987 and $3 billion the following year, compared to Sino-North Korean trade worth $519.4 million in 1987 (Delfs, *FEER*, 8 December 1988, pp. 21–22). Trade offices have been opened with Hungary, Yugoslavia and the Soviet Union (Soviet-South Korean trade amounted to around $150 million in 1987; Susan Chira, *IHT*, 2 February 1989, p. 1). Bulgaria and Poland are to follow suit. Trade pacts have been signed with Bulgaria, Poland and Yugoslavia. A joint venture is to be set up in 1989 between a South Korean company and the Soviet Union involving a tourist hotel in Moscow (part of the company's plan for a chain extending to countries such as China and Hungary), while others have been agreed in principle in construction, manufacturing and fisheries. It is interesting to note that the GDR, although it attended the Olympics, has avoided such links, no doubt sympathetic to the other 'split nation'.

President Kim Il Sung practises a strong cult of personality and his policy of *Chuch'e* (*Juche*) or 'self-reliance' means that man is capable of mastering his own environment. This has made North Korea one of the most isolated of the socialist countries. Kim Il Sung has described *Chuch'e* as 'holding fast to the principle of solving for oneself all the problems of the revolution and construction in conformity with the actual conditions at home and mainly by one's own effort.... man, a social being that is independent and creative, is master of everything and decides everything' (quoted in Rhee 1987: 890). This stresses the human factor in development and downgrades the importance of material incentives. Also downgraded is the importance of foreign trade and its accompanying specialization, due to the fear of possible domination by larger powers. In recent years, however, there has been a greater stress on foreign trade, capital, and technology, especially with and from Western countries. In January 1984 Kim Il Sung expressed an interest in expanding links with 'friendly' Western states (Rhee 1987: 888), a call repeated at the Democratic Republic's 40th anniversary celebrations some four years later. Kim Jong Il called for a stricter implementation of an 'independent accounting system of enterprises', a gradual increase in the managerial independence of state enterprises, greater use of economic criteria in decision-making and improved worker incentives, although there has been no notable decline in party influence (Koh 1988: 63). The *EIU* (*Country Report* 1988, no. 1, p. 33), however, detected a swing back to *Chuch'e* in early 1988.

Development strategy has been dominated by a stress on heavy industrialization (especially machinery), with light industry and agriculture developed together. The Third Seven-year Plan was begun in April 1987 after a delay of two years,[2] with the following elements: (1) increases in gross industrial output by 1.9 times, gross agricultural output by 1.4 times, national income by 1.7 times and the value of foreign trade by 3.2 times, with grain output increasing by 50 per cent to 15 Mt by 1993, coal output rising from 70 Mt to 120 Mt and 300,000 hectares of tideland to be reclaimed by 1993; (2) the basic task is to lay the material and technical foundation for the victory of socialism by following *Chuch'e*, modernization and science and technology; (3) the plan aims to solve the problems of clothing, feeding and housing the people (Koh 1988: 62–63). In a report on the new seven year plan, Prime Minister Yi Kun-mo warned against an overemphasis on economic management and material incentives at the expense of political work (p. 64).

In a significant article in *IHT* (27 November 1987, p. 4) Selig Harrison concluded, on the basis of a visit to North Korea (23 September–2 October 1987), that economic pressure seemed to be forcing North Korea into reducing military spending by means of an improvement in relations with South Korea and the United States and into allowing a rapid importation of advanced industrial technology via a Chinese-style economic opening to the West.[3] In January 1988, however, the United States, accepting the evidence of North Korean involvement in the destruction of a South Korean airliner in November 1987, added North Korea to its list of countries that support terrorism (alongside Iran, Libya, Syria, Cuba and South Yemen), with adverse economic consequences for any future links (e.g. the US voting against loans by international organizations).

North Korea has one of the world's largest standing armies.[4] Rhee estimates that defence accounts for about a quarter of GNP (1988: 898).

Economic background

In the 1930s the area now constituting the North was more rapidly industrialized, especially in terms of heavy industry, than the South (Suh 1983: 199). In 1946 agriculture contributed almost 60 per cent of national product (Yoon 1986: 61), while more than 90 per cent of industrial establishments was nationalized (Chung 1986: 189). The population was 20.7 million in 1987 (compared to 42.7 million for the South), nearly 70 per cent being urbanized. Energy needs are dominated by coal (70 per cent), backed up by hydroelectric power, with a deliberately low importance attached to oil, which it lacks. Minerals include coal, iron ore, and non-ferrous metals such as gold, silver, zinc and lead.

The dearth of official statistics makes any real assessment difficult (see Table 14.1). In the mid-1980s, however, the World Bank described North Korea as a lower middle-income economy, with a $900 per capita income, well above that of Vietnam ($150) and China ($300). The *EIU Country Report* (1988, no. 1, p. 38) estimates that per capita GNP was $2,296 in South Korea, compared with only $860 in North Korea in 1986, and that the latter's per capita national income now probably slightly exceeds $1,000 (compared with the South's likely $3,700 in 1988; *The Economist*, 17–23 December 1988, p. 56). *The Financial Times* gives per capita GDP as $2,500 for the South and $1,200 for the North (25 October 1988, p. 24). The official North Korean figure for national income per head in 1986 is $2,400 (*EIU Country Report*, 1989, no. 1, p. 40). One of the world's dramatically successful newly industrialized countries (NICs), South Korea vividly illustrates the relative inertia and technological lag experienced by socialist economies in general and their desperate need to attract foreign capital and technology. This is not to underestimate North Korea's achievements, especially its industrial development, compared with that of other socialist countries, after substantial destruction in the Korean War. In 1985 a 220 per cent increase in industrial ouput was reported for the period 1977–84. National income increased 1.8 times over the period 1978–84 (Suh 1986: 84).

Table 14.1 North Korea: national income

Average annual rate of growth of national income (%)

1954–56	1957–61	1961–70	1971–75	1976–80	1981–84	1986	1987
30.1	20.9	7.5	10.4	4.1	4.3	2.1	3.3

Sources: Chung (1983: 172); Lee (1988: 1267); Pauley (*FT*, 21 March 1989, p. 4).

Economic planning

North Korea has a rigid command economy, with economic plans containing very detailed output targets for each industrial enterprise (Pak 1983: 214). Rationing is, in fact, more common than in the traditional economic system in more normal times, with the workshop and residential areas used as means of distributing highly subsidized basic commodities (e.g. rice). As regards manpower, moral incentives are stressed, and school-leavers are allocated in groups to particular jobs. Income tax was abolished in 1974. In 1958 a sort of Chinese-style Great Leap Forward was begun, involving a mass mobilization of people inspired by moral rather than material incentives. In February 1973 the 'Three Revolution Teams' (ideological, technological and cultural) were initiated. Teams of young people were sent to enterprises to encourage workers to greater effort and to teach them new techniques (Rhee 1987: 899–900). Campaigns and the accompanying exhortations are still a feature of economic decision-making. In 1974 there was a '70 day battle', in 1980 a '100 day battle' and between 20 February and 9 September 1988 a '200 day battle', the last concentrating on major construction projects in energy, the metal industry, and chemicals. Electricity, coal, and steel are seen as the key to the successful fulfilment of the Third Seven-year Plan (1987–93), and agricultural success involves increased irrigation, electrification, mechanization and chemicalization (the so-called four 'technical revolutions') (*EIU Country Report*, 1988, no. 2, p. 37; Koh, Asian Survey, 1989, vol.XXIX, no. 1, p. 40).

The First Five-year Plan actually ran from 1957 to 1960 and the First 'Seven-year Plan' from 1961 to 1970. Between the seven-year plans for 1978–84 and 1987–93, no annual economic plans were launched. Since 1961 an economic management system called the '*Taean* (machine plan) Work System' has been in operation, where the party committee (60 per cent of its members being workers) rather than the manager makes the decisions necessary to carry out the state plan. The manager is merely a member of the committee, which instructs him to implement these decisions (*EIU Country Report*, 1988, no. 2, pp. 894–95).

Economic reform has been very limited. The *EIU Country Profile* on North Korea for 1987–88 reports that in the late 1950s there was a steamlining of economic ministries into a lesser number of 'commissions' and a further reorganization a year later (p. 56), and the 1960s saw a strengthening of material incentives, especially in agriculture (p. 57). Recently some ministries have been split up (*EIU Country Profile*, 1988, p. 40). In the 1986 Report (no. 2) there is a report on what appears to be GDR-style combine reforms in 1985, where enterprises in related areas of activities (e.g. supplier-user) are encouraged to co-ordinate their operations in a formal manner. Output targets are still set, but the quantity and source of inputs are, in some cases, no longer pre-specified. Some managers have greater powers to fix bonus rates and incentives for the work-force, and to decide the share of profits to reinvest (p. 39). The 1985 Report (no. 3, p. 34) notes that within the enterprise, teams of four to six workers plan their own work schedules and determine their bonus rates. Enterprise managers have greater say over manpower, equipment, materials and funds and may devote up to 50 per cent of excess profits to increasing output, welfare benefits or bonuses. Party committees dominate enterprises (*EIU Country Report*, 1989, no. 1, p. 39). Harrison (1987: 38) considers that there has been a rejection of a Chinese-style decentralization of decision-making to the managers of industrial enterprises.

Rhee (1987: 889) reports the August 1984 mass movement to increase basic consumer goods production by teams of part-time workers from locally available inputs such as waste and by-products. According to Lee (1988: 1268), small groups of workers in industrial enterprises, in co-operative farms and at home produce basic necessities for direct sale to consumers in markets. The *EIU Country Profile* for 1988–89 notes that provinces are responsible for consumer goods production, receiving no central investment but having to transfer tax revenue (p. 72).

Agriculture

In the *March 1946 agrarian reform* land was redistributed to the tillers. Land was confiscated without payment from landlords who leased land to tenants (62.1 per cent of total arable land confiscated, itself 54 per cent of total arable land); landlords owning more than five hectares (23.8 per cent); Japanese (11.3 per cent); the church (1.5 per cent); and national traitors and expatriates (1.3 per cent). Those benefiting were landless peasants (61.5 per cent), small land-owning peasants (35.2 per cent), agricultural employees (2.3 per cent), and landlords who returned to farms (1.0 per cent). The land reform took less than a month to complete (Pak 1983: 216–17). *Collectivization* spanned the period 1954–58, moving Chinese-style through three types of co-operatives. There were increasing degrees of co-operative activity, ranging from the pooling of labour and some collective use of implements and animals to the distribution of income based solely on work contribution. Co-operatives were designated 'collectives' in 1962, and each collective is broken down into work brigades (specializing in activities such as crops, livestock and machines) and these in turn into work teams ('specialized', 'mixed', or 'all-purpose') (Pak 1983: 217–19). According to the *EIU* (*Country Profile*, 1988–89, p. 66) there are now 'subwork teams', where three or four families are allocated a piece of crop land and the necessary implements.

In 1970 land used by the collective farms accounted for 94 per cent of all arable land, while the state farm figure was 4 per cent. Note that all natural resources and forests were nationalized in 1947. There are still agricultural machine stations (Pak 1983: 222). *Private plots* are 0.02 of an acre at most (before 1977, 0.04 of an acre), but peasants were, until recently, only allowed to consume the produce themselves and not to sell it on markets (*EIU Country Profile*, 1987–88, p. 59). The *EIU* (*Country Report*, 1988, no. 1, p. 38), however, states that farmers' markets are now held two or three times a month, for an hour or so, for the sale of produce grown on the tiny plots (some 200 square metres each) and household goods manufactured by 'sideline work teams'. Urban workers help at harvest time. Koh (1988: 64) detects no measurable increase in the sphere of individual initiative, while official rhetoric still underlines the need to convert co-operatives into state farms. The increase in agricultural output is to be attained not through greater incentives, but via an increase in cultivable land, mechanization and use of chemical fertilizers.

Economic policy (Pak 1983) has, in general, given priority to heavy industry, but light industry and agriculture have been developed together. Industry provides support for agriculture in order to industralize it. Intensive farming is practised, especially involving the use of fertilizers and mechanization, and there are large infrastructural schemes – irrigation to protect against the effect of drought, and land reclamation, including from the sea. Moral incentives have been stressed. The *Ch'ollima* ('flying horse') movement, which began in 1958, mimicked the Chinese Great Leap Forward in that it was designed to increase productivity by means of a stress on ideological incentives to work hard. After the middle of the 1960s the work brigade was stressed (Pak 1983: 223–4). The *Ch'ongsalli* method of managing co-operative farms, started in 1960, stressed party direction of agriculture, strong one-man management, and ideological motivation, and established work brigades and teams (p. 224).

Harrison (1987: 38) sees retrogression in policy: (1) He argues that there has been a recent decline in the autonomy enjoyed by co-operative farms: this has the aim of turning over control of co-operative property to the state in order to end the class differences between workers and farmers. (2) Free markets for farmers now operate only once a month rather than weekly.

Foreign trade and payments

Economic links with South Korea have been largely severed and the commission set up in 1985 to deal with the re-establishment of commercial links became bogged down by intense rivalry. Nevertheless, the two countries have recently (November 1988) started to trade on a small scale, with no duties on the North's imports into South Korea (Maggie Ford, *FT*, 17 January 1989, p. 6; Susan Chira, *IHT*, 2 February 1989, p. 1, and 3 February 1989, p. 2; *EIU Country Report*, 1989, no. 1, p. 31).

The policy of 'self-reliance' extends also to Comecon, where it has only observer status, preferring industrialization and rejecting integration and specialization on minerals. It relies on the Soviet Union and China, however, for machinery, oil, coal and modern arms. The Soviet Union also builds plants in exchange for a percentage of the output. In contrast, Vietnam changed strategy after the 1975 reunification and China after the Cultural Revolution.

In 1984 it was decided to pay greater attention to foreign trade, although three years later foreign trade totalled only $4 billion compared with $88 billion for South Korea (Robin Pauley, *FT*, 21 March 1989, p. 4). Despite a policy of 'self-reliance' and in order to modernize its capital stock, North Korea purchased Western technology, machinery, equipment and even whole plants on a grand scale in the early 1970s. In the period 1970–82 80 per cent of imports and 48 per cent of exports were with capitalist countries (quoted in Rhee 1987: 901). A debt of about $2 billion with the West (about $3 billion in total) was run up by 1982 (*EIU Country Profile*, 1987–88, p. 68).[5] Western banks' loans in the mid-1970s were used to finance infrastructural investments such as roads.

North Korea defaulted in 1976,[6] the causes including the fall in mineral exports after 1974 and the difficulties in exporting manufactured products (Suh 1983: 209). Several debt reschedulings and delayed payments for imports have made North Korea a poor credit risk. Between March 1984 and June 1988 North Korea paid neither interest nor principal, but even before the former date interest payments were irregular (the last before that being in 1979) and principal repayments were non-existent. In September 1986 Japan's Ministry of International Trade and Industry compensated domestic firms for their trade losses with North Korea (Koh 1988: 64), and in August of the following year Western commercial bank creditors declared a formal default. This allows the seizure, in this case by Swiss and British courts, of North Korean assets in the West such as gold and property. The debts were consolidated into two bank syndicates. North Korea was forced into a reopening of re-scheduling talks in September 1988. A scheme suggested by one of the syndi-cates in June 1988 involves the following (a token initial repayment of $5 mil-lion was made on 1 July): a new loan of $900 million, with a formal North Korean Government guarantee;[7] there would be a separate schedule of pay-ments on the so-called settlement loan (30 per cent of the $900 million), on which a fixed interest rate of 8 per cent is payable, with a final payment due on 15 December 1991. If this repayment schedule is maintained, the remaining 70 per cent will be written off; otherwise the whole $900 million will fall due. The scheme, however, has led to disagreement between the bank syndicates (Fid-ler 1988: 25).

The Soviet Union's share of North Korea's imports rose from around a quarter in the early 1980s to almost half in 1985. Non-ferrous metals, includ-ing gold, are important exports, especially for earning hard currencies. In 1987 work was being carried out on fourteen major Soviet assisted industrial pro-jects, including a plan to build a nuclear power station. Sixty four major indus-trial projects have already been undertaken in the past 40 years with Soviet aid (Koh 1988: 64). The long-term programme for economic and technical co-operation to the year 2000 sees North Korea providing labour in particular for construction and food production in the Soviet Far East (Quinn-Judge, *FEER*, 8 December 1988, p. 22).

The stress on self-reliance has been modified over time, with the foreign trade-income ratio rising from 19.2 per cent in 1961–67 to 30.3 per cent in 1971–76 (Suh 1983: 207). There have also been marked changes in the import-ance of trade with the other socialist countries over time, falling from 99.6 per cent in 1955 and a low of 60.6 per cent for exports in 1975 and a low of 45.9 per cent for imports in 1974 (Chung 1986: 84). In terms of commodity structure exports during the 1950s consisted of more than 70 per cent mineral ores and during the 1960s and 1970s manufactured goods (mainly metals and pig iron), and inedible raw materials such as mineral ores and silk, more than 60 per cent. Among imports during 1970 machinery and transport equipment were the biggest items, followed by mineral fuels and food (Suh 1983: 208).

In 1986 North Korea opened up to tourists[8] in the drive to earn convertible currencies, and two years later (in October) South Korea lifted its trade em-bargo and allowed northern goods in duty free. The United States followed with a slight easing of its trade embargo, imposed in 1950, allowing North Korean purchases of humanitarian items such as medicines.

Joint equity ventures

In September 1984 a joint venture law was promulgated in order to attract Western capital, technology and know-how, but with limited success to date. Harrison (1987: 38) estimates that 50 are under way (44 with Japanese-

Koreans) (Table 14.2), and Koh believes that only one involves a non-Korean resident in Japan (1988: 64). The North Korean International Joint Venture General Company was founded in August 1986 in partnership with Japanese Koreans. This is a sort of holding company which both establishes and acquires other enterprises (Lee 1988: 1264). Minerals and high technology are the areas favoured, but actual examples include hotel construction (France), clothing, food processing, car components, construction materials, chemical products, and department stores (Japan – mostly Japanese Koreans) (Rhee 1987: 888). For example, the Rakwon (Paradise) department store is operated by Japanese-Koreans. Purchases, however, are restricted to hard currency spenders such as foreign diplomats and privileged North Koreans who possess the 'red won' (a special form of currency with a red stamp), which can be converted into hard currency (Harrison 1987: 37). There are also joint ventures with socialist countries, including a shipping enterprise with Poland, joint Soviet-North Korean timber projects in Siberia and four joint Chinese-North Korean power stations. A joint venture with the Soviet Union for the production of milling machines in North Korea is planned (Quinn-Judge, *FEER*, 8 December 1988, p. 22). In early February 1989 it was announced that the first North-South Korean joint ventures, situated in North Korea, had been agreed upon in principle, involving the development of a tourist area, a ship repair yard, and a railway rolling stock plant.

Table 14.2 North Korea: statistical survey

Average annual rate of growth of national income (%)

1954–56	1957–61	1961–70	1971–75	1976–80	1981–84	1986	1987
30.1	20.9	7.5	10.4	4.1	4.3	2.1	3.3

Foreign debt ($ billions)

			1982		1986		
			3 (total)		2.23 (West)		
			2 (West alone)		1.83 (Socialist countries)		

Joint ventures (1987)	50
Population (1986)	19.06 million

Sources: Chung (1983: 172); Suh (1986: 84); Economist Intelligence Unit, *Country Profile* (1987–88: 68); Harrison (1987: 38).

The private non-agricultural sector

In 1985 individuals were allowed to engage in small private handicraft production such as in knitting (*EIU Country Report*, 1985, no. 3, p. 34). The dominance of state and collective enterprises in the economy can be seen in the figures given by Suh (1983: 199) for 1946 and 1956, respectively: national income, 14.6 per cent and 85.8 per cent; manufacturing, 72.4 per cent and 98.7 per cent; agriculture (1949), 3.2 per cent, and 1956, 73.9 per cent.

Conclusion

North Korea is one of the most isolated socialist countries, adopting, for instance, a policy of *Chuch'e* or self-reliance. A rigidly controlled society and economy are subjected to the cult of personality of 'the great leader' Kim Il Sung and 'the dear leader', Kim Jong Il (the son and heir). North Korea is in the same position as the GDR in being the poorer half of a divided nation, and it may not be a coincidence that both are reluctant reformers. North Korea retains a highly centralized economic system, and moral incentives are high on the agenda. Few reforms are being applied or are in prospect in either the industrial or agricultural sectors. The country has run into debt repayment problems, the private sector remains severely constrained, and the September 1984 joint venture legislation has produced only a limited response, mainly from Japanese citizens of Korean descent.

Postscript

The South Korean Government has vetoed, for security reasons, the proposed shipyard and rolling stock joint ventures, but has agreed to tourist schemes (*EIU Country Report*, 1989, no.2, p. 33).

Notes

1. North Korean troops crossed the 38th parallel on 25 June 1945. Since July 1953 the two Koreas have been separated by the Demilitarized Zone, which runs to the south of the 38th Parallel in the West and to the north in the East. North Korea occupies 55 per cent of the whole.
2. The Second Seven-year Plan (1978–84) and the Six-year Plan (1971–76) were also extended by two years.
3. See also an extended article in *FEER*, 3 December 1987.
4. *The Economist* (23–29 January 1988, p. 44) puts it at 840,000. The army is backed up by 5 million reservists. A more recent estimate is 870,000 men under arms compared with 650,000 in South Korea (*IHT*, 31 December 1988, p. 2).
5. At the end of 1986 $2.23 billion was owed to the West and $1.83 billion to the socialist countries, mainly to the Soviet Union. Officially the hard currency debt is estimated at only $1 billion (Harrison 1987: 38). The United States imposes a ban on loans to North Korea.
6. The end-of-year hard currency debt was $1.4 billion, with a further $1 billion owed to the socialist countries.
7. The Foreign Trade Bank, which signed the previous loan agreements, has been eclipsed by the Korea Gold Star Bank, which now handles most of the external economic relations.
8. Except those from Japan (ban lifted July 1987), the United States, Taiwan, Israel, and South Africa.

Chapter fifteen

The Mongolian People's Republic

Background

A country of pastoral nomads,[1] Mongolia was ruled by China during the Qing dynasty (1644–1911), although Mongolia actually ruled China during the Yuan dynasty (1271–1368). Genghis Khan (1162–1227) was proclaimed ruler of 'All the Mongols' in 1206. Requesting Russian protection, Mongolia declared its independence from China in December 1911.[2] Although China recognized Mongolia's autonomy in 1913, the latter reverted to a Chinese province 1919–21, after Chinese troops re-established control. On 11 July 1921 independence was once again declared after Soviet troops had arrived in Mongolia in pursuit of White Russian forces. The Mongolian People's Republic formally came into being in November 1924, the second socialist country after the Soviet Union, with the latter's strong support. Soviet troops stayed on until 1925; five divisions were stationed in Mongolia in 1966 and one was taken away in 1987. According to Milivojevic (1987: 562), Soviet forces were 'officially' stationed in Mongolia from 1921 to 1925, from 1936 to 1956 and from 1966 to the present, but unofficially at least some Soviet forces have been stationed there every year since 1921; also, uniquely, Mongolia has no domestic armaments industry (p. 564).[3]

Yumjaagiyn Tsedenbal became General Secretary of the Mongolian People's Revolutionary Party in 1940, Prime Minister in 1952, and (after removal 1954–58) President in 1974. In August 1984 Jambyn Batmonh (sometimes written Batmunkh) replaced Tsedenbal as party leader.[4] Other political events of note include the establishment of diplomatic relations with nationalist China in 1946 and with socialist China three years later, membership of the United Nations since 1961 and the establishment of diplomatic relations with the United States on 27 January 1987. In 1985 border trade with China was resumed, but relations with China improved noticeably after Gorbachev's Vladivostok speech in July 1986, in which he said that Mongolia and the Soviet Union were discussing a partial withdrawal of Soviet troops.[5] In 1987 Mongolia renewed scientific and technical co-operation with China, after a span of two decades.

The population of this arid country reached 2 million in September 1987, of which just over half is now urbanized. The population is growing at an annual rate of nearly 3 per cent, a cause of some concern because of factors such as rising youth unemployment (Sanders, *FEER*, 27 October 1988, p. 42). Sanders (1987a: 84–85) vividly describes the desperately poor state of the economy in 1921: (1) It was dominated by nomadic cattle-rearing. Ninety per cent of the population were nomadic herdsmen who owned no land. Fifty per cent of livestock was owned by feudal secular and church lords constituting just 7.8 per cent of the population (serfdom persisted until the revolution). (2) Foreigners owned what little there was of industry (e.g. in coal mining, gold mining, power stations, armouries, and the telegraph system; nationalization took place soon after the assumption of power. (3) There was heavy foreign indebtedness. (4) There was no national currency; mediums of exchange included sheep, foreign notes, and silver bullion and coins.[6] Resource endownment comprises mainly land suitable for livestock, timber, brown and coking coal, copper, molybdenum, gold, fluorspar, iron ore, wolfram and lead. Approximately 60 per cent of the country has never been subjected to a proper geological survey (*EEN*, 1987, vol. 1, no. 8).

Planning

The first attempt at a five-year plan was for the period 1931–35, but it was only after the Second World War that systematic planning took place. Annual plans began in 1941. School leavers are directed to their place of work by the Directorate of the Mongolian Organized Work Force (Sanders 1987a: 119). Enterprises and institutions are still mainly responsible for housing their own work-forces (p. 123).

Economic reform

When he first took over, and before Gorbachev became General Secretary, Batmonh attacked waste, losses, and mismanagement, describing the system of economic management as the weakest link in economic work (Heaton 1986: 86). At the Nineteenth Congress of the Mongolian People's Revolutionary Party in May 1986 he attacked bureaucracy, ill-discipline, irresponsibility, narrow thinking, and mere slogans (Heaton 1987: 79). There is now criticism of the 1960s and 1970s as an era of stagnation (*EEN*, 1988, vol. 2, no. 10, p. 4), obviously echoing Soviet sentiments. Tsedenbal was not explicitly named, however, until Batmonh's speech at the end of December 1988 (Sanders,*FEER*, 19 January 1989, p. 21).

Ministerial reorganization took place in 1968. Ministerial amalgamations have also included the 1986 decision to allow the Ministry of Agriculture to take over the Ministry of Water Supply in October and the establishment of one body in charge of construction (the State Construction Committee) in December (Sanders 1987a: 62). In the early 1970s industrial production associations along Soviet lines began to be formed. A 'commission for perfecting management and the economic mechanism' was formed in 1987 as well as a 'standing commission for agriculture and food supply' and two committees for increasing efficiency in the use of materials and for improving the repair of machinery and vehicles imported from the Soviet Union. The current ministerial position is as follows (see Sanders, *FEER*, 11 February 1988, p. 62, and Asian Survey, 1989, vol. XXIV, no. 1; *EEN*, 1988, vol. 2, no. 4, pp. 6–7), the changes being designed to streamline the planning process:

1. The State Construction Committee. This was formed in early 1987 out of the Ministry of Construction and two design institutes and is under the control of Vice-Premier Sonomyn Luvsangomso.
2. In December 1987 the Ministry of Light and Food Industry and the Ministry of Agriculture were reorganized into the Ministry for Light Industry and the Ministry for Agriculture and Food Industry, the latter thus taking over food processing from the former.
3. The Ministry of Foreign Economic Relations and Supply has assumed the functions of the Ministry of Foreign Trade, the State Committee for Material and Technical Supply, and the State Committee for Foreign Economic Relations.
4. The Ministry of Power, Mining, and Geology, formed out of the Ministry of Fuel and Power Industry and the Ministry of Geology and Mining Industry.[7]
5. A new Ministry for Environmental Protection.
6. The State Committee for Planning and the Economy. This was formed at the end of January 1988 out of the State Planning Commission and the two committees for prices and labour and is under the control of Vice-Premier Puntsagiyn Jasray.[8]
7. The State Committee for Science and Technology. This has absorbed higher education in order to improve the link between university training and the research institutes.

Over 100 enterprises were taking part in a new '*economic experiment*' in financial autonomy. The participating sectors included light industry, food production, fuel and power, public catering, and transport and communications. Construction, timber and services were to be included during 1987. Plan fulfilment must cover all the relevant products (Sanders, *FEER*, 11 February 1988, p. 64). At the June 1987 Central Committee meeting Batmonh stressed the need for the restructuring of economic management, intensive growth and raised efficiency. In an earlier speech, in May of the same year, he listed a number of problems: the stress on fulfilling net plan indices, the continuing shortages of foodstuffs and consumer goods, the poor quality of many products, bureaucracy, lack of initiative and deficient housing (Jarret 1988: 84). Prime Minister Dumaagiyn Sodnom referred to overcentralization as the main problem of economic management and planning, and said that the remedy lay in the need to limit the role of the State Planning Commission to general capital investment policy and broad targets, with ministries and state committees making decisions on aspects such as the purchase of machinery and equipment. Provincial and town administrations and enterprise managers will have greater autonomy and are to be financially accountable (as will be work teams within the enterprise), while enterprise performance will be judged by the fulfilment of export orders and sales contracts (Sanders, *FEER*, 10 December 1987, pp. 40–41). The 1988 plan avoids the subjection of every enterprise to highly detailed plan targets, enterprises being allowed, for the first time, to fill in the details of their own plans on the basis of a restricted number of central plan targets (Sanders, *FEER*, 11 February 1988, p. 62). Personal material incentives have also been given increased attention (in 1988 pay scales dependent on enterprise revenue were introduced in the light and food industries, internal trade, and supply: Sanders, Asian Survey, 1989, vol. XXIV, no. 1, p. 52). There have also been experiments in electing enterprise managers and team leaders. Local authorities[9] have been given greater power over enterprises in their areas and are able to use a portion of the funds of enterprises for infrastructural purposes (*EEN*, 1988, vol. 2, no. 10, p. 5).

Although Mongolia seems to be following in Soviet footsteps the system as it stands is still largely run along traditional lines. Kaser (1987b) considers that the reform proposals do not amount to as far-reaching a reform as in the other socialist countries of Asia, and a growing labour force and available land and natural resources make the drive for intensive growth less urgent.[10]

Industrial development and policy

Up to the start of the Second World War the limited amount of industrial activity largely concentrated on the processing of livestock products. The next two decades saw diversification into such activities as metalworking, timber-processing and consumer goods, followed by full-scale industrialization, with intra-branch diversification and modernization (Sanders 1986: 86–87). Soviet aid has been of substantial importance. In the five years to 1986 Soviet aid may have amounted to around $3 billion (*EEN*, 1987, vol. 1, no. 12, p. 6). Some 35,000 Soviet advisers are in the country. One source suggests that aid, largely from the Soviet Union and in the form of long-term, low interest credit, financed about 50 per cent of investment during the late 1960s and the 1970s (Wallace and Clarke 1986: 98). The 1986–90 and 1985–2000 plans focus on agriculture and improving food supplies (Heaton 1986: 86).

Agriculture

In 1919 90 per cent of national income originated in agriculture.[11] The first state farms were established in 1922–23 for controlling arable land and for cereal cultivation. By the end of 1930 nearly 30 per cent of poor and middle peasant households had been forced into collectives, but unrest led to a retreat.[12] Among the policies implemented during the Second World War was the imposition of state procurements and obligatory wool deliveries upon individual households. Collectivization took place during the 1950s.

Within the collectives are teams (brigades) and further down 'bases', comprising a few households, each with its own equipment and production tasks. Some fodder is grown by the collective, but this is done mainly by state farms. In 1969 the livestock machine stations were transferred to the collectives. Herdsmen's families live in permanent settlements, and the herdsmen themselves drive the livestock to pasture according to season. From 1979 onwards collective members became entitled to state old-age pensions. Members have to work a minimum number of workdays for the collective (raised from 150 to 250 in 1967). There are controls on the number of livestock that can be held by individual members. In December 1987 co-operative members were permitted to own 100 head of stock per family living in the Gobi zone and 75 per cent in the forest-steppe zone, compared with 75 and 50 per cent respectively, before that date (Sanders, *FEER*, 11 February 1988, p. 62). Almost 25 per cent of livestock of a total of 22.6 million in 1987) is in private hands, either in townspeople's plots or in the herds of co-operative members (p. 62). The 52 state farms are the main producers of cereals and other crops (Sanders, *FEER*, 10 December 1987, p. 44). *Individual holdings* of workers, employees and citizens are currently (since January 1986) allowed 8 to 25 livestock per household depending on areas. The same decree, as well as increasing the number of livestock allowed, permitted the sale of surplus produce through the co-operative trade network in addition to the state procurement system (the 1978 decree had fixed compulsory state procurements for some products).

A number of state farms have been developed into 'agro-industrial complexes', with their own processing plants (e.g. fruit and vegetables and flour)[13] and utilizing industrial techniques in farming. Since 1986 state farms and co-operatives have benefited from higher state prices for procurements above the annual average rate of growth attained over the period of the last five-year plan.[14]

The division of arable land is as follows: state farms, 69 per cent; herding collectives, 21 per cent; *personal holdings*, 10 per cent. The corresponding figures for livestock are: 6 per cent, 70 per cent, and 22 per cent, respectively. Sanders reports several years of stagnant agricultural output, due to declining productivity in the livestock sector, with falls in average slaughter weight, per capita meat production trailing behind population growth, and meat exports declining. Livestock numbers totalled 22.6 million in 1986 and 1987, the same as in 1970 (*FEER*, 11 February 1988, p. 62).

Foreign trade

Comecon trade is overwhelmingly dominant. According to Sanders, 1985 figures show the division of Mongolian exports as: CMEA, 94.5 per cent; other socialist countries, 1.6 per cent; and capitalist countries, 3.9 per cent. The respective figures for imports are: 97.5 per cent, 1.5 per cent, and 1.0 per cent (1987a: xvi). Mongolian exports in terms of commodities were mineral raw materials, 42.6 per cent; non-food manufactures (e.g. clothing and footwear), 24.5 per cent; and foodstuffs, 15.4 per cent, while imports were: machinery and industrial equipment, 36.2 per cent; fuels, 28.7 per cent; and consumer goods, 17.3 per cent. In 1986 ores and concentrates (copper, molybdenum, and other non-ferrous metals) accounted for about 45 per cent of exports and non-foodstuff raw materials and processed products about 25 per cent (Sanders, *FEER*, 10 December 1987, p. 42).

Soviet trade is dominant within socialist trade, although the exact proportions have varied depending on Mongolia's relations with China. The Soviet Union was the only trading partner from the mid-1920s to 1953, when trade with China began. Eighty five per cent of trade turnover was accounted for by the Soviet Union in 1956, 70 per cent in 1960 (when Mongolian trade with China reached 18 per cent), 60 per cent in 1966 (Sanders 1987a: 100), and then rose to around 80 per cent, where it is at present (Sanders, *FEER*, 10 December 1987, p. 42). In 1986 machinery and equipment took over 36 per cent of imports from the Soviet Union, the remainder being oil and petrol, textiles, consumer goods, and foodstuffs (p. 42). The first five-year trade agreement was signed with China in 1986. The 1984 and 1985 agreements were short-term and concerned with border trade exchanges.

The state foreign trade monopoly was set up in 1930. Foreign trade associations specialize by commodity. Mongolia became a member of Comecon in 1962. One factor inhibiting foreign trade is the dependence on Soviet railways. The road network was built with links to the Soviet rail network in mind, and air transport has increased recently (Ebon 1987: 20). The expectation was that Mongolia would sign a transit agreement with China in the first half of 1989, especially encouraging links with the Southeast Asian market (Margie Lindsay, *FT*, 1 November 1988, p. 8). In 1987 total trade turnover was 5.4 billion togrog (£920 million). The small size of Western trade is expected to increase to 30 per cent of the total by the year 2000 as the government introduces such changes as hard currency auctions and decentralization of decision-making. Japan is the leading 'Western' trading partner ($20 million turnover annually), others including Switzerland, West Germany and Britain (p. 8).

Joint stock companies

The earlier Soviet-Mongolian joint stock companies (pre- and early post-Second World War), such as those in banking, trade, transport, and mineral extraction were subsequently handed over into full Mongolian ownership. There are, however, a number of joint companies operating today (in transport, power supply and mineral extraction, for example), mainly in co-operation within the Soviet Union, but also with Bulgaria and Czechoslovakia. Two new joint ventures with the Soviet Union are to be set up, involving the production of sheepskin coats and felt footwear, and discussions are going on about projects in agriculture, building materials, the timber industry and energy (*EEN*, 1988, vol. 2, no. 10, p. 5).

A law on joint ventures with Western countries is in prospect, especially in activities such as mineral extraction and processing, and the processing of agricultural products.

The non-state, non-agricultural sector

From the start of the 1960s policy centred on the merging of workers and herdsmen and of state and co-operative property, with the possibilities of private property thought to be exhausted. Current policy is to encourage co-operatives and private enterprises in the food industry and in services (*EEN*, 1988, vol. 2, no. 10, p. 5); Sanders reports a recent ordinance of the Council of Ministers encouraging the setting up of private co-operatives providing services, manufacturing, and processing on a small scale (*FEER*, 30 June 1988, p. 27).

Conclusion

Mongolia, freed from Chinese control with Soviet help, formally became the second people's republic in 1924. This small country (in terms of population) of pastoral nomads gradually became more industrialized with Soviet aid and under effective Soviet control. The current leader Jambyn Batmonh, has begun to criticize aspects of society and of the economy in the style of Gorbachev, although actual reform has been limited. See especially the 1987–88 ministerial reorganization and the small-scale experiment in financial autonomy in the industrial sector. The system at present is still largely run along traditional lines and reform proposals are relatively modest. Nevertheless, Mongolia can be expected broadly to follow the Soviet lead at some stage.

Notes

1. There are around 3 million Chahar Mongols in Inner Mongolia (an autonomous region of China) and Buryat Mongols in Siberia, mostly in the Buryat and Kalmyk

  autonomous republics.
2. It was formerly the Chinese province of Outer Mongolia.
3. For the general background see Green (1986).
4. Batmonh became Premier in 1974 and President in 1986.
5. A Soviet motorized rifle division withdrew between April and June 1987, a 25 per cent cutback of the roughly 60,000 Soviet troops still left in Mongolia (Jarret 1988: 81). In his famous speech to the United Nations (7 December 1988) Gorbachev promised that a 'large portion' of the troops would be withdrawn, subsequently quantified at three-quarters.
6. The Togrog (=100 Mongo) was issued in 1925 and became the only legal tender three years later.
7. Note the importance of coal in power generation.
8. Membership of the Council of Ministers has fallen by about 25 per cent, and four vice-premiers are now largely in charge of economic planning and management.
9. *Hurals* are assemblies of deputies.
10. Sanders reports a labour surplus in urban areas and a shortage in rural areas, since migrants are attracted to the former by higher incomes (*FEER*, 30 June 1988, p. 27).
11. In 1985, by contrast, 25 per cent (Heaton 1987: 80); industry 32.3 per cent (Heaton 1986: 87). Sanders (1987a: xvii–xviii) gives figures for agriculture of 18.3 per cent of GDP, industry 32.4 per cent, and trade and supply 31.6 per cent.
12. Milivojevic (1987: 565) argues that there was a nationwide revolt against both the regime and Soviet control, leading to the abandoning of collectivization and the reintroduction of large Soviet forces.
13. Sanders reports on the recent start of production of preserves at the Sharyn Gol Fruit and Vegetable Industry Association, a 10-year project built with aid from Bulgaria.
14. See Sanders (1987a: 64).

Chapter sixteen

The Socialist Republic of Vietnam

Political background

France began the colonial period for Vietnam in 1858 with the capture of present-day Da Nang, seized Saigon in 1861, and formed the protectorates of Annam and Tonkin by 1883. On 19 August 1945 a communist government was first proclaimed in North Vietnam, without the assistance of external forces. War with France began the next year, following the reimposition of colonial rule. Recognition of the Democratic Republic of Vietnam by the socialist countries took place in January 1950. France's defeat at Dien Bien Phu in 1954 was followed by the Geneva Accords in July of the same year that divided Vietnam along the 17th parallel and promised elections within two years in order to create a unified government and country. Saigon fell to North Vietnamese forces in April 1975 after a long struggle with the United States and 30 years of war in total. The United States had withdrawn its combat troops by March 1973, although formal reunification as the Socialist Republic of Vietnam did not occur until 2 July 1976. The reunification represents the only example of a socialist country incorporating a relatively large capitalist area. Over the period 1976–78 there came about a unified financial system (including one currency), banking system and budget (Spoor 1988: 104–5). The constant official aim has been 'to build socialism and defend the Fatherland'. A major theme of the 1988 book by Beresford is that the imposition of the northern model on the south resulted in such serious problems that reforms became necessary from 1979 onwards.

Ho Chi Minh founded the Vietnamese Communist Party on 3 February 1930, and this became the Vietnamese Workers' Party in February 1951 and the Communist Party of Vietnam in 1976. He left in 1911 and did not return until until 30 years later, although communist resistance dated from the 1920s. Ho died in 1969 and was succeeded by a collective leadership under Le Duan. Le Duan died in July 1986, to be followed by a stop-gap General Secretary of the Workers' Party, Truong Chinh, and his replacement on 11 December, Nguyen Van Linh. The Sixth Congress of the party in December 1986 was a major event in both a political and an economic sense. Many of those who had led the country to triumph in war gave way: Truong Chinh (who was also President), Pham Van Dong (Premier) and Le Duc Tho (chief negotiator with the United States at the Paris talks which ended January 1973) left the Politburo, although they were named as 'comrade advisors' to the new Politburo and the Central Committee in January 1987. In June Pham Hung and Vo Chi, both in their mid–70s, became Premier and President, respectively. The former died in March 1988; his stand-in was First Vice-Premier Vo Van Kiet. A new, more technocratic, and provincially based leadership was left to deal with economic problems so serious that the 'renovators' ('renovation' is *doi moi*, also translatable as 'transformation' or 'radical change') coined the phrase, 'The North won the war, the South must manage the economy.' Do Muoi (71) became Premier in June 1988.

Relations with China deteriorated to the extent of a border war in February 1979 after the December 1978 invasion of Kampuchea (Cambodia), which overthrew the tyrannical Pol Pot regime. Further clashes took place later on. A treaty of friendship and co-operation was signed with the Soviet Union on 3 November 1978. Vietnam now has the world's fifth largest military organization.[1]

Economic background

The 311,620 square kilometres of Vietnam are poorly endowed in terms of soil and are periodically hit by typhoons. In the mid-1980s only about 21 per cent of the land area was usable for agriculture – there are less than 0.1 hectares of cultivated land per capita, the third lowest in the world after Singapore and Japan (Esterline 1988: 88). The forested area has almost halved since the early 1940s, partly the result of enormous wartime damage caused by mass bombings, land clearances, and defoliation through the use of 'Agent Orange'. The country is also not generously endowed with raw materials (coal being the principal energy resource), but self-sufficiency in oil is expected by 1990 (the target is 3.0 Mt). The population is nearly 65 million (around 80 per cent rural), the largest socialist country after China and the Soviet Union, having approximately doubled over the 40 years prior to the mid-1980s. In 1985 population growth was 2.3 per cent; the 1990 target is 1.7 per cent (*Vietnam Courier*, 1987, no. 2, p. 6).[2] One of the major tasks after reunification was to socialize the economy of the South.

In 1954 the North's economy was overwhelmingly agrarian and technologically backward, with only 1.5 per cent of material product originating in modern industry (Beresford 1988: 129, quoting Chau). Beresford points out the contrast between this and the economy of the South in 1975, where a third of the population was urbanized and there was a large, market-oriented farm sector, with a fairly egalitarian distribution of landownership in the Mekong delta, the main rice producing area, after the 1970–72 reforms. There was a flourishing tertiary sector and a small, import-dependent manufacturing sector accounting for 11 per cent of GDP in 1960 and 6.5 per cent in 1972. When US aid was suddenly cut off there was immense dislocation (Beresford 1988: 147–55). By 1975 industry and mining accounted for 11 per cent of the workforce in the North (p. 60), with the same percentage of the population urbanized (p. 156).

Table 16.1 shows official statistics for rates of growth of national income and total agricultural output and for 'paddy and paddy equivalent' (rice and rice equivalent) in millions of tonnes. Agricultural production declined in 1979 and 1980 (*Vietnam Courier*, 1987, no. 1, p. 4) and in 1987 food production fell by 2 per cent, available grain per capita declining from 304 kg in 1985 to 280 kg in 1987 (Hiebert, *FEER*, 14 January 1988, p. 48). Vu Khoan, Assistant Minister for Economic Affairs in the Foreign Ministry, said on 6 April 1988 that annual food production per capita was 620 pounds (280 kg), compared with 748 pounds in 1985. Farms were being divided into smaller units because of the lack of mechanized farm machinery like tractors; the situation was aggravated by a fuel shortage (reported by Barbara Crossette in *EIU*, 7 April 1988, p. 6). Rice and equivalent output fell in 1977 and 1978 (*Vietnam Courier*, 1987, no. 2, p. 18) and in 1987. The 1988 target of 19 Mt is likely to be achieved and the growth of agricultural production as a whole is likely to be of the order of 4.1 per cent. In May 1988 there was official recognition that more than 3 million people in 12 northern provinces were living 'at the edge of starvation', while nearly 8 million in the North would be 'seriously short of food' until the next harvest (Hiebert, *FEER*, 26 May 1988, p. 18). Hiebert lists the causes of

Table 16.1 Vietnam: national income, agricultural output, inflation, and debt

Average annual rate of growth of national income (%)

1955–65	1966–75	1976–80	1981–85	1986
6.5	6.0	0.4	6.4	4.6

Average annual rate of growth of agricultural output (%)

1976–80	1981–85
1.9	4.9

Paddy and paddy equivalent (rice and equivalent) (million tonnes)

1976–80 (Average)	1975	1982	1983	1984	1985	1986	1987	1990 (Plan)
11.5	11.6	16.6	17.0	17.3	18.2	18.5	17.6	22.0

Inflation (%)

1982	1983	1986	1987	1988
80.0	55.0	Over 700	700–1,000	700

Foreign debt (end 1987) ($ billions)

Non-convertible currency debt to socialist countries	Convertible debt owed to about 30 countries and to international organizations
6.5	2.7

Sources: Economist Intelligence Unit, *Country Profile* (1987–88: 14); *Vietnam Courier* (1987), no. 1, p. 4, and no. 2, p. 18; Michael Richardson, *IHT*, 19 December 1988, p. 2; Esterline (1988: 91); John Elliott, *FT*, 14 March 1989, p. 6.

the stagnation in food production over the last three years as natural disasters, shortages of fertilizers and pesticides and poor farm prices. *The Daily Telegraph* quotes a Vietnamese source as saying that about 10 million people faced hunger, 4 million faced serious hunger and 21 people had died of starvation in various Northern provinces (12 July 1988, p. 9). Conditions eased in early June when the new harvest began.

Kimura (1986: 1043–44) notes the incomplete and reliable nature of Vietnam's statistics. He draws a clearer distinction between the average annual growth rate achieved during the Second Five-year Plan period (1976–80) of 1.5 per cent and the 5.9 per cent figure for the Third Five-year Plan period (1981–85). Vietnam is classified as one of the poorest countries in the world in terms of per capita income (Kimura presents a range of Western estimates, varying between $125 and $200 in 1983–84; 1988: 1040). Finkelstein (1987: 982) quotes the US Department of State's 1984 figure of $160. *The Economist* (26 December 1987–8 January 1988, p. 59) gives a figure of $265 for per capita GDP. There was large scale unemployment, despite the fact that 50,000 to 60,000 people were working in other socialist countries. Of the 1 million young people entering the labour market each year, only 40 per cent are employed (Hiebert, *FEER*, 14 January 1988, p. 48) By the end of 1986 inflation was more than 700 per cent compared to 80 per cent in 1982 and 55 per cent in 1983. According to Hiebert, the figure was between 700 and 1,000 per cent in 1987 (*FEER*, 14 January 1988, p. 48) and to Elliott 700 per cent a year later (*FT*, 14 March 1989, p. 6).

By the end of 1987 non-convertible debt to the socialist countries, especially the Soviet Union, amounted to $6.5 billion, which is partly being repaid by sending workers to Eastern Europe (Esterline 1988: 91). Moreover, debts of $2.7 billion were owed to about 30 countries and international organizations (p. 105). In 1981 foreign debt was $3 billion, the debt-service ratio was 77 per cent of total exports and 218 per cent of exports to the convertible currency area (Spoor 1988: 109). During the period 1955–64 China and the Soviet Union were roughly equally important aid donors; Spoor feels that the figure of 23.8 per cent for foreign financing as a proportion of total budgetary revenue is probably an underestimate (1987: 343). China cut off aid altogether after the 1978 invasion of Kampuchea, but between 1979 and the mid-1980s Soviet aid ran at an average of about $2 billion annually, roughly equally divided between economic and military aid. Ligachev (the Soviet representative at the December 1986 Congress) promised to double economic aid, mostly loans repayable over 30 years, over the next five years. This was despite open admission by the Vietnamese that much had been squandered on poorly chosen projects, delayed commissioning of plant, and so on, and despite Western pressure to use aid as a lever for troop withdrawal from Kampuchea. The *EIU* (*Country Profile*, 1987–88, p. 15) suggests that Soviet aid is now supplied on a project basis, rather than being integrated into the state budget associated with the plan. The IMF cut off loans in January 1985 because of Vietnam's inability to pay off its debts, which amounted to $34 million. The United States has imposed a trade embargo since May 1975; the only exception permitted is deliveries of humanitarian aid. In 1987 the United States agreed to urge private charities to help the war disabled with artificial limbs and so on. The UN World Food Programme has contributed only modest amounts. By early 1987 gold and foreign exchange reserves had fallen to $15 million (about two weeks' imports) (Esterline 1988: 88).

Economic reforms

After the July 1954 Geneva agreement, early phases of reform involved the 1955–57 'reconstruction' and creation of the 'national economy' and the 1958–60 Three-year Plan. During the period 1958–59 Ho Chi Minh was attracted by Maoist thought. Increased emphasis was given to mass mobilization methods (socialist emulation and political activation, consciousness raising, and exhortation), and in October 1958 a new system of management was introduced: 'Cadres take part in work, workers take part in management.' This followed Ho's September suggestions that leading officials do one day's manual labour a week and the others a half of each day, while workers should be trained in administration (see Post 1988: 143–50). Doubts about the efficacy of mass mobilization techniques had set in by the end of 1959 and Post sees the September 1960 Third Congress of the Workers' Party as marking a decisive shift, in that Vietnam definitely became caught up in the Soviet pattern. The following five-year plan laid emphasis on skills and firm managerial control as the means of increasing production (Post 1988: 150).

During the 1970s there was a general shift towards the co-ordination of plans at the provincial level, which, in 1979, allowed provinces to retain a certain percentage of foreign exchange earnings for their own use (White 1985: 101). The September 1979 reforms pointed in the direction of decentralization, under which enterprises were permitted to produce unplanned products and output above obligatory sales, which could be sold on the free market or to the state at negotiated prices. Two years later encouragement was also given to the use of the piece rate system of wage payment (Beresford 1988: 160–63). The enterprise production plan, as from January 1981, consisted of three parts: state-assigned output manufactured with state supplied inputs; output resulting from inputs procured by the enterprise itself; and by-products. Retained profits are higher for the last two, and by-products may be sold on the free market, if the state is not interested (Spoor 1988: 107; 1988a: 119). According to the *EIU*, workers themselves are now able to use enterprise facilities on their own account to make goods for sale on the free market or to the state (*Country Profile*, 1987–88, p. 190). The Fifth Congress of March 1982 stressed the need to shift priorities away from heavy industry and towards agriculture and light industry (and their exports). The period 1982–85 saw criticism of 'bureaucratic centralism in economic policy' and the need for decentralization of decision-making to enterprises to free them from the day-to-day control of government agencies, to encourage more direct links between enterprises, to remove subsidies and introduce 'socialist accounting', and to tie pay to performance. But Stern (1987) sees this as only amounting to tinkering with the planning system, with the state at the same time emphasizing the need for control of commerce and markets.

The Sixth Congress in 1986 confirmed the new approach. The 1986–90 five-year plan stresses the importance of the grain harvest and an increase in the production of consumer goods for both domestic production and exports (Finkelstein 1987: 986).The lack of progress in implementing these reforms led to their reaffirmation by the August 1987 Central Committee Plenum, which outlined the programme of implementation, starting with enterprises jointly operating with Soviet enterprises and with those producing consumer goods in 1988 and, finally, covering all enterprises by 1990 (Hiebert 1987b: 94).

A number of ministerial mergers were made in 1987 (e.g. a new Ministry of Agriculture and Food was set up), to reduce bureaucracy and overcome empire building, and many ministers were changed. Financial control was emphasized: strict controls over investment spending, reduced employment in the state sector to combat excessive bureaucracy, and state organizations to move towards 'financial self-government and the acceptance of resonsibility for profits and losses'.

As in the Soviet Union, during the 1980s in Vietnam there have been attacks on corruption, abuses of power, complacency and obstruction, together with numerous personnel changes. There has been a growing realization that winning wars is not at all the same as winning the peace. In July 1986 Truong Chin declared that 'we have held on too long to the system of centralism, bureaucratism, and subsidization'. There would be no more target dates for socialist transformation. Since he became General Secretary in December 1986, Nguyen Van Linh has talked about the 'serious errors' of the previous ten years and the need for a 'complete and radical socio-economic *renovation*'.[3] This is needed in order to eliminate the managerial system characterized by a 'subsidy-based bureaucratic centralism mechanism' and replace it with a planning mechanism based on socialist cost accounting and business activities, consonant with the principle of democratic centralism. Nguyen Van Linh (1987: 15) says that state purchases of farm produce for sale at low prices involve subsidies equalling nearly a third of the budget. In June 1988 Linh said, 'The national economy has collapsed largely because the situation of faked profits and true losses has prevailed. We have been calculating the prices of equipment and materials too low for too long, compelling the state to make up for losses that were too big' (reported in *IHT*, 18–19 June 1988, p.

2). Renovation is needed in 'economic thinking' (economic laws have been ignored), production structure, and economic management. While central planning should remain (there would be no return to chaotic capitalism), the plan must (supposedly) be worked out from the bottom upwards, although, it is stressed, under the guidance and regulation of the centre in order to ensure balance. More use should be made of economic levers, the operational decisions of production units should not be interfered with and branch and territorial planning should be closely combined. Beresford's (1988: 174) reading is that legally binding plan targets are to be scrapped except for 'a few essential areas' as it is put, such as foreign trade commitments.

The country had been left without an economic and social strategy, and those who could not adapt had to be retrained or replaced. The three major programmes relate to food grain and foodstuffs, consumer goods and exports, these constituting the main content of the 1986–90 plan. Inflation is of paramount concern and much stress is laid on stabilizing the situation, partially closing the gap between the amount of money in circulation and the supply of goods and services. There must be a far stricter credit and interest policy, encouragement of saving by index-linking savings deposits to the rate of inflation, temporary and selective price freezes, a reduction in investment and in the budget deficit (by lowering subsidies and investment spending for example).[4] On the other side of the equation, the supply of goods must be increased, by, for example, stimulating the private sector. Price determination should fully take account of costs and regard should also be paid to import prices.

A notable event was the election, by secret ballot, of the manager of the Thanh Long Paper Mill by 133 representatives of cadres and workers, the provincial authorities subsequently officially confirming the appointment. Normally the provincial authorities or the competent ministry appoint managers on the basis of the local party committee and administration (*Vietnam Courier*, 1987, no. 8, p. 13).

Hiebert calculates that, since late 1986, the reforms have not been introduced in most of Vietnam, being only spasmodically applied in certain provinces and companies, due to resistance from officials and managers (*FEER*, 17 March 1988, p. 21). He reports the slow implementation of the reforms due to the lack of people with sufficient experience and know-how (*FEER*, 28 July 1988, p. 21). Thayer (1988: 4) sees the proponents of economic reform as a coalition of Southerners (or officials with long experience in the South) and another group centred in the Northern port of Haiphong. A municipal district in the port introduced an incentive-based contract system in agriculture in 1979 which was later adopted as a national model. The reformers are at present in the ascendancy despite the 1986 figures which show that 73 per cent of the 1.8 million party members are in the North (p. 4). From an ideological point of view it is seen as possible to progress directly towards socialism by bypassing the capitalist stage, but not to miss out on the development of the market production stage.

Besides extreme centralization and subsidization, which stemmed from running a perpetual war economy, other problems include: unemployment; an acute shortage of managers and other skilled manpower (many business-men, including the entrepreneurial Chinese minority, have left the country); bottlenecks in energy, raw materials and transport and communications; the familiar 'scattering' of investment resources; foreign debt and exchange prob-lems; and isolationism.

Large-scale migration to the cities caused the *'redistribution' of the work-force* in 1986, which uprooted 1.3 million people in five years. Workers, mainly young people, were sent to the new economic zones (Esterline 1987: 93–94). A resettlement plan was first put forward in 1973. Recently the aim has been to resettle up to 250,000 people annually, mostly from the North, in zones in central and southern Vietnam. Farmers are able to market that proportion of the crop remaining after the state extracts its share (Barbara Crossette, *IHT*, 28 April 1988, p. 6). Beresford (1988: 70, 151–52) sees the aims as increasing cultivated land area and transferring people from overcrowded cities and densely populated deltas in the the North. Between 1975 and 1985 around 2 million people had moved to the zones (p. 152).

Financial reforms

Between 1954 and 1960 state enterprises were not separate financial units, but came under the budget, with the state covering all investment and any losses and draining off any profits. But although the latter year saw the start of the implementation of a *khozraschyot* system, Spoor (1987: 342) argues that it is doubtful if it was actually achieved; for example, significant cash transactions still took place. The February 1959 reform involved a rate of exchange of one dong (the currency unit) for 1,000 old dong, with an upper limit of 2,000 new dong to the amount of money that could be exchanged.

April 1985 saw a massive devaluation of the dong against the US dollar, from just below 12 to 100 dong to the dollar. In September a new dong re-placed the old at a rate of one to ten, although immediate exchange was limited to 20,000 dong per family in order to penalize the free market traders. In fact, however, this penalized many state enterprises as well, since they used cash to purchase scarce inputs, this further increasing the goods shortage. Two weeks' advance warning, however, allowed black marketeers to get rid of old dong and hoard hard currencies. Workers and cadres received extra cash to compensate for the loss of the coupon ration books (which were sup-plemented with some cash previously; Esterline 1987: 93). Wage and price reforms thus meant that employees' heavily subsidized ration certificates were replaced by pay increases to compensate for the rise in retail prices. Subsequent wage increases were to be dependent on merit and productivity increases. The 'two price system' (free market and state ration prices) was to be replaced by the 'one price system' in order to eliminate black markets. Subsidies to state enterprises, too, were to be replaced by a system of wholesale prices that was to reflect costs, while there was to be some further decentralization of decision-making. In 1984 production in excess of quotas could be sold at free market prices.

The following results ensued:

1. Soaring inflation (see Table 16.1).
2. Some reversal of policy (e.g. reintroduction of rationing for some basic necessities in January 1986 and of subsidies for some low-income earners).
3. The January 1986 sacking of Tran Phuong (Vice-Premier for Economic Affairs) and the June 1986 replacement of To Huu (a Vice-Premier of the Council of Ministers) by Vo Chi Cong.
4. A wholesale replacement of ministers (e.g. of Finance, Transport and Communications, Foreign Trade, Coal and Mining).

Anti-inflation policies include restrictions placed on wage and price increases; reductions in government subsidies and spending in general; the suspension of investment projects; and the sale, since mid-November 1987, of government bonds with a 2 per cent interest rate, State employees are forced to buy bonds worth half a month's salary, and private operators of market stalls and restaurants are pressed to buy bonds at the value of one month's income (Hiebert, *FEER*, 17 March, p. 21). Nguyen Xuan Oanh summarizes fiscal and monetary policies: tax rates are being increased (at present there is no income tax, and other taxes contribute a mere 13 per cent of government revenue) and collection improved. The State Bank is to concentrate on credit regulation and control of the money supply, while new commercial and specialized banks are being set up to provide loans to the whole of the business sector, including private enterprises and joint ventures. The aim is to eliminate the multiple exchange rate system and to end up with no more than two rates, one for commercial transactions and the other for fund transfers, both much closer to free market rates. State enterpises will have to price imports at market rates with exchange rate reform (Oanh 1988: 4).

Transactions in present-day Vietnam involve the dong, the US dollar, gold, Western consumer goods, barter and State Express 555 cigarettes. In July 1987 the Ho Chi Minh City Industrial and Commercial Bank was opened, the first commercial bank, with part of the stock sold to private citizens for the first time. Keith Richburg reports the Haiphong Shipping Company's experiment to sell up to 49 per cent of its shares to private individuals and co-operatives, compensated by dividend checks; the purchase of five shares is accompanied by the entitlement to a company job (*IHT*, 13–14 August 1988, p. 14).

Agriculture

Land reform was implemented as early as 1953–54, involving land appropriation and redistribution, the colonial legacy having left most peasants as tenant farmers. *Collectivization* did not begin in the North until 1959, but by 1968 more than 90 per cent of peasants formally belonged to higher-level co-operatives. Beresford (1988: 130) points out Chinese influence in the staged process. 'Mutual aid' teams or 'production solidarity' groups were first set up, building on the existing wet rice practices of joint transplanting and harvesting and the lending of tools and draft animals. There next followed 'lower-level co-operatives' ('production collectives'), in which individual income depended on both labour and contributed land and means of production, and, finally, 'higher-level co-operatives', in which labour was the sole source of remuneration. The Chinese commune, however, was not emulated. Five per cent of the collective's land was devoted to *private plots*, while agriculture was largely left alone during the war and a de facto reversion to family farming was permitted in many areas (Beresford 1988: 134). Co-operatives dominated agricultural output, state farms contributing only a small percentage (specifically 0.5 per cent of gross agricultural output in 1960 and 1.1 per cent in 1963; Spoor 1987: 347). In 1963 quotas were fixed for a given period, initially three years on the basis of the average results for 1961–62, as an incentive to increase output. As far as the South is concerned, the decision to collectivize was taken in early 1977, the aim, stated the following year, being to complete the process by 1980. In pre-1979 co-operatives there were compulsory procurement quotas for rice and pork, with a dual system of quotas and above-quota prices, while other products were subject to contract. During the 1970s the trend was towards locally negotiated procurements (White 1985: 100–101), and in June 1982 stress was laid on district and provincial self-provision of food (p. 101). From the late 1970s onwards the role of the district (between province and village) increased as regards transactions with the state, and integrating agricultural and industrial development at the local level (Werner 1988: 158). In 1976 the farm tax was based on the estimated gross output of the normal average crop, but this was changed nine years later to average yield per hectare in various geographical situations, tax rates being fixed for a three year period (Spoor 1988: 111).

In the mid-1980s about 71 per cent of the working population was employed in agriculture. Grain is the principal crop, especially rice, and the figures for 'paddy and paddy equivalent' are shown in Table 16.1. There were improving harvests up to 1986, although rice production has not kept pace with population growth since 1979 (malnutrition is widespread as noted earlier), and losses arise from a poor system of distribution. Part of the explanation for the improvement is to be found in the reforms introduced to amend the traditional agricultural model, although the ultimate aim is still full collectivization. By mid-1985 75 per cent of both the southern farm population and cultivated land area was accounted for by production solidarity teams, production collectives and co-operatives (Duiker 1986: 109). The *EIU* estimate is that by the end of 1985, on paper at least, some 90 per cent of peasant households and 85 per cent of the cultivated acreage in the South had been collectivized (*Country Profile*, 1987–88, p. 16).

In January 1981, after experiments starting in Haiphong in 1978, a *'production contract' system* was introduced in the North, but this was not widespread in the South until the following year. In this system individual peasant households, or sometimes work teams, lease land from the co-operative and take over most stages of production in exchange for contracted deliveries, keeping produce over the contracted amount (fixed on the basis of the average productivity of land over the preceding three years and set for a two- to three-year period) to be consumed by themselves or sold on the free market. Any shortfall in contracted deliveries must be made good the following year. The remaining *private farms* sign contracts with the state. Collectives provide inputs and communal services such as irrigation and ploughing (White 1985: 97; Beresford 1988: 162; Vo Nhan Tri 1988: 80).

From the mid-1980s, the movement towards collective farming was to be achieved with a greater emphasis on incentives such as the redistribution of land to poor southern peasants enrolled in semi-socialized 'production solidarity teams' or 'production collectives', and the product contract system, in which collectives lease out land to peasants in return for a grain quota (Duiker 1986: 109).

In April 1987 it was decided that agricultural tax rates and product-contract quotas (the amount of grain peasants have to sell to the state) were to be reviewed and stabilized. The tax rate and contract quotas are to remain unchanged until 1990. Peasants were no longer to be pressurized into providing rice to the state beyond the tax and quota obligations (Hiebert 1987: 101).

In 1987 further measures were taken to combat problems with the supply and distribution of foodstuffs. In March the government removed checkpoints on roads, originally designed to prevent illegal private trading, and later formally authorized private individuals to form transport businesses in order to convey foodstuffs to market; thus controls on cross-provincial movement of goods were removed. An *April 1988 Politburo resolution* called for the following: a reduction in the size of co-operatives; the conversion of co-operatives in highland regions into 'work-exchange teams or private holdings'; the main type of co-operative in the South is to be the 'production group', in which tools are shared and mutual aid given during peak periods; and ten-year contracts for land plots to be permitted in order to provide incentives to look ahead (Hiebert, *FEER*, 28 April 1988, p. 76). Individual farmers are now allowed to perform most tasks in the rice-growing cycle, while under the revised contract system farmers will be able to retain 45 to 50 per cent of their output instead of the previous 25 per cent (Hiebert, *FEER*, July 1988, p. 22;

Cima, *Asian Survey*, 1989, vol. XXIV, no. 1, p. 66). The August 1988 Directive involved the return of land in the Mekong Delta to its previous owners in the form of individual plots, land which had been taken over in the late 1970s. Land still belongs to the state, but the guaranteed use of land by peasants is now 15 years (Hiebert, *FEER*, 17 November 1988, p. 110). Nguyen Van Phuoc (a Deputy Minister of Agriculture) acknowledges Chinese experience as providing the pattern for the new tenure system (reported by Keith Richburg in *IHT*, 16–17 July 1988, p. 2).

Nearly 75 per cent of co-operative members' income is derived from the 'family economy' and 90 per cent of the meat and fish and all fruit and vegetables sold in urban markets is accounted for by private plots (Hiebert, *FEER*, 17 November 1988, p. 76).

An interesting innovation that sprang from the food problems of the late 1970s was the establishment in 1980 of a food supply organization, the Food Company of Ho Chi Minh City, under Madam Nguyen Thi Thi, outside the existing procurement and distribution system. Bank credits were used to purchase agricultural inputs and industrial consumer goods, which were then traded for food in the countryside. In 1983 the organization became an independent state enterprise, rather than a subdivision of the city's food department, and now processes foodstuffs and feedstuffs. It has a monopoly of the city's rice trade; it runs rice mills, noodle factories, bakeries and its own retail outlets; it has a small oil refinery, trading oil products for agricultural goods. It plans to build a solar power station to ensure electricity supply: piece rates provide an incentive for hard work. It now runs 7,000 retail stores. Plans are submitted to central authorities for incorporation into national economic plans.

Factors that affect agricultural pricing include price stability, especially for basic foodstuffs; average cost pricing plus profit markup; and, since 1975, attention to world prices (White 1985: 101–6). Agriculture is now the priority sector.

Foreign trade and investment

Foreign trade

Comecon dominates Vietnam's foreign trade to the tune of about 75 per cent, the Soviet Union alone around 65 per cent in the early 1980s. Japan, however, which also offers long term loans, is actually second to the Soviet Union as a partner. Exports are mainly primary products, such as coal, timber, crude oil and foodstuffs, including sea products such as shrimps. Imports are chiefly capital goods, such as fishing equipment, oil, raw materials, and fertilizers. Imports were 13 per cent of GNP in 1984 (Beresford 1988: xiv). Within Comecon during the 1980s there has been a shift towards greater specialization in tropical products and light manufactures (p. 175). In February 1987 a commission for economic relations with foreign countries was set up to develop links with Third World and Western nations. There are already assembly plants operating with licences from, for example, Japanese companies. A 70 per cent increase in exports is planned for 1986–90. There has been a US embargo since May 1975. In 1987 Vietnam sought diplomatic relations with the European Community, and is already a member of the IMF, the World Bank, and the Asian Development Bank.

The September 1979 reforms allowed exporting enterprises, with the approval of the Ministry of Foreign Trade, to sign contracts directly with foreign companies. In 1981 Ho Chi Minh City, Hanoi, Haiphong and Da Nang were allowed to set up their own foreign trade corporations. The 1979 reforms allowed enterprises to use 10 per cent of planned and 50 per cent of above-plan foreign exchange earnings for the import of raw materials and spare parts, while in late 1981 all localities were permitted to export directly and to retain 70 to 90 per cent of foreign exchange earnings for the import of raw materials, machinery, and consumer goods for their own use (Spoor 1988a: 121–22). Managers of state enterprises in Ho Chi Minh City were allowed, in 1987, to borrow funds from abroad in order to import modern equipment and technology, to enter into joint ventures with overseas companies and to employ 'overseas Vietnamese and technical advisors and managers'. Relatives of exiled Vietnamese were promised the facility of foreign currency accounts and a favourable rate of exchange, and the tourist door was opened to all foreigners and expatriates.

Foreign investment

Vietnam is critically short of advanced technology and know-how. The 1977 law failed to attract very much foreign capital, because of the imposition of such restrictions as 49 per cent maximum foreign ownership and the necessity of local management. Power shortages still act as a deterrent. The last four Western companies exploring for oil left in 1981. Negotiations resumed in the mid-1980s and in 1988–89 offshore exploration agreements were signed with Shell and Petrofina, Total, and BP (oil drilling ventures were also signed with Indian companies), with production sharing the basis. Exploration continued during the hiatus through Vietexopetro, the Vietnamese-Soviet oil and gas company. A new law, which became operational on 1 January 1988, permits the setting up of solely foreign-owned companies and foreign companies to own up to 99 per cent of the equity of joint ventures; foreigners may be managing directors, but a Vietnamese must be at least deputy chief executive; profits and capital may be repatriated and nationalization is ruled out. Expatriates may be employed if local skills are lacking; profit tax is normally charged at 15 to 25 percent, but concessions are possible in remote areas or in special sectors such as timber. Subject to Vietnamese law and an arbitration process, foreign employers are able to hire and fire employees (Ungphakorn, *FT*, 19 January 1988, p. 4). Examples are to be found in small-scale oil refining, electronic telephone switchboards, television set assembly, and aluminium windows. A joint venture with an Indonesian bank is planned for 1989. Under the new arrangements nearly 30 joint ventures have been licensed, whose partners include the Soviet Union, Australia, Belgium, Britain, and India (*FT*, 20 October 1988, p. 4). A more recent figure is over 50, mainly in oil exploration and exploitation, marine products and tourism (*The Guardian*, 15 December 1988, p. 10).

The non-state, non-agricultural sector

Handicrafts began to be converted into co-operatives in 1958. Twenty years later a 'socialist transformation' campaign was launched against large private traders in the South. This and the attempt to transfer private businessmen to the new economic zones led to the flight of the 'boat people'. Particularly affected were the Hoa people of Chinese descent (Finkelstein 1987: 980). Ungar (1987–88: 609) lists a number of reasons, in addition to the restrictions on private enterprise and the impact of the new economic zones, to explain the exodus of the Hoa people, including fear of a war between China and the Soviet Union and the prospect of military service. In 1979, however, small-scale private activity was once more encouraged. Until recently there was a legal limit on employment of one to two people, although family labour was largely unregulated (Fforde 1987: 25). Now privately owned industrial enterprises are permitted to employ 10 to 15 workers (Beresford 1988: 65).

There is now a more relaxed attitude to the private sector. In 1978 private trade was formally abolished (although the black market survived), in 1983 taxes were increased on private establishments such as restaurants, and a further attack was made in 1985 via taxation and the occasional forcing through of 'joint ventures' with the state. In 1986 attitudes began to change and by the following year licences were no longer required for small businesses (such as bicycle repair, coffee shops and hairdressers), while workers and civil servants (including teachers and doctors) were openly encouraged to take a second job during off-duty hours. Family businesses and co-operatives were encouraged by a whole series of measures. These included tax holidays and exemptions for exporters; availability of state credit and inputs on equal terms as the state sector and even foreign exchange, those producing exports allowed to retain some of the foreign exchange for imports of materials and equipment; freely set prices; trademarks; sale of patents allowed; inventors to be entitled to between 15 and 20 per cent of the profits resulting from applications of their ideas (see, for example, *Vietnam Courier,* 1987, no. 7, p. 5). In August 1987 private vehicles were allowed to carry passengers and freight, with fares regulated for established routes, but free for special services. In 1986 the Hanoi Party Committee permitted registered individuals to have up to five employees (Stern 1987: 480). By late 1985 the 'private and individual sector' (including craftsmen, peasants who have not yet joined co-operatives, small traders, individual suppliers of services, and self-employed people) produced one-third of the gross social product and accounted for 32.7 per cent of national income; the sector provided a living for about one-third of the population (*Vietnam Courier*, 1987, no. 4, p. 14). Since 1985 there have been joint stores between the state and private individuals (Stern 1987: 487). Hiebert reports on a Hanoi workshop with 30 employees, an example of the private firms stemming from the relaxation of controls there (*FEER*, 28 July 1988, p. 20). The Rising Sun Torch enterprise, producing battery-free torches, is a family firm that contracts out to some 1,000 people working in their own homes the inputs needed to produce the final product (reports by David Watts in *The Times*, 11 November 1987, p. 8, and Murray Hiebert, *FEER*, 17 March 1988, p. 20).

The latest decree ensures that 'all commercial and service activities undertaken by economic instititutions in the country are protected according to state law....Individuals are entitled to pool their capital and set up their own business organizations or privately run corporations, which, however, must be registered.' All individuals and businesses are entitled to loans and accounts at the state bank, and all products produced by legitimate businesses can be distributed freely around the country (reported in *IHT*, 3 January 1989, p. 2).

Conclusion

Unlike North Korea and the GDR, Vietnam has managed to reunite the country, in 1975, after decades of war against the Japanese, the French, and the Americans. This third largest socialist country in terms of population is currently in a desperate situation, with rampant inflation, debt repayment problems and severe food shortages among other things. Reforms have been introduced, such as the 1981 'group contract' system in agriculture, some limited experiments in the industrial sector and a recent expansion of the private sector (Table 16.2). The new General Secretary Nguyen Van Linh (appointed December 1986) has made a Gorbachev-type attack on problems and adopted a recognizable set of solutions. It is not yet clear how far the reforms will go, but Linh has stressed that a 'complete and radical socio-economic renovation' is needed in order to eliminate what he calls a 'subsidy-based, bureaucratic centralism mechanism'. The reform proposals call for the creation of a planning mechanism based on 'socialist cost accounting and business activities'. This seemingly involves a greater indirect control of the economy via economic levers, and enhanced decision-making powers to production units. The current 1986–90 plan pays particular attention to food grain and foodstuffs, consumer goods, and exports. Vietnam is extremely anxious to expand links with the West, held back by political factors such as troops stationed in Kampuchea. The withdrawal of these troops and the seeking of improved relations with China in general are key elements in the aim of switching resources into the civilian sector of the economy. It is interesting to speculate on the relative influence of the Soviet and Chinese reforms. The latter's influence is clearly to be seen in Vietnam's agrarian policy.

Table 16.2 Vietnam: statistical survey

Private and individual sector (1985)	
(including farmers who have not joined co-operatives)	32.7% of national income
Population (1988)	65 million

Source: Vietnam Courier (1987), no. 4, p. 14.
For growth rates of national income and agricultural output, 'paddy and paddy equivalent' in Mt, inflation, and foreign debt, see Table 16.1, this volume.

Postscript

There are reports of success on the inflation front. Murray Hiebert (*FEER*, 6 July 1989, p. 53), for example, gives an average monthly figure of around 3.5 per cent for April and May 1989.

Notes

1. The standing army, some 1.1 million regular troops, is backed up by 3 million reservists. The navy, naval infantry, and air defence unit comprise 150,000; there is also a border defence force of 60,000 and various paramilitary groups totalling 1.5 million (Michael Richardson, quoting Thayer, in *IHT*, 6 December 1988, p. 1). Richardson also quotes Western estimates of one-third to one-half of the budget being devoted to defence, although it should be noted that since 1975 the army has been actively involved in civilian work (p. 6). Vietnam itself puts the standing army at 750,000 (April 1989), and plans to reduce it to 500,000. In May 1988 a detailed staged withdrawal programme was announced for Vietnamese troops from Kampuchea (now Cambodia once again), with an end-of-1990 deadline (since moved forward to September 1989). In November 1988 Laos claimed that all Vietnamese troops had been withdrawn, having been there since 1975.
2. The *EIU* (*Country Profile*, 1987–88, pp. 9–10), provides further demographic details: crude birth rate, 47 per thousand in 1960 and 35 per thousand in 1984; crude death rate, 21 and 8, respectively; infant mortality, 157 and 50, respectively; 1.5 to 2 million deaths from military action, 1960–80, and 750,000 emigrants after 1975; life expectancy, 43 years in 1960 and 65 in 1984; 85 per cent of the population literate. In October 1988 a tougher population control policy was announced (the previous one based on taxes and economic incentives was ineffective). Normally, a family with more than two children will be penalized by contributing towards education and medical care, extra community work, a lower priority in housing waiting lists or building land allocation, and higher rents for more living space. More than three children means the inability to move into cities. Free

contraceptives and abortion will be available and a 'commendation and award scheme' will encourage vasectomy and sterilization. Ethnic minorities in the northern mountains and central highlands are permitted three children (Hiebert, *FEER*, 8 December 1988, p. 32).

3. See *Vietnam Courier*, 1987, nos 1 and 2, and Nguyen Van Linh (1987) for his major speeches at the Sixth Congress of the CPV, 15–18 December 1986, and at the Second Plenum of the Central Committee, 1–9 April 1987. Linh was dropped from the Politburo in 1982 for opposing the rapid socialization of South Vietnam after 1975, but he remained the Party Secretary for Ho Chi Minh City and his successful economic policies led to his reinstatement as a Politburo member in June 1985.
4. See Spoor (1988) for an analysis of the mounting budget deficits. In 1978 budgetary revenue derived from taxes (20 per cent) and most of the remainder from state enterprises in the form of turnover tax, profit transfers, and depreciation funds.

Part four

Conclusion

Chapter seventeen

Summing up

About 1.6 billion of the world's population of 5.1 billion (mid-1988) reside in the 14 socialist countries studied here and this is leaving aside others such as Nicaragua, Burma, Kampuchea, Laos, and Ethiopia, which could justifiably be included within the fold. On the eve of their socialist development only the East German and Czechoslovak economies were industrially advanced. The traditional Soviet economic model was initially imposed upon or adopted by them all regardless of circumstances, but today there is a perhaps surprising variety of economic systems to be found.

The planning changes are not easy to summarize, but a crude ranking may be attempted. At one extreme are Albania and North Korea with their old-fashioned command economies, while Cuba is retrenching and even retrogressing in some respects; in all three moral incentives play an important role. At the other extreme Yugoslavia and Hungary are in the front line of reform and the future points firmly in the direction of the market, especially for the former. China has made spectacular changes, even though the reform programme is currently stuck in the 'rectification' process. On paper Poland offers Hungarian-style changes and even more radical ones in some respects, while the Soviet proposals, if implemented in full, would signify a marked departure from the traditional system. Vietnam shows genuine willingness to get to grips with its problems. Mongolia's modest proposals may be expected to blossom in the future under the all-pervading Soviet influence. Czechoslovakia and Bulgaria are dragging their feet, while the GDR and Romania are the most reluctant to introduce radical reforms.

Some of the reasons for the reforms have been spelled out in detail, such as the infamous micro-economic problems, the 'scattering' of investment resources, and declining rates of growth, but stress should also be laid on the exogenous pressure exerted by the achievements of the leading Western countries. The growing technological gap is a cause of particular anxiety to the socialist countries. Even within the group pressure builds to especially emulate China's achievements.

A number of current problems have also been highlighted, such as inflation and foreign debt. As regards the former, the picture varies significantly. Vietnam's recent record is extraordinary, with figures of over 700 per cent in 1986, perhaps up to 1,000 per cent the following year and an estimated 700 per cent for 1988. Yugoslavia's annual rate was 290 per cent in January 1989 and Poland's may have been 70 per cent in 1988. Hungary achieved about 17.0 per cent in 1988, and China's 18.5 per cent in 1988 has contributed enormously to the 'rectification' process. Likewise, the foreign debt situation is far from homogeneous, with Yugoslavia, Poland, Hungary, Cuba, North Korea, and Vietnam experiencing various degrees of repayment difficulties. Romania's extreme austerity measures stem from Ceausescu's concern to eliminate the debt as soon as possible (he announced that this had been fully paid off by the end of March 1989).

As far as particular aspects of the economy are concerned, the roles of private enterprise and foreign capital are arousing considerable interest:

1. Socialized agriculture is still dominant in general, although Poland and Yugoslavia stand out as exceptions (see Table 17.1). The distinctions between private and socialized activities, however, are becoming increasingly blurred. For example, the household responsibility system now characterizes Chinese agriculture, although land is still publically owned and state quotas are imposed. If adopted on as wide a scale as promised, the Soviet leasing system would represent a distinct shift away from the traditional system. Hungary and Bulgaria show how to achieve an effective symbiosis between private and socialized agriculture, as when co-operatives provide both services for the private plots and credits to construct buildings in which animals can be raised under contract.

Table 17.1 The socialist countries: private agriculture (mid-1980s)

Country	Agricultural land (%)	Agricultural output (%)
Albania (Private plots allowed within co-operatives)	Not known	Not known
Bulgaria	13.0	25.0
China	Dominated by household responsibility systems	
Czechoslovakia	3.0	10.0
Cuba	8.0	< 10.0
GDR	9.0	3.7 (Excluding private plots)
Hungary	13.0	34.0
Mongolia	10.0	22.0 (of livestock)
North Korea	Not known	Not known
Poland	72.0	78.0
Romania	9.0	Not known
Soviet Union	3.0 (Sown area)	25.0
Vietnam	Not known	Not known
Yugoslavia	80.0	69.0

Source: Compiled by author from sources used in the text.

2. In non-agricultural activities the socialized sector is even more typically dominant and likely to remain so. The basic production unit in industry is still the state-owned enterprise ('socially owned' in Yugoslavia), one that has tended to increase in size over time. Treatment of the private sector varies considerably (see Table 17.2). At one extreme Albania does not permit private enterprise in industry, while in Bulgaria, Czechoslovakia, North Korea, Romania, and Cuba the private non-agricultural sector is not flourishing. Hungary, the Soviet Union, Vietnam, China, and the GDR, on the other hand, are, to varying degrees, actively encouraging it. Poland's 1 January 1989 legislation even awards it, in theory, equal status with the state and co-operative sectors. Again, however, the appearance of stocks and shares of various sorts in countries like China and Hungary is beginning to blur distinctions.

Table 17.2 The socialist countries: the private (legal) non-agricultural sector

Country	Percentage of national income	
Albania	Zero	
Bulgaria	Small	
China (1987)	3.6 (Industrial output)	13.0 (Retail sales)
Czechoslovakia	Small	
Cuba	Small	
GDR (1985)	2.8 (Including private farmers)	
Hungary (1984)	5.5	
Mongolia	Not known	
North Korea	Small	
Poland (1987)	7.0	
Romania	Small	
Soviet Union	Small	
Vietnam (1986)	32.0 (Including private farmers)	
Yugoslavia	5.7	

Source: Compiled by the author from sources used in the text.

3. Most of the socialist countries have now passed legislation permitting direct foreign investment from the West in order to obtain capital goods embodying modern technologies and managerial and marketing skills. Mongolia is contemplating such legislation. Even wholly foreign-owned enterprises are now allowed or are to be allowed in China, Hungary, Poland, and Yugoslavia: the Soviet Union itself is considering them. In Albania, on the other hand, there is a constitutional ban even on foreign credits, while the GDR offers no promise of acceptance of joint ventures – at the moment at least. China's 'open door' policy has been the most successful, but, in general, Western capital has shown reluctance. The reasons are not too difficult to determine, given problems such as input supply in planned economies and profit repatriation in situations where

domestic sales earn inconvertible currencies.

Some general comments may be in order, by way of conclusion:

1. The present is, of course, only understandable in the perspective of history. Albania's and Cuba's policies today have to be seen in the light of a history of foreign domination, and it is no coincidence that North Korea and the GDR, both the poorer half of a divided nation, are reluctant reformers, given that this would be tantamount to acceptance of having lost the race. It is also worth remembering, on the other hand, that the GDR shows that a relative success can be made of a command economy, given factors such as a tradition of skill, discipline and hard work, although it is helped by concessions from the FRG.
2. A successful call for increased individual initiative, responsibility, and performance almost invariably requires material incentives in the form of improved supplies of consumer goods and services. The lesson here seems to be that China and Hungary may have the answer in reforming agriculture first and in rapidly expanding the private sector.
3. With the gradualist approach to reform there is the danger that new elements may disturb the operation of the existing system during the transitional stage. The Soviet Union itself seems to be such a case.
4. It is probably the case that political liberalization is a precondition for successful economic reform, in order to release the individual traits mentioned above. Poland seems to need a form of 'social contract', whereby power is conceded in return for public acceptance of austerity. China, however, makes us pause, since political change has noticeably lagged behind economic reform. Nevertheless, economic reform tends to lead to at least demands for political liberalization, and sustained economic progress probably needs these demands to be met.

One thing is certain. Economic life in the socialist countries is a boiling cauldron. Only a small glimpse has been afforded here.

Bibliography

Periodicals and reports

Abecor Country Reports are distributed in Britain by Barclays Bank on behalf of an association of European banks. The Vietnam Courier is published in Hanoi.
Periodicals and reports mentioned in the text are abbreviated as follows:

CDSP	Current Digest of the Soviet Press
EEN	Eastern Europe Newsletter
EIU	Economist Intelligence Unit
FEER	Far Eastern Economic Review
FT	Financial Times
IHT	International Herald Tribune

Books and journals

Abalkin, L. (1988) 'Restructuring the system and methods of planned management', *Problems of Economics*, vol.XXX, no. 9.
Adam, J. (1987) 'The Hungarian economic reform of the 1980s', *Soviet Studies*, vol. XXXIX, no. 4.
—— (1989) *Economic Reforms in the Soviet Union and Eastern Europe since the 1960s*, London: Macmillan.
Aganbegyan, A. (1988) 'The Economics of perestroika', *International Affairs* (London), vol. 64, no. 2.
—— (1988a) *The Challenge: Economics of Perestroika*, London: Hutchinson.
Amann, R. and Cooper. J. (1982) *Industrial Innovation in the Soviet Union*, New Haven, CT: Yale University Press.
Arnot, B. (1988) *Controlling Soviet Labour*, London: Macmillan.
Arthur Anderson (1984) *The People's Republic of China: Perspectives*, London.
Ash, R. (1988) 'The evolution of agricultural policy', *The China Quarterly*, no. 116.
Åslund, A. (1984) 'The Functioning of Private Enterprise in Poland', *Soviet Studies*, vol. XXXVI, no. 3.
—— (1985) *Private Enterprise in Eastern Europe*, London: Macmillan.
Azicri, M. (1988) *Cuba: Politics, Economics and Society*, London: Pinter.
Babić, M. and Primorac, E. (1986) 'Some Causes of the Yugoslav External Debt', *Soviet Studies*, vol.XXXVIII, no. 4.
Barkin, D. (1981) 'Cuban agriculture: a strategy of economic development' in Horowitz (ed.).

Batt, J. (1988) *Economic Reform and Political Change in Eastern Europe: A Comparison of the Czechoslovak and Hungarian Experiences*, London: Macmillan.

Bauer, T. (1988) 'Economic reforms within and beyond the state sector', *American Economic Review*, Papers and Proceedings, (May).

Baum, R. (1986) 'China in 1985: the greening of the revolution', *Asian Survey*, vol.XXVI, no. 1.

Baylis, T. (1986) 'Explaining the GDR's economic strategy', *International Organisation*, vol. 40, no. 2.

Bechtold, H. and Helfer, A. (1987) 'Stagnation problems in socialist economies' in Gey, Kosta, and Quaisser (eds).

Beresford, M. (1988) *Vietnam: Politics, Economics and Society*, London: Pinter.

Bergson, A. (ed.) (1953) *Soviet Economic Growth*, New York: Row, Peterson.

—— (1961) *The Real National Income of Soviet Russia since 1928*, Cambridge, MA: Harvard University Press.

—— (1985) 'A visit to China's economic reform', *Comparative Economic Studies*, vol.XXVII, no. 2.

Berliner, J. (1976) *The Innovation Decision in Soviet Industry*, Cambridge, MA: MIT Press.

Bernado, R. (1981) 'Moral stimulation and labour allocation in Cuba' in Horowitz (ed.).

Bethkenhagen, J. (1987) 'The GDR's energy policy and its implications for the intensification drive', *Studies in Comparative Communism*, vol.XX, no. 1.

Betz, H. (1989) 'Recent changes in the system of management in the GDR' in Adam (1989).

Bideleux, R. (1985) *Communism and Development*, London: Methuen.

Birman, I. (1978) 'From the achieved level', *Soviet Studies*. vol.XXXI, no. 2.

Blazyca, G. (1980a) 'An assessment of Polish economic development in the 1970s', *European Economic Review*, vol. 14.

—— (1980b) 'Industrial structure and the economic problems of industry in a centrally planned economy: the Polish Case', *Journal of Industrial Economics*, (March).

—— (1982) 'The degeneration of central planning in Poland' in Woodall, J (ed.) *Policy and Politics in Contemporary Poland: Reform and Crisis*, London: Pinter.

—— (1985) 'The Polish economy under martial law – a dissenting view', *Soviet Studies*, vol. 37, no. 3.

—— (1986) *Poland to the 1990s: Retreat or Reform*, London: EIU (August).

—— (1987) 'The new round of economic reform in Eastern Europe', *National Westminster Review* (November).

Bleaney, M. (1988) *Do Socialist Economies Work? The Soviet and East European Experience*, Oxford: Basil Blackwell.

Bova, R. (1987) 'On perestroyka: the role of workplace participation', *Problems of Communism*, (July–August).

Bowers, S. (1989) 'Stalinism in Albania: domestic affairs under Enver Hoxha', *East European Quarterly*, vol.XXII, no. 4.

Boyd, M. (1988) 'The performance of private and socialist agriculture in Poland: the effects of policy and organization', *Journal of Comparative Economics*, vol. 12, no. 1.

Brabant, J. (1980) *Socialist Economic Integration*, Cambridge: Cambridge University Press.

Brezinski, H. (1987) 'The second economy in the GDR – pragmatism is gaining ground', *Studies in Comparative Communism*, vol.XX, no. 1.

Brodzka, T. (1987) 'Stage two of the reform', *Polish Perspectives*, vol.XXX, no. 3.

Brus, W. (1982) 'The economic policy of Poland', in Höhmann, Nove, and Seidenstecher (eds).

Bryson, P. (1984) *The Consumer under Socialist Planning: the East German Case*, New York: Praeger.

Bryson, P. and Melzer, M. (1987) 'The Kombinat in GDR economic organisation' in Jeffries, Melzer, and Breuning.

Buck, H.F. (1987) 'The GDR financial system', Jeffries, Melzer, and Breuning.

Cavoski, K. (1988) Comment in Winiecki (1988a).

Cerny, R. (1988) 'The restructuring of the economic mechanism in agriculture', *Czechoslovak Economic Digest*, no. 4.

Cervinka, A. (1987) 'The State Enterprise Act', *Czechoslovak Economic Digest*, no. 6.

Chamberlain, H. (1987) 'Party-management relations in Chinese industry: some political dimensions of economic reform', *The China Quarterly*, no. 112 (December).

Chan, T. (1986) 'China's price reform in the 1980s', discussion paper no. 78, Department of Economics, University of Hong Kong.

Chelstowski, S. (1988) 'The second stage scenario', *Polish Perspectives*, vol.XXXI, no. 1.

Cheung, S. (1986) *Will China Go Capitalist?*, London: Institute of Economic Affairs (Hobart Papers).

Childs, D. (1987) *East Germany to the 1990s: Can it Resist Glasnost?*, London: EIU (December).

Chung, J. (1983) 'Economic planning in North Korea' in Scalapino and Kim.

—— (1986) 'Foreign trade of North Korea: performance, policy and prospects' in Scalapino and Lee.

CIA Analyst (1986) 'Polish agriculture: policy and prospects' in US Congress, Joint Economic Committee, Washington, DC: US Government Printing Office.

Cochrane, N. (1986) 'Yugoslav agricultural performance in the 1980s and prospects for 1990', US Congress, Joint Economic Committee, Washington DC: Government Printing Office.

—— (1988) 'The private sector in East European agriculture', *Problems of Communism*, (March-April).

Collier, I. (1987) 'Intensification in the GDR: a postscript', *Studies in Comparative Communism*, vol.XX, no. 1.

Comisso, D. and Marer, P (1986) 'The economics and politics of reform in Hungary', *International Organisation*, vol. 40, no. 2.

Conyngham, W. (1982) *The Modernisation of Soviet Industrial Industrial Management*, Cambridge: Cambridge University Press.

Cook, E. (1984) 'Agricultural reform in Poland: background and prospects', *Soviet Studies*, vol.XXXVI, no. 3.

—— (1986a) 'Prospects for Bulgarian agriculture in the 1980s', US Congress, Joint Economic Committee, Washington DC: Government Printing Office.

—— (1986b) 'Prospects for Polish agriculture', US Congress, Joint Economic Committee.

Cornelsen, D. (1987) 'The GDR Economy in the eighties: economic strategy and structural adjustments', *Studies in Comparative Communism*, vol.XX, no. 1.

Costa, N. (1988) 'Albania: a nation of contradictions', *East European Quarterly*, vol.XXII, no. 2.

Crane, K. (1986) 'Foreign trade decision-making under balance of payments pressure: Poland versus Hungary', US Congress, Joint Economic Committee, Washington DC: Government Printing Office.

Crowther, W. (1988) *The Political Economy of Romanian Socialism*, New York:

Praeger.

Csaba, L. (1988) 'CMEA and the challenge of the 1980s', *Soviet Studies*, vol.XL, no. 2.

Cumings, B. (1988) 'Korea', *The Guardian*, 17 June 1988, p. 14 (author of *The Origins of the Korean War*, Vols 1 and 2. Princeton, NJ: Princeton University Press.

Cummings, R. (1986) 'Agricultural performance and prospects in Czechoslovakia through the Eighties', US Congress, Joint Economic Committee, Washington, DC: Government Printing Office.

Debardeleben, J. (1985) *The Environment and Marxism-Leninism: the Soviet and East German Experience*, Boulder, CO: Westview Press.

Delfs, R. (1987) 'China 1987', *FEER*, 19 March.

Dellin, L. (1970) 'Bulgaria's economic reform', *Problems of Communism* (September-October).

Dennis, M. (1988) *The German Democratic Republic: Politics, Economics and Society*, London: Pinter.

DIW Handbuch (1985), Hamburg: Rowohlt.

Dominguez, J. (1986) 'Cuba in the 1980s', *Foreign Affairs*, vol. 65, no. 1.

Donnithorne, A. (1967) *China's Economic System*, London: Allen and Unwin.

Do Rosario (1987), *FEER*, 16 July.

—— (1987) 'China's Special Economic Zones', *FEER*, 1 October.

Duiker, W. (1986) 'Vietnam in 1985: searching for solutions', *Asian Survey*, vol.XXVI, no. 1.

Dyker, D. (1981) *The Process of Investment in the Soviet Union*, Cambridge: Cambridge University Press.

—— (1985) *The Future of the Soviet Planning System*, London: Croom Helm.

—— (ed) (1987) *The Soviet Union under Gorbachev: Prospects for Reform*, Chapters 3, 'Industrial planning', and 4, 'Agriculture', London: Croom Helm.

—— (1988) 'Restructuring and "radical reform": the articulation of investment demand' in Linz and Moskoff.

Ebon, M. (1987) in *FEER*, 5 March.

Eckstein, S. (1981) 'The debourgeoisement of Cuban cities' in Horowitz (ed).

Economist (1985) Survey on Comecon, 20 April.

—— (1988) Survey on the Soviet Economy, 9–15 April.

Economist Intelligence Unit (EIU) (1987–88) *Country Profile*: China; North Korea; East Germany; Cuba ; Czechoslovakia; Hungary; Indochina (Vietnam) ; Romania; Soviet Union; Yugoslavia.

Edwards, G. (1985) *GDR Society and Institutions*, London: Macmillan.

Elek, P. (1989) 'Symbiotical coordination of the plan and private sector in Eastern Europe and China since the 1970s', *East European Quarterly*, vol.XXII, no. 4.

Ellman, M. (1986) 'Economic reform in China', *International Affairs*, vol. 62, no. 3.

—— (1989) *Socialist Planning*, 2nd edn, London: Cambridge University Press.

Esterline, J. (1987) 'Vietnam in 1986', *Asian Survey*, vol.XXVII, no. 1.

—— (1988) 'Vietnam in 1987', *Asian Survey*, vol.XXVIII, no. 1.

Estrin, S. (1983) *Self-Management: Economic Theory and Yugoslav Practice*, Cambridge: Cambridge University Press.

Estrin, S., Moore, R. and Svejnar, J. (1988) 'Market imperfections, labour management and earnings in a developing country: theory and evidence for Yugoslavia', *Quarterly Journal of Economics*, vol.CIII, no. 3.

Fallenbuchl, Z. (1984) 'The Polish economy under martial law', *Soviet Studies*, vol.XXXVI, no. 4.

—— (1986) 'The Economic Crisis in Poland and Prospects for Recovery' in US Congress, Joint Economic Committee, Washington DC: US Government Printing Office.

Fang Lizhi (1989) 'Long march to democracy', *The Independent*, 18 January.

Fangui, Huang (1987) 'China's introduction of foreign technology and external trade: analysis and options', *Asian Survey*, vol.XXVII, no. 5.

Federal Ministry for Inner-German Relations (1985) *DDR Handbuch*, Bonn.

Feiwell, G. (1968) *New Economic Patterns in Czechoslovakia*, New York: IASP.

—— (1979) 'Economic reform in Bulgaria', *Osteuropa Wirtschaft*, no. 2.

—— (1982) 'Economic development and planning in Bulgaria in the 1970s' in Höhmann, Nove, and Seidenstecher.

Fforde, A. (1987) 'Industrial development in the Democratic Republic of Vietnam', London: Birkbeck College Discussion Paper 2.

Fforde, A. and Paine, S. (1987) *The Limits of National Liberation: Economic Management and the Re-unification of the Democratic Republic of Vietnam*, London: Croom Helm.

Fidler, S. (1988) 'Banks at odds over North Korean deal', *The Financial Times*, 19 July 1988, p. 25.

Field, R. (1984) 'Changes in Chinese industry since 1978', *The China Quarterly* (December).

Filtzer, D. (1989) 'The Soviet wage reform of 1956–1962', *Soviet Studies*, vol.XLI, no. 1.

Financial Times (various surveys)
>   Bulgaria: 7 December 1984; 27 October 1988.
>   China: 9 December 1985; 20 August 1986; 5 September 1986; 22 September 1986; 29 September 1986; 30 September 1986; 18 December 1986; 18 December 1987.
>   Counter-trade: 11 February 1986; East-West Trade: 13 December 1988.
>   Cuba: 17 February 1989.
>   Czechoslovakia: 23 October 1985.
>   Hungary: 11 September 1987.
>   Yugoslavia: 18 June 1984; 21 December 1984; 21 June 1985; 17 December 1985; 17 June 1986; 16 December 1986; 22 December 1987; 22 June, 1988; 6 December 1988.

Finkelstein, D. (1987) 'Vietnam: a revolution in crisis', *Asian Survey*, vol.XXVII, no. 9.

Fitzgerald, F. (1988) 'The "Sovietization of Cuba thesis" Revisited' in Zimbalist (ed.).

Gagnon, V. (1987) 'Gorbachev and the collective contract brigade', *Soviet Studies*, vol.XXXIX, no. 1.

Garland, J. (1987) 'The GDR's strategy for intensification', *Studies in Comparative Communism*, vol.XX, no. 1.

Garvy, G. (1977) *Money, Financial Flows and Credit in the Soviet Union*, Cambridge, MA: Ballinger.

Gey, P. (1987) 'The Cuban economy under the new system of management and planning: success or failure?' in Gey, Kosta and Quaisser.

Gey, P., Kosta, J., and Quaisser, W. (1987) *Crisis and Reform in Socialist Economies*, London: Westview Press.

Ghai, D., Kay, C., and Peek, P. (1988) *Labour and Development in Rural Cuba*, London: Macmillan.

Gilberg, T. (1975) *Modernization in Romania since World War II*, New York: Praeger.

Gold, T. (1989) 'Urban private business in China', *Studies in Comparative Communism*, vol. XXII, nos 2 and 3.

Goldman, M., and Goldman, M. (1988) 'Soviet and Chinese economic reforms', *Foreign Affairs*, vol. 66, no. 3

Gomulka, S. and Rostowski, J. (1984) 'The reformed Polish economic system 1982–3', *Soviet Studies*, vol. 36, no. 3.

Gorbachev, M. (1987) *Perestroika: New Thinking for Our Country and the World*,

London: Collins; New York: Harper & Row.

Granick, D. (1975) *Enterprise Guidance in Eastern Europe*, Princeton, NJ: Princeton University Press.

Green, E. (1986) 'China and Mongolia: recurring trends and prospects', *Asian Survey*, vol.XXVI, no. 12.

Gregory, P.and Stuart, R. (1986) *Soviet Economic Structure and Performance*, 3rd edn, New York: Harper & Row (2nd edn, 1981).

Guardian (various surveys)

> China: China 13 October 1986; Regional China-Jiangsu and Guangdong 16 October 1987; Shanghai 19 November 1987.
>
> Hungary: 31 October 1985; 20 October 1986; 5 May 1988.
>
> Soviet Union: 6 November 1987; 24 June 1988; 13 December 1988; 5 April 1989.
>
> Yugoslavia: 27 October 1986; Slovenia, 16 May 1988.

Hagelberg, G. (1981) 'Cuba's sugar policy' in Horowitz (ed.).

Halpern, N. (1985) 'China's industrial economic reform: the question of strategy', *Asian Survey*, vol.XXV, no. 10.

Hamel, H. and Leipold, H. (1987) 'Economic reform in the GDR: causes and effects' in Jeffries, Melzer, and Breuning (eds).

Hanson, P. (1989) 'The Soviet economy at the end of year IV', *Detente*, no. 14.

Hare, P. (1987) 'Resource allocation without prices: the Soviet economy', *The Economic Review*, vol. 5, no. 2.

Hare, P. , Radice, H. and Swain, N. (1981) *Hungary: a Decade of Reform*, London: Allen and Unwin.

Harrison, S. (1987), *FEER*, 3 December.

Hartford, K. (1985) 'Hungarian agriculture: a model for the socialist world?', *World Development*, vol. 13, no. 1.

—— (1987) 'Socialist countries in the world food system: the Soviet Union, Hungary and China', *Food Research Institute Studies*, vol.XX, no. 3.

Heaton, W. (1986) 'Mongolia in 1985: from plan to plan', *Asian Survey*, vol.XXVI, no. 1.

—— (1987) 'Mongolia in 1986: new plan, new situation', *Asian Survey*, vol.XXVII, no. 1.

Heinrich, H-G. (1986) *Hungary: Politics, Economics and Society*, London: Francis Pinter.

Hewett, E. (1988) *Reforming the Soviet Economy: Equality versus Efficiency*, Washington DC: the Brookings Institution.

Hiebert, M. (1987a) *FEER*, 7 May.

—— (1987b) *FEER*, 1 October.

Höhmann, H-H., Nove, A. and Seidenstecher, G. (eds) (1982) *The East European Economies in the 1970s*, London: Butterworths.

Holesovsky, V. (1968) 'Financial aspects of the Czechoslovak reforms' in Bornstein, M. (ed.) *Plan and Market*, New Haven, CT: Yale University Press.

—— (1973) 'Planning and the Market in the Czechoslovak Reform' in Bornstein, M. (ed.) *Plan and Market*, New Haven, CT: Yale University Press.

Holzman, F. (1976) *International Trade under Communism*, New York: Basic Books.

—— (1987) *The Economics of Soviet Bloc Trade and Finance*, Boulder, CO and London: Westview Press.

Hongkong and Shanghai Banking Corporation (1985) *The People's Republic of China*.

—— (1986) *China Briefing*, no. 23.

—— (1987) *China Briefing*, no. 26.

—— (1987) *China Briefing*, no. 27.

Horowitz, I. (ed.) (1981) *Cuban Communism*, 4 edn, New Brunswick and London:

Transaction Books.

Hristov, E. (1987) 'Perestroika', *Bulgaria* (September-October).

Hu, Teh-wei., Li, Ming., and Shi, Shuzhong (1988) 'Analysis of wages and bonus payments among Tianjin urban workers', *The China Quarterly*, no. 113.

International Herald Tribune (various surveys)
China: 15 September 1986; 9 July 1986.
Hungary: 12 June 1985.
Soviet Union: 7–8 November 1985; 7 November 1988.

Ishihara, K. (1987) 'Planning and the market in China', *The Developing Economies*, vol.XXV, no. 4.

Jackson, M. (1986a) 'Recent economic performance and policy in Bulgaria' in US Congress, Joint Economic Committee, Washington DC: Government Printing Office.

—— (1986b) 'Romania's debt crisis: its causes and consequences', US Congress, Joint Economic Committee.

Jackson, S (1986) 'Reform of State Enterprise Management in China' in *The China Quarterly*, No. 107.

Jacobsen, H-D. (1987) 'The foreign trade and payments of the GDR' in Jeffries, Melzer, and Breuning (eds).

Jae Ho Chung (1988) 'South Korea-China economic relations', *Asian Survey*, vol.XXVIII, no. 10.

James Capel Hong Kong Research (1988) *China's Thirteenth Party Congress*, London.

Janeba, V. (1988) 'Experience gained from the comprehensive experiment', *Czechoslovak Economic Digest*, no. 4.

Jarret, K. (1988) 'Mongolia in 1987', *Asian Survey*, vol.XXVIII, no. 1.

Jeffries, I. (ed.) (1981) *The Industrial Enterprise in Eastern Europe*, New York: Praeger.

Jeffries, I., Melzer, M. (eds) and Breuning, E. (advisory ed.) (1987) *The East German Economy*, London: Croom Helm.

Jerome, R. (1988) 'Sources of economic growth in Hungary', *East European Quarterly*, vol.XXII, no. 1.

Jiménez, A. (1987) 'Worker incentives in Cuba', *World Development*, vol. 15, no. 1.

Johnson, D. (1988) 'Economic reforms in the People's Republic of China', *Economic Development and Cultural Change*, vol. 36, no. 3.

—— (1988a) 'Agriculture' in Cracraft, A. (ed.) *The Soviet Union Today*, Chicago, IL: The University of Chicago Press.

Jones, C. (1988) *The Banker* (February).

Juviler, P. , Kimura, H. (eds) (1988) *Gorbachev's Reforms: US and Japanese Assessments*, New York: De Gruyter.

Kaczurba, J. (1988) 'The external context', *Polish Perspectives*, vol.XXXI, no. 1.

Kaplan, N. (1953) 'Capital formation and allocation' in Bergson (ed.).

Kaser, M. (1981) 'The industrial enterprise in Bulgaria' in Jeffries (ed.).

—— (1986) 'Albania under and after Enver Hoxha', US Congress, Joint Economic Committee, Washington DC: Government Printing Office.

—— (1987a) 'One economy, two systems: parallels between Soviet and Chinese reforms', *International Affairs*, vol. 63, no. 3.

—— (1987b) 'Mongolia and the Asian wave of socialist economic reform', paper presented at the conference on 'Mongolia Today', 27 November, at the SOAS, University of London.

Katsenelinboigen, A. (1977) 'Coloured markets in the Soviet Union', *Soviet Studies*, vol. 29, no. 1.

Kay, C. (1988) 'Cuban economic reforms and collectivisation', *Third World Quarterly*, vol. 10, no. 3.

Keren, M. (1973) 'The New Economic System in the GDR', *Soviet Studies*, vol.XXIV, no. 4.

Kerner, A. (1988) 'Reflections on the draft bill on the state enterprise', *Czechoslovak Economic Digest*, no. 2.

Kerpel, E., and Young, D. (1988) *Hungary to 1993: Risks and Rewards of Reform*, London: EIU.

Kimura, T. (1986) 'Vietnam-ten years of economic struggle', *Asian Survey*, vol.XXVI, no. 10.

Klein, W. (1987) 'The role of the GDR in Comecon: some economic aspects' in Jeffries, Melzer, and Breuning (eds).

Koh, B. (1988) 'North Korea in 1987', *Asian Survey*, vol.XXVIII, no. 1.

Kolankiewicz, G. (1987) 'Polish trade unions "normalised" , *Problems of Communism* (November-December).

Kolankiewicz, G. and Lewis, P. (1988) *Poland: Politics, Economics and Society*, London: Pinter.

Kornai, J. (1986) 'The Hungarian reform process: visions, hopes and reality', *Journal of Economic Literature*, vol.XXIX (December).

Korzec, M. (1988) 'Contract labour, the "right to work" and new labour laws in the People's Republic of China', *Comparative Economic Studies*, vol.XXX, no. 2.

Kosta, J. (1987) 'The Chinese economic reform: approaches, results and prospects' in Gey, Kosta, and Quaisser.

Kostakov, V. (1988) 'Labour problems in the light of perestroyka', *Soviet Economy*, vol. 4 (Jan-March).

Kroll, H. (1988) 'The role of contracts in the Soviet economy', *Soviet Studies*, vol.XL, no. 3.

Kurakowski, S. (1988) *Poland: Stagnation, Collapse or Growth?*, London: Centre for Research into Communist Economies.

Kyn, O. (1970) 'The rise and fall of economic reforms in Czechoslovakia', *American Economic Review*, Papers and Proceedings.

Lampe, J. (1986) *The Bulgarian Economy in the Twentieth Century*, London: Croom Helm.

Lang, I., Csete, L. and Harnos, Z. (1988) 'The enterprisal system of an adjusting agriculture in Hungary', *European Review of Agricultural Economics*, 15 nos.2–3.

Lee, Hy-Sang (1988) 'North Korea's closed economy', *Asian Survey*, vol.XXVIII, no. 12.

Lee, P. (1986) 'Enterprise autonomy in post-Mao China: a case study of policy-making, 1978–83', *The China Quarterly*, no. 105.

Leptin, G. and Melzer, M. (1978) *Economic Reform in East German Industry*, Oxford: Oxford University Press..

Lin, J. (1988) 'The household responsibility system in China's agricultural reform; a theoretical and empirical study', *Economic Development and Cultural Change*, vol. 36, no. 3 (Supplement).

Ling, L. (1988) 'Intellectual responses to China's economic reforms', *Asian Survey*, vol.XXVIII, no. 5.

Linz, S. (1988) 'Managerial autonomy in Soviet firms', *Soviet Studies*, vol.XL, no. 2.

Linz, S., and Moskoff, W. (1988) (eds) *Reorganisation and Reform in the Soviet Union*, Armonk, NY and London: M.E.Sharpe.

Litvin, V. (1987) 'On perestroyka: reforming economic management', *Problems of Communism* (July-August).

Lockett, M. (1987) 'China's development strategy: the Seventh Five-Year Plan and after', *Euro-Asia Business Review*, (July).

Loncarevic, I. (1987) 'Prices and private agriculture in Yugoslavia', *Soviet Studies*, vol.XXXIV, no. 4.

Lydall, H. (1989) *Yugoslavia in Crisis*, Oxford: Clarendon Press.

MacEwan, A. (1981) *Revolution and Economic Development in Cuba*, London: Macmillan.

Makarov, V. (1988) 'On the strategy for implementing economic reform in the USSR', *American Economic Review*, Papers and Proceedings (May).

Marer, P. (1986a) 'Economic reform in Hungary: from central planning to regulated market', US Congress, Joint Economic Committee, Washington DC: Government Printing Office.

—— (1986b) 'Hungary's balance of payments crisis and response, 1978–84', US Congress, Joint Economic Committee.

—— (1986c) 'Economic policies and systems in Eastern Europe and Yugoslavia: commonalities and differences', US Congress, Joint Economic Committee.

Marr, D., and White, C. (eds) *Postwar Vietnam: Dilemmas in Socialist Development*, New York: Cornell University Southeast Asia Program.

Marrese, M. (1986a) 'Hungarian agriculture: moving in the right direction', US Congress, Joint Economic Committee.

—— (1986b) 'CMEA: effective but cumbersome political economy', *International Organisation*, vol. 40, no. 2.

Mason, D. (1988) 'Glasnost', perestroika and Eastern Europe', *International affairs*, vol. 64, no. 3.

Matousek, J. (1988) 'Draft law on cooperative farming', *Czechoslovak Economic Digest*, no. 1.

McCauley, M. (1983) *The German Democratic Republic since 1945*, London: Macmillan.

McConnell, C. and Brue, S. (1986) *Contemporary Labour Economics*, New York: McGraw-Hill.

McFarlane, B. (1988) *Yugoslavia: Politics, Economics and Society*, London: Pinter.

McIntyre, R. (1988) *Bulgaria: Politics, Economics and Society*, London: Pinter.

—— (1988a) 'The small enterprise and agricultural initiatives in Bulgaria: institutional invention without reform', *Soviet Studies*, vol.XL, no. 4.

Melzer, M. (1981) 'Combine formation and the role of the enterprise in East German Industry' in Jeffries (ed.).

—— (1982) 'The GDR – economic policy caught between pressure for efficiency and lack of ideas' in Höhmann, Nove, and Seidenstecher, (eds) *The East European Economies in the 1970s*, London: Butterworths.

—— (1983) 'Wandlungen im Preissystem der DDR' in G.Gutmann (ed.) *Das Wirtschaftssystem der DDR*, Stuttgart: Fischer Verlag.

—— (1987a) 'The pricing system of the GDR: principles and problems' in Jeffries, Melzer, and Breuning (eds).

—— (1987b) 'The new planning and steering mechanisms in the GDR', *Studies in Comparative Communism*, vol.XX, no. 1.

—— (1987c) 'The perfecting of the planning and steering mechanisms' in Jeffries, Melzer, and Breuning (eds).

Mencinger, J. (1987) 'The crisis and the reform of the Yugoslav economic system in the eighties' in Gey, Kosta, and Quaisser (eds).

Merkel, K. (1987) 'Agriculture' in Jeffries, Melzer, and Breuning (eds).

Mesa-Lago, C. (1981) 'Economics: realism and rationality' in Horowitz (ed.).

Michel, J. (1987) 'Economic exchanges specific to the two German states', *Studies in Comparative Communism*, vol.XX, no. 1.

Milivojevic, M. (1987) 'The Mongolian People's Army', *Armed Forces*, vol. 6, no. 12.

Mirkovic, D. (1987) 'Sociological reflections on Yugoslav participatory democracy and social ownership', *East European Quarterly*, vol.XXI, no. 3.

311

Miskiewicz, S. (1987) 'Social and economic rights in Eastern Europe', *Survey*, vol. 29, no. 4.

National Westminster Bank (1985) *China: an Economic Report* (October).

Nguyen Van Linh (1987) *Some Pressing Problems on the Distribution and Circulation of Goods*, Hanoi: Foreign Languages Publishing House.

Noti, S. (1987) 'The shifting position of Hungarian trade unions amidst social and economic reforms', *Soviet Studies*, vol.XXXIX, no. 1.

Nove, A. (1961) *The Soviet Economy*, London: Allen and Unwin.

—— (1981) 'The Soviet industrial enterprise' in Jeffries (ed.).

—— (1986) *The Soviet Economic System*, 3rd edn, London: Allen and Unwin.

—— (1987) 'Soviet agriculture: light at the end of the tunnel?', *Detente*, nos. 9–10.

Nuti, D. (1977) 'Large corporations and the reform of Polish industry', *Jahrbuch der Wirtschaft Osteuropas*.

—— (1981a) 'Industrial enterprises in Poland, 1973–80: economic policies and reforms' in Jeffries (ed.).

—— (1981b) 'The Polish crisis: economic factors and constraints' in Miliband, R., and Savile, J. (eds) *The Socialist Register*, London: Merlin Press.

Oanh, Nguyen Xuan (1988) *International Herald Tribune*, 13 December.

Ofer, G. (1987) 'Soviet economic growth: 1928–1985', *Journal of Economic Literature*, vol.XXV (December).

Pak, Ky-Hyuk (1983) 'Agricultural policy and development in North Korea' in Scalapino and Kim (eds).

Palovics, I., and Ujhelji, I. (1988) 'European agriculture in a global context: the European CMEA countries', *European Review of Agricultural Economics*, 15, nos.2–3.

Panova, G. (1988) 'Recent developments in Soviet banking', *National Westminster Bank Quarterly Review* (August).

Parker, J. (1987) 'A survey of China's economy', *The Economist*, 1 August.

Parsons, J. (1986) 'Credit contracts in the GDR: decentralised investment decisions in a planned economy', *Economics of Planning*, vol. 20, no. 1.

Pekshev, Y. (1988) *International Herald Tribune*, 7 November.

Pérez-López, J. (1986) 'Cuba's economy in the 1980s', *Problems of Communism*, vol.XXXV, no. 5.

Perkins, D. (1988) 'Reforming China's economic system', *Journal of Economic Literature*, vol.XXVI, no. 2.

Phillips, D. (1986) 'Special Economic Zones in China's modernisation: changing policies and changing fortunes', *National Westminster Review* (February).

Post, K. (1988) 'The working class in North Viet Nam and the launching of the building of socialism', *Journal of Asian and African Studies*, vol.XXIII, no. 1–2.

Prescott, L. (1986) 'Farming policy in Albania', *Albanian Life*, no. 2 (no. 35 in the series).

Prout, C. (1985) *Market Socialism in Yugoslavia*, London: Oxford University Press.

Prybyla, J. (1985) 'The Chinese economy: adjustment of the system or systemic reform?', *Asian Survey*, vol.XXV, no. 5.

—— (1986) 'China's economic experiment: from Mao to market', *Problems of Communism*, vol.XXXV, no. 1.

—— (1987) 'On some questions concerning price reform in the People's Republic of China', Working Paper 9–87–16, Pennsylvania State University.

Putterman, L. (1988) 'Group farming and work incentives in collective-era China', *Modern China*, vol. 14, no. 4.

Quaisser, W. (1986) 'Agricultural price policy and peasant agriculture in Poland', *Soviet Studies*, vol.XXXVIII, no. 4.

—— (1987) 'The new agricultural reform in China: from the people's communes to peasant agriculture' in Gey, Kosta, and Quaisser (eds).

Radice, H. (1981) 'The state enterprise in Hungary' in Jeffries (ed.).

Reut, A. (1987) *International Herald Tribune*, 7–8 November.

Rhee, Kang Suk (1987) 'North Korea's pragmatism: a turning point?', *Asian Survey*, vol.XXXVII, no. 8.

Richman, B. (1969) *Industrial Society in Communist China*, New York: Random House.

Riskin, C. (1987) *The Political Economy of Chinese Development since 1949*, London: Oxford University Press.

Roca, S. (1981) 'Cuban economic policy in the 1970s: the trodden paths' in Horowitz (ed.).

Rodriguez, J. (1987) 'Agricultural policy and development in Cuba', *World Development*, vol. 15, no. 1

—— (1988) 'Cubanology and the provision of basic needs in the Cuban revolution' in Zimbalist (ed.).

Rohlicek, R. (1987) 'Fundamental principles of the restructuring of the economic mechanism', *Czechoslovak Economic Digest*, no. 7.

Rosen, S. (1987) 'China in 1986: a year of consolidation', *Asian Survey*, vol.XXVII, no. 1.

—— (1988) 'China in 1987', *Asian Survey*, vol.XXVIII, no. 1.

Rostowski, J. (1989) 'The decay of socialism and the growth of private enterprise in Poland', *Soviet Studies*, vol.XLI, no. 2.

Roucek, L. (1988) 'Private enterprise in Soviet political debates', *Soviet Studies*, vol.XL, no. 1.

Rychetnik, L. (1981) 'The industrial enterprise in Czechoslovakia' in Jeffries (ed.).

Sacks, S. (1983) *Self-Management and Efficiency: Large Corporations in Yugoslavia*, London: Allen and Unwin.

Salem, E. (1987) 'China 1987', *FEER*, 19 March.

Sanders, A. (1987a) *Mongolia: Politics, Economics and Society*, London: Pinter.

—— (1987b) *FEER*, 16 July.

—— (1987c) *FEER*, 10 December.

Santana, S. (1988) 'Some thoughts on vital statistics and health status in Cuba' in Zimbalist (ed.).

Scalapino, R., and Kim, Jun-Yop (eds) (1983) *North Korea Today: Strategic and Domestic Issues*, Berkeley, CA: Institute of Asian Studies, University of California.

Scalapino, R., and Lee, H. (eds) (1986) *North Korea in a Regional and Global Context*, Berkeley, CA: Institute of East Asian Studies, University of California.

Schäuble, W. (1988) 'Relations between the two states in Germany: problems and prospects', *International Affairs*, vol. 64, no. 2.

Schnytzer, A. (1982) *Stalinist Economic Strategy in Practice: the Case of Albania*, London: Oxford University Press.

Schram, S. (1988) 'China after the 13th Congress', *China Quarterly*, no. 114.

Schroeder, G. (1982) 'Soviet economic "reform" decrees: more steps on the treadmill', US Congress, Joint Economic Committee, Washington DC: Government Printing Office.

—— (1986) *The System versus Progress: Soviet Economic Problems*, London: The Centre for Research into Communist Economies.

—— (1988) 'Organisations and hierarchies: the perennial search for solutions' in Linz and Moskoff (eds).

—— (1988a) 'Property rights issues in economic reforms in socialist countries', *Studies in Comparative Communism*, vol.XXI, no. 2.

Schüller, A. (1988) *Does Market Socialism Work?*, London: The Centre for Research into Communist Economies.

Shafir, M. (1985) *Romania: Politics, Economics and Society*, London: Pinter.

Shcherbakov, V. (1987) 'The wholesale restructuring of wages', *Problems of Economics*, vol.XXX, no. 6.

Sicular, T. (1988) 'Plan and market in China's agricultural commerce', *Journal of Political Economy*, vol. 96, no. 2.

—— (1988a) 'Grain pricing: a key link in Chinese economic policy', *Modern China*, vol. 14, no. 4.

—— (1988b) 'Agricultural planning and pricing in the post-Mao period', *The China Quarterly*, no. 116.

Sirc, L. (1979) *The Yugoslav Economy under Self-Management*, London: Macmillan.

—— (1981) 'The industrial enterprise in Yugoslavia' in Jeffries (ed.).

Sit, V. (1988) 'China's export-oriented open areas: the export processing zone concept', *Asian Survey*, vol.XXIII, no. 6.

Skinner, G. (1985) 'Rural marketing in China: repression and revival', *The China Quarterly*, no. 103.

Skorov, G. (1987) 'Economic reform in the USSR', Working Paper no. 24, World Institute for the United Nations Library (August).

Slider, D. (1987) 'The brigade system in Soviet industry: an effort to restructure the labour force', *Soviet Studies*, vol.XXXIX, no. 3.

Smith, A. (1980) 'Romanian economic reforms' in *Nato Economic Reforms in Eastern Europe and Prospects for the 1980s*, London: Pergamon Press.

—— (1981) 'The Romanian industrial enterprise' in Jeffries (ed.).

—— (1983) *The Planned Economies of Eastern Europe*, London: Croom Helm.

Spigler, I (1973) *Economic Reform in Rumanian Industry*, Princeton, NJ: Princeton University Press.

Spoor, M. (1987) 'Finance in a socialist transition: the case of the Democratic Republic of Vietnam (1955–1964)' in *Journal of Contemporary Asia*, vol. 17, no. 3.

—— (1988) 'Reforming state finance in post-1975 Vietnam', *The Journal of Development Studies*, vol. 24, no. 4.

—— (1988a) 'State finance in the Socialist Republic of Vietnam', in Marr and White (eds).

Stahnke, A. (1987) 'Kombinate as the key structural element in the GDR intensification', *Studies in Comparative Communism*, vol.XX, no. 1.

Staller, G. (1968) 'Czechoslovakia: the new model of planning and management', *American Economic Review*, no. 2.

Stern, L. (1987) 'The scramble toward revitalisation: the Vietnamese Communist Party and the economic reform programme', *Asian Studies*, vol.XXVII, no. 4.

Strassburger, J. (1985) in *DDR Handbuch*.

Suh, Dae-Sook (1986) 'North Korea in 1985: a new era after forty years', *Asian Survey*, vol.XXVI, no. 1.

Suh, Sang-Chul (1983) 'North Korean industrial policy and trade' in Scalapino and Kim (eds).

Swain, N. (1987) 'Hungarian agriculture in the early 1980s: retrenchment followed by reform', *Soviet Studies*, vol.XXXIX, no. 1.

Tam, On-Kit (1988) 'Rural finance in China', *The China Quarterly*, no. 113.

Tedstrom, J. (1987) 'On perestroyka: analysing the "basic provisions"', *Problems of Communism* (July-August).

Teichova, A. (1988) *The Czechoslovak Economy 1918–80*, London: Routledge.

Thalheim, K. (1981) *Die wirtschaftliche Entwicklung der beiden Staaten in Deutschland*, Opladen: Leske Verlag & Budrich GmbH.

—— (1986) *Stagnation or Change in Communist Economies*, London: The Centre for

Research into Communist Economies.

Thayer, C. (1988) 'A Haiphong-Ho Chi Minh axis leads Vietnam toward reform', *International Herald Tribune*, 15 April.

The Times (1986) *Survey on China*, 10 October.

Trehub, A. (1987) 'Social and economic rights in the Soviet Union', *Survey*, vol. 29, no. 4.

Treml, V. (1988) 'Perestroyka in Soviet statistics', *Soviet Economy*, vol. 4 (January-March).

Tröder, M. (1987) 'The 1981–5 Order of Planning' in Jeffries, Melzer, and Breuning (eds).

Tsantis, A. and Pepper, R. (1979) *Romania: the Industrialization of an Agrarian Economy under Socialist Planning*, Washington DC: World Bank..

Turits, R. (1987) 'Trade, debt and the Cuban economy', *World Development*, vol. 15, no. 1.

Turnock, D. (1986) *The Romanian Economy in the Twentieth Century*, London: Croom Helm.

UNCTAD Secretariat (1987) 'Trading with the GDR', *Foreign Trade Review* (Oct-Dec).

Ungar, E. (1987–8) 'The struggle over the Chinese community in Vietnam, 1946–86', *Pacific Affairs*, vol. 60, no. 4.

US Congress, Joint Economic Committee (1977) *East European Economies Post-Helsinki*, Washington, DC: US Government Printing Office.

—— (1979) *Soviet Economy in a Time of Change*, Washington, DC.

—— (1982) *Soviet Economy in the 1980s: Problems and Prospects*, Washington, DC.

—— (1986) *East European Economies: Slow Growth in the 1980s, vol. 3: Country Studies on Eastern Europe and Yugoslavia*, Washington, DC.

van Brabant, J. (1988) 'Planned economies in the Gatt framework: the Soviet case', *Soviet Economy*, vol. 4 (Jan-March).

Vankai, T. (1986) 'Hungarian agricultural performance and prospects during the Eighties', US Congress, Joint Economic Committee.

Vetrovsky, J., and Hrinda, V. (1988) 'Direct relations: clearing operations in the national currencies of Czechoslovakia and the Soviet Union', *Czechoslovak Economic Digest*, no. 4.

Vid, L. (1988) *International Herald Tribune*, 7 November.

Vo Nhan Tri (1988) 'Party policies and economic performance: the Second and Third-year Plans examined', in Marr and White (eds).

von Beyme, K., and Zimmerman, H. (1984) *Policymaking in the German Democratic Republic*, Aldershot: Gower.

von Czege, A. (1987) 'Hungary's New Economic Mechanism: upheaval or continuity', in Gey, Kosta, and Quaisser (eds).

Vortmann, H. (1985) in *DIW Handbuch*.

Wädekin, K-E. (1982) *Agrarian Policies in Communist Europe*, Totowa, NJ: Rowman and Allanheld.

—— (1988) 'Soviet agriculture: a brighter prospect' in Wiles (ed.).

Walker, K. (1984) 'Chinese agriculture during the period of the readjustment', *The China Quarterly* (December).

Wallace, W., and Clarke, R. (1986) *Comecon, Trade and the West*, London: Pinter.

Wanless, P. (1980) 'Economic reform in Poland 1973–9', *Soviet Studies*, vol.XXII, no. 1.

Watson, A. (1988) 'The reform of agricultural marketing in China', *The China Quarterly*, no. 113.

Werner, J. (1988) 'The problem of the district in Vietnam's development policy', in

Marr and White (eds).

White, C. (1985) 'Agricultural planning, pricing policy and cooperatives in Vietnam', *World Development*, vol. 13, no. 1.

White, G. (1987a) 'Cuban Planning in the Mid-1980s: Centralisation, Decentralisation and Participation' in *World Development*, vol. 15, no. 1.

—— (1987b) 'The politics of economic reform in Chinese industry: the introduction of the labour contract system', *The China Quarterly*, no. 111.

—— (1988) 'State and market in China's labour reform', *The Journal of Development Studies*, vol. 24, no. 4.

White, G., and Bowles, P. (1988) 'China's banking reforms: aims, methods and problems', *National Westminster Bank Quarterly Review* (November).

Wiedemann, P. (1980) 'The origins and development of agro-industrial development in Bulgaria', in R.Francisco, B.Laird, and R.Laird (eds), *Agricultural Policies in the USSR and Eastern Europe*, Boulder, CO: Westview Press.

Wiles, P. (ed.) (1988) *The Soviet Economy on the Brink of Reform*, London: Unwin Hyman.

Winiecki, J. (1988) *The Distorted World of Soviet-type Economies*, London: Croom Helm.

—— (1988a) *Gorbachev's Way Out?*, London: CRCE.

Wong, C. (1986) 'The economics of shortage and the problems of reform in Chinese industry', *Journal of Comparative Economics*, vol. 10, no. 4.

—— (1988) 'Interpreting rural industrial growth in post-Mao China', *Modern China*, vol. 14, no. 1.

Wong, E. (1987) 'Recent developments in China's Special Economic Zones: problems and prognosis', *The Developing Economies*, vol.XXV, no. 1.

World Bank (1984) *China: Socialist Economic Development*, Volumes 1 and 2, Washington DC.

—— (1988) Report in *Polish Perspectives*, vol. XXXI, no. 1.

Wu, J., and Reynolds, B. (1988) 'Choosing a strategy for China's economic reform', *American Economic Review*, Papers and Proceedings (May).

Yoon, Suk Bum (1986) 'Macroeconomic interaction between domestic and foreign sectors in the North Korean economy: a schematic interpretation', in Scalapino and Lee (eds).

Zimbalist, A. (1987) 'Cuba's socialist economy toward the 1990s', *World Development*, vol. 15, no. 1.

—— (ed.) (1988) *Cuban Political Economy*, Boulder, CO and London: Westview Press.

—— (1988a) 'Cuba's statistical and price systems: interpretation and reliability', *Latin American Perspectives*, vol. 15, no. 2.

—— (1988b) 'Cuba's external economy: reflections on export dependence, Soviet aid and foreign debt', *Comparative Economic Studies*, vol.XXX, no. 2.

—— (1989) 'Incentives and planning in Cuba', *Latin American Research Review*, vol.XXIV, no. 1.

Zimbalist, A., and Eckstein, S. (1987) 'Patterns of Cuban development: the first twenty five years', *World Development*, vol. 15, no. 1.

Zimbalist, A., Sherman, H., and Brown, S. (1989) *Comparing Economic Systems: A Political-Economic Approach*, 2nd edn, New York: Harcourt Brace Jovanovich.

Index